# STRATEGIC MARKETING

**FOR**

# EDUCATIONAL INSTITUTIONS

SECOND EDITION

## Philip Kotler
*Northwestern University*

## Karen F.A. Fox
*Santa Clara University*

PRENTICE-HALL, Inc., Englewood Cliffs, New Jersey 07632

*Library of Congress Cataloging-in-Publication Data*

Kotler, Philip.
    Strategic marketing for educational institutions / Philip Kotler,
Karen F.A. Fox.
        p.    cm.
    Includes bibliographical references and index.
    ISBN  0-13-668989-2
    1. Education—Marketing.   2. Public relations—Schools.
3. Educational fund raising.   4. Educational planning.   I. Fox,
Karen F.A., 1944–    . II. Title.
LB2847.K68   1994
371.2'06—dc20                                    94-24025
                                                      CIP

Production Editor: Northeastern Graphic Services, Inc.
Project Manager: Alana Zdinak
Acquisitions Editor: Dave Borkowsky
Assistant Editor: Melissa Steffens
Interior Design: Northeastern Graphic Services, Inc.
Cover Design: Bruce Kenselaar
Design Director: Jayne Conte
Copy Editor: Donna Mulder
Proofreader: Northeastern Graphic Services, Inc.
Manufacturing Buyer: Marie McNamara
Editorial Assistant: Aviva Rosenberg
Production Assistant: Renee Pelletier

 © 1995, 1985 by Prentice-Hall, Inc.
A Simon and Schuster Company
Englewood Cliffs, New Jersey 07632

Printed in the United States of America

10 9 8 7 6 5 4 3 2 1

ISBN  0-13-668989-2

Prentice-Hall International (UK) Limited, *London*
Prentice-Hall of Australia Pty. Limited, *Sydney*
Prentice-Hall Canada Inc., *Toronto*
Prentice-Hall Hispanoamericana, S.A., *Mexico*
Prentice-Hall of India Private Limited, *New Delhi*
Prentice-Hall of Japan, Inc., *Tokyo*
Simon & Schuster Asia Pte. Ltd., *Singapore*
Editoria Prentice-Hall do Brasil, Ltda., *Rio de Janeiro*

**THIS BOOK IS DEDICATED**

*To Milton and Neil Kotler,*
*who were my first students,*
*later my teachers,*
*and now my colleagues.*

P. K.

*To Sylvia and Karl Fox,*
*my parents and first teachers,*
*who are exemplars*
*of lives enriched by learning.*

K. F.

# Contents

## PART IV
## Designing Marketing Programs    *273*

## PART V
## Applying Marketing    *389*

# Preface

The decade since the publication of the first edition of *Strategic Marketing for Educational Institutions* has been marked by rapid change in the education marketplace at all levels, from preschool through university and beyond. Many readers have told us that the first edition has served as an indispensable handbook in addressing these changes—some have even referred to our book as "the Bible" of educational marketing.

This response has been both gratifying and challenging, as we are well aware that the forces affecting American education have continued to evolve. Our purpose in this second edition is to revisit the education marketplace, offer a fresh reappraisal of the challenges facing today's educational institutions, and present readers with updated tools and perspectives.

Educators are well aware of the multiplying pressures and even attacks on education in the United States. Public officials and their constituents are raising questions about the performance of this sector of society: Are educational institutions teaching the right things? Are schools preparing U.S. students with the skills needed to compete globally in the twenty-first century? Are professors putting enough time and effort into teaching, or are they short-changing their students by focusing on research and outside activities? Are schools spending money on the right things?

While questions mount, most educational institutions have very limited financial resources with which to make major changes. Tuition, the financial lifeline for most private educational institutions, increased rapidly in the 1980s, but increases have since slowed as family incomes have flattened. Publicly-supported institutions have also raised their tuitions and fees, eliciting protests from students and their families.

Despite tuition increases, many institutions—including such mighty universities as Yale and Stanford—have sustained large deficits and have resorted to such actions as eliminating courses, deferring building maintenance, and freezing hiring—which could result in problems in the future. Smaller and less well-funded educational institutions, public and private, are scrambling to do more with less, while investing additional resources in development programs to attract additional financial support.

Educational institutions in many parts of the United States will be competing for a smaller pool of students, as already-apparent demographic realities are played out. The "baby boomlet" is passing through high school and into college during the 1990s, after which the youth population will decline.

In short, many educational institutions are facing a financial crisis, a student enrollment crisis, and even an identity crisis.

In the midst of this turbulent environment, some educational institutions have met the new challenges well, mostly as a result of taking a strategic, market-oriented view of the changing educational marketplace. These institutions have implemented major new policies and adopted new tools, some borrowed from business, to increase their effectiveness. They have paid attention to total quality management, customer satisfaction, and organizational restructuring and reengineering, in an effort to transform their institutions and improve their performance. In our view, a strategic marketing perspective provides the underpinning for these efforts.

To provide the reader with a cumulative understanding of marketing and an ability to apply these ideas directly to educational institutions, we have divided our book into six sequenced segments:

> Part I, Understanding Marketing, introduces marketing concepts and the marketing perspective, and shows how these apply to the institution's relationships with its publics and markets. The importance of service quality, value, and customer service are emphasized as the hallmarks of excellent educational institutions and the foundation for effective marketing, and useful marketing research techniques are identified.

> Part II, Planning Marketing, introduces the process by which the institution develops strategic and operational plans, beginning with understanding the internal and external environments, assessing its tangible and intangible resources, and formulating its mission, goals, and objectives. Based on these steps, the institution can determine where it should focus its efforts and what organizational changes will be needed to support the strategic plan.

> Part III, Understanding Markets, describes the ways marketers analyze the market, segment it, and select those markets that the institution can best serve. After selecting target markets, the institution will seek to understand how consumers decide what programs and services they want.

> Part IV, Designing Marketing Programs, presents the steps in planning programs and services and in pricing, locating, scheduling, and communicating about them.

> Part V, Applying Marketing, illustrates how marketing applies to recruiting, enrolling, and retaining students, as well as attracting financial support.

> Part VI, Evaluating Marketing Activities, presents guidelines for evaluating the institution's marketing effectiveness to ensure that the institution remains responsive and relevant in the future.

This edition has greatly benefited from the comments and questions of readers, and our contacts with educators. In traveling around the country and abroad, visiting a wide variety of educational institutions and talking with educators, we found that many of our 1985 prescriptions are proving effective in practice, though many educational institutions still resist these approaches. We also found that many new tools and strategies must now be added to cope with today's and tomorrow's challenges.

Our work has also benefited from the growing body of work in services marketing, service quality, and educational marketing and strategy. Over the past decade the field of services marketing and quality has received the attention of such experts as John Bateson, Leonard Berry, Mary Jo Bitner, William Davidow, Christian Grönroos, Christopher Lovelock, A. Parasuraman, Daniel Seymour, Valarie Zeithaml, and Ron Zemke.

A number of writers have focused on educational marketing and strategy, among them Robert Cope, William Ihlanfeldt, George Keller, Larry Litten, and James Scannell. Their work and ours follow on the pioneering work of John Maguire, Eugene Fram, and others who, as early as two decades ago, realized that marketing had something to offer to educational institutions.

We wish to thank the many people who commented on the manuscript at various stages of its development. In particular, we thank Richard Burke, Carole Custer, Peter Davies, John Maguire, Linda Maguire, and Daniel Saracino, who have probably read the manuscript and its preceding edition as many times as the authors have, and who have contributed stellar insights based on years of firsthand acquaintance with the challenges of educational marketing. Additional helpful reviews came from Maureen McNulty, Jeff Totten, and Elizabeth Tidwell. Others have graciously assisted us by reading individual chapters of the manuscript and offering us the benefit of their specialized knowledge: Patti Crane, Bonnie Farber, Kathy Kurz, Joel Leidecker, James Scannell, Charles Sizemore, and Ernest Theodossian.

Many others have helped us obtain needed information to update our examples, check facts, and in other ways improve this edition. These helpful sources include John Vaccaro of the College Board office in San Jose, California; Lorraine Bazan and George Carlson, librarians at Santa Clara University; and Barbara Celone, Head, Social Science Resource Group, Stanford University Libraries, and her colleagues at Cubberley Library at Stanford University School of Education, who over many years have provided access and assistance in using that library's extensive collection.

Karen Graul, Administrative Assistant for the Marketing Department at Santa Clara University, was involved with the manuscript from the beginning, and ably handled several complex tasks with the assistance of students Gerald Gonzales and Sean Scullen. Their competence and cheerfulness greatly eased the process.

Nancy Allen, who provided superb research assistance on the first edition while an M.B.A. student at Santa Clara University, now has a Ph.D. from Harvard. M.B.A. student Beverly Swanson did a thorough update of the review of literature in 1990, before taking a management position at Stanford University. So any gaps in research for this edition are the sole responsibility of the authors.

We are grateful to the fine staff at Prentice-Hall who have worked with us in the lengthy process from idea to manuscript to finished book. Sandy Steiner was our editor at the start and, after a promotion, handed the responsibility on to David Borkowsky. Assistant marketing editor Melissa Steffens was our always-helpful direct link to Prentice-Hall. Alana Zdinak was our project manager, and Donna Mulder our copy editor. Vanessa Sanchez of Northeastern Graphic Services, Inc. lived with our manuscript through its transformation from a very full floppy disk into the book you now hold in your hands. We also thank John Connolly, formerly of Prentice-Hall, who many years ago proposed that we collaborate on this book.

We take particular satisfaction in presenting a book that addresses the key tasks of educational institutions. Having attended several educational institutions, served on the faculty of others, and consulted with educational institutions, we support the importance of their educational missions and value their contributions to improving individual lives and society as a whole. We hope that this book will make a contribution to furthering the aims of education.

# I

# Understanding Marketing

# 1

# The Education Marketplace

*While chancellor of the University of Maine System, Robert Woodbury wrote an opinion piece in which he proposed, "Why not run a business like a good university?":*

*"If you only ran your college like a business…" is a phrase we in university administration hear almost daily from our friends in the business world.*

*Frankly, we in higher education have learned much about operating in a more businesslike manner. The stringencies of the last few years in particular have helped us weed out unnecessary functions, use technology more effectively, plan more strategically, and use limited resources more efficiently. Most of us are better managers than we would have been if we had been less attentive to recent developments in the private sector.*

*Those in the private sector, however, might reflect on some comparisons and strengths in the university world that might be helpful, in turn, to them.*

*First, higher education is one of the few U.S. "industries" universally recognized as the best in the world. This is no longer true of cars or electronics or most other areas of manufacturing. But our colleges and universities dominate the globe as do few sectors other than the entertainment industry, munitions, and soft drinks.*

*Second, our favorable balance of payments is estimated to exceed $5 billion and is expanding. Almost 420,000 foreign students, the vast majority funded from abroad, study full-time on our* *campuses. Perhaps 80,000 U.S. students study abroad and then only for brief periods and mostly for "cultural" reasons.*

*Third, higher education has been a growth industry for four decades, despite a dramatic decrease in the college-age population [over the past 15 years]. We have expanded from 2 million students to more than 14 million since World War II. Growth in related areas, such as continuing education or sponsored research, has grown as dramatically.*

*Fourth, cases of college bankruptcy, defaults on loans, or high-level malfeasance are all but unknown. Certainly many colleges are run better than others, but the overall record of fiscal stewardship would be the envy of many boards of directors.*

*Fifth, no other industry that I know has assembled, retained, and energized so much educated talent at such low cost. At a single institution, thousands of people have studied an average of six full years past their bachelor's degree (more than many M.D.s) and earn only $45,000 (the average salary of a university professor in the United States).*

*Sixth, undergraduates get a bargain, despite the perceptions of parents or taxpayers. A college supplies housing, food, association with the best minds in many fields, art centers, athletic events, entertainment, libraries, and all the amenities and intellectual resources of a small city. Who else can do this for an average cost of $12,000 a year?*

*Seventh, the return on investment is enviable. Aside from any benefits of a human or cultural dimension, a graduate of a four-year institution earns approximately 50 percent more than a high school graduate, or $500,000 more over a lifetime. The contributions of university research and ancillary activities to society are incalculable.*

> **Source:** Robert L. Woodbury, Chancellor of the University of Maine System, "Why Not Run a Business Like a Good University?" *The Christian Science Monitor*, March 23, 1993, p. 19, with minor adaptations.

---

Making a direct comparison between a university and a business would have been shocking a few decades ago. Educational institutions educated students, relying on money from tuition and gifts to pay teachers' salaries and the other expenses of operating their programs. Their aim was to impart knowledge and skills that would improve the lives and work opportunities of their graduates. Businesses, in contrast, aimed to make a profit, defined in narrowly financial terms. Education and business were considered distinct "worlds," with little or nothing in common.

American educational institutions have learned much from business, including improved budgeting systems, endowment investing, and other financial management procedures, as well as increased professionalization of human resource management functions. Development and admissions professionals borrow relevant business concepts and adapt them to their roles in attracting resources to their institutions. Over the past decade, the vocabulary of marketing—especially marketing research, market segmentation, and strategic planning—has become widely used and applied, and even comfortably familiar.

As long as schools received enough resources and students, they tended to carry on their marketing activities without much conscious reflection. The admissions office staff continued to contact prospective students, the alumni association kept in touch with alumni, and the development office contacted alumni and foundations, inviting donations. The faculty prepared for classes, taught, met with students, and wrote articles, while the support staff carried out the myriad functions that made the school run. Students attended class, studied at the library, joined in campus activities, and got career advice at the career center. All the while, everyone at the school might have claimed that "this school does no marketing."

Educational institutions eventually recognized that they had marketing problems. Declines in prospective students, enrollment, donations, and other resources in the face of mounting costs reminded them of their dependence on the marketplace they served. Many faced changing student needs and societal expectations, increasing competition for scarce students and funding resources, and unabating financial pressures. Board members, legislators, and community groups began putting tough questions to educational administrators about their institutions' missions, opportunities, and strategies. One result was that educators were often forced to take a hard look at marketing to see what this discipline might offer to keep their institutions viable and relevant.

This book presents marketing concepts and tools that are directly relevant to the application of marketing in schools, colleges, universities, and other educational institutions. Examples from educational contexts demonstrate how these marketing concepts and tools can be applied effectively. This first chapter describes what marketing is and how it is embodied in a marketing orientation. The chapter then reviews the educational marketplace today, and the benefits of adopting a marketing orientation.

## WHAT IS MARKETING?

The fact that people have needs and wants lays the groundwork for marketing. *Marketing exists when people decide to satisfy their needs and wants through exchange.* Educational institutions need to receive certain resources in order to offer their services to others. Schools and colleges depend on tuition payments, taxpayer dollars (for public institutions), donations, and grants for financial support; on students and other clients as recipients of the institution's services; and on administrators, faculty, and staff as providers of the educational and other services for which the institution was founded. Without the ability to attract students, money, staff, faculty, facilities, and equipment, the institution would cease to exist. Several private educational institutions have closed in the past few years alone.

Most educational institutions obtain the resources they need through exchange. *Exchange is the act of obtaining a desired product or benefit from someone by offering something in return.* The institution offers satisfactions—courses, degree programs, career preparation, and other services and benefits—to its markets. In return, it receives needed resources—tuition payments, donations, volunteers, money, time, and energy. This exchange is shown in Figure 1-1. Participating in the exchange process is voluntary, with each party participating with the expectation of being better off as a result of the exchange.

Marketing is a central activity of modern institutions, growing out of their quest to effectively serve some area of human need. To survive and succeed, institutions must know their markets; attract sufficient resources; convert these resources into appropriate programs, services, and ideas; and effectively distribute them to various markets and publics. The participants in these tasks do so voluntarily because they expect to benefit personally and/or to contribute to the well-being of society at large. The modern institution aims to achieve its goals mainly by offering and exchanging values with various markets and publics.

The concept of exchange is central to marketing. Through exchanges, social units—individuals, small groups, institutions, whole nations—attain the inputs they need. By offering something attractive, they acquire what they need in return. Since both parties agree to the exchange, both see themselves as better off after the exchange.

A professional marketer is skilled at *understanding, planning, and managing exchanges.* The marketer knows how to research and understand the needs of the other party; to design a valued offering to meet these needs; to communicate the offer effectively; and to present it at the right time and place. Here is our definition of *marketing*:

> *Marketing* is the analysis, planning, implementation, and control of carefully formulated programs designed to bring about voluntary exchanges of values with target markets to achieve institutional objectives. Marketing involves designing the institution's offerings to meet the target markets' needs and desires, and using effective pricing, communication, and distribution to inform, motivate, and service these markets.

Several things should be noted about this definition of marketing. First, marketing is defined as a managerial process involving analysis, planning, implementation, and control. This definition emphasizes the role of marketing in helping educators face very practical marketing problems.

Second, marketing manifests itself in carefully formulated *programs*, not just random actions. Effective marketing activity depends upon thorough advance planning and careful implementation.

FIGURE 1-1    Exchanges between an educational institution and its various markets

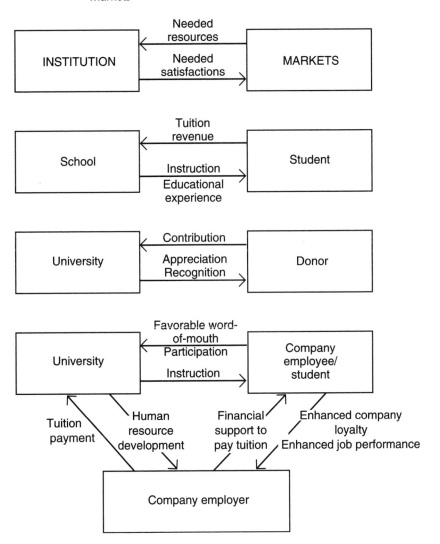

Third, marketing seeks to attract customers by *serving their needs*. A college that is seeking students will offer a strong academic program, financial aid, career advice, jobs, and other benefits to those who choose to attend.

Fourth, marketing means the selection of *target markets* rather than an attempt to be all things to all people. Marketers routinely distinguish among possible market segments and decide which ones to serve on the basis of the school's mission and resources. Educational institutions operate in a complex environment of publics and customers, making effective targeting even more vital to marketing success.

Fifth, marketing helps institutions survive and prosper through serving their markets with *greater effectiveness*. Marketing planning requires that an institution be very specific about its objectives.

Sixth, marketing relies on designing the institution's offering in terms of the target market's *needs and wants*. Efforts to impose a program, service, or idea that is not matched to the market's needs or wants will fail. Effective marketing is client-oriented, not seller-oriented.

Seventh, marketing of services utilizes and blends a set of tools called the *marketing mix*—programs, price, place (delivery systems), promotion (including advertising, public relations, personal contact, and other activities), processes, physical facilities, and people. Marketing is more than advertising, and requires an understanding of all the factors influencing consumers' decisions. For example, a school may do no advertising and yet attract a large following because of its location or its reputation for effective teaching. The most effective institutions understand the role and importance of each component of the marketing mix and use the tools in an integrated way to appeal to and serve their selected target markets.

## WHAT IS A MARKETING ORIENTATION?

Many people think adding a marketing position or office means that the institution has adopted a marketing orientation. This could not be further from the truth. Most educational institutions have admissions offices, fund-raising programs, and alumni offices, and they may even include advertising and public relations experts on their staffs. They are using some marketing tools, but they are not necessarily marketing-oriented. What distinguishes an institution with a marketing orientation?

## MEETING CUSTOMERS' WANTS AND NEEDS

A *marketing orientation* holds that the main task of the institution is to determine the needs and wants of target markets and to satisfy them through the design, communication, pricing, and delivery of appropriate and competitively viable programs and services.

Educational institutions sometimes confuse wants and needs. A person experiences a *need* as a state of deprivation of some satisfaction. The most basic human needs include food, clothing, shelter, safety, belonging, esteem, and other survival needs. While formal education is not required for physical survival, most people need a good education to participate effectively in modern society and to earn an adequate salary.

How the person strives to meet the need for education—as well as other needs—is usually culturally defined. We describe these culturally shaped expressions of needs as *wants*. For example, an American who wants to study medicine will start by enrolling in a college or university, rather than by becoming an apprentice to a doctor. Within the same culture, individual wants will vary. One person may feel well educated and successful upon completing high school, while another strongly desires a Ph.D. from a prestigious university.

Institutions that focus on their existing programs and fail to understand underlying needs suffer from "marketing myopia."[1] They are so enamored of their programs that they lose sight of what their students, donors, and other publics need or will need in the future. A vocational school may think that the student needs a course in welding when the student really needs a job. That is, a school may get caught up in what it has to offer and miss the consumer's real concern. A school may offer students less (or more) than what they expect because the school doesn't understand their wants and needs. The student who finds another school that provides a better program will have a new want but the same need. Educational institutions that hold tightly to traditional programs often act as though students' needs and wants should never change. Or the alumni office may continue offering pregame barbecues when alumni want continuing education and career-change assistance.

An institution with a marketing orientation concentrates on satisfying the needs of its constituencies. These institutions recognize that efficiency and good programs and services are all means or results of satisfying target markets. Without satisfied target markets, institutions would soon find themselves adrift and would sink into oblivion. The employees in a marketing-oriented institution work as a team to meet the needs of their specific target markets, focusing on creating and projecting a climate of service and continuous improvement.

Satisfying target markets does not, however, mean that an educational institution ignores its mission and its distinctive competencies to provide whatever educational programs happen to be "hot" at the moment. Rather, the institution seeks out consumers who are or could be interested in its offerings and then adapts these offerings to make them as attractive as possible.

## Serving the Long-Term Interests of Consumers and Society

Is meeting consumers' perceived needs and wants too narrow an objective for an educational institution? Probably so. First, students often have long-range needs that they do not yet perceive. Although students may say that they prefer to "take it easy," their longer-range interest may require not only a diploma but also real mastery of information and skills that the diploma stands for. Education also serves the larger needs of society by preparing people to be productive and to carry out their societal and civic roles and responsibilities.

Second, most educational institutions have multiple objectives. Students may view the school as a sort of retail store whose function is to sell them what they want to purchase, but the school's mission is usually much broader. For example, the mission statement of a church-supported college may emphasize academic excellence, educating the whole person, and deepening religious commitment; some students may prefer easy courses, multiple-choice exams, and sleeping in on Sunday morning. An educational institution must weigh the needs and preferences of students while preserving the institution's academic reputation and other institutional goals and commitments.

A growing number of marketers see their responsibility to take four factors into account in their marketing decision making: consumer needs, consumer wants, consumers' long-term interests, and the interests of society. This orientation can be called a *societal marketing orientation*:

> A *societal marketing orientation* holds that the main task of the institution is to determine the needs, wants, and interests of its consumers and to adapt the institution to deliver satisfactions that preserve or enhance the consumer's and society's well-being and long-term interests.

This broader definition of marketing is quite compatible with the aims of most educational institutions. For example, a college might use an ad showing a successful alumnus saying, "If college turns out to be the best four years of your life, maybe you went to the wrong college," emphasizing that the long-term outcomes of college attendance go beyond the immediate college experience.[2]

## THE EVOLUTION OF MARKETING
## BY EDUCATIONAL INSTITUTIONS

Marketing is not a new activity for educational institutions. In an article several decades ago, Scott Cutlip tells about American colleges and universities, both public and private, which turned to advertising, publicity, lobbying, fund raising, and student recruitment activities in the middle of the last century![3]

Over this long history, the acceptance and focus of educational-institution marketing has evolved. Attracting students continues to be a focus for marketing application, but marketing is now achieving greater importance in attracting financial resources, enhancing the institution's image and public awareness, and in other areas. Exhibit 1-1 describes the six stages in the evolution of marketing applied to enrollment.

EXHIBIT 1-1    Stages in the evolution of enrollment marketing

---

**1. Marketing is unnecessary.** Many educational institutions assumed that the value of education was obvious, and that those who valued education would make their way to the school doors to enroll. The school's curriculum changed very slowly because it was based on decades—even centuries—of tradition and had "stood the test of time." Students enrolled because they wanted exactly what the school offered—or because there were no alternatives. The school felt it did not need any recruiting—or marketing. The school had a registrar. Highly attractive schools set up procedures to select the most promising candidates from those who wanted to attend.

**2. Marketing is promotion.** Schools found that they were not enrolling enough students, or enough of the students they most wanted to attract. They assumed that prospective students either didn't know about them or that they lacked the motivation to approach the school independently. Schools actively sought out students and stepped up their recruiting activities. They established a recruiting function (perhaps a faculty committee) and later an admissions office, which functioned primarily as a sales department for the school. The head of the admissions office was the director of admissions. The admissions-office staff operated as salespeople, making "sales calls" and sending out catalogs, brochures, and posters.

**3. Marketing is segmentation and marketing research.** The more advanced—or most distressed—schools began to realize that the admissions office's resources could be used more effectively if they could be directed to the most attractive and likely prospects. If the admissions office could better understand those who enrolled, the admissions staff could direct their efforts to attract similar students. If the admissions staff understood how the college-choice decision was made, they could provide the right information at the right time. The admissions office either developed a research capability, worked with the school's director of institutional research (if there was one), or hired outside consultants to conduct, analyze, and draw implications from marketing research.

**4. Marketing is positioning.** As more schools intensified their recruiting and promotion activities and sharpened them with research, some schools sought a new basis for competition. Some began to appreciate the importance of achieving distinctiveness in the minds of prospective students. They realized they could not offer all programs and be the best school for all students. They decided to examine their histories, distinctive characteristics, and opportunities, and to "take a position" in the constellation of educational institutions.

Positioning goes beyond image making. Positioning is an attempt to distinguish the school from its competitors along real dimensions that students value in order to be the preferred school for certain student segments. Positioning aims to help prospects to know the real differences the school represents, so that they can match themselves to the school that can satisfy their needs best.

**5. Marketing is strategic planning.** Some schools were buffeted not only by competition from other schools, but also by major changes in the economy, in demo-

EXHIBIT 1-1    (continued)

graphics, in values, and other areas outside the institution's direct control. These schools began to realize the interconnection between these external changes and the school's image, its positioning, its programs, and many other facets of the school—including its ability to attract and serve students. These schools extended their planning efforts to identify major trends and to assess how well the school was responding to these trends. The school revised its programs, procedures, and other activities to better align its efforts with these trends.

**6. Marketing is enrollment management.** A few schools realized that the admissions office, while effective, was attending to only part of "the big picture." Attracting students, processing their applications, end encouraging admitted students to enroll were all extremely important activities, but these schools began asking themselves what it would take to optimize the students' experience at the school.

Their answer was to view each student admission as the *beginning* of a relationship with the school that would continue through the period of enrollment to graduation and extend into many years as a satisfied alumna or alumnus and, hopefully, as a donor and supporter of the school.

Treating each student as a valued partner in a relationship called for significant additional changes in policies, procedures, and services. The collaboration between the admissions office and the financial aid office became even closer. In fact, many schools named a dean or vice-president of enrollment management to spearhead coordination among admissions, financial aid, registration, academic advising, residence life, career development and placement, and on-campus employment. Instead of asking students to walk around to various offices to get their questions answered, systems were devised to provide better information and smoother handling of both routine situations and problems. Enrollment management also called for greater attention to research on student retention, student and alumni satisfaction, career placement, and other measures of effectiveness to guide improvements.

Enrollment management also involved a change in the usual way of thinking. The objective was no longer to "do one's job" but rather to respond to student needs. Faculty members spent time talking with prospective students about courses and careers in their field, viewing themselves as members of the enrollment management effort. The instructor offering to help a student cope with academic difficulties realized that he or she was aiding retention every bit as much as was the counselor or the financial aid officer.

## TURMOIL IN THE EDUCATION MARKETPLACE

Just at the time that many educators have begun to accept the idea of marketing, the pace of change for educational institutions has quickened.

Now some university presidents are floating the idea of a three-year bachelor's degree program so that able students can save time and money. Once-tuition-free state colleges and universities are rapidly raising tuition charges. Federal and state student aid has dropped, tuition rises faster than inflation, and family incomes stay flat. Computer and video technology has improved the range of teaching and learning tools while further raising the cost of education. Some existing public schools and some new ones have been established as "charter schools," which allow parents, teachers, and others to design the curriculum and policies, free from many public school regulations. If these charter schools receive approval from the local school district or the state, they are eligible to receive the same per-pupil payment that would go to other public schools in the area.[4] Some public figures and many parents are pushing the idea of school vouchers, so that public and private schools will compete for students. A growing number of parents are considering or are already "home schooling" their children, reflecting concerns about the values taught or basics untaught by other educational options. An estimated half million children, 1 percent of the U.S. school-age population, are being home schooled. School board members are pushing total quality management (TQM) and other approaches to improve efficiency and effectiveness. In the midst of these changes, guiding an educational institution is likely to attract more conflict and more demands than ever before.

The huge and diverse American educational system involves one out of every four Americans. In 1992 this included about 61 million students at all levels, 3.5 million teachers, and 3 million administrators, professional and support staff. Annual expenditures for education were about $425 billion, representing about 7.5 percent of the country's gross domestic product.[5] This amount does not include what companies spend on educating and training their workers, nor does it include education provided through informal classes and other non-school-based learning.

There are 3,600 public and private colleges and universities in the United States, striving to maintain or increase enrollment, improve program quality, and increase donations and grants to cover educational costs. These and other educational institutions face significant challenges, as the following discussion highlights.

## State-Supported Colleges and Universities

Despite their many contributions to society, state-supported educational institutions in the 1990s face some of their stiffest challenges in many decades. When job growth is sluggish, state and local governments receive less in tax revenues, and financial support for education often loses out as entitlement programs claim a growing share of government budgets. State funding for state colleges and universities has diminished to the point that some institutions claim they are "state-*assisted*" rather than "state-*supported*."

The pressure to do more with less—much less—has intensified, while demand for educational services is growing, with more high school graduates overall and increases in lower-income and minority applicants. Slower growth in family incomes has put private education farther out of reach for most families, spurring more applications for admission to lower-cost public institutions. California, the most populous state, will need to accommodate over 700,000 additional college students, most in public colleges and universities, by the year 2000—yet the resources to do so are not likely to be available.[6] In fact, public and private institutions alike have been deferring maintenance on campus facilities, cutting back library purchases, and falling behind in computer technology.

## Community Colleges

Public community colleges constitute about one-third of all institutions of higher education in the United States, and meet a wide range of educational needs, including remediation, the first two years of baccalaureate study, vocational skills training, and leisure enhancement. Community colleges also have helped move many minority students into higher education.

Community colleges continue to grow in size, importance, and influence in their communities. Most were founded as open-access institutions with a commitment to serve all those who could benefit from additional education. During the 1970s and 1980s, success of community colleges was often defined as growth in student enrollment, rather than in student outcomes. In some cases this has created a lingering image of community colleges as "centers for leisure-time activity, social-welfare institutions, or places for underprepared learners, but not as educational institutions providing opportunities with excellence . . . ."[7] Some community colleges are striving to heighten their academic reputations, offering honors programs with small seminars for the best entering students, while continuing to meet other community needs for education for vocational and career advancement as well as college transfer.

Funding limitations have pushed many community colleges to raise tuition and fees to cover a larger share of costs. How to do this in the most equitable way has been a challenge. Some community colleges with high demand but reduced funding have raised fees to cover budget shortfalls, and then find enrollments dropping. Some community colleges now charge one tuition level for those who do not already have a baccalaureate degree or who are unemployed, and another much higher level for everyone else. Community colleges also strive to attract a larger market to their short courses and workshops, which are priced to recover all costs.

## Public Schools

Public elementary school enrollment rose 12 percent between 1985 and 1991, while public high school enrollment declined by 7 percent during that period.[8]

The "baby boomlet" that swelled the elementary schools will soon reach the high schools, but this phenomenon will be short-lived and will be concentrated in just three states: California, Texas, and Florida.[9] After the year 2000, the total number of youth will decline and the percentage of minority youth will increase.

Many public schools are inadequate in materials, curriculum, and quality of instruction, and need more funds and major reforms to meet the needs of their students. Even schools that are "good enough" must improve to help students deal with the knowledge explosion, technological advances, and increased global competitiveness based on highly trained "human capital." Even the most outstanding public school districts find they must communicate more effectively with taxpayers, state legislators, and with parents to build their involvement and to increase their support for bond issues and education legislation.

In addition to limited funding, American public schools suffer from a negative public image. To some extent this negative public image is undeserved. Studies of educational achievement reveal that American students compare very favorably on international rankings in reading and mathematics,[10] and that American students know as much and do as well as students in previous generations.[11] The 1993 Phi Delta Kappa/Gallup Poll found that only 19 percent of a national sample of American adults awarded the nation's schools a grade of A or B. In contrast, 72 percent of public school *parents* rated the schools attended by their oldest children an A or B,[12] suggesting a high level of satisfaction with local schools, but deep skepticism about American education as a whole.

To meet diversity goals and demand for more varied educational offerings, many public school districts have established magnet schools and other specialized schools. But the existence of such schools does not guarantee that parents and students will learn about them and choose them. School districts find they must have information campaigns to explain school choices, and in some instances they have revised curricula, streamlined bus schedules, and added special programs to increase their appeal.

### Selective Private Colleges and Universities

The very best American colleges and universities could fill their freshman classes several times over with students whose families would willingly pay full tuition and fees. Yet Harvard University, which rests at the pinnacle of the prestige hierarchy and accepts about one of every six applicants, awards financial aid to many of these applicants in order to admit a geographically, socially, and racially diverse—rather than wealthy—class.

But prestige does not pay the bills, particularly for research in medicine, engineering, and other sciences. Government cutbacks have pushed topnotch institutions into greater reliance on corporate donations and alliances.

Alumni giving to these institutions for scholarships and other purposes is often strong, but the resource gap persists almost everywhere. Stanford University, among others, had to make deep expenditure cuts in the early 1990s and yet faced more red ink. Increasing donation rates and levels will be important in the years ahead, as well as increasingly skillful management of scarce resources.[13]

## Less Selective Private Colleges and Universities

These institutions are typically small and heavily tuition-dependent, with moderately selective or unselective admissions policies, limited state and federal support, and often strong church affiliations. This description fits approximately one-third of all the four-year colleges in the United States. These colleges provide well-prepared and less well-prepared students with individual attention and opportunities for active participation in a campus community setting that most larger institutions cannot match.

Many of these less selective institutions are concerned less with increasing admissions standards than with simply attracting enough students to keep operating because these institutions rely on tuition payments to cover as much as 90 percent of their operating expenses. Their prospective students are often dependent on financial aid grants, loans, and jobs to pay the bills. When financial aid is in short supply, these prospects attend lower-cost public institutions, and private colleges fail to meet their enrollment goals.

Demographic shifts create new concerns. There was virtually no population growth during the 1980s in states where many of these less selective colleges are located: Illinois, Indiana, Massachusetts, Michigan, New York, Ohio, and Pennsylvania.[14] Colleges in these states may turn more diligently toward attracting prospects from the faster-growing states, further increasing competition among less selective institutions.

## Nonpublic Elementary and High Schools

Nonpublic elementary and high schools enroll about 11 or 12 percent of American students and include a wide variety of school types.[15] There are thousands of schools with a religious affiliation—Catholic, Episcopal, Lutheran, Jewish, and others—which are supported and controlled by individual religious entities (a particular parish or congregation) or controlled by dioceses or denominations.

The more than 8,400 Catholic schools make up the largest single segment of nonpublic schools, enrolling 2.5 million of the 5.3 million students in nonpublic schools in 1992–93. Mostly nonresidential, these tuition-dependent Catholic schools compete with no-cost public schools and are turning to marketing to develop and retain their constituencies. The number of Catholic schools has steadily declined since 1964, as the official Church position on Catholic schooling changed from one of mandates ("All Catholic parents are bound to send their children to the parish school"[16]) to one of encouragement.

In the late 1980s the rate of Catholic school closings slowed significantly, and enrollment has increased. More sophisticated management and improved marketing programs appear to be responsible for these trends. Lay boards of directors and trustees now assist in long-range and operational planning, policy formulation, evaluation, and resource development, although in many instances the boards have advisory authority only. With this groundwork, Catholic schools are establishing comprehensive development programs, including annual giving and planned giving for endowment growth, to bring a Catholic education within reach of more children.

There is considerable overlap between schools with religious affiliations and independent schools, with many Episcopal and Quaker schools fitting both categories. The term *independent schools* is sometimes attached only to the most elite nonpublic schools, but in its broadest meaning the term refers to any school governed by a board of trustees.

Independent schools in the United States vary tremendously in philosophy, organization, and style. As characterized by Pearl Rock Kane, some are traditional, others progressive; some are residential, some are day, some combine both; some are single-sex, some coeducational; some are academic and selective, others are "second-chance" schools for those who failed elsewhere; some are expensive, others are free. The independent schools share six basic characteristics: They are self-governing and self-supporting, they control selection of their teachers and students, they define their own curricula, and they are typically small in size.[17]

These schools face the same demographic changes as other institutions. Few can passively wait for applications. Most independent schools are heavily tuition-dependent and must provide more financial assistance to keep up enrollment and/or try to identify and enroll international students who can afford to pay, as well as offer additional services to serve these students.[18]

## Proprietary Vocational Schools

While most educational institutions in the United States operate under not-for-profit charters, independent vocational schools are privately owned and operated to cover costs and generate a profit for the owners/investors. Secretarial and cosmetology schools are among the earliest examples, followed by various technical and other vocational schools. The earliest proprietary schools sprang up long before the community college movement brought low-cost programs within reach of most Americans. Successful proprietary schools have maintained their position by offering highly focused, practical, short-duration programs in high-growth vocational fields. Proprietary vocational schools typically rely on mass-media advertising and telemarketing to attract students.

Some proprietary institutions have attracted government scrutiny because they have enrolled students who receive government grants and loans, pay the school, then fail to complete the program and pay back their debt. Some proprietary schools have focused more on profit than on delivering customer value, which has created an image problem for many institutions of this type.

To succeed, proprietary vocational schools must strive for excellent job placement records. They must attract and serve employers as well as students, building long-term relationships with employers by meeting their needs for well-qualified employees who have up-to-date training and good work skills.

## Other Organizations with an Educational Mission

Education is not limited to formal education leading to a diploma, degree, or certificate. Many religious, cultural, and health organizations also have education as one of their purposes. Many churches and synagogues offer extensive educational programs, from general-interest community programs to specialized religious education. Museums, symphony orchestras, and operas offer short courses on related topics. Many cultural organizations offer educational programs for prospective docents. Hospitals offer fitness, stress management, and smoking cessation programs for patients, employees, and community members. These and similar organizations often seek more participants and the funding necessary to carry out their educational programs.

Education has become a valued mode of leisure for many Americans, including retired people. Adult education programs, colleges, and private organizations provide special events, individual courses, and residential and travel programs which combine learning and sociability. These leisure programs often must "pay their own way," which increases the importance of planning and promoting the most attractive programs to the right markets.

Most companies offer job-related training programs for their employees, ranging from on-the-job training to degree programs to management training. Many large corporations subsidize their employees to attend degree programs at nearby universities, on site, and/or via teleconferencing at company facilities. A 1992 survey of 36 large companies found that each company spent an average of nearly $2 million on executive education alone, most conducted internally but with one-fourth obtained from university-based programs.[19] Companies paying for these programs are demanding evidence that programs help employees to accomplish their work assignments more effectively and creatively.

## Educational Institutions Abroad

Population growth and improvements in economic well-being have expanded demand for and access to education around the globe. Some American institutions have become involved in "exporting" education through establishing branch campuses overseas to serve students in other locations. Also, many U.S. colleges and universities educate substantial numbers of international students who then return to their countries of origin.

In developing countries governments recognize the equation between education and economic development and push for construction of additional classrooms and expansion of opportunities for secondary and university education. Especially where governments have been unable to meet the demand, private institutions have expanded to serve those who can pay. For example, the Monterrey Institute of Technology grew from one campus in Monterrey, Mexico, to a system of 26 private campuses throughout Mexico and Central America.[20]

In the United Kingdom, educational reforms between 1988 and 1992 changed many traditional assumptions about the control and funding of post-secondary education. Colleges of further education (vocational and continuing education, as well as courses for the university-bound) now must appeal to and satisfy the marketplace to achieve the government's growth targets for enrollment levels, rather than being funded solely for following policies and procedures set by local education authorities. The colleges actively compete for students by offering innovative courses and programs, and have implemented marketing activities, aided by workshops on marketing for educational institutions, and by marketing handbooks and other resources.[21]

Access to university-level education has been enhanced by elevating the status of the country's polytechnic institutes to that of universities. University-level institutions can no longer depend upon receiving funding purely on an historical basis, with annual increments. Instead, each institution must propose to the University Funding Council the number of students the institution can serve in each field, and is then funded on a "core" and "margin" basis. Institutions compete for these margin funds according to criteria designed to encourage greater efficiency. This radical change in higher education funding pressures institutions to be more focused, to pay attention to costs and quality, to satisfy current students while attracting new ones, and to look for new sources of income.

In Japan, private schools, colleges, and universities are starting to think about marketing.[22] Parents seek to get their children admitted to "the best" schools to improve their chances of entering a prestigious university. *Jukus*— for-profit "cram schools"—provide after-school tutoring and instruction to improve students' scores on the fact-laden university admissions tests. One chain of jukus is so big that it is one of the largest companies listed on the

Tokyo Stock Exchange. The jukus advertise widely for students and some are quickly adopting such innovations as offering practice tests students can take using a touch-tone telephone, with immediate feedback on correct answers. These examples of how marketing concerns and activities have grown beyond the United States are likely to presage similar developments in other parts of the world in the decades ahead.

### THE SPHERE OF MARKETING INFLUENCE

Every educational institution has several publics, and the institution should strive to have responsive relations with most or all of them. We use the term *public* to describe a person or group that has an actual or potential interest in or effect on the institution. Figure 1-2 shows 16 major publics, individuals,

FIGURE 1-2   The university and its publics

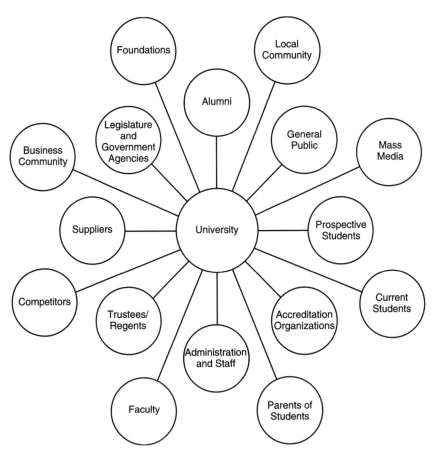

and groups that have an actual or potential interest in and/or effect on a university. We will discuss the most important ones here.

**Faculty.** The faculty consists of the skilled practitioners—professors, teachers, and other instructors—who deliver the institution's educational services. The extent of the faculty's formal and informal power varies from one institution to another, but in most colleges and universities the faculty also play a role in institutional governance. At the most responsive institutions, faculty members clearly understand and are fully committed to the institution's mission. In others, faculty may be at odds with the trustees and administration over the institutional mission and other issues. A school where professors are student-oriented is much more likely to attract and retain students and donors than one where professors are indifferent, all other things being equal. The school's trustees and administration need to work alongside faculty to build a shared commitment to the institution and its students.

**The President.** To succeed, an educational institution must deal effectively with its many publics and generate a high level of satisfaction. The top administration of the institution usually carries a particular responsibility for these areas. Clark Kerr, former president of the University of California at Berkeley, described the position this way:

> The university president in the United States is expected to be a friend of the students, a colleague of the faculty, a good fellow with the alumni, a sound administrator with the trustees, a good speaker with the public, an astute bargainer with the foundations and the federal agencies, a politician with the state legislature, . . . a persuasive diplomat with donors, [and] a champion of education generally. . . .[23]

The president is not solely responsible for the institution's effectiveness, but he or she has the potential to move the institution forward. According to Robert Birnbaum in his study of college presidents,

> Most presidents have short-term, marginal . . . effects on their colleagues . . . [which] would likely not be different under another president with similar qualifications . . . [and they] satisfy the basic leadership needs of most colleges.
>
> Over the longer term, colleges also need the inspiration and motivation of interpretive leadership. This can be provided in two ways. Occasionally it is provided by an exemplary president who is seen as taking the role of faculty, listening, respecting the culture, and being subject to influence. The legitimation and support developed by these presidents may permit them powerful episodic leverage to renew their colleges. . . . [M]odal presidents may be "good enough," as long as they are not in office for extended periods.[24]

**Other Administrators.** The administration is responsible for running the institution. Reporting to the president are high-level administrators organized by function, program, market, and/or geographical area. Thus, reporting to a college president are administrators taking care of functions (such as the vice president for business), programs (such as the dean of the engineering school), and markets (such as the dean of students).

**Board of Trustees.** The president and other administrators are usually responsible to a board of trustees or regents. The board's job is to oversee the institution and to make sure it is operating efficiently to realize its objectives.[25] Among the board's more important responsibilities are the following:

1. Selects or approves the chief officer of the institution.
2. Participates in setting or approving long-range strategy for the institution.
3. Develops or approves policies for the conduct of institutional affairs.
4. Develops or approves compensation levels and salaries of higher management.
5. Participates in fund raising.
6. Considers major issues that have come before the institution.
7. Adds members who are influential and can provide further contacts with other influentials.
8. Legitimizes the institution in the eyes of others.
9. Provides such specialized skills and advice as would come from lawyers and businesspeople.

Clearly, the board is an important part of the institution. Board members must be carefully selected. Most institutions seek prestigious members, some seek "ordinary citizen" members, and others seek a combination. Some boards are so involved in the institution that they are a major force in driving the institution to its best performance. They make demands on the administration to produce plans and results. Other boards are a drag on the institution. They are too conservative and reluctant to change. They remember the school in the past and do not let it change with the times. Administrators must move these trustees to shift their perspective so they will deliberate about the institution's present problems and help the institution to prepare for its future challenges. This transformation may require an action plan. In addition, the institution cannot assume that new trustees will automatically understand their responsibilities and know how to fulfill their obligations as trustees. Many schools and colleges arrange for training programs for new (and continuing) trustees.

**Staff.** The staff consists of the institution's other employees who work on a paid basis. This could include middle management, secretaries, security officers, telephone operators, residence and food service managers and employees, and so on.

The administration faces the normal issues of building an effective staff: defining job positions and responsibilities, recruiting well-qualified people, training them, motivating them, compensating them, and evaluating them. All employees need to be trained in a "customer-service" orientation, whether their "customers" are students or other staff or both. For example, the service-oriented controller's office can choose to help departments and programs to improve and simplify their systems, or constantly complain that other offices "don't know what to do." The positive approach involves looking at other offices as internal customers to be served with helpfulness and skill.

Motivating the staff requires understanding what employees value: fair salaries, appropriate treatment, respect, recognition, an opportunity to learn and develop skills, and the feeling of working for a worthwhile organization. The institution must offer these benefits and create a positive climate in order to expect solid work performance, high morale, and continuous support in return. Educational institutions often feel they are unable to match business-sector salaries, but limited budgets should not compromise efforts to follow the best personnel practices and to deal with employees in a just and constructive manner.[26]

**Volunteers.** Volunteers are unpaid participants in the institution's work, often in fund raising and recruiting. In some educational institutions, volunteers also serve as tutors, instructors, or assistants to staff.

Volunteers usually have a special commitment to the institution and its success. They may be alumni or parents of current students. They want to see others enjoy the benefits the institution offers. When the institution's quality and reputation grow, they are proud and their commitment increases. Often the volunteers include current students, who organize events for prospective students, host campus visits, make visits to their former schools, and in other ways share their own commitment to the institution with others.

The competent volunteer staff manager will be skilled in identifying, attracting, and motivating good volunteers. Understanding the volunteer's needs, the manager will meet them in a way that draws their support and hard work. The institution will sponsor social functions for volunteers, confer awards for many years of service, and arrange other ways to recognize their contributions.

**Consumers.** Marketers use the term *consumer* to refer to the person who uses and benefits from the product or service, and the term *customer* to mean the person who selects a particular source for this product or service.

Educational institutions have many customers: students, staff, faculty, alumni, donors, and others. The term *customer* is most often used in talking about attracting and serving students. Some educators feel uncomfortable with the term *customer* because the term places the teacher-student relationship on a commercial basis, suggests that the professor's activities in teaching and research are "products," and implies that the professor should be reactive and please students at all costs—even at the expense of learning. This is an overly narrow interpretation of the term, as we will demonstrate in this book. Some educators avoid the term by using *client, student,* or *program participant.*

Educational institutions often have several sets of consumers and must distinguish these consumer groups and their relative importance. Consider the issue in relation to a state college. Who is the state college's primary consumer? Is it the students because they consume the product? Is it the students' parents, who expect the college to transmit knowledge and ambition to their sons and daughters? Is it employers, who expect the college to produce people with marketable skills? Is it taxpayers, who expect the college to produce educated people? Or is it the college's alumni, who expect their alma mater to do notable things to make them proud? Educational institutions need to delineate their various customer groups, examine their needs and expectations, and consider how to meet them.

No educational institution can flourish without a sincere appreciation for the needs of its students, which begins with how the institution treats those who inquire about admission, and follows those who enroll through graduation and through their subsequent years as alumni.

**Donors.** Donors are those individuals and organizations that make gifts of money and other assets to the institution. Thus, a university's donors include alumni, alumni parents, friends of the university, foundations, corporations, and government agencies. The university development office has a professional fund-raising staff that develops a philosophy of fund raising and specific proposals that might excite potential donors. The staff tries to match the university's financial needs with appropriate donors and donor groups. The university tries to build value in the eyes of its donors so that donors can enjoy the satisfaction of being part of the institution's success.

Educational institutions also attract the attention and interest of publics beyond the campus.

**Government Publics.** Most educational institutions have some obligations to, and oversight by, government agencies and bodies. Receiving funding from state and/or federal government sources imposes certain standards of performance and financial reporting. Changes in policies and funding levels can have a direct impact on the institution's functioning. Public institutions depend on the goodwill of the state legislature and also have government-appointed boards of regents. Private institutions must meet certain guidelines to assure their students' eligibility for federal assistance.

**Local Publics.** Every institution is physically located in one or more areas and comes in contact with local publics such as neighborhood residents and community organizations. These groups may take an active or passive interest in the school's activities. Thus, the residents surrounding a high school may be concerned about potential vandalism, parking congestion, and other things that may go with large concentrations of teenagers in the neighborhood. An educational institution often has a community relations officer responsible for building cooperative relations with the community before potential conflict issues emerge.

Occasionally an educational institution takes the initiative to improve the surrounding neighborhood in constructive ways. For example, the president of Marquette University was concerned about the dangerous and decaying neighborhood surrounding the campus, and spearheaded a major community renewal program in the early 1990s that included rehabilitating commercial and residential property, while retaining the community's ethnic and economic diversity.[27]

**Activist Publics.** Educational institutions are increasingly being petitioned by interest groups for certain concessions or policy changes. For example, universities have faced demands from environmental groups to limit construction of new facilities, and from animal rights activists to halt research on animals. Attacking or ignoring demands of activist publics is shortsighted. Instead, the institution should intensify its efforts to stay in touch with those groups and to communicate its goals, activities, and intentions more effectively.

**General Public.** Members of the general public carry around images of the institution that affect their patronage and legislative support. The institution needs to monitor how it is seen by the public and to take concrete steps to improve its public image where it is weak or negative. (This is discussed in greater detail in Chapter 9.)

**Media Publics.** Media publics include media companies that carry news, features, and editorial opinion—specifically, newspapers, magazines, and radio and television stations. Getting more and better coverage calls for an understanding of what the press is really interested in. The effective media relations manager has contacts with the major media and systematically cultivates a mutually beneficial relationship with them. The manager offers interesting news items, informational material, and quick access to top administration and faculty specialists. In return, the media are likely to give the institution more and better coverage. (This topic is discussed in Chapter 14.)

Clearly an educational institution should take the interests of all its publics into account. Balancing the needs and demands of each group, however, is a demanding task. At times, the institution will aim to increase its service to one group more than another. Most of the time, the administration is busy balancing and reconciling the interests of diverse groups rather than favoring one group all the time at the expense of the other groups.

What is the relationship between a public and a market? A public becomes a market when the institution decides it wishes to attract certain resources (participation, tuition, donations, and the like) from that public through offering a set of benefits in exchange. The institution will strive to learn more about that public and to design an offer that will prompt the public-turned-market to engage in exchange.

## WHAT BENEFITS CAN MARKETING PROVIDE?

Institutions that understand marketing principles often achieve their objectives more effectively. In a free society, institutions depend upon voluntary exchanges to accomplish their objectives. They must attract resources, motivate employees, and find customers. Proper incentives can help stimulate these exchanges. Marketing is the applied science most concerned with managing exchanges effectively and efficiently, and it is relevant to educational institutions as well as to profit-making firms.

Marketing is designed to produce four principal benefits:

**1.** *Greater success in fulfilling the institution's mission.* Marketing provides tools for comparing what the institution is actually doing with its stated mission and goals. Careful analysis prepares the groundwork for programs to address the real problems. For example, analysis may indicate that few people are attracted to a school because its mission and resulting programs are too narrow. Knowing this, the administrators may decide either to increase public interest in the school's specific mission, or to continue to serve the smaller number of students who find its present mission and programs appealing. Marketing helps identify problems and plan responses that will help the institution fulfill its mission.

**2.** *Improved satisfaction of the institution's publics and markets.* To succeed, institutions must somehow satisfy consumer needs. If the institution fails to develop satisfactory programs for its customers—students, donors, and others—the resulting bad word of mouth and turnover will ultimately hurt it. Institutions that are insensitive to their markets' needs and desires may find more apathy and lower morale. Such institutions ultimately find it difficult to attract new students and adequate alumni support. Marketing, in stressing the importance of measuring and satisfying consumer needs, tends to produce an improved level of service and customer satisfaction.

**3.** *Improved attraction of marketing resources.* In striving to satisfy their customers, institutions must attract various resources, including students, employees, volunteers, donations, grants, and other support. Marketing provides a disciplined approach to improving the attraction of these needed resources.

**4.** *Improved efficiency in marketing activities.* Marketing emphasizes the rational management and coordination of program development, pricing, communication, and distribution. Many educational institutions make these decisions without considering their interrelationship, resulting in more cost for the given result. Even worse, uncoordinated marketing activities may completely miss the mark or turn away the very groups they were designed to attract. Since few educational institutions can afford to waste resources, they must achieve the maximum efficiency and effectiveness in marketing activities. An understanding of marketing can help in this task.

## THE PLAN OF THIS BOOK

The book is divided into six parts. The topics are carefully sequenced to provide the reader with a cumulative understanding of marketing and an ability to apply these ideas directly to educational institutions. Most readers will be best served by reading the chapters in the sequence presented, while specialists may wish to skip to specific topics.

Part I, Understanding Marketing, introduces marketing concepts and the marketing perspective, and shows how these apply to the institution's relationships with its publics and markets. Service quality, value, and customer service are emphasized as the hallmarks of excellent educational institutions and the foundation for effective marketing. We present frameworks for identifying marketing problems and for conducting research to understand the dimensions of these problems.

Part II, Planning Marketing, introduces the process by which the institution develops strategic and operational plans. To plan successfully, the institution needs to understand its internal and external environments, assess its tangible and intangible resources, and formulate its mission, goals, and objectives. These steps precede strategy formation, determining where the institution should focus its efforts and what organizational changes will be needed to support the strategic plan.

Part III, Understanding Markets, describes the ways marketers determine the actual and potential market size, divide the market into market segments, and select those markets that the institution can best serve. After selecting target markets, the institution will seek to understand how consumers decide what programs and services they want. Therefore this section includes the buying decision process for individual consumers of educational services and for organization buyers such as companies.

Part IV, Designing Marketing Programs, presents the steps in planning programs and services and in pricing, locating, scheduling, and communicating about them.

Part V, Applying Marketing, illustrates how marketing applies to recruiting, enrolling, and retaining students; and attracting financial support.

Part VI, Evaluating Marketing Activities, presents guidelines for evaluating the institution's marketing effectiveness to ensure that the institution remains responsive and relevant in the future.

## SUMMARY

Marketing is of growing interest to schools, colleges, universities, and other educational institutions that seek ways to increase their effectiveness in attracting and serving students and in obtaining the resources they need.

What is marketing? Marketing is more than the use of selling, advertising, and promotion to create or maintain demand. Marketing is the skill of planning and managing the institution's exchange relations with its various publics. Our definition is this: Marketing is the analysis, planning, implementation, and control of carefully formulated programs designed to bring about voluntary exchanges of values with target markets for the purpose of achieving institutional objectives. Marketing involves the institution in studying the target market's needs, designing appropriate programs and services, and using effective pricing, communication, and distribution to inform, motivate, and serve the market. Marketing helps the institution to develop viable programs and to price, communicate, and deliver them effectively, and also helps to attract the financial and other resources to fulfill its educational mission.

### Notes

1. Theodore Levitt, "Marketing Myopia," *Harvard Business Review* (July–August 1960), pp. 45–56.

2. Advertising concept developed by Dr. Barbara Shrager, President, Attainment Marketing Partners, Inc., New York, New York.

3. Scott M. Cutlip, "'Advertising' Higher Education: The Early Years of College Public Relations," *College and University Journal*, Part I: 9, no. 4 (Fall 1970), 21–28; Part II: 10, no. 1 (January 1971), pp. 25–33.

4. Sarah Lubman, "Parents and Teachers Battle Public Schools By Starting Their Own," *The Wall Street Journal*, May 19, 1994, pp. A1, A6.

5. National Center for Education Statistics, *Digest of Education Statistics 1992* (Washington, DC: U.S. Department of Education, Office of Educational Research and Improvement, 1992), p. 6.

6. Roberto P. Haro, "Coping With the Human Fallout of California's Education Crisis," *The Chronicle of Higher Education*, April 21, 1993, pp. B3–B4.

7. Richard C. Richardson, Jr., "The Presence of Access and the Pursuit of Achievement," in Judith S. Eaton, ed., *Colleges of Choice: The Enabling Impact of the Community College* (New York: American Council on Education and Macmillan Publishing Company, 1988), p. 26.

8. National Center for Education Statistics, *Digest of Education Statistics 1992*, p. 43.

9. Harold L. Hodgkinson, *Independent Higher Education in a Nation of Nations* (Washington, DC: National Institute of Independent Colleges and Universities, 1993), p. 11. (Prepublication copy)

10. Gerald W. Bracey, "The Third Bracey Report on the Condition of Public Education," *Phi Delta Kappan*, 75 (October 1993), pp. 105–117.

11. Dale Whittington, "What Have Our 17-Year-Olds Known in the Past?" *American Educational Research Journal* (Winter 1992), pp. 776, 778.

12. Stanley M. Elam, Lowell C. Rose, and Alec M. Gallup, "The 25th Annual Phi Delta Kappa/Gallup Poll of the Public's Attitudes Toward the Public Schools," *Phi Delta Kappan*, 75 (October 1993), pp. 137–152.

13. Don Hossler and Larry H. Litten in *Mapping the Higher Education Landscape* (New York: The College Board, 1993) present a comprehensive description of selective institutions of higher education.

14. Harold L. Hodgkinson, *Independent Higher Education in a Nation of Nations*, p. 5.

15. NCEA Data Bank, *United States Catholic Elementary and Secondary Schools 1992–93 Annual Statistical Report on Schools, Enrollment, and Staffing* (Washington, DC: National Catholic Educational Association, 1993).

16. Mandate of the Third Plenary Council at Baltimore, 1884.

17. Pearl Rock Kane, "What Is an Independent School?" *Independent Schools, Independent Thinkers* (San Francisco: Jossey-Bass, 1992), pp. 5–19.

18. Steve Stecklow, "The New Preppies: Boarding Schools Go Overseas for Students; Money Is the Object," *The Wall Street Journal*, February 25, 1994, pp. A1, A7.

19. 1992 budget data from 36 companies surveyed for Executive Education in Major Corporations, a study led by Albert A. Vicere of Pennsylvania State University, cited in "Executive Education," special section of *The Wall Street Journal*, September 10, 1993, p. R3.

20. Instituto Tecnologico y de Estudios Superiores de Monterrey.

21. The Staff College, located in Blagdon, Bristol, has been the primary source of marketing training in the United Kingdom through short courses, workshops, and publications. For two very useful leading marketing guides, see Peter Davies and Keith Scribbins, *Marketing Further and Higher Education* (York, United Kingdom: Longman, 1985); and Michael Baber and Christine Megson, *Taking Education Further: A Practical Guide to College Marketing Success* (Stratford-upon-Avon, United Kingdom: MSE Publications, 1986).

22. One sign of this interest was the translation and publication of the first edition of this book in Japan in 1989, at the request of a major Japanese publishing company.

23. Clark Kerr, *The Uses of the University* (Cambridge, MA: Harvard University Press, 1964), p. 29.

24. Robert Birnbaum, *How Academic Leadership Works: Understanding Success and Failure in the College Presidency* (San Francisco: Jossey-Bass, 1992), p. 169.

25. See Richard T. Ingram and Associates, *Handbook of College and University Trusteeship: A Practical Guide for Trustees, Chief Executives, and Other Leaders Responsible for Developing Effective Governing Boards* (San Francisco: Jossey-Bass, 1980), for a comprehensive discussion of the responsibilities of trusteeship in higher education. See also Richard P. Chait and Barbara E. Taylor, "Charting the Territory of Nonprofit Boards," *Harvard Business Review* (January–February 1989), pp. 44–54. Catholic elementary and secondary school boards can benefit from *Catholic School Management—on Boards*, a bimonthly newsletter (published by Catholic School Management, 24 Cornfield Lane, Madison, CT 06443) on developing more effective boards and on agenda setting; and from a booklet entitled *A Handbook for Agenda Planning and Preparation for Catholic School Boards*, available from the same source.

26. Sunny Merik, "The Claims We Make Make Claims on Us," working paper, University Communications, Santa Clara University, August 1993. This paper reports on the financial difficulties of low-salary employees in higher education, defines central issues of justice and fairness, and proposes ways to provide valued benefits targeted to low-salary employees.

27. Joseph N. Boyce, "Marquette University Leads Urban Revival of Blighted Environs," *The Wall Street Journal*, February 1, 1994, pp. A1, A8, tells about the efforts of the Rev. Albert DiUlio, S.J.

# 2

# Providing Quality Service, Value, and Customer Satisfaction

*In spring 1991 Jim Scannell, a vice president at the University of Rochester, attended a "Quality Day" at Xerox and became an enthusiastic supporter of total quality management (TQM) concepts and techniques.*

*EPARD—an acronym for enrollment, placement, alumni relations, and development, Scannell's unit is responsible for two of the most critical income streams of the university—net tuition revenues and gifts. He shared his enthusiasm for TQM with Kathy Kurz, associate vice president for EPARD. Kurz eventually became the division's quality champion.*

*Scannell and Kurz quickly saw several ways in which an increased focus on quality could help the unit to successfully meet its responsibilities in both the short and long term. The keys, in their judgment, are organization, customer and market responsiveness, fact-based management, and value-driven decisions— in other words, quality management.*

*Here is an excerpt from Kathy Kurz's memo explaining these keys to the division:*

*ORGANIZATION:*
*Everything we do is in support of the lifeblood of the University, from the most obvious functions—admissions and development, to the less obvious—student employment and research. What makes our unit unique is the merger of functions traditionally viewed as disparate in a manner that*

31

*enables synergy and enhanced communication to meet our mission. Although a number of institutions will cease to exist in the next ten to fifteen years, and many will merge or change their basic mission, a few will rise to the occasion and exit this dynamic/chaotic period stronger than they entered. Creative leadership at all levels will in fact make the difference. We believe that our unique organization will make that creative leadership possible.*

*What functions, then, comprise the EPARD division? Enrollment functions have traditionally been viewed as limited to the admissions office. Our unit brings together the functions involved in recruiting, funding, tracking, and retaining, empowering, and replacing students, as well as functions facilitating connections between students and alumni. The links between development and enrollment are obvious, though seldom acknowledged structurally.*

*In higher education institutions, development has traditionally involved fundraising through annual giving, corporate and foundation relations, and major donor cultivation. EPARD incorporates all of those traditional functions with the function of alumni relations. We believe that to be successful fundraising must be built on a solid base of connection with and service to our alumni. This relationship begins to be built before students even enroll, and continues through their life via involvement in such activities as reunions, regional clubs, and volunteer activities linking them to current students. Students are future alumni, and their experience as undergraduates is critical to their lifelong connection to the University and their willingness to contribute not only financial resources, but also their time in recruiting prospective students, and assisting them with career exploration. . . . By merging these functions under the vice president, creative programming and leadership can emerge.*

*CUSTOMER RESPONSIVENESS*

*The best organization in the world will be ineffective if the focus on customers is lost. In the EPARD division, this responsiveness takes a number of forms. First and foremost is our treatment of individual students, alumni, parents, friends and each other (internal customers). We believe that every contact counts, and strive for responsiveness to any and all individual customer concerns.*

*Second, our strategic planning efforts rely on continual development of our capacity to anticipate immediate and long-term customer interests and methods of improving the institution's ability to provide for these interests. Close communication with the Colleges (as the "production" side of the University) is crucial to implementing the institu-*

*tion's response. One clear example of this responsiveness is the role Center for Work and Career Development takes in empowering students. They strive to create a series of academic and experiential programs and opportunities for students to develop the necessary confidence, knowledge and tools to be empowered to take on the new challenges which await them after graduation. Other examples are the programs and opportunities created by Alumni Services that enable alumni to grow as individuals, as contributing members of their communities, and as supporters of future generations of Rochester students through giving their time, talents, and resources. Coordination with the gift processing and development computer programming staffs is critical to the accomplishment of this goal.*

*Finally, our marketing efforts strive to reach out to future customers with a clear and compelling message about the University that will allow us to attract outstanding students in sufficient numbers during a period of national enrollment declines and will enable us to compete effectively for the scarce resources of our alumni, parents and friends. A critical piece of the enrollment marketing effort is our pricing and financial aid strategies. We strive to implement pricing, financial aid, payment plan, and receivables strategies that will optimize the institutions' ability to attract and fulfill the desired academic, racial/ethnic, and socio-economic mix of students.*

## FACT-BASED MANAGEMENT

*The existence of a separate office (Enrollment Management Systems and Research) charged with conducting research and expanding our use of information systems attests to the importance of data in our planning efforts. We are experimentally oriented, and believe in assessing the impact of our programs through sound research techniques. We believe that fact-based decision making is the responsibility of every staff member (not solely the role of the Systems and Research group). Only through data can we truly understand our markets, evaluate our programs, and plan new strategies.*

## VALUE-DRIVEN DECISIONS

*Older structural models found our higher education organizations budget-driven. With the decline in growth in the numbers of new students participating in higher education as well as the increasing competition for gifts, foundation funding, and research grants, colleges and universities became more market driven in the 80's. Our premise is that the most successful organizations, as we head to the 21st century, will be neither budget nor market-driven but rather value-driven. They will understand the two or three core, fundamental qualities and attributes that distinguish the institution and hold on to those principles regardless of the challenges. It is this orientation that will secure and guarantee the integrity and future of the institution into the next century.*

**Source:** Based on two University of Rochester memos, "History of UR Quality" and "What is EPARD+?" by Kathy Kurz.

---

Educational institutions are paying attention to quality principles because they see how improved institutional functioning will benefit students and enhance productive use of limited resources. Responsive institutions want to understand the needs and preferences of their students, faculty, staff, and other constituencies, so they can provide the things these groups value.

Basic human consideration sometimes gets lost in the functioning of often bureaucratic institutions. Over a decade ago, the president of Samford University, Thomas Corts, wrote in a memo that "as surely as there are 'Fifty Ways to Leave Your Lover,' as the popular song goes, there are fifty ways and fifty reasons for a student to end his love affair with his college." At that time the terms *service quality* and *total quality management* were little known in academic circles, yet this college president grasped the essence of these new movements extremely well. His specific proposals, among others, include the president taking an active role in setting expectations for the entire institution about the importance of a service orientation; training employees to have a positive problem-solving attitude when working with students; rewarding those employees who consistently "go the extra mile"; and inviting and responding to student complaints and concerns.

Intensified competition has sharply focused businesses' attention on their customers, customer satisfaction, customer value, and the importance of service quality. Many American companies, inspired by the Malcolm Baldrige National Quality Award competition launched in 1987, have applied the Baldrige award criteria to improving their own processes, output, and customer service. Exhibit 2-1 shows the core values underlying these awards. The Baldrige criteria are now being applied at several higher education institutions, and the State of New York has already implemented an award.[1]

Educational institutions must gather relevant information and implement well-designed and coordinated systems, which provide what their customers value most, in a manner that pleases customers. This chapter presents modes of thought and practices applicable to both businesses and to educational institutions aspiring to high levels of customer satisfaction and service excellence.

EXHIBIT 2-1     The core values underlying the Baldrige awards

---

**Customer-driven quality:** The customer defines quality. The organization should be sensitive to emerging customer and market requirements, and strive to retain customers over the long term.

**Leadership:** The organization's leaders must be personally involved in the quality-improvement effort, and must create a customer orientation, and review and recognize employees for superior performance.

**Continuous improvement:** This must be approached with a well-defined and executed plan, based on information, preferably quantitative.

**Employee participation and development:** Employee satisfaction and customer satisfaction are closely linked. Employees need to be highly trained and involved in decision making.

**Fast response:** Faster and more flexible response to customers means implementing procedures that reduce the time to completion while also reducing errors.

**Design quality and prevention:** Through review of existing processes and careful design of new ones, the institution prevents future problems.

**Long-range outlook:** The institution has a strong and directed focus on the future, with a long-term commitment to developing employees and exceeding customers' requirements.

**Management by fact:** The institution collects and seeks out data to help in planning, assessing performance, and comparing quality against benchmarks.

**Partnership development:** Institutions need to build internal and external partnerships to better accomplish their goals.

**Institutional responsibility and citizenship:** The institution's objectives and practices should support publicly important purposes, such as business ethics, and protection of public health, safety, and the environment.

---

Source: Based on Daniel Seymour, "The Baldrige Cometh," *Change* (January/February 1994), pp. 17–18, which draws on the Baldrige award criteria, available from the National Institute of Standards and Technology, Gaithersburg, MD 208–9.

## ESTABLISH A CLIMATE OF RESPONSIVENESS

*Responsive* institutions focus on the customer—identifying who is the "real" customer, striving to see things from the customer's viewpoint, and satisfying the customer's needs and concerns. The institution makes every effort to sense, serve, and satisfy the needs and wants of its customers and publics within the constraints of its mission and resources. Once it understands customers' needs and preferences, the institution can determine how responsive it can be and then implement programs to manage responsive relations with its customers. The institution that does so reaps tremendous benefits. People who come in contact with the customer-oriented institution report high personal satisfaction:

- "My college was terrific—the faculty really cared about students and taught well."
- "This adult education class is the best I've ever taken."
- "Our local high school offers a quality program for both college prep and vocational students. Students get a good education here."

These publics become the best promoters of the institution. Their goodwill and favorable word of mouth reach others and make it easy to attract and serve more people. Alumni take pride in the institution and are glad to contribute to its future success. The institution receives favorable attention from the news media, further spreading its story.

## Levels of Institutional Responsiveness

Educational institutions vary considerably in their level of responsiveness. Here we distinguish three levels, shown in Table 2-1 and described in the following paragraphs.

**The Unresponsive Institution.** Unfortunately, some educational institutions are not very responsive to their students and to their other internal and external publics. While administrators would like the institution to be more responsive, they sometimes feel they lack the resources or influence over employees. The budget may be insufficient to hire, train, and motivate good faculty and staff. Or administrators may feel they lack the power to require employees to give good service, since employees often are unionized or under civil service and cannot be disciplined or fired for being insensitive to students and others. One inner-city high school principal complained that his problem was not poor students but poor teachers, many of whom were "burned out" and uncooperative but could not be removed.

Unresponsive institutions usually reflect a bureaucratic mentality. Bu-

TABLE 2-1    Three levels of institutional responsiveness

|  | UNRESPONSIVE | CASUALLY RESPONSIVE | HIGHLY RESPONSIVE |
|---|---|---|---|
| Complaint system | No | Yes | Yes |
| Surveys of satisfaction | No | Yes | Yes |
| Surveys of needs and preferences | No | No | Yes |
| Customer-oriented personnel | No | No | Yes |

reaucracy is the tendency of institutions to routinize their operations, replace personal judgment with impersonal policies, specialize the job of every employee, create a rigid hierarchy of command, and convert the institution into an efficient machine.[2] Bureaucrats are not concerned with innovation, with problems outside their specific authority, or with nuances that affect specific situations or, for that matter, with the institution as a whole. They will serve people as long as the people's problems fall within the limits of their jurisdiction. People's problems are defined in terms of how the bureaucratic institution is set up rather than having the institution set up to respond to people's problems. This narrow view of the institution's sphere of action often stands in the way of implementing more effective—and more responsive—systems. For example, employees may be demoralized by restrictive rules imposed from above that prevent them from providing good service.

Administrators in unresponsive educational institutions often assume that they know what people need. Such overconfidence has been eroded in recent years by the realization that students—and donors—have many options. The unresponsive educational institution is probably already out of business or on the way. Even public elementary and secondary schools have competition—both for students and for public support for bond issues and other funding.

Some institutions seem—and are—unresponsive to students because they are more concerned with other things than customer satisfaction. Some universities focus on research and treat undergraduate students as nuisances. As long as institutions exist by mandate (as do government agencies) or are without competition, they will often behave bureaucratically toward their publics. By contrast, responsive institutions realize that to attract students and other needed resources, they must offer programs and other benefits that their publics desire in exchange.

**The Casually Responsive Institution.** When American universities began to experience a decline in student applications in the early 1970s, they began to pay more attention to their students and publics. College administrators who had focused on the problems of hiring faculty, scheduling classes, and running efficient administrative services began to listen more to the students. They left their doors open, made occasional surprise appearances in the student union, encouraged suggestions from students, and added student members to university committees. These steps moved the university into being casually responsive.

The result is a better feeling among the institution's consumers, building a partnership between the servers and the served. Whether or not the increased consumer satisfaction continues depends on whether the institution makes a show of listening or actually does something about what it hears. The institution may merely offer a semblance of openness and interest without intending to use the results in any way. If so, some consumers will resent the institution and may try to force it into greater responsiveness.

**The Highly Responsive Institution.** A highly responsive institution differs from a casually responsive institution in two additional ways: It not only surveys current consumer satisfaction but also researches unmet consumer needs and preferences to discover ways to improve its services. It builds its processes to deliver that quality routinely, and it selects, trains, and empowers its people to become customer-minded.

Many educational institutions fall short of being highly responsive. Most rarely take formal surveys of their students' real needs and desires, nor do they encourage and train their faculty and staff to be student-minded. A small liberal arts college recognized this failing, and it developed the following statement to guide its administrators, professors, and staff.

Students are:

- The most important people on the campus; without them, there would be no need for the institution.
- Not cold enrollment statistics, but flesh-and-blood human beings with feelings and emotions like our own.
- Not dependent on us; rather, we are dependent on them.
- Not an interruption of our work, but the purpose of it; we are not doing them a favor by serving them—they are doing us a favor by giving us the opportunity to do so.

If this philosophy can be successfully implemented, the college will have moved a long way toward being highly responsive.

Some educators will recoil at these assertions, believing that students are not "the most" important people on campus, but rather are the recipients of the valuable programs the school provides. Some schools that narrowly held to this product-centered view of education have already closed, and many others are scrambling for students.

Institutions which succeed in implementing a customer orientation are typically those where *customer orientation* has been defined from a systems perspective, where quality customer service reflects excellent management support. Benjamin Schneider's research on perceptions of service quality found that bank customers reported better service in those branches where *employees* independently reported that they received a lot of support for excellent service—where the branch manager emphasized service, where there were enough tellers and good training, and where equipment was well maintained and supplies plentiful.[3] To build quality customer service, administrators and other managers need to create the conditions for employees to excel.

## Steps in Building a Responsive Institution

Transforming an unresponsive institution into a highly responsive institution requires major commitments and changes in the institution. As noted by Edward S. McKay, a long-time marketing consultant:

It may require drastic and upsetting changes in organization. It usually demands new approaches to planning. It may set in motion a series of appraisals that will disclose surprising weaknesses in performance, distressing needs for modification of operating practices, and unexpected gaps, conflicts, or obsolescence in basic policies. Without doubt, it will call for reorientation of business philosophy and for the reversal of some long-established attitudes. These changes will not be easy to implement. Objectives, obstacles, resistance, and deep-rooted habits will have to be overcome. Frequently, even difficult and painful restaffing programs are necessary before any real progress can be made in implementing the concept.[4]

Many educational institutions start by seeking marketing advice and expertise from outside advisors or from administrators or staff with marketing backgrounds. When the institution decides to become more responsive, it needs to develop a plan for institutional change. Achieving a marketing orientation calls for several steps, the sum of which will, it is hoped, produce a marketing-oriented institution within three to five years. A description of these steps follows.

**Top-Administration Support.** An institution is not likely to develop a strong marketing orientation until its president (or other top leadership) believes in it, understands it, wants it, and wins the support of other high-level administrators for building this function. The president is the institution's highest "marketing executive" and has to create the climate for marketing. A university president, for example, must remind the faculty, registrar, director of student services, and others of the importance of serving students. By setting the tone that the institution must be service-minded and responsive, the president prepares the groundwork for introducing further changes later.

If the president doesn't personally understand, support, and operate with a marketing perspective, the institution will almost always have a hard time changing its direction. To gain this understanding, the president can read, attend conferences and workshops, and visit with leaders at other institutions which reflect a marketing orientation in serving others.

**Effective Organization Design.** The president cannot do the whole marketing job. Certain roles are, or should be, major marketing positions, including the admissions director, director of development, director of alumni affairs, and public affairs director. They should be acutely aware of the importance of their various external markets to the well-being of the institution, and should represent their interests. They should be well-informed about marketing through seminars, workshops, and reading and stay abreast of the professional applications of marketing in their areas of responsibility and for the entire institution. A school with an enrollment management structure often finds that marketing expertise and activities can be better coordinated.

**Internal Marketing Training.**  Ideally there is a widespread awareness and understanding of marketing, so that each employee—administrator, staff, and faculty—understands how his or her role contributes to attracting and serving the institution's various publics and markets. The importance of a marketing orientation must be diffused throughout the institution, starting with top administrators and trustees, since their understanding and support are essential if marketing is to "take" in the institution. The key administrators with marketing positions may take major responsibility for working with their employees, but the institution as a whole may need to develop greater awareness of the market and marketing factors. Those who serve exclusively internal customers should understand that they too can and should reflect a marketing orientation. For example, the media-service employees can see their jobs as protecting the equipment and following scheduling policies, or as flexibly and graciously responding to the instructional needs of faculty and students.

**Marketing-Oriented Hiring Practices.**  Training can go only so far in inculcating the right attitudes in administrators, faculty, and other employees. If administrators have been rewarded for consistency, staff for unbending efficiency, and faculty for concentrating on research, it may be difficult to change the reward system in midstream.

The first principle in developing a caring faculty and staff is to hire caring people. The school can start to hire faculty who are more teaching- and student-oriented. Some people are more naturally service-minded than others, and this can be a criterion for hiring.

New employees (including faculty) should go through an initial training program that emphasizes the importance of a customer orientation. Periodic workshops on listening skills, advising, and on classroom presentation skills and techniques for evaluating student learning can help faculty feel more confident in working with students.

**Hiring Marketing Specialists.**  Many educational institutions eventually consider adding a marketing expert and wonder what the job description should look like and how it would fit in the school's organizational structure. Marketing is a relatively new function, and one that is intertwined in all the institution's activities. In a service business, every encounter with the providing institution is a "moment of truth" that shapes the customer's image of and satisfaction with the service. Thus, there is no consensus about whether it is even possible to have "a marketing person" and what this person would do.

For example, if there is a vice president for marketing, some people in the institution may assume that this person is "in charge of marketing," and feel that they have little or no responsibility for marketing. A vice president for marketing might be viewed primarily as an expert on institutional relations (alumni and development), with little interest or expertise in admissions and the other areas that directly affect students. A director of marketing services could end up in a "service" position, reacting to requests for help from various parts of the institution but without the clout to strengthen the institution's overall marketing orientation and effectiveness.

## FOCUS ON CUSTOMER SATISFACTION

Most educational institutions want to be more effective, but they are not sure how to proceed. Focusing on enhancing customer satisfaction and customer value is a good place to begin. According to Daniel Seymour:

> Developing a lot of happy, satisfied customers—whether they are students, parents of students, alumni, professors, or industry employers—should be a primary goal of causing quality in higher education.[5]

### The Nature of Satisfaction

What determines whether the consumer is highly satisfied, somewhat satisfied, somewhat dissatisfied, or highly dissatisfied with a decision, such as the decision to attend a particular school or college? The satisfaction level is determined by the difference between the service performance as perceived by the customer and what the customer expected: *perceived performance* and *expectations*.

A person could experience one of three broad levels of satisfaction. If the institution's performance falls short of expectations, the person is dissatisfied. For example, if a college fails to perform as the student was led to expect, the student will revise his or her attitude toward the college and may drop out, transfer, or stay but bad-mouth the college. On the other hand, if the college meets expectations, the student will tend to be satisfied and stay. If the institution's performance exceeds the person's expectations, the person is highly satisfied, pleased, or even delighted.

Of course, various publics and customers of the institution may have differing expectations and perceptions of the school's performance. Parents may focus on the school's academic outcomes and consider a school excellent in every respect, while their children may consider the classes boring or school policies too restrictive. Donors may judge the school by one set of criteria, while faculty may use another.

Two people may see the same performance but evaluate it differently because their expectations and interpretations are different. For example, consider two students enrolled in the same class, where the instructor always lectures, never provides time for questions, and is rarely available outside of class. One student may reduce the gap between expectations and performance by concluding—correctly or not—that the instructor is a very knowledgeable and busy person and that students should consider themselves lucky just to be able to take that class. The second student, in contrast, may be highly critical and may find fault with the instructor's performance in other ways as well. The second student will be more prone to drop the class or, if his or her response to other aspects of the school is also negative, to leave the school.

## How Expectations Are Formed

How do the various publics form their expectations? Expectations are formed on the basis of the person's prior experience, statements by friends and associates, and communications with the institution and others like it. If the institution raises expectations too high ("All our graduates move into high-paying careers"), some publics may be disappointed when the institution fails to deliver. On the other hand, if a school underclaims, it may create high satisfaction among students and other publics; but by downplaying the benefits it offers, the school may discourage applicants who would in fact be quite satisfied with the institution. The safest course is for the school to plan for and to deliver a certain consistent level of performance and to communicate this level to its students and other publics.

In the business sector, some of today's most successful companies are raising customer expectations and delivering service to match. These companies are aiming for TCS—total customer satisfaction. Xerox, for example, guarantees "total satisfaction" and will replace at its expense any dissatisfied customer's equipment with the same or comparable product for a period of three years after purchase. Cigna advertises "We'll never be 100% satisfied until you are, too." These companies are aiming high because customers who are *just satisfied* will still find it easy to switch when a better offer comes along.

In like manner, educational institutions seeking to attract and retain customers must track their customers' expectations, their perceptions of the school, their level of satisfaction, and their perceptions of competitors as well.

## ENHANCE CUSTOMER VALUE

So far we have emphasized the importance of satisfying customers' needs and expectations, but we have not considered the cost of providing this level of satisfaction. In general, customers estimate the value of each choice they have, and select the alternative that will deliver the most value. The student selects the school that will provide the best educational experience and/or career outcomes, the faculty or staff member selects the job offer that provides the blend of income, location, and work situation preferred, and the donor considers the impact of a donation to school A versus school B.

From the standpoint of the institution, the resources used in delivering the satisfactions its constituents desire is a *cost*. From the customer's standpoint, acquiring the desired satisfactions has a *price*, which includes money spent plus time, effort, and opportunity cost—other things the customer could have done with the same time and/or money. The *value* received is a matter of customer perception and judgment, not of the monetary price paid or the monetary cost. A recent study concludes,

> Today's consumer is looking for a strong return on educational investment. The question being asked is, "With my academic background, my financial means and personal goals, where can I get the education that will be best for me?"[6]

Several magazines, notably *U.S. News and World Report* and *Money*, annually publish ratings of undergraduate education at U.S. colleges and universities. *U.S. News* rates institutions on their reputations (as judged by higher education leaders), their resources (endowment income, students' academic standing, and so on), and such outcomes as graduation rates and alumni donation rates. *Money* considers the tuition price in relation to each school's outcomes, measured by the number of graduates who receive doctorates or become business leaders, among other categories. *Money's* ratings try to relate the cost (tuition) against the outcomes (achievement).

Of course this is a somewhat narrow definition of value. The quality of the educational experience, the opportunities for personal development and leadership, and other aspects of college life cannot be measured before matriculation nor, with much precision, even after graduation. Besides, each student approaches college with a somewhat different set of needs, abilities, and expectations.

The Institute for Research in Higher Education found that "you get what you pay for" does not apply directly in higher education. They compared institutional ratings on reputation and student quality (from *U.S. News)* and outcomes (from *Money)* for 138 private liberal arts colleges. Considering annual tuition (vertical axis) and results (horizontal axis), they found two distinct horizontal bands of schools, yet each "band" ranges from ordinary to very good/excellent results (Figure 2-1):

> The distinct horizontal bands . . . suggest that institutions may charge the same sticker price for very different performance. The institutions closer to the upper left-hand corner charge dearly for what they produce, while the outliers tending toward the lower-right corner would be the smart choice of full-paying students seeking the best results for their money.[7]

Since value is the relationship between price and quality, the institution can increase value in two ways: reduce price (across the board or through financial aid for certain students) and/or increase quality. Forward-looking educational institutions are trying to enhance value in both ways. While few are actually lowering current tuition, most are looking for ways to *slow the rate of increase* in tuition to the rate of inflation. Slowing tuition increases requires reducing costs in the school's operations by becoming more efficient

FIGURE 2-1   Defining customer value: tuition vs. results

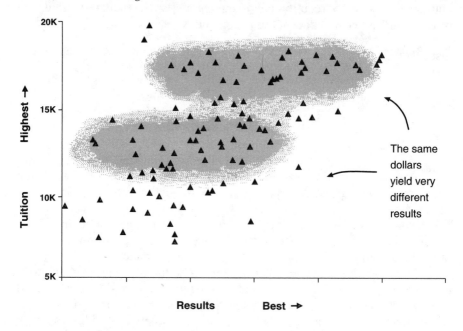

*Institutions may charge the same tuition for very different performance.*

Source: The Institute for Research on Higher Education at the University of Pennsylvania, "Three R's of Higher Education: Choosing the Cream of the Crop," *Change*, Vol. 25, No. 6 (November/December 1993), p. 62.

in using current resources. Various forms of financial aid—including grants, work, and loans—are being used more effectively. Schools also look for ways to save their customers time and effort by, for example, streamlining time-consuming registration procedures. Schools also attempt to enhance quality by improving career services, residence life, and academic programs.

Quality enhancement and cost-reduction efforts need to be guided by the institution's mission and by consideration of what the institution's customers and publics value most, followed by a search for better ways to deliver the desired satisfactions in the most cost-effective manner. We will have more to say about price and value in Chapter 13.

## CREATE A QUALITY-DELIVERY SYSTEM IN THE INSTITUTION

Improving quality and increasing customer satisfaction are *continuous processes*, not discrete events. Consider the self-study and other documents schools prepare before periodic accreditation reviews. After the review and implementation of the required changes, these documents can be filed for the next five to ten years until the next accreditation visit. This treats quality as a checkpoint, deserving of attention only when required by external evaluators. Institutions pursuing quality improvement need to adopt a system and processes to define customer needs, collect performance-relevant information, refine or revise procedures, implement new initiatives, and review progress and improvements on a continuous basis.

Institutions new to total quality management often begin by educating a core group about quality principles and then initiating a few pilot projects, often in administrative services. For example, the first project might involve identifying causes and process improvement to shorten the time to reply to information requests, to reduce the average duration of remodeling jobs, or to reduce errors in billing. These are often easiest to implement because they are frequently repeated processes, amenable to the application of manufacturing-based TQM methods.

*Total quality* for an educational institution includes but goes beyond administrative services. In the United Kingdom, *institutional quality assurance* is a required part of government inspection procedures for every institution of further education. The government's 1993 *Charter for Further Education* sets out the rights of those who attend further education colleges, and requires these colleges to survey customer satisfaction at least annually.

During the 1980s the North Dakota University System tried everything—including "desperate measures"—to deal with demands for quality while cuts in state funding exacerbated the problem of keeping up with growing enrollment. But there was little success and no confidence that the system could survive the 1990s, until the board examined the potential of TQM (total quality management) and concluded that "TQM holds great promise for higher education institutions." In its "Partners for Progress Plan for 1990–97," the board established goals for setting and achieving constantly improving standards of service that meet the needs of students, citizens, economic enterprises, and colleagues in education, as appropriate for each operating unit and level of the system.[8] The plan spelled out 1997 goals for graduates; faculty, research, and public service personnel; creating a campus community; and ensuring quality.

## MEASURE SERVICE QUALITY

Educational institutions offer a range of services, not just one. The *core service* is usually instruction, but the other services of a college often include residential, dining, counseling, advising, career planning, tutoring, library, computer, and other services. Even nonresidential schools include many of these additional services.

Who defines what quality means? The ultimate judge is the customer, the person who decides which services to buy and which to avoid. Customer-defined quality is determined by expectations and perceived performance, as discussed earlier in this chapter. Judgments about quality often reflect one or more of the following four views:

**1.** *Conformance to standards or specifications.* In this view, the most important determinant of quality is performing the service according to the stated guidelines. For example, if confirmation of registration is supposed to be mailed in five days, is it in fact mailed in five days or less?

**2.** *Consistency.* Is the service always performed exactly the same way every time? Achieving consistency is very important in mass-producing a manufactured product, but is it important for services to be performed the same way every time? What does consistency mean in situations where service clients' needs may vary? Educational institutions should aim to produce routine services in a consistent manner—consistently very good. Consistency by itself isn't enough: *Consistent* service quality could translate into "dependably mediocre" or "always outstanding" service.

**3.** *Outcome quality.* Did the service result in the client receiving what was desired? Did the student get the scholarship or career information he or she sought? Did the graduate succeed in getting a job? Services must be designed to provide the outcomes customers value.

**4.** *Process quality.* Process quality describes how the service was delivered. Was the service delivered in a manner that was appropriate and positive for the consumer? Did the career counselor listen attentively to the student's questions, explain the information in a clear manner, ask for feedback, and try to reassure the student that the Career Center would help with his or her job search? For example, a student could get the information he or she needed (good outcome quality), but the process might have been slow and confusing, and the personnel unpleasant (poor process quality).

Each of these perspectives on quality has merit. Those responsible for quality improvement should seek out what customers value most and then apply the approach(es) most relevant to particular situations.

### Implement Complaint and Suggestion Systems

The simplest approach to assessing service quality is to establish complaint and suggestion systems, so that people who are dissatisfied or who see ways to improve service can express their views and ideas. A responsive institution will make it easy for its students and other publics to complain if they are disappointed.

The institution will want complaints and suggestions to surface for three reasons: First, a responsive institution will want to know when its students or other publics are dissatisfied. They are often the best and the only observers of certain aspects of the institution's performance. Second, the institution may need to make significant changes, and complaints and suggestions can help identify the most important areas for attention. To ignore or fail to ask for complaints and suggestions leaves the institution without this potentially valuable information.

Third, some people will take the initiative and complain when they are dissatisfied, but others will simply bad-mouth the school, drop out, or stop donating if they feel the school is not interested in hearing about its failings or in receiving suggestions to make it better. More than one prospective donor has decided against donating because the institution's president or dean did not respond to their letters or calls.[9]

Good complaint and suggestion systems will provide much valuable information for improving the institution's performance. Such systems may not uncover the amount of real dissatisfaction nor identify all good suggestions, since:

1. Many people who are disappointed may not complain because they either feel too angry or believe that complaining would do no good. One study found that only 34 percent of a group of dissatisfied people said they would complain.
2. Some people overcomplain (the chronic complainers), and this introduces bias into the data.
3. Some people with good suggestions will not bother to write them down, believing that they will be ignored anyway.

Some critics have argued that complaint and suggestion systems do more harm than good. If people get an opportunity—indeed, an invitation—to complain or make suggestions, they are more likely to feel dissatisfied. Instead of having their disappointment ignored, they are asked to spell it out and are led to expect redress. If redress is not forthcoming or if suggestions are not implemented, they will be more dissatisfied. Although this might happen, we believe that the value of the information gathered by soliciting complaints and suggestions exceeds the cost of stimulating dissatisfaction or raising expectations, as long as the institution takes action to correct identified problems.

How can complaints and suggestions be facilitated? The school can make it easy for dissatisfied (or satisfied) people to express their feelings by placing suggestion boxes in the corridors and by surveying students or other publics (discussed in more detail later).

Educational institutions could also borrow practices from service-oriented companies. Many restaurants and hotels provide comment cards for guests to report their likes and dislikes. Hospitals often have an appointed "patient advocate" who listens to patients' complaints and suggestions, resolves problems, and formulates plans to prevent future problems. Some customer-oriented companies—Procter & Gamble, General Electric, and Whirlpool—have toll-free 800-number telephone "hot lines" to maximize the ease with which customers can inquire, make suggestions, or complain. This continuous flow of information from consumers provides these companies with many good ideas and enables them to act more rapidly to resolve problems.

New technologies create new feedback systems. Many higher education institutions now provide electronic-mail access for faculty, staff, and students. By providing an electronic "mailbox" and publicizing its existence ("Have a suggestion? E-mail to SUGGEST"), the school could make it even easier for people to make suggestions. On-line terminals in campus libraries and other locations can be used by those who don't have computer E-mail accounts.

Once complaints and suggestions are received, the school must have procedures for handling them speedily and equitably. Handling complaints is different from handling suggestions. The institution should follow the following guidelines in handling complaints:

1. Take pains to learn about complaints quickly, by making it easy for dissatisfied customers to complain. Provide comment cards, telephone numbers, or other easy-to-use mechanisms.
2. Be prompt in taking responsibility for mistakes when they are discovered or brought to the school's attention by others.
3. Strive to make amends as rapidly and thoroughly as possible by empowering those who receive the complaints to respond whenever possible.

In addition to addressing individual complaints, the school should try to identify the major categories of complaints. Often most of the complaints will cluster around a small number of areas, which can then be the focus of attention. The school might count the number of complaints about quality of instruction, residence-hall facilities, food, and other areas, and then rate the seriousness and remediability of complaints in each area. The school should focus its corrective actions on those categories showing high frequency, high seriousness, and high remediability.

In the case of suggestions, a committee or other review process should also be established to handle them in a timely manner. For example, many university libraries have a designated bulletin board where typed copies of user queries are displayed, along with carefully researched responses by the library staff.

## Prepare Service Report Cards

The next step is to collect the perceptions and evaluations of customers and publics in more systematic and proactive ways. This is often done by asking consumers to fill out *service report cards*, which vary from very simple checklists to more comprehensive surveys.

The school may prepare a service report card covering the entire institution or prepare questionnaires to assess service quality for individual programs or services. A service report card to alumni will naturally be different from one for new freshmen or currently enrolled students. A focus on quality requires the institution to continuously seek customer evaluations at various levels.

Preparing a service report card requires identifying the categories or service attributes the respondents will evaluate. There are several ways to prepare lists of categories or service attributes:

1. *Ask managers—but be careful.* The administrators responsible for each service area can list the most important areas. The food-service director would list aspects of that service, the library would add others, and so on. This is a speedy way to construct a report card, but managers may not focus on the service items that are most important to the respondents (in this case, students) or they may word the items in a confusing manner. For example, the food-service director might list "quality of food" and mean freshness, while students might interpret it to mean the variety and tastiness of the food.

2. *Conduct focus group interviews with respondent groups.* Groups of 10 to 12 members of the intended respondent group (e.g., undergraduate students living on campus) could be invited to attend an informal discussion led by a trained moderator. (Focus groups are described in greater detail in Chapter 3.) Respondents could be asked to list and discuss the various services they believe are of greatest concern to students, and then to fill in the other services that deserve attention.

3. *Collect critical incidents.* The critical incident technique (CIT), developed by John Flanagan in the 1950s, has become a central tool for identifying service problems and training needs. The researcher interviews (or sends paper-and-pencil surveys to) people who work in a particular occupation or are customers of such businesses or organizations, asking them to relate specific examples—incidents—of outstanding and of poor service. Content analysis of these incidents helps to identify training gaps and/or areas of customer sensitivity, so that training programs can be developed to increase excellent performance and overcome barriers to its achievement.[10]

4. *Administer the SERVQUAL instrument.* Parasuraman, Zeithaml, and Berry developed a standard-format questionnaire called SERVQUAL (for SERVice QUALity) to obtain consumers' expectations and evaluations of various types of services and service providers.[11] The SERVQUAL instrument is used to obtain the respondents' opinions about what the service provider *should do* (the respondent's expectations) and what the particular service provider *actually does* (the respondent's perceptions of the institution's per-

formance). Several researchers have adapted the original SERVQUAL instrument for use by educational institutions.[12]

The authors of SERVQUAL identified five types of gaps that reduce service quality, which are here translated into an educational context[13]:

*Gap 1.* The gap between student expectations and university administrators' perceptions of those expectations.

*Gap 2.* The gap between administrators' perceptions of student expectations and their translation of these expectations to faculty and staff.

*Gap 3.* The gap between stated university policies, procedures, and other performance specifications and the actual delivery or implementation of services by the university's faculty and staff.

*Gap 4.* The gap between actual service delivery and the university's external communications (promotion) about its services.

*Gap 5.* The gap between a student's expected and perceived experience at the university. The SERVQUAL instrument addresses this fifth gap.

### Finalize the Instrument and Collect Customer Judgments

At this stage the researcher must transform the list of service attributes or categories into a clear and useful survey format. (The SERVQUAL questionnaire includes this step.) Service report cards typically solicit the respondent's appraisal of what the current situation is and what it ought to be; what the respondent expected and what he or she experienced; or how important a series of attributes are to the respondent, and how well the institution performs on each attribute.

Any service report card needs to be pretested with a small number of respondents similar to the intended respondent group(s). For example, if the survey is for upper-division students, the pretesting should be conducted with upper-division students. The researchers will seek to clarify the wording and organization of the questionnaire to assure that the answers will be meaningful and interpretable.

The researchers will decide how many respondents to survey, what their characteristics should be (a sample of all students? of transfer students? and so on), and how they will be reached to participate in the study. The researchers will see that the surveys are distributed and returned, and that the data are coded (or precoded) and entered for computer analysis as appropriate.

### Analyze Results and Seek Implications

Statistical analysis of the results will vary by the type of survey selected. Three basic types of analysis are described here, with references for greater depth.

*Gap analysis.* SERVQUAL and similar surveys ask respondents to describe what they expected and what they experienced. The results of such surveys can be usefully expressed in terms of the *gaps* between expectations and performance, between what should be and what is, and so on. The gaps are often expressed numerically as the respondent group's mean rating (for example, on a scale from 1 to 7) of expectation for each attribute compared with the group's mean rating of actual performance on an equal scale. The data can also be displayed graphically with one line connecting the ratings of "Is" and another the ratings of "Ought" (see Figure 6-5 on discrepancy ratings). The institution would look at the areas in which respondents indicate the greatest discrepancies and relatively high expectations and take steps to bring the actual performance closer to the respondents' expectations.

*Root-cause analysis.* Root-cause analysis involves a close examination of the factors that contribute to a negative outcome. The antecedents of the negative outcome are traced back to identify ways in which the system or process can be changed to reduce or eliminate the same outcomes in the future. Exhibit 2-2 illustrates root-cause analysis applied to a student's weak academic performance. Root-cause analysis is an example of *formative evaluation,* since the analysis helps decision makers to improve an ongoing process.

*Importance-performance analysis.* If the service questionnaire is appropriately designed to collect respondents' ratings of the *importance* of each attribute and the institution's *performance* on each attribute, the researcher can construct a graphical display of the relative positions of the attributes for the institution.[14]

Figure 2-2 shows an example of an importance-performance grid for a small liberal arts college. Pleasant College (name disguised) was once exclusively a women's college but had begun admitting men. The college also had launched a B.S. in nursing program that attracted mostly older, returning students. Figure 2-2 shows the results for one segment: female students under age 24, the traditional market for this college.

Since the college had several significantly different segments (men, returning women, and nursing students), separate importance-performance grids were prepared for each segment in order to identify major differences. For example, the importance-performance grid for male students showed that athletic facilities were very important and totally inadequate, while the nursing students had such a hectic schedule of hospital assignments and course work that many of the college's amenities went unused and were therefore very unimportant to them. Such results can direct the institution in matching its offerings to its key segments.

It is useful to plot the segment-level importance-performance grids onto transparency material (preferably with a different color ink on each) so that the grids for multiple segments can be superimposed and visually compared.[15]

EXHIBIT 2-2    An application of root-cause analysis

Paula had never been a strong student, but she worked hard. She was on financial aid, and needed to keep "above C-level." Her transcript was mostly C's peppered with some D's and an occasional B. But when she got her grade report for the previous quarter, she was alarmed—one C, one D, and one F! "What will happen to me? What can I do now?"

The D average for the quarter would place her financial aid status in jeopardy. Her loans and grants wouldn't pay for F's and she couldn't pay for those units herself. She would be on academic probation and might have to drop out of school for a quarter or two to earn money to return.

How did it happen? Because she was devoting almost every hour she wasn't in class to working. She didn't have much time to study, and did a lousy job in courses that required team projects because she had a hard time coordinating meetings with team members. They resented her lack of contribution, and she felt guilty, but work came first. The result: Exhaustion.

Why? Because the past quarter's workload was tougher than ever. The courses Paula bombed in were in her major, but she wasn't well-prepared for them. She had taken the prerequisites the preceding quarter, but she now realized she just hadn't learned enough to provide a foundation for the more advanced courses.

Why? Because the prerequisite courses were taught by part-timers who were hired, handed textbooks, and given classroom assignments and a "welcome." The part-time faculty members developed their syllabi as best they could, and taught their courses. But they received no feedback from other professors about their syllabi, assignments, or exams. Therefore professors in prerequisite courses didn't always know what their students would need to master to do well in succeeding courses. Why?

Because the full-time faculty were so busy with teaching and committee work that they never thought of, let alone implemented, an orientation plan for new part-time faculty. In fact, new full-time faculty got very little guidance either. Thus new faculty were unacquainted with the overall framework of the major or how their courses fit into that framework.

Because only full-time faculty attended department meetings—and they never thought to invite part-timers to attend.

Because part-timers taught primarily undergraduate courses during the day, because it was widely held that "anyone" could teach the basic undergraduate courses—the prerequisites. And that way the full-time faculty could teach the advanced electives and graduate courses.

Sometimes a cursory analysis of a problem is not enough to identify its real origins. On first glance, it appears that Paula failed. But as we look deeper, it becomes clear that the professors and, ultimately, the system were major causes of her failure.

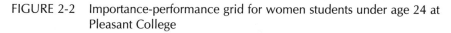

FIGURE 2-2   Importance-performance grid for women students under age 24 at Pleasant College

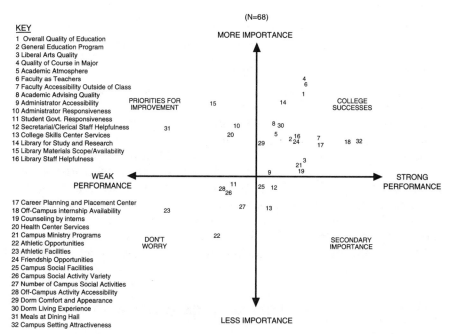

The researcher would then direct the institution's attention to the attributes that respondents rated as very important and on which the institution was rated strong (the upper-right-hand quadrant). These factors often can be highlighted in communications about the institution, as long as they are sufficiently important. ("Good food in dining halls" does not save a college rated weak on curriculum, advising, and career outcomes.)

To focus improvement efforts, the researcher would direct attention to the upper-left-hand quadrant, the location of attributes respondents considered important but on which the institution performed poorly.

*Care in using averages.* Gap analysis (including SERVQUAL) and importance-performance analysis rely on using *means* (averages) of respondents' judgments about their expectations and about the institution's performance. The institution should be very careful to determine whether mean ratings are appropriate. If the study finds that students are reasonably content, does this average mask the fact that half the students are enthusiastic while half are miserable and angry?

In addition to segment-by-segment analysis described previously, the institution should look for wide dispersion of opinions and, where found, look deeper into the factors contributing to them. The institution may choose to carry out (or hire specialists to carry out) more elaborate research studies and data analysis to identify underlying predictors that may not show up in univariate and bivariate analyses.

*Measuring long-term impact.* Evaluations of service quality are typically gathered soon after the service has been received. (A typical example is the hotel feedback card asking "How did we do?" and asking if the room was clean, the bed comfortable, and the staff courteous.) But most educational institutions aim to have a lasting impact on their students and others who come in contact with them.

Appropriate systems for monitoring longer-term effects should be established. Most service-quality evaluations by educational and other service institutions imitate hotel feedback cards rather than measuring their stated longer-term customer-oriented objectives.[16] For example, a professor's performance ("service quality") is often assessed in the short term by student evaluations of specific courses at the end of each term. A longer-term perspective would also consider the professor's impact on students through the skills and habits of mind transmitted, the academic and career advising during the students' enrollment, and through informal mentoring after they graduate.

## BENCHMARK WITH EXCELLENT ORGANIZATIONS

Current students and other clients come to an educational institution with certain expectations. A school or college can generate strong satisfaction by meeting or exceeding these expectations. But to continue to improve, the institution may have to look beyond its current operating assumptions and the expectations of current customers, to identify better policies and practices, and even to raise its sights and/or broaden its scope.

The practice of benchmarking refers to measuring an institution's processes and performance by comparing them with the processes and performance of other institutions or businesses known for being "the best" on some attribute. Many of the world's most successful companies have turned to benchmarking to enhance their improvement efforts. Du Pont, for example, conducted a study of outstanding companies to identify the characteristics and practices that contributed to their reputation for delivering superior value to their customers.[17]

A college engaging in benchmarking could undertake one or more of the following three approaches. First, the college could compare its own *performance statistics* with other *similar colleges* to identify those which are outstandingly better on some measure. For example, the college might discover another college that has a much higher retention-to-graduation rate, and then contact (and even visit) the college to learn how it accomplished this success.

Relevant benchmark information for higher education can be obtained from several sources, including the federal government, the Higher Education Data Sharing (HEDS) organization, and the Association of Governing Boards of Universities and Colleges.[18]

Second, the college could identify other colleges that have adopted procedures and practices that are promising. For example, colleges that were early to introduce highly efficient, computerized course registration procedures became models for many other institutions. Colleges that have implemented effective residence-hall enhancement programs, diversity training, and other innovations are sought out by institutions interested in adopting the best available practices.

Third, the college could compare its performance on selected dimensions with "the best" businesses and organizations *outside the field of education* to identify ways to increase effectiveness. Hospitals have learned "hospital-ity" from examining the best practices of the top hotels. A college could learn from how Nordstrom department store has earned an outstanding reputation for attentive salespeople. A university-wide task force at Stanford University looked at ways to "re-engineer" the university and its systems, and included study visits to outstanding companies around the United States.

The goal of benchmarking is to identify promising new practices for the institution to implement. For example, a university experiencing a decline in residence-hall occupancy could benchmark against other university residence-hall programs but they could—and should—also benchmark against their competition, which in many cases are local apartment complexes.

Benchmarking is a valuable but humbling experience. Examining the successes of others can (and should) jolt the institution out of its complacency and lead to greater efficiency and effectiveness and ultimately to enhanced customer satisfaction.

## IMPROVE SERVICE QUALITY

All the attention to gathering and analyzing customer complaints, suggestions, performance evaluations, and benchmarking data is just the first stage in quality and satisfaction improvement. Next the institution must take action to close the gaps between what is currently being done and what the institution aims to become.

Appropriate and feasible actions to address quality gaps will vary from one institution to another. Excellent resources on improving service quality have appeared in the past few years. Here we will illustrate the range of service quality improvements.

**Redesign Services.** The service may need to be completely redesigned and offices reorganized to correct fundamental design flaws. A common source of student frustration is student financial services. Enrolled students and their parents complain that they "can't get a straight answer" to their questions about bills, balances, financial aid, and other matters. Exhibit 2-3 describes how Pratt Institute redesigned its administrative services for students to be both more efficient and more appropriate for their customers.

**Select, Train, and Motivate Employees.** A service-oriented institution needs to reflect its service culture in designing positions, advertising them, and selecting the best candidates. Providing training—continuous training—communicates better ways to perform the job and, at the same time, the institution's serious interest in facilitating more effective performance. Enhancing employee motivation is often related to the nature of the work environment, the collegiality and mutual support, and expressions of genuine appreciation for a job well done.

Institutions that value their clients and customers, and that show the same care and consideration for their employees as they expect employees to give to customers, often achieve strong internal support for efforts to improve service quality. Changes in procedures need to be clearly communicated, along with the reasons behind them, and the appropriate training and technology need to be in place to facilitate them.

Many colleges and universities overlook a large pool of employees when they plan training and quality-improvement programs: their own students, employed on campus under the work-study program. Those students who work for "excellent bosses" gain tremendous career advantages along with their paychecks, while too often student workers are not held to appropriate standards of training, attentiveness, and dependability. Even students who depend on them for services—for example, in the gym or library—hold low service expectations because the work-study students "are just doing this to get through school." This view, if widely held, will assure poor service on many campuses to the detriment of student workers and their customers.

**Empower Front-Line Service Providers.** Many services are delivered in face-to-face or telephone *service encounters* between the customer and the provider. The congeniality, helpfulness, and expertise of the service provider will largely determine the satisfaction of the customer. Relevant training (including problem analysis and role playing) and well-organized information, coupled with the authority to resolve most problems, can help front-line providers to perform their jobs better.

**Enhance Technological Supports for Service.** Attributing service disappointments to providers' "bad attitudes" or "lack of training" can mask the fundamental problem of a lack of the appropriate or most effective tools. Equipped with computer access to an up-to-date database, the financial services employee can answer student requests for information. Academic advisors cannot give tailored advice about course selection unless they have access

EXHIBIT 2-3    Redesigning administrative student services

Student administrative services are often ineffective for three reasons. First, students often get inadequate advise and direction from these offices. Staff who interact with students often are responsible both for counseling students and for handling transactions. At the beginning of a term, the processing of transactions takes precedence, advising is short-changed, and students are confused. According to Julie Karns, vice president for finance and administration, financial counseling is especially important for young students. Eighteen-year-olds, including many from modest-income families, are expected to negotiate a $20,000 to $30,000 annual investment at private colleges and universities, or $10,000 to $15,000 costs at public and state institutions. Given the number of separated and divorced families, the economic squeeze on middle-income families, and the variety of grants, loans, jobs, and work-study jobs, most undergraduates live on the edge financially and are confused about financial aid possibilities.

Second, staff in the bursar, registrar, and financial aid offices often are narrowly trained and cannot respond to student questions about other offices and procedures, and cannot make correct referrals. Third, the offices of the bursar, registrar and student records, and financial aid often report to different institutional divisions, leading to fragmented decision making and inconsistent policies. (Furthermore, financial aid is typically separate from admissions, although from the applicant's viewpoint the institution's "offer" is a combination of admission and aid.)

Pratt Institute engaged in an extensive planning process to develop a new model for administrative services based on three new functions. In place of the three traditional offices of bursar, registrar, and financial aid, Pratt grouped its services by functions: information and counseling; operations and processing; and analysis, reporting, and services. At the Information Center students can make inquiries about academic, financial, or record keeping matters with minimal waiting. Or for complex matters or detailed counseling, students can make appointments with a counselor. The first staff person to discuss the problem summarizes the student's problem in writing and begins the research process before the student comes for the appointment. The office also runs information sessions on financial aid, helps find campus jobs, and carries out other duties.

The operations and processing group staff are trained to answer basic student questions about policy and procedures, but their primary role is to process academic and financial information promptly and accurately. The third group issues reports and studies, but also assists the operations group with instruction about data processing and use of technology.

Implementing these changes required a major reorganization, with attention to reassigning of employees by skills. Management and staff development included listening skills, telephone technique, offering appropriate referrals, and how to provide students with advice on a single visit. Systems enhancements will eventually offer students access to the transcripts and financial accounts through ATM-like systems.

Source: This section draws on Julie Karns, "Redesigning Student Services," *Planning for Higher Education*, 21 (Spring 1993), 27–32.

to advisees' transcripts. A department secretary cannot handle administrative tasks, produce manuscripts and correspondence, answer student questions, and answer all phone calls coming for faculty because the institution resists installing separate voice-messaging capabilities.

Sometimes the tools—for example, personal computers and networks —are available, but aren't being used effectively. One university, about to enroll a deaf student for the first time, advised all department secretaries and key administrators to come for training in the use of special telecommunications equipment (TDD) the university planned to buy and install. It was then pointed out that all administrators, faculty, staff, *and* students already had access to electronic mail messaging, which was more useful (since it reached everyone) and carried no additional costs.

**Train Customers to Help Themselves.** Many service firms have discovered time and cost savings *and* often enhanced customer satisfaction by training customers to do part of the job themselves. Customers thus become "partial employees" of the institution.[19] Examples abound in the commercial sector: motorists pump their own gas, customers get cash from automated teller machines, and dial their own phone calls. Cafeteria customers bus their own trays in return for faster service and lower prices. Some institutions combine customer training with technology to enlist customers to do much more work themselves. Students equipped with personal identification numbers and computer access can check their own transcripts and registration records, rather than line up at the registrar's office. "Smart" software that matches courses taken with graduation requirements can make more time for faculty and advisees to discuss issues other than rather than completion of requirements.

**Lead with High-Visibility Actions.** Sometimes the institution recognizes that many areas need to be improved but lacks the resources to make major changes quickly. The new president of a good but struggling liberal arts college wanted to communicate to students that he recognized their importance and that he aimed to make the college better and stronger. The college needed academic enhancement, athletic facilities, and other changes that would require vigorous fund raising. Taking office in the summer, he first directed that the interiors of all the student residences be repainted and the most urgent deferred maintenance problems addressed. These actions alone are not substitutes for other, longer-range service-quality improvements, but they can reassure students and publics that the institution is "on the move."

**Communicate with Customers.** When institutions engage in service-quality improvement, they may assume that the improvements are obvious to their customers. Institutions not only need to offer quality and value, they need to communicate it. Pratt Institute will want to publicize its reorganized administrative services, featuring how the changes will make life easier for students. Employees in the new offices wear name badges, so students and others can ask for specific employees and also thank them for good service. If the library computerizes its catalog and checkout system, users need to be trained in how to use the new system and to be informed about how these enhancements will help them.

## AIM FOR CONTINUOUS IMPROVEMENT

Educational institutions operate in an environment of constant change. Not only does the external environment change, but four-year colleges see at least a quarter of their student population change each year, and community colleges have a wave of new faces every term. Faculty and staff don't stay the same forever, nor do the colleges and schools that employ them.

Since it is impossible to reach the pinnacle of service excellence once and for all time, educational institutions must constantly identify and implement improvements in what they do and how they do it. Curricula need updating and revision, procedures need to be upgraded as new needs and technologies emerge, and all employees—faculty, staff, and administrators—need access to constant training and development opportunities. The process of continuous improvement requires a mindset of constant monitoring, problem identification, and research. Effective marketing action depends upon well-designed, accurate marketing research, which is addressed in the next chapter.

## SUMMARY

Educational institutions provide valued services to their students and other customers, and aim to meet customer needs and expectations. While many institutions want to be responsive and effective, they are not sure what responsiveness is or how to achieve it. Some institutions seem unresponsive because they are concerned with other things than customer satisfaction. They are bureaucratic, impersonal, rigid, and reject innovation. Highly responsive institutions, in contrast, survey current customer satisfaction but also look for unmet needs and ways to enhance their services.

Creating a highly responsive institution requires major commitments and changes, including top-administration support, effective organization design, internal marketing training, and marketing-oriented hiring practices, among others.

Effective, responsive institutions deliver customer satisfaction, striving to meet and exceed customers' expectations. They understand that customers seek value—the results received for their expenditure of time, effort, and money—and they try to increase value by operating efficiently and effectively.

The institutions look at service quality as it is defined by their customers, measuring customers' judgments of their service quality through complaint and suggestion systems, service report cards, and the feedback from these systems. Some techniques for appraising service quality include gap analysis, root-cause analysis, importance-performance analysis, and benchmarking with other educational institutions, businesses, and other organizations.

With the results of this service-quality analysis, the institution must take action to close the gaps between what is currently being done and what the institution aims to become. The institution must determine which gaps are most important to customers and, therefore, most worth the time and effort to reduce. Areas for action include redesigning services, empowering frontline service providers, enhancing technical supports for service (for example, with computers, training, telecommunications facilities, and so on), training customers to help themselves, leading with high-visibility actions, and communicating with customers.

Service quality is not achieved once and for all, but must be preserved and enhanced through efforts at continuous improvement. Institutions that care about quality and produce quality have a strong advantage in implementing marketing. They know their customers, and they have identified the critical processes that must be carried out well to generate a high level of customer satisfaction. They continually collect data to guide productive planning and action and to increase the likelihood that the most valued activities are done right the first time.

## Notes

1. Daniel Seymour, "The Baldrige Cometh," *Change* (January–February 1994), pp. 16–27.

2. See Anthony Downs, *Inside Bureaucracy* (Boston: Little, Brown, 1967).

3. Benjamin Schneider, "The Service Organization: Climate Is Crucial," *Organizational Dynamics* (Autumn 1980), pp. 52–65.

4. Edward S. McKay, *The Marketing Mystique* (New York: American Management Association, 1972), p. 22.

5. Daniel T. Seymour, *On Q: Causing Quality in Higher Education* (Phoenix, AZ: The Oryx Press, 1993), p. 42.

6. The Institute for Research on Higher Education at the University of Pennsylvania, "Three R's of Higher Education: Choosing the Cream of the Crop," *Change*, 25, no. 6 (November/December 1993), pp. 59–62.

7. Ibid., pp. 61–62.

8. Daniel T. Seymour, *On Q: Causing Quality in Higher Education*, pp. 35–36.

9. One such story is told about Leland and Jane Stanford, who returned to the United States after the death of their only child in Italy. They stopped to see the president of Harvard College, intent upon making a major donation in memory of their son. Reportedly they were snubbed and so decided to return to their farm in California where they established and endowed Stanford University in 1891.

10. Sandra Wilson-Pessano, "Defining Professional Competence: The Critical Incident Technique 40 Years Later," invited address, Annual Meeting of the American Educational Research Association, Division I (April 1988).

11. A. Parasuraman, Valarie Zeithaml, and Leonard Berry, *SERVQUAL: A Multiple-Item Scale for Measuring Customer Expectations of Service Quality* (Cambridge, MA: Marketing Science Institute, Report No. 86–108, 1986).

12. Matt Shanks, Mary Walker, and Thomas J. Hayes, "University Service Expectations: A Marketing Orientation Applied to Higher Education," *Proceedings of the 1993 Symposium for the Marketing of Higher Education* (Chicago, IL: American Marketing Association, 1993), pp. 100–111, includes such a modification of SERVQUAL. The study asked solely for expectations, however, and not for perceived performance of the subject university's MBA program.

13. Dale A. Lunsford, "The Gap Model of Service Quality: A Research Paradigm for the Marketing of Higher Education," *Proceedings of the 1992 Symposium for the Marketing of Higher Education* (Chicago, IL: American Marketing Association, 1992), p. 95; Valarie A. Zeithaml, A. Parasuraman, and Leonard L. Berry, *Delivering Service Quality: Balancing Customer Perceptions and Expectations* (New York: The Free Press, 1990).

14. John A. Martilla and John C. James, "Importance-Performance Analysis," *Journal of Marketing*, (January 1977), pp. 77–79.

15. Each point on the grid represents the mean importance rating and the mean performance rating on an attribute. Two specific refinements aid in the practical use of importance-performance analysis. First, the resulting data points may tend to cluster close together and be located predominantly in the upper-right-hand quandrant. Respondents often rate "everything" as "important," and—despite years of complaining—students often rate the school's performance as pretty good. Also, few students are in a position to compare the performance of the school they attended with that of other schools. The school's decision makers could gain additional insight by moving the underlying grid toward the upper-right-hand corner of the diagram to identify those areas that rate "less well" than others in a relative sense.

Second, to facilitate multisegment visual comparisons, all the ratings must be charted on grids using the same dimensions. Then the resulting grid for, say, male students can be printed on a transparency and superimposed on the grids for other segments to do a visual comparison of the ratings of each attribute.

16. See Peter Seldin, "The Use and Abuse of Student Ratings of Professors," *The Chronicle of Higher Education*, July 21, 1993, p. A40.

17. Bill Siefkin, "Review of Research on Organizations Providing Superior Value to Their Customers," internal working paper, Du Pont Corporate Plans, 1991.

18. See William F. Massy, "Meaningful Performance: How Colleges and Universities Can Set Meaningful Goals and Be Accountable," Discussion Paper, Stanford Institute for Higher Education Research, Stanford University, Stanford, CA, especially pp. 16–19.

19. Peter K. Mills and James H. Morris, "Clients as Partial Employees of Service Organizations: Role Development in Direct Participation," *Academy of Management Review*, 11 (1986), pp. 726–735; and Richard B. Chase, "Where Does the Customer Fit in a Service Operation?" *Harvard Business Review*, 56 (November–December 1978), pp. 137–142.

# II

# Planning Marketing

# 3

# Identifying and Researching
# Marketing Issues

*Calderdale College in Halifax, England, is a college of further education (similar to an American community college). The administration became aware that a growing number of local residents were self-employed, running their own small businesses. Many of the first-time small business owners were struggling to make ends meet due to their inexperience. The college felt that this segment could greatly benefit from business-related training and support.*

*The college already offered a variety of full- and part-time courses in business, leading to certificates, but few of the local small business owners ever enrolled. The college, therefore, set out to find out why the college was not attracting them.*

*Investigating the market, they found that many of these small business owners shared certain characteristics. They were all very busy trying to keep their businesses afloat and could not spare the time to attend classes. Most had left school at the earliest possible opportunity and, therefore, lacked any formal qualifications. Their memories of formal education were often negative. To them, a college was no different from school. College instructors, like schoolteachers, were thought to be "academic," out of touch with reality, and incapable of providing the practical advice the businesspeople so desperately needed. Many felt they needed to learn more about modern information technology, but they were afraid to tackle it, thereby exposing their ignorance about it in public.*

*When the college compared this profile with the marketing mix it currently offered, it was obvious why it was not attracting the small business segment of the market:*

*Most existing business programs required regular attendance over a long period of time and led to formal certificates, which this segment considered irrelevant. The courses emphasized theoretical "textbook" knowledge as much as practical skills. The college's publicity emphasized features of the colleges and its courses, rather than any resulting benefits to participants. The vast majority of the college's students were young people, and adults did not feel "at home" in that environment. The classes were held in traditional classrooms in Victorian-era buildings.*

*The result of the college's analysis was the development of a separate marketing mix targeted at small businesses.*

*The program consisted of short courses which could be taken on flexible schedules and at convenient locations. Thus, the* product *and the* process *of delivery were changed to match the market. The courses were delivered away from the college's main buildings, in a small business industrial complex. The facilities were attractive and the location convenient. This took into account the* place *and the* physical facilities. *The instructors were carefully chosen for their practical, down-to-earth approach. They invited successful businesspeople to speak to the class, which gave the courses more credibility because the* people *were right. Trainees were able to learn at their own pace, on up-to-date equipment, with opportunities for one-on-one help in privacy, a change in the* product *that increased its appeal. Supporting publicity material—*promotion*—emphasized the practical benefits to businesses and their owners.*

*This new program took time and money to establish, but the college was able to get additional funding from government sources. This meant that the cost of attending—the* price*—could be set at a level that struggling businesspeople could afford. The outcome of the initial research was that Calderdale College now provides a highly regarded and popular service for local small businesses.*

**Source:** Adapted from Peter Davies and D. Pardey, *Making Sense of Marketing* (London: Macmillan, 1990).

Problem identification and problem solving are important tasks for educational administrators and other decision makers. When problems become clear, most institutions take action to resolve them. But recognizing emerging problems can tax the attention of busy educators and, once the problems emerge, it takes time and effort to gather the most useful information and come to a decision. Before undertaking the process, decision makers should take pains to identify the "right" problem, and take seriously the results of data-gathering and marketing research in coming to a decision. If those in charge already have committed themselves to a course of action, resources devoted to research will be wasted and should be spent elsewhere. If research is undertaken, the cost of the research should be proportionate to the likely contribution to making better decisions.

This chapter considers how an institution can identify its marketing problems and how the marketing information system can be structured to provide the information required for resolving marketing problems and building on opportunities. We use the term *marketing information system* to describe the institution's activities for gathering, analyzing, storing, and disseminating market-relevant information.

The components of a school's marketing information system are illustrated in Figure 3-1. At the left is the marketing environment that the institution must monitor—specifically, target markets, marketing channels, competitors, publics, and key trends external to the institution. (In Chapter 4 we term this the macroenvironment.) Using the institution's records and other data sources and conducting new research studies as needed, the school develops analyses to guide decision making. This information then flows to the appropriate administrators to help them in marketing planning, implementation,

FIGURE 3-1  Components of the marketing information system

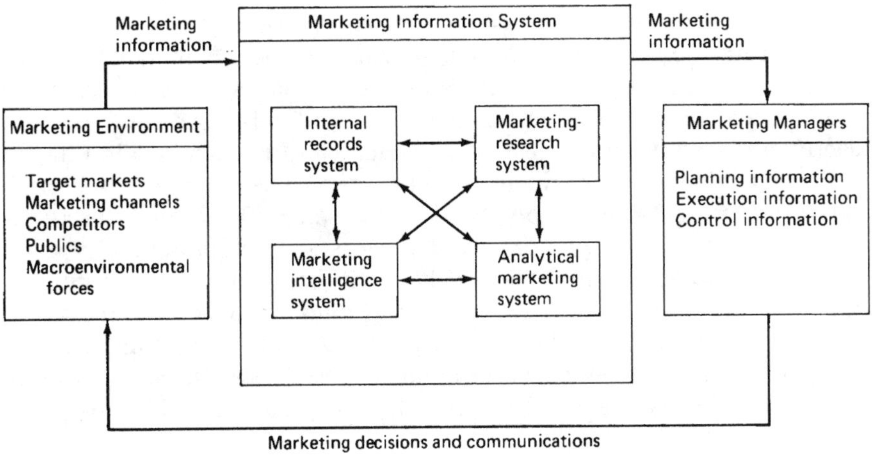

and control. The resulting decisions and communications then flow back to the marketing environment, which must be continuously monitored.

Many educational institutions fail to see that internal records and marketing intelligence can play an important part in helping to identify and resolve marketing problems. Formal marketing research projects ideally build on a base of existing data and marketing intelligence, rather than starting from zero.

We strongly believe that good information and appropriate marketing research are indispensable for effective marketing planning and action. This chapter provides an overview of the marketing information system and the process of conducting research, including the following topics:

1. Identifying marketing issues
2. Using the institution's existing records
3. Gathering marketing intelligence
4. Conducting marketing research
5. Analyzing marketing research data

This chapter introduces these topics and indicates useful approaches. The reader will find many examples of applications of marketing research in subsequent chapters, where the methods can be more fully developed in the context of real marketing problems.

## IDENTIFYING MARKETING ISSUES

Each educational institution needs to identify the specific marketing-related issues to address. Correct problem identification is essential to avoid wasting resources on irrelevant issues. The story of "Paula" in Chapter 2 underscores the challenge of getting deeply enough into a problem to truly understand its root causes. Once issues have been identified, the institution can study the important ones in detail and develop institutional responses.

An educational institution can systematically identify marketing issues in four ways. First, administrators can use complaint systems, importance-performance analysis, SERVQUAL, and other research-based approaches to identify problems from the customers' standpoint (all discussed in Chapter 2). Second, administrators can list observed problems in a *marketing problem inventory* and can ask others to do the same. Third, they can assess the demand for various programs and services and *determine the demand patterns* that present problems for the institution. Fourth, the institution can undertake a comprehensive *marketing audit* to determine the status of its current marketing activities. A marketing audit replaces the need for the first two approaches because an audit considers each potential problem area and demand state. The latter three approaches will be discussed in this chapter.

### The Marketing Problem Inventory

A *marketing problem inventory* is a list of the marketing problems the institution has identified. The inventory should include those situations that might suggest present or future difficulties with the school's markets and publics. No two people or groups within the institution will see precisely the same problems. The admissions director may identify "difficulty meeting the announced decision notification date" as a problem, whereas applicants are more concerned about getting a thorough review and (hopefully) a positive decision. Those compiling the marketing problem inventory may want to include lists from others as well.

Figure 3-2 shows a marketing problem matrix to compare the problems facing the college as a whole and each separate department.

An institution carrying out a marketing problem inventory may be surprised at the number of problems it identifies and the extent to which some problems emerge that were never examined from a marketing perspective. For example, private schools tend to cite the need to increase salaries and benefits to attract able teachers and to provide for capital improvements and repairs on aging facilities. All Saints High School (name disguised) was a

FIGURE 3-2    The marketing problem matrix

| | College | Dept. 1 | Dept. 2 | Dept. 3 | . . . . . . . . . . . . . . . N |
|---|---|---|---|---|---|
| Declining Overall Enrollment/ Credit Hours | | | | | |
| Declining Enrollment in Selected Disciplines | | | | | |
| Insufficient Attraction of High-Quality Students | | | | | |
| Poor Image | | | | | |
| Low Retention/ Student Satisfaction | | | | | |
| Low Faculty Satisfaction | | | | | |
| Insufficient Attraction of Funds | | | | | |

Catholic high school for girls that had "gone co-ed" in the 1970s. After growing to a high of 700 students in 1980, the school's enrollment slipped to 250 students a decade later. The school's administrators and the most loyal parents felt that the school was good and the school simply needed to "get the word out" to attract more students.

A problem analysis for All Saints identified the following specific problems that had an impact on enrollment and the ability to attract more students:

**1.** Some specific administrative decisions in the past about priorities for admission alienated previously enthusiastic parents, who then placed their children in other schools.

**2.** The absence of priests, sisters, or brothers as teachers at the school made the school seem "less Catholic" to parents, but there was little All Saints could do, since the number of priests and members of Catholic religious orders has declined precipitously in the United States in the past 25 years, and fewer of these are selecting work in teaching.

**3.** The principal's refusal to communicate openly to parents about school issues and policies angered even the most supportive parents and created a climate of distrust. Otherwise-eager prospective donors lacked confidence that the money would be used effectively.

**4.** As enrollment declined, the school no longer was perceived as the inclusive "neighborhood school" it had once been, so there was less incentive to consider All Saints as the obvious choice for a Catholic secondary education.

**5.** To recoup enrollment, All Saints began to accept every applicant, regardless of academic record. While continuing to require the Catholic high school admissions examination, the school used test results to make placement rather than admissions decisions. Weak students were admitted conditionally and were required to attend summer school. The effect was a decline in students' and parents' perceptions about the academic quality of the school.

**6.** Recruiting materials and activities were minimal. The school hosted an annual meeting for eighth-grade teachers and counselors to tell them about All Saints. The publications were perfunctory rather than welcoming, and the school handbook (distributed to students, parents, and prospects) was poorly organized and contained serious typographical and factual errors.

This problem inventory revealed more areas for investigation and improvement that would never have been uncovered if the school had simply intensified their student recruitment program or made appeals for more donations. Some of these problems are more important than others, and the school will need to rank them and determine the factors that contribute to them.

Problem identification can be painful because some of the problems are of the school's own making, not simply failures to respond to changes in demand or in the economy. Uncovering past mistakes and facing up to continuing issues is unpleasant, and resolving them is likely to require considerable effort and expense.

The pain of this process is not specific to small, private schools. Some of the most prestigious universities in the United States have undergone wrenching reviews, with implications for budgets and staffing.

## Determining Demand States

An educational institution usually has some idea of what level of demand it seeks. A residential college in a rural area may be constrained by available residential facilities to enroll no more than 800 students but must enroll at least 725 in order to meet its financial commitments. A Sunday school may seek to enroll as many children as can be encouraged to attend, whereas a public school program for physically handicapped children seeks to serve only those children who need special services.

Marketing arises when an institution determines the *desired level of transactions* that it wants with a target market. At any one time, the actual demand level may be below, equal to, or above the desired demand level. The task of marketing management is to influence the level, timing, and character of demand in a way that will help the institution achieve its objectives. By comparing the actual demand state and the desired state, the institution can identify problem areas. For example, a college may have too few applicants for its business school but so many majors and would-be majors in communication that it cannot provide enough class sections.

## The Marketing Audit

Although the marketing problem inventory and the analysis of demand states will assist in identifying problems areas, most educational institutions will benefit from undertaking a *marketing audit.* The person or team carrying out the marketing audit gathers information critical to evaluating the institution's marketing performance. The auditor examines existing information, such as application and enrollment trends, fund-raising results, and other institutional reports, and also interviews administrators, faculty, staff, students, and others.

The marketing audit is not a marketing plan but an independent appraisal by a competent consultant of the main problems and opportunities facing the institution, and what it can do about them. The auditor's independence increases the likelihood of fresh perspectives on the institution's activities, accomplishments, and problems. Yet the auditor must rely heavily on the school's own data and on interviews with school administrators, faculty, staff, students, and other publics to make this appraisal. So if data are lacking or respondents are not candid, the marketing audit will be less complete and useful.

The auditor will produce some short-run and long-run recommendations of actions the institution could take to improve its performance. The administration has to weigh these recommendations and implement those it feels would contribute to improved marketing performance. Since many educational institutions would benefit from conducting a marketing audit, we provide a separate chapter on the methods, components, and outcomes of a marketing audit in Chapter 17.

## USING THE INSTITUTION'S EXISTING RECORDS

The most basic information system and one of the most important is the school's *internal records system*. Every institution accumulates information in the regular course of its operations. A college will keep records on its students, including names, addresses, ages, courses taken, grades received, major fields, test scores, payments, financial aid awards, and so on. From academic transcripts, student files, and applications, the college can develop statistics on the number of applications received, the acceptance rate, the average high school grade-point average and admissions test scores of students who enroll, the frequency distribution of majors, and other useful statistics. The college will also have records on faculty, administrators, staff, costs, billings, assets, and liabilities, all of which are indispensable for making management decisions.

The college's career center will keep records on students who use its services and can determine graduates' job-hunting success, fields selected, and typical salary offers. The career center may also have reports from employers on graduates hired in the past, their promotions, and intended job areas for future recruiting.

The development office will keep track of alumni and other donors, their addresses, past contributions, and other data. Its campaign progress file will show the amount raised to date from each major source, such as individuals, foundations, corporations, and government grants. Its cost file will show how much has been spent on direct mail, advertising, brochures, salaries, consulting fees, and so on.

This information often needs to be subdivided, graphed, compared, or otherwise processed to understand exactly what the numbers mean and to see the interrelationships. For example, the university's business school enrollment may be steady but, unless divided by level (graduate/undergraduate), this observation can mask an increase in undergraduate majors and a decline in M.B.A. students. The business school will want to further analyze the enrollment data on graduate enrollment in order to prepare an action plan.

TABLE 3-1    Questionnaire for determining marketing information needs of decision makers

---

1. What types of decisions are you regularly called upon to make?
2. What types of information do you need to make these decisions?
3. What types of information do you regularly get?
4. What types of special studies do you periodically request?
5. What types of information would you like to get that you are not now getting?
6. What information would you want daily? Weekly? Monthly? Yearly?
7. What magazines and reports would you like to see routed to you on a regular basis?
8. On what specific topics would you like to be kept informed?
9. What types of data analysis programs would you like to see made available?
10. What do you think would be the four most helpful improvements that could be made in the present marketing information system?

---

Educational decision makers need appropriate, accessible information in order to make decisions about current and future programs, as well as to anticipate marketing-related problems. Some administrators find that the most basic information was never collected or never recorded. In other cases, the information was sloppily kept or even destroyed by those who did not understand its potential value. Some educational institutions have collected lots of information but do not know how that information might be usefully organized and interpreted to aid in decision making.[1]

Every internal records system can be improved in its speed, comprehensiveness, accuracy, and accessibility. Periodically, an institution should survey its administrators for possible improvements in the internal records system. Table 3-1 shows the major questions that can be put to them. Once their opinions are gathered, the information system designers can design an internal records system that reconciles (1) what decision makers think they need, (2) what decision makers really need, and (3) what is economically feasible.

Most internal records systems were devised to *record* data, not to make them useful. Some educational institutions have taken great strides in making data easily accessible via networked computers, but at other institutions the time lag between request and reply is so great that administrators stop asking and instead make decisions on information already in hand. Records of currently enrolled students and budget information are always the first data to be made available, but decision makers could benefit from a wider range of readily available data. The continuing development of institutional information systems will increase their scope and ease of use.

## GATHERING MARKETING INTELLIGENCE

Whereas the internal records system supplies decision makers with information on the past, the *marketing intelligence system* supplies them with information on current happenings and emerging trends. Here is our definition:

> The *marketing intelligence system* is the set of sources and procedures by which managers obtain their everyday information about developments in the environment beyond the institution.

Gathering marketing intelligence is not a "cloak-and-dagger operation." Most of the useful information is readily available. A specialist in intelligence for business corporations claims that 95 percent of the information companies need to make business decisions is available and accessible to the public.[2] They can learn about competitors by accessing public databases of financial statistics, reading company reports and public records, attending trade shows, and observing competitors' activities in the marketplace. So it is for educational institutions also.

Educational administrators can gather considerable marketing intelligence by reading newspapers and other publications and talking to people inside and outside the institution, including at meetings and conferences. This informal approach can spot important developments, but administrators may learn too late of some other important developments, such as pending legislation affecting the school's activities.

An institution can improve the quality of its marketing intelligence efforts. First, the institution must communicate with administrators, faculty, and staff about the sorts of information that are useful for decision making and urge them to pass information to others in the institution as rapidly as possible.

Second, the institution should encourage outside parties with whom it deals—professional associations, lawyers, accountants, and others—to pass on any useful bits of information. For example, a tax advisor may have clients interested in making bequests to the college, or may be aware of tax law changes that could help the development office to be more effective in informing prospective donors about the tax advantages of donations.

Third, the institution's employees can carry on specific intelligence-gathering activities. Admissions staff can compile information on enrollments, tuition levels and increases, and other data from published sources. The institution should continually try to identify "best practices" of other similar institutions—or even from commercial firms—and adopt them as rapidly as feasible. Exhibit 3-1 tells how administrators at James Madison University visited other campuses to learn from them. "Mystery shoppers" could also be useful to learn how other colleges serve prospects, contacting the admissions offices of several colleges and reporting back on how well they deal with inquiries. Quite probably, the "shopper" will report receiving widely different receptions, some of which may be "turnoffs" and others highly effective. Specialized intelligence gathering can also reveal whether the institution's own staff is really practicing a customer orientation and suggest the need for additional training.

EXHIBIT 3-1    Learning from other institutions

---

Many institutions send administrators to other campuses to look for ways to improve their own colleges. But officials at James Madison University decided to take a cloak-and-dagger approach.

Unlike other campus visitation teams, the U-2 Committee—so dubbed after the military reconnaissance plane—traveled incognito. Armed with cameras and videotape recorders, James Madison officials took notes on how Georgetown and Pennsylvania State Universities and the University of Maryland at College Park operated their bookstores, dining halls, and other services.

The U-2 Committee was called the Committee for Campus Visitations until officials decided to have a little fun and rename it. Besides, they didn't want a formal visit: They wanted to view the campus the way parents and prospective students would.

None of the colleges complained about the visits, but some newspapers, including *The Washington Post*, wrote about James Madison's covert operations. "We understand the principle of visiting other campuses," said Vicki Fong, a Penn State spokesperson. "A lot of campuses are looking for ways to serve students better. I just hope they had a good time."

---

Source: "Notebook," *The Chronicle of Higher Education*, (September 1, 1993), p. A44.

Fourth, the institution can establish an office specifically responsible for gathering and disseminating marketing-relevant information. Many universities have an institutional research office which—with additional personnel and resources—could carry out or at least coordinate this function. The staff would scan relevant publications, abstract useful information, and disseminate it to appropriate people inside the institution. The office would install suggestion and complaint systems so that students and others would have an opportunity to express their attitudes toward the institution. It would index the information so that all the past and current information could be easily retrieved. It would work with decision makers to plan and carry out surveys and other marketing research studies. The staff would assist administrators and others to evaluate the results of research. These and other services would greatly enhance the quality of the information available for making marketing-related decisions.

## CONDUCTING MARKETING RESEARCH

Every school has occasions when it needs to carry out research studies to make better marketing decisions. For example, educational institutions often seek answers to such questions as these:

1. What are the demographic characteristics of residents of this community college district?
2. What academic majors are likely to be in greatest demand in the local job market over the next five years?
3. What proportion of graduates of regional high schools select this college?
4. Would a job-skills course for re-entry women be well received? How many students might enroll?
5. How much should the college charge for the computer-skills course? How much would/could potential students pay?
6. What improvements in campus facilities would yield the greatest increase in student satisfaction?

To answer these and other questions, institutions turn to marketing research:

> *Marketing* research is the systematic design, collection, analysis, and reporting of data and findings relevant to a specific marketing situation or problem facing an institution.

Who conducts these studies for educational institutions? A large university will typically have a research director (with the title of director of institutional research, vice president for planning, or the like) who coordinates other professionals. The institutional research office selects problems or clarifies problems posed by others in the institution, designs studies, and either carries them out or contracts with outside marketing research companies.

The institution may hire a marketing consultant or research firm to design and carry out the research, or the project may be carried out by administrators or faculty members trained in research techniques.[3] Many universities have experts in research design, statistics, and testing and measurement on their own faculties. Finally, the institution might contact local business schools about assistance from marketing faculty or students.

Useful research does not have to be expensive, but it does need to be carried out with care.[4] Given the increasing sophistication and cost of marketing research, when a major study is deemed essential the institution should be willing to hire the right professional expertise to meet the institution's research needs. Underfunded, unprofessional research may lead to fuzzy research results and poor decisions. The cost of the research should be weighed in relation to the expected value of the results. For example, if a college is losing $400,000 each year because 100 residence-hall places are vacant ($100 \times \$4,000$), the college should strive to quickly put this fixed asset to good use. It is well worth paying for top-notch professional marketing research assistance to guide this effort.

Decision makers need to know enough about the potential and limitations of marketing research to get the right information at a reasonable cost and to use it intelligently. One protection is to work with experienced researchers. In addition, administrators should know enough about marketing

FIGURE 3-3   The marketing-research process

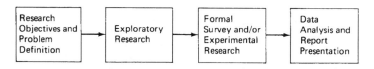

research procedures to review the plan, determine its appropriateness, and evaluate the interpretation of results.[5]

Figure 3-3 shows the four basic steps in sound marketing research, which are described in the sections that follow.

## Research Objectives and Problem Definition

The first step in research is to define the research objectives. The overall objective may be to learn about a market, to determine the most attractive program to offer, or to measure the effect of a communications program. In any case, the problem guiding the research must be clearly specified. If the problem statement is vague, if the wrong problem is defined, or if the uses of the research are unclear, the research results may be useless or even misleading.

A useful way to clarify the research objectives in advance is to use "backward" marketing research, shown in Figure 3-4. Alan Andreasen, the developer of this approach, urges researchers and decision makers to determine what decisions need to be made and what the final research report will look like *before* the research process is launched.

## Exploratory Research

Before carrying out a formal (and therefore more expensive) research study, researchers often review secondary (existing) data, do observational research, and interview individuals and groups informally to arrive at an understanding of the current situation.

**Analysis of Secondary Data.** Marketing researchers typically begin by gathering and reviewing secondary data, if any exist. *Secondary data* are relevant data that already exist somewhere, having been collected for another purpose. Secondary data are normally quicker and less expensive to obtain and provide the researcher with a start on the problem. Afterward, the researcher can gather *primary data*—namely, original data collected to address the problem at hand. There are numerous sources of existing data:

1. *Internal records.* The institution's internal records system should first be examined to determine relevant data are already there.

FIGURE 3-4    The process of "backward"
marketing research

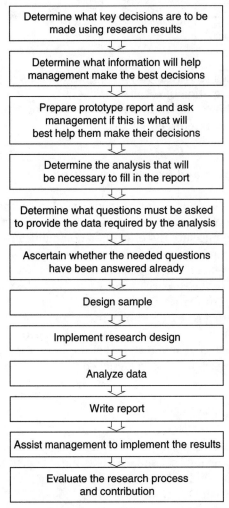

Source: Alan R. Andreasen, *Cheap But Good Marketing
Research* (Homewood, IL: Dow Jones-Irwin, 1988), p. 65.

2. *Government.* The federal government publishes more marketing data than
does any other source in the country. The U.S. Bureau of the Census issues
the *Census of Population* and *Census of Housing.* The National Center for
Education Statistics, state departments of education, and local school districts are other sources of data.

3. *Educational associations.* National and local associations often compile

data about member institutions. Many such associations publish special studies from time to time which give statistics about similar institutions.
4. *Competitors and other private organizations.* Catalogs and reports provide information about enrollment levels and trends.

Secondary data from these and other sources can be useful as long as researchers are careful to check them for relevance, impartiality, validity, and reliability. Increasingly data are becoming available on diskettes or through on-line information services, making this information easier to use and quicker to access.

**Observational Research.** Primary data can be gathered by observing the relevant people and settings. For example, students' satisfaction with the university food service can be measured not only by how many students sign up for the meal plan, but also by observing their reactions as they go through the meal lines, what items they select, and what food goes uneaten.

**Qualitative Interviewing.** In addition to observation, researchers often need to conduct some interviews during the exploratory stage of a marketing research project. Interviewing can suggest factors that play a role in the marketing problem. In the exploratory stage, interviewing should emphasize uncovering new qualitative information rather than obtaining quantifiable results. Therefore, exploratory interviews are open-ended to stimulate respondents to share their thoughts and feelings regarding the issue being studied.

Qualitative research can be used (1) to probe deeply into consumers' underlying needs, perceptions, preferences, and level of satisfaction; (2) to gain greater familiarity with and understanding of marketing problems whose causes are not known; and (3) to develop ideas that can be further investigated through quantitative research. Qualitative research is not only a desirable first step, it is sometimes the only step permitted by limited budgets, and it can often reveal important insights that help sharpen understanding of important issues. (Quantitative research, on the other hand, seeks to produce statistically reliable estimates of particular market or consumer characteristics. Quantitative research usually entails interviewing or surveying a much larger number of people than does qualitative research, and it assumes that the interviewer knows in advance what specific questions to ask.)

When seeking information about individuals, the researcher could conduct individual interviews or group interviews. *Individual interviewing* consists of interviewing one person at a time, either in person or over the telephone. *Group interviewing* consists of inviting from six to ten people to gather for a few hours with a trained interviewer to discuss a program, service, or institution. The group interviewer needs objectivity, some knowledge of the subject matter of the study, and an understanding of group dynamics and consumer behavior; otherwise, the results can be worthless or misleading.

Group interviews are typically held in pleasant surroundings—a hotel meeting room or a home, for example—and refreshments are served to increase the informality. Sometimes representatives of the commissioning institution will observe the focus group from behind one-way glass, but this requires use of a special facility.

The group interviewer starts with a broad question related to the research theme. For example, in a study of private education, parents might be asked, "What experiences do you feel will make the greatest contribution to your child's future success?" Questions would then move to the subject of educational experiences, then to schooling, and then to the specific school relative to others.

The interviewer encourages free and easy discussion among the participants, hoping that the group dynamic will bring out real feelings and thoughts. At the same time, the interviewer "focuses" the discussion, and hence the name *focus group interviewing.* The comments are recorded through note taking or tape recording, and then studied to understand the participants' attitudes.

Focus group interviewing is becoming one of the major marketing research tools for gaining insight into consumer thoughts and feelings.[6] In many cases, the results of focus group interviews are used to guide the development of survey instruments or of marketing experiments.

Individual interviews and focus groups are very useful to identify attitudes and opinions of individuals, but sometimes the institution wants to learn about the marketing-related concerns of other organizations. For example, suppose a community college provides job-related training under contract to a local company. If the community college wanted to know about the company's satisfaction level, who should they ask? The participating employees? The company's training director? The employees' bosses?

The college would probably benefit by conducting a *customer visit.*[7] A team of college representatives, carefully identified and prepared, would visit with key people at the company one at a time. The college group should be *cross functional* and prepared. For example, the group visiting the company might include an instructor in the program, the head of the job-skills division, and an administrator from an area that provides support for the job-skills program. The team would read and discuss (or get formal training on) how to conduct customer visits and develop and list of key questions. The customer visit would take place at the company's office, with interviews scheduled in advance. Table 3-2 gives examples of objectives that can often be accomplished through customer visits.

## Formal Research

After defining the problem and doing exploratory research, the researchers may wish to carry out more formal research to measure magnitudes or to test

TABLE 3-2    Sample objectives for customer visits

---

*Identify* unmet customer needs.
*Identify* new market oppotunities.
*Explore* likes and dislikes concerning the current product offering.
*Explore* how customers perceive the intangible aspects of the product (i.e. its delivery and support).
*Describe* the role played by the product within the customer's operation or business strategy.
*Describe* the customer's decision model and process for choosing among vendors.
*Generate* possible explanations for observed market trends.
*Generate* alternative ways of segmenting the market.

---

Source: Edward F. McQuarrie, *Customer Visits: Building a Better Marketing Focus* (Newbury Park, CA: Sage Publications, 1993), p. 36. Reprinted by permission of Sage Publications, Inc.

hypotheses. At this point, the marketing researchers can design a formal survey or a marketing experiment. A description of each follows.

**Survey Research.** Many educational decision makers assume that marketing research is synonymous with conducting a survey. In fact several approaches to conducting marketing, including focus groups and use of existing data, require no surveys at all.

When a survey is deemed appropriate, the decision makers must understand that that approach is not as simple as it may first appear. Some people have an overly simplistic view of conducting a survey. They think the process consists of writing a few obvious questions and finding an adequate number of people in the target market to answer them. In fact designing a reliable survey requires training and experience. Here we will describe the main considerations in developing the research instrument, selecting the sample, and collecting the data.[8]

*Designing the research instrument.* The main survey research instrument is the questionnaire. Constructing good questionnaires calls for considerable skill. In fact, experienced researchers usually begin by searching for existing survey questionnaires that address the same issues. In some instances the existing survey questionnaires can be purchased and/or adapted for use in the new study, thus reducing expense and complications. For example, when a new questionnaire is developed, it must go through several small pretests to identify any confusion in wording or responses before the questionnaire is used with the larger sample of respondents.

A common error occurs in the *types of questions asked:* the inclusion of questions that cannot be answered, or would not be answered, or need not be answered, and the omission of other questions that should be answered. Each question should be checked to determine how it serves the research objectives. Questions should be dropped that are merely interesting (except for one or two to start the interview) because they lengthen the time required and try the respondent's patience.

The *form of questions* can affect the response. An *open-ended question* is one to which the respondent is free to answer in his or her own words; for example, the respondent is asked, "What is your opinion of this school?" and is invited to write a response. A *closed-ended question* is one to which the possible answers are supplied on the questionnaire, and the respondent marks the "best answer." Types of questions are described and illustrated in Exhibit 3-2.

The *choice of words* also calls for considerable care. The researcher should strive for simple, direct, unambiguous, and unbiased wording. The *sequencing of questions* in the questionnaire is also important. The lead questions should create interest, if possible. Open-ended questions are usually better here. Difficult or personal questions should be introduced toward the end in order not to create an emotional reaction that may affect subsequent answers or cause the respondent to break off the interview. The questions should be asked in as logical an order as possible in order to avoid confusing the respondent.

Questions about the respondent (age, income, educational level, and so forth) are usually asked last because they tend to be more personal and less interesting to the respondent.

*Selecting the sample.* The marketing researchers must identify respondents who can supply information relevant to the research objective. Three decisions are required:

**1.** *Sampling unit.* This answers the question, *Who is to be surveyed?* The proper sampling unit is not always obvious from the nature of the information sought. In the case of a survey about important factors in selecting a school, should the sampling unit be the student, the mother, the father, or all three? Who is the usual initiator, influencer, decider, user, and/or purchaser? For a private elementary school, the parents' opinions will be most important; for a college, the prospective student's opinions will probably be most important, but the parents are likely to play a significant role.

**2.** *Sample size.* This answers the question, *How many people should be surveyed?* Large samples give more reliable results than small samples do. Thus, the decision makers can have greater confidence that the statistical results closely reflect the actual characteristics, attitudes, and opinions of the group represented by the sample respondents. However, it is not necessary to sample the entire target market or even a substantial part of it to achieve satisfactory precision. Carefully chosen samples, although small, can often provide good reliability.

**3.** *Sampling procedure.* This answers the question, *How should the respondents be chosen?* Table 3-3 shows types of samples. To draw valid and reliable inferences about the target market, a random probability sample of the relevant population should be drawn. Random sampling allows the calculation of confidence limits for sampling error. But random sampling is almost always

EXHIBIT 3-2    Types of Survey Questions

| A. CLOSED-ENDED QUESTIONS | | |
|---|---|---|
| NAME | DESCRIPTION | EXAMPLE |
| Dichotomous | A question offering two answer choices. | "In selecting this school, did you visit the campus?"<br>Yes ☐    No ☐ |
| Multiple choice | A question offering three or more answer choices. | "With whom did you discuss your college decisions?"<br>No one ☐<br>Parents ☐<br>School counselor ☐<br>Friends at school ☐<br>Other ☐ |
| Likert scale | A statement with which the respondent shows the amount of agreement/ disagreement. | "Smaller colleges generally provide a better education than larger colleges."<br>Strongly disagree        1 ☐<br>Disagree        2 ☐<br>Neither agree nor disagree  3 ☐<br>Agree        4 ☐<br>Strongly agree        5 ☐ |
| Semantic differential | A scale is inscribed between bipolar words, and the respondent selects the point that represents the direction and intensity of his or her feelings. | *East Ridge College*<br>Large      _:_:_:_:_:_ Small<br>Difficult   _:_:_:_:_:_ Easy<br>Modern   _:_:_:_:_:_ Old-<br>fashioned |
| Importance scale | A scale calling for rating the importance of some attribute from "not at all important" to "extremely important." | "For me, attending a college close to my home is":<br>Extremely important   1 __<br>Very important        2 __<br>Somewhat important    3 __<br>Not very important    4 __<br>Not at all important  5 __ |
| Rating scale | A scale calling for rating some attribute from "poor" to "excellent." | "East Ridge College's residence facilities are":<br>Excellent        1 __<br>Very good        2 __<br>Good        3 __<br>Fair        4 __<br>Poor        5 __ |

EXHIBIT 3-2   (continued)

## B. OPEN-ENDED QUESTIONS

| NAME | DESCRIPTION | EXAMPLE |
|------|-------------|---------|
| Completely unstructured | A question that respondents can answer in an almost unlimited number of ways. | "What is your opinion of East Ridge College?" |
| Word association | Words are presented, one at a time, and respondents mention the first word that comes to mind. | "What is the first word that comes to your mind when the you hear following?" College _____ East Ridge _____ Study _____ |
| Sentence completion | Incomplete sentences are presented, one at a time, and respondents complete the sentence. | "In selecting a college, the most Important consideration in my decision is _____ |
| Story completion | An incomplete story is presented and respondents are asked to complete it. | "Jane was trying to decide what college to attend. She visited several colleges, including East Ridge. As she walked across the East Ridge campus, she noticed the students walking toward the library. This aroused in her the following thoughts and feelings. *Now complete the story.*" |

more costly than nonrandom sampling. Some marketing researchers feel that the extra expenditure for probability sampling could be put to better use. Specifically, more of the money of a fixed research budget could be spent in designing better questionnaires and hiring better interviewers to reduce response and nonsampling errors, which can be just as fatal as sampling errors. This is an issue that marketing researchers and administrators must carefully weigh.

*Contacting the respondents.* Respondents are typically surveyed by telephone, mail, or personal interviews. *Telephone interviewing is* the best method for gathering information quickly. It also permits the interviewer to tailor the sequence of questions for each respondent and to clarify questions if they are not understood.

Telephone interviewing to randomly selected respondents often means that only short, not too personal, interviews can be carried out because many people resist telephone interviewers. But when educational institutions are

TABLE 3-3    Types of samples

| A. *Probability sample:* | |
|---|---|
| Simple random sample | Every member of the population has a known and equal chance of selection. |
| Stratified random sample | The population is divided into mutually exclusive groups (such as age groups), and random samples are drawn from each group. |
| Cluster (area) sample | The population is divided into mutually exclusive groups (such as city blocks), and the researcher draws a sample of the groups to interview. |
| B. *Nonprobability sample:* | |
| Convenience sample | The researcher selects the easiest, most available members of the population from whom to obtain information. |
| Judgment sample | The researcher uses his or her judgment to select population members who are good prospects for relevant information. |
| Quota sample | The researcher finds and interviews a prescribed number of people in each of several categories (e.g., age, sex, education level). |

surveying their own applicants, current students, alumni, and parents, telephone interviewing is very effective because it is much more personal than a mail questionnaire. When calling to interview high school students, including a client institution's prospective students, at least one major educational marketing research firm sends letters a week or two in advance to announce that the students will be called about their attitudes about colleges on a particular evening. Students are given an 800 number to call if they want to reschedule the time. The resulting interviews often take 20 to 30 minutes and many respondents seem to enjoy the opportunity to talk freely about their concerns about college selection.

Telephone surveys should always be conducted by selected, well-trained interviewers who can relate well to the study respondents. Interviewers should be provided with professionally designed and pretested *scripts*, which guide the wording and sequence of the questions to be asked.

The *mail questionnaire* may be the best way to reach people who would not give personal interviews or who might be biased by interviewers. On the other hand, mail questionnaires require simple, clearly worded questions, and the return rate is usually low and/or slow.

*Personal interviewing is* the most versatile of the three methods. The interviewer can ask more questions and can supplement notes on the respondent's comments with personal observations. Personal interviewing is the most expensive method, since it requires skilled interviewers and more technical and administrative planning and supervision. If the interview consists primarily of open-ended questions, the interviewer needs to take excellent notes and the researcher needs to devote time to interpreting the responses.

**Experimental Research.** We have talked about formal research in its most common form, the survey. Decision makers often want to go beyond measuring the perceptions, preferences, and intentions of a target market and seek to measure actual cause-and-effect relationships. For example, the school may want to assess different advertisements or viewbooks before publication to find out which are drawing the most attention and interest from prospective students. The experimental method is often worth the additional effort and expense because the results are usually more conclusive and reliable. Exhibit 3-3 illustrates one approach, electronic focus groups, a state-of-the-art quantitative group interviewing process.

## Data Analysis and Report Presentation

The final step in the marketing research process is to develop meaningful information and findings to present to the decision maker who requested

EXHIBIT 3-3   Electronic focus groups

Marketing research techniques continue to evolve. Maquire Associates, a marketing research firm, uses MagNet, an electronic focus group, as a way to gather individuals' opinions about publications, videos, copy themes, design concepts, products, and/or ideas in "real time."

Each participant in the electronic focus group holds a handset with a dial connected to a central data recorder and processor. The participant turns the dial (from a low of zero to a high of ten) to indicate immediate reactions to the stimulus.

For example, the participant may be shown a college's video describing the campus, academic programs, and student life. The computer records each participant's dial position once every second, so that the flow of responses can be traced and matched to specific aspects of the video.

After watching and rating the video, the focus group moderator conducts a discussion, during which participants continue to use the dial to indicate their agreement or disagreement with other participants' remarks.

MagNet provides a continuous indicator of the representativeness of each speaker's comments from every participant, including the less verbal ones. Collecting data with MagNet reduces some problems characteristic of typical focus groups where, for example, less verbal participants may not express their opinions, while more forceful personalities can dominate or affect the perceptions and comments of others.

Afterward, the researcher can go back through the recording of the session and the recorded participant responses to identify the statements, concepts, or images that were most responsible for changes in opinion.

the study. In the case of survey data, the researcher will tabulate the data and develop one-way and two-way frequency distributions to show the relationships between variables. Averages and measures of dispersion will be computed for the major variables. The researcher should apply more advanced statistical techniques when they are appropriate and useful in discovering additional relationships in the data. In particular, if the researcher relies on looking at each variable one at a time, there is no direct way to identify possible relationships between variables, such as the relationship between a prospective student's intended major and the student's decision to select college A over college B. Finding such relationships requires bivariate statistics, including cross-tabulation and correlation analysis. To examine more complex interactions between variables, the researcher must design the study and data collection to permit the use of multivariate statistics, including multiple regression analysis and other approaches described in Exhibit 3-4.

The researcher's purpose is not to overwhelm decision makers with numbers but to present major findings that will help them make better marketing decisions. Before preparing the written report, the researcher should think about the reader's perceptual style (quantitative? visual?), level of research sophistication, and role in the institution.[9] Most research reports would be better understood if authors gave greater attention to creating easy-to-grasp visual displays of their results.[10]

A marketing research report should clearly describe the following:

1. The objective or principal question the research was designed to answer
2. The research questionnaire or experimental procedure
3. The characteristics of the sample
4. The qualitative and/or quantitative results
5. Clear statements of the research findings
6. The implications of the research findings
7. Recommendations for action

In addition to preparing a written report, the researcher should meet with the decision makers who requested the study to go over the major findings of the research and to explain the recommendations. This meeting is an opportunity to make sure the results are clearly understood before any action plans are implemented.

The decision maker is then responsible for charting a course of action that will help the institution to gain the most benefit from the research. Sadly, many research studies end up filed away and ignored because the decision maker doesn't understand the results, or the time for action passed while the research was in progress, or because there are inadequate resources to implement the recommendations.

Some decision makers experience "analyis paralysis," fearful of making decisions without "complete" knowledge of "all" the facts. Some decision

EXHIBIT 3-4   Quantitative tools for marketing research

*Chi-square.* A statistical technique for determining the association between two variables, either (1) to determine whether the observed data match expectations, or (2) to determine whether the distribution of one variable is associated with another.

Examples: A community college can determine whether the ethnic diversity of its enrolled students matches the distribution of ethnic backgrounds of its surrounding community to verify that the college is serving the whole community.

A public high school can determine whether public or private elementary school graduates are more likely to graduate from high school.

*T-test.* A statistical technique for comparing the means or proportions of two independent samples to determine whether the samples are drawn from the same population. (*ANOVA, analysis of variance*, is used to test means for three or more samples.)

Example: A private high school could determine the mean high school grade-point averages of its graduates who attended private and public elementary schools, and then use the t-test of the means to see if the two groups' academic performance was similar or distinguishably different.

*Multiple regression.* A statistical technique for estimating how the value of one variable changes with changes in the values of a number of independent variables.

Example: The university can estimate how its number of matriculants varies by different levels of ability as measured by the American College Test. This example is explained in Chapter 8.

*Cluster analysis.* A statistical technique for separating objects (schools, places, things, and so on) into a specified number of mutually exclusive categories which are internally homogeneous.

Example: A researcher wants to divide a set of private colleges into "sets" of schools that are considered very similar to other colleges in the same set. The perceptual map relating Yale and its competitors in Chapter 7 (Figure 7-7) is similar (but not identical) to the results of cluster analysis.

*Factor analysis.* A statistical technique used to determine the key underlying dimensions of a larger set of interrelated variables.

Example: A researcher wants to categorize a list of many college characteristics into a smaller set of factors that would influence students' satisfaction with their school. The SERVQUAL questionnaire, discussed in Chapter 2, was constructed in this manner—starting with many service characteristics and then reducing them to ten and later five broad categories.

*Discriminant analysis.* A statistical technique for classifying people (or objects) into two or more categories.

Example: A school wants to understand the differences between those admitted students who choose to attend and those who choose to attend another school. Chapter 16 on attracting students describes the use of matriculant/nonmatriculant surveys for this purpose.

***Chi-Square Automatic Interaction Detector (CHAID).*** A statistical technique which identifies interactions among factors using a branching approach.

Example: A school can examine data on admitted students who enrolled and those who did not enroll to identify the factors which influenced each subsequent subgroup. Identifying the most influential factors for subgroups enables the school to increase its student yields. An application of this technique is presented in Chapter 10.

***Conjoint analysis.*** A statistical technique that allows determining a person's preferences for a set of product or service attributes and the importance of each attribute, based on the person's ranked preference for certain offers.

Example: In designing a new academic program (or redesigning an existing program), the school can determine what *combination* of program features would be most attractive to the largest number of prospective participants. An example is presented in Chapter 11.

makers keep gathering more information to make the "best" decision, when they should use the information already at hand to make better decisions with greater efficiency. On the other hand, much competently conducted research never gets used in decision making because it gets buried in file cabinets. When there is turnover in administrators or managers, the existence of these studies may be forgotten or overlooked.

Marketing research can help the institution to be more effective, but only if the process is purposeful and timely, and the results are used.

## ANALYZING MARKETING RESEARCH DATA

The preceding sections presented the categories of problem identification and information gathering undertaken by educational institutions. The evolution of commercial marketing research techniques, their rapid adoption by educational institutions, and the availability of powerful personal computers and easy-to-use software mean that schools have greater access to sophisticated and useful approaches for gathering and analyzing research data.

*Advanced statistical procedures* can be used to learn more about relationships within a set of data and their statistical reliability. It allows management to go beyond frequency distributions, means, and standard deviations in the data to answer such questions as these:

- What are the best predictors of persons who are likely to apply to our school versus competing institutions?
- What are the best variables for segmenting our donor market, and how many segments will be created?
- What combination of program elements would make the most attractive management program for mid-career professionals?

Exhibit 3-4 briefly describes some of these more advanced statistical procedures. We will present examples of applications of these approaches in subsequent chapters.

In addition, some educational institutions have developed useful *statistical models* for decision making. For example, some universities now use models of the admissions process to predict the relationship between inquiries, applications, acceptances, and enrollment. Others have developed models to predict the comparative academic success of applicants for admission based on prior academic record and other variables. These and other models will be more widely developed and used as educational institutions strive to refine their marketing strategies.

## SUMMARY

Each educational institution must identify its marketing issues, and then gather marketing information to clarify the nature of its problems and to guide marketing activities. The necessary work can be done within the institution, by professional staff and/or faculty experts, or with the help of outside consultants. Marketing research takes time and money. When setting the budget for marketing research, the decision makers should consider the magnitude and urgency of the issue, and the likelihood of useful research results.

Problems can be systematically identified in four ways. First, the school can use complaint systems, importance-performance analysis, SERVQUAL, and other research-based approaches to identify problems from the customers' standpoint (all discussed in Chapter 2). Second, the school can prepare a marketing problem inventory. A marketing problem inventory includes problems and situations that might suggest present or future difficulties with the school's markets and publics.

Third, the school can compare the actual demand state it is experiencing with its desired state to determine where discrepancies—and therefore problems—exist. Fourth, the school can carry out a marketing audit to examine its marketing environment, objectives, strategies, and activities. Once the problems are identified, the school needs marketing information to clarify the problem areas and to guide planning to solve them.

Four systems make up the marketing information system. The first, the internal records system, consists of all the information that the institution gathers in the regular course of its operations. It includes information on students, programs, and finances. Many research questions can be answered by analyzing the information in the internal records system, yet so far few institutions systematically gather and organize their records to make them useful for decision making.

The second, the marketing intelligence system, describes the set of sources and procedures by which administrators obtain their everyday information about developments in the marketplace. An institution can improve the quality of its marketing intelligence by motivating its managers to scan the environment and report useful information, and by hiring intelligence specialists to find and disseminate information within the institution.

The third, the marketing research system, consists of the systematic design, collection, analysis, and reporting of data and findings relevant to a specific marketing situation or problem facing an institution. The marketing research process consists of four steps: developing the research objectives and problem definition; exploratory research; formal survey and/or experimental research; and data analysis and report presentation. Each step involves a series of judgments about the central questions to answer and the most appropriate methods of obtaining the needed information.

The fourth, the analytical marketing system, consists of advanced statistical procedures for analyzing the relationships within a set of data and their statistical reliability, and quantitative models that help make better marketing decisions.

## Notes

1. A provocative book on the effective gathering, coordination, and use of information within companies is Vincent Barabba and Gerald Zaltman, *Hearing the Voice of the Market: Competitive Advantage Through Creative Use of Market Information* (Boston, MA: Harvard Business School Press, 1991).

2. Leonard Fuld, cited in "'Competitor Intelligence': A New Grapevine," *The Wall Street Journal*, March 12, 1989, p. B2.

3. George Dehne, David L. Brodigan, and Peter Topping, *Marketing Higher Education: A Handbook for College Administrators* (Washington, DC: Consortium for the Advancement of Higher Education, 1991) includes an excellent chapter on choosing and using a marketing consultant on pp. 81–90.

4. Alan R. Andreasen, *Cheap But Good Marketing Research* (Homewood, IL: Dow Jones-Irwin, 1988).

5. Books on marketing research for educational institutions include Larry H. Litten, Daniel Sullivan, and David L. Brodigan, *Applying Market Research in College Admissions* (New York: College Entrance Examination Board, 1983); and Robert S. Lay and Jean J. Endo, eds., *Designing and Using Marketing Research*, New Directions for Institutional Research, no. 54, vol. XIV, no. 2 (San Francisco, CA: Jossey-Bass, 1987). For a brief guide to interpreting research reports, see Karlene H. Roberts, *Under-*

*standing Research: Some Thoughts on Evaluating Completed Educational Projects,* ERIC ED032759.

6. Sources on conducting focus groups include Richard A. Krueger, *Focus Groups: A Practical Guide for Applied Research* (Beverly Hills, CA: Sage Publications, 1989); David L. Morgan, ed., *Successful Focus Groups: Advancing the State of the Art* (Newbury Park, CA: Sage Publications, 1993); and Alfred E. Goldman and Susan Schwartz McDonald, *The Group Depth Interview* (Englewood Cliffs, NJ: Prentice-Hall, 1987).

7. See Edward F. McQuarrie, *Customer Visits: Building a Better Marketing Focus* (Newbury Park, CA: Sage Publications, 1993).

8. There are numerous guides to marketing research, survey research, questionnaire preparation, and data collection and analysis. Alan Andreasen's book (cited in note 4) is a highly readable handbook. Gilbert A. Churchill's *Marketing Research: Methodological Foundations*, 4th ed. (Chicago, IL: Dryden, 1991) is a classic marketing research textbook.

9. Peter T. Ewell, "Putting It All Together: Four Questions for Practitioners," *Enhancing Information Use in Decision Making,* New Directions for Institutional Research, no. 64 (San Francisco, CA: Jossey-Bass, Winter 1989), pp. 85–90.

10. Edward Tufte, *The Visual Display of Quantitative Information* (Cheshire, CT: Graphics Press, 1983).

# 4

# The Marketing Planning Process

*Heights University (name disguised), with an enrollment of 6,000, half undergraduate, is a tuition-dependent private university striving to improve its academic stature and its financial condition. Like many other institutions of its type, the university is struggling to maintain enrollment while increasing selectivity. While some of its graduate programs are well respected, undergraduate admissions standards are modest—a high school grade average of C will open the door.*

*For several consecutive years the university experienced operating deficits of up to $1 million a year. Tuition was increased steeply every year to cover the short-fall, resulting in further decreases in student enrollment, a painful trend for a university dependent on tuition for most of its operating income. Unrestricted annual giving for the operating budget averaged half a million dollars a year, and the budget for undergraduate scholarships was little more than $2 million.*

*The trustees supported stiff budget cuts to stabilize the university's situation. The president and trustees then began formal planning meetings to determine how best to move toward a solid financial situation and enhanced academic quality.*

---

Most educational institutions first acknowledge the value of formal planning when they encounter serious enrollment and revenue declines, or find that their admissions or development programs have been poorly managed and unsuccessful. At first administrators may hope the situation is an aberration that will right itself in time without concerted action. When they realize the magnitude of the situation, they begin to investigate ways to monitor problems and develop plans to address them.

Recognizing the need for planning is only the first step. Marketing planning relies on skills that may be somewhat new to those administrators who have specialized in successfully managing day-to-day operations and have not been involved in planning. Many institutions have hired planning specialists to direct the planning process and to assist administrators in planning.

In this chapter, we lay out and illustrate the steps in the marketing planning process at both the strategic and tactical levels. By *strategic marketing planning*, we mean planning of the overall direction of the institution to respond to its markets and opportunities. By *tactical marketing planning*, we mean planning of the specific action steps needed to take advantage of the marketing opportunities identified through strategic planning.

The marketing planning process consists of six components, each of which is discussed in depth in a subsequent chapter. In this chapter, we address the following questions about planning:

1. How is marketing planning used?
2. What are the steps in strategic planning?
3. What are the components of a tactical marketing plan?
4. What can formal planning systems contribute to institutional effectiveness?
5. How can marketing control systems assist in assessing marketing success?

## STRATEGIC MARKETING PLANNING

The general notion of planning is not new to education. Three levels of planning are used. The first level encompasses the budgeting and scheduling process. All schools must plan at this level, and many are turning to computer-based budgeting models and additional highly trained financial managers to improve the process. Despite these improvements, many private institutions continue to rely on year-to-year budgets and are slow in adopting five- to ten-year budgets.

A second level is short-range tactical planning—recruiting of students, physical-plant decisions, development efforts, and program and curriculum changes. Most colleges, universities, and private schools are engaged to some degree in short-range planning. In fact, some institutions compound their problems by relying on many short-range plans, each addressing one problem or symptom, when they should be proceeding to the third level, strategically oriented long-range planning, to focus their short-range plans. Strategic planning involves clarifying the institution's mission, assessing its resources, and examining the environment to determine what the institution's priorities and strategies should be.

We believe that educational institutions should be carrying out formal planning of two types, strategic planning and tactical planning. Strategic planning answers the question, "How can this institution best operate, given its goals and resources and its changing opportunities?" The second type, tactical marketing planning, grows out of the strategic plan and guides the execution of the strategy.

Consider the case of Heights University. The president and the board of trustees were determined to improve the university's stature. They hired a team of consultants to work with a high-level planning committee of trustees, vice chancellors, deans, and others. The consultants talked with or surveyed key informants in the institution. The consultants then guided the planning committee in analyzing environmental trends and the school's mission, strengths, and weaknesses. In the financial category, for example, the university had a balanced budget and little debt. Its financial weaknesses included a small endowment and rising fixed-cost overhead.

Heights University's trustees decided on a strategy of improving the institution's academic quality and thus enhancing its national reputation. The trustees' plan called for the university to achieve several specific objectives, including to increase enrollment to specified levels, to be ranked within *Barron's* "very competitive" category, to qualify for membership in the Association of Research Libraries, and to move toward Association of American Universities status. This is a challenging set of objectives, as it is difficult to build enrollment and selectivity at the same time.

The tactical plan followed and was based on the strategic plan. The tactical plan included objectives and an action plan for each area—enrollment, finances, and so on. In each area, the planning committee considered the threats that might affect the plan and, where possible, set up contingency plans to deal with them. The tactical plan can be updated each year as new information becomes available.

## STEPS IN STRATEGIC PLANNING

Strategic planning is new to most educational institutions. We define *strategic planning* as follows:

> *Strategic planning* is the process of developing and maintaining a strategic fit between the institution's goals and capabilities and its changing marketing opportunities. It relies on developing a clear institutional mission, supporting goals and objectives, a sound strategy, and appropriate implementation.

The definition suggests the appropriate steps an educational institution can take to improve its effectiveness. This chapter presents an overview of the strategic planning process (Figure 4-1), and subsequent chapters give details on each step.

FIGURE 4-1    Strategic planning process model

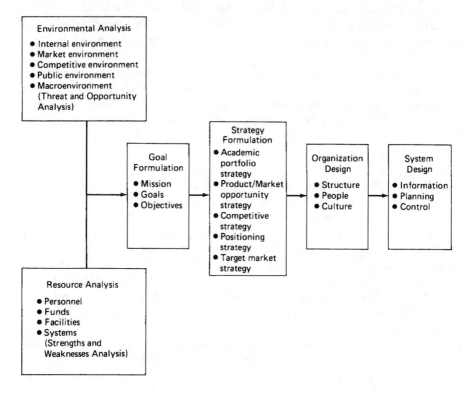

First, the institution must analyze its present and future environment (Chapter 5). Second, it reviews its major resources to suggest what it can accomplish. Third, the institution establishes its overall goals and its specific objectives (Chapter 6). Fourth, the institution reviews its mission and selects the most cost-effective strategy for reaching these goals and objectives (Chapter 7). Finally, implementing the strategy usually requires changes in the institution's structure and systems of information, planning, and control (Chapter 3 and the final section of this chapter). When these components are aligned, they promise improved performance.

The strategic planning process should be completed at each major institutional level because each level or component has somewhat different goals, resources, and marketing opportunities. In the case of a university, a high-level committee which includes top administrators and others should undertake strategic planning as it affects the university as a whole and state institutional assumptions and goals to guide planning at other levels. Similarly selective committees should then formulate strategic plans for each school (for instance, engineering school, business school, music school). In turn, each department chairperson, working with faculty, can carry out strategic planning for the department.

If a university operates branches in different locations, each branch will need to do strategic planning, since each will have different threats and opportunities. All these plans would be sent up to top administration for review and perhaps further development with the original planners. The final plan is often presented to the university board of trustees for approval. In a smaller educational institution, the strategic planning process will be simpler and involve fewer levels, but the elements remain the same.

Strategic planning typically involves faculty and key staff, as well as administrators. The faculty senate or other faculty representatives have a crucial role to play in planning, and their support is essential. Some administrators alienate potential supporters of strategic planning, failing to recognize that all planning introduces change, which can disrupt or even destroy familiar ways of doing things.[1] Planning committee members need to be provided with extensive, timely information to carry out their roles, and participants need to have confidence that successful plans will be implemented and will provide clear benefits to the institution.[2]

### Identifying and Analyzing Environmental Trends

We will illustrate the stages in the strategic planning process with the case of Beloit College.

The first step in strategic planning is to analyze the environment because changes in the environment usually call for new institutional strategies. An *environmental audit* answers three questions: (1) What are the major trends in the environment? (2) What are the implications of these trends for the institution? (3) What are the most significant opportunities and threats? These question must be examined for each of the institution's major environments: its internal environment, its markets, its publics, its competition, and the larger macroenvironment. The aim of environmental analysis is to produce a documented picture of the most significant environmental developments the institution must consider in formulating its future goals, strategies, structures, and systems. Methods for carrying out environmental scanning and forecasting are presented in Chapter 5.

From the environmental audit, the planners should draw out several major threats and opportunities for further examination. An *environmental threat* is a trend or potential event that will harm the institution or one of its programs unless the institution takes action.

Beloit College detected the following threats in the environmental audit:

1. In the market environment, they found that most of their students came from northern and eastern states, where the college-age population is projected to decline most.

2. In the public environment, they determined that the local community was rather apathetic toward the college and might not continue to employ students or cooperate with class projects.

3. In the competitive environment, Beloit officials hoped to compete with such prestigious private colleges as Carleton, Grinnell, and Oberlin. Beloit expected these institutions to become more aggressive in competing for students.

4. In the macroenvironment, Beloit is a private school with high tuition costs. Changes in the economic environment pose a threat to it.

By identifying and classifying threats, this college can determine which environmental threats to monitor, plan for, or ignore. The most serious threats—those that Beloit must monitor and be prepared to respond to—are those with a *potentially severe impact* and *high probability of occurrence*. It can ignore threats that are low in both severity and probability. Beloit should monitor—but need not prepare contingency plans for—threats such as competition from other colleges.

Opportunity analysis can be potentially more important than threat analysis. By managing its threats successfully, an institution can stay intact but does not grow. But by managing its opportunities successfully, the school can make great strides forward. A *marketing opportunity* is one in which the institution is likely to enjoy superior competitive advantages.

Beloit College officials identified several marketing opportunities:

1. In the market environment, Beloit surveyed employers and found that the demand for liberal-arts graduates with some emphasis in applied areas was strong.

2. In the public environment, they detected that legislators and government officials would continue to support public scholarship aid for small colleges. (Subsequent changes in the economy and in federal government policy challenged this expectation.)

3. In the competitive environment, Beloit noted that its location was reasonably close to a major metropolitan area (Chicago) and was perceived to be not too far from eastern cities.

These opportunities then can be evaluated on the bases of attractiveness and probability of success.

## Assessing Institutional Resources

Following the environmental analysis, the institution should identify the major resources it has (its strengths) and lacks (its weaknesses). Beloit carried out a resource audit (discussed in Chapter 6) focusing on people, money, and facilities. The audit determined that teaching quality was good but that the college was overstaffed. Faculty positions were cut by one-third. Beloit's financial situation was neither a clear strength nor a clear weakness. The college's small size and pleasant campus seemed to be strengths, but the location in the Snowbelt was perceived to be a weakness. Of course, Beloit must prepare a much more extensive list of intangible as well as tangible strengths and weaknesses. In particular, the school should look for its *distinctive competencies*, those resources and abilities in which it is particularly strong, and for those strengths that give it a differential advantage over its competition.

## Formulating the Institution's Mission and Goals

The environmental and resource analyses provide the background and stimulus for thinking about the institution's basic *goals* and *objectives*. As the environment changes, top administration and the board should review and reassess the institution's basic mission, goals, and objectives. At some schools, a review will convince participants in the planning process that the current goal structure is still clear, relevant, and effective. Other institutions will find their goals clear but of diminishing appropriateness to the new environment and resource situation, and some will discover that their goals are no longer clear and that the institution is drifting.

The *goal-formulation process* involves establishing, first, the mission of the institution; second, the long- and short-run goals; and third, what the specific current objectives will be.

**Mission.** An educational institution exists to accomplish some purpose, its mission. A useful way to examine the school's *mission* is to answer the following questions:[3] What is our function in society? What do we offer? Whom do we serve? What do we offer to those we serve? What will we offer? What should we offer?

Beloit College has to define a particular concept or brand of education if it is to stand out. Consider these possibilities: Is Beloit College in the *intellectual training business*, so that its students are highly knowledgeable and perceptive about the world they live in? Is it in the *personal-growth business*, aiming to help students develop their total personhood, intellectually, emotionally, and socially? Is it in the *college fun-and-games business*, providing students "the best time of their lives" before becoming adults? Each definition implies a different consumer and a different way of rendering value to the consumer.

Beloit altered its mission statement to include career preparation as well as intellectual training: "An awareness of the available career options, together with the skills to pursue those options."

**Goals.** The institution's *goals* are the variables it will emphasize. Each institution has a potential set of relevant goals from which to select. For example, a college might be interested in increasing its national reputation, attracting better students, improving teaching, building a larger endowment, and so on. A college cannot successfully pursue all these goals simultaneously and must choose to emphasize certain ones. For example, if Beloit's enrollment were to fall, it would probably make increased enrollment a paramount goal.

**Objectives.** Next, the institution's goals for the coming years should be stated in operational and measurable form, called *objectives*. The goal of increased enrollment must be turned into an objective such as "increasing enrollment of the next academic-year class by 15 percent." Typically, the institution will evaluate a large set of potential objectives for consistency and priority before adopting a final set of objectives.

## Formulating and Implementing the Strategy

Strategic planning culminates in an overall strategy for the institution or planning unit (department, program, and so on). An *institutional strategy* includes decisions about its current programs (whether to maintain, build, or drop them), and about future new programs and market opportunities. Heights University decided to take steps to enhance the quality and stature of the whole institution. Beloit College decided to retain its commitment to the liberal arts while helping students acquire career-related skills. The institution also needs to develop strategies for selecting target markets, for positioning the institution, and for addressing competition.

Strategies are not simply inspirations or "bright ideas." Nor is strategy formulation the same thing as goal formulation. Strategies grow out of and reflect the environmental analysis, resource analysis, and goal-formulation steps. Unless the institution has goals it wishes to accomplish, there is no need for strategy formulation. According to an old adage, "If you don't know where you're going, any road will take you there." Only when the environmental analysis, resource analysis, and goal-formulation steps have been carefully done can the institution's administrators and other planning participants feel confident that they have the necessary background for reviewing current programs and markets and considering changes.

Several analytical tools help educational planners to carry out this review. Two are particularly appropriate for education: *academic portfolio strategy*, which involves reviewing existing programs for market attractiveness, program quality, and centrality to the institution's mission; and *product/market opportunity strategy* to identify potential program changes and markets. These and other tools are presented in Chapter 7, which considers marketing strategy in depth.

**Organizational Design.** The institution must have the *structure*, *people*, and *culture* to carry out its strategies. For example, Bradley University combined admissions, financial aid, orientation, career development, placement, retention, and advising services into a division of student affairs. The new division employs a marketing framework in planning its activities. Other institutions have changed the top-administrative structure or combined academic departments to implement a strategy.

Implementing the strategy may require not only changes in organizational structure but also the retraining or replacing of personnel in key positions. For example, if an institution changes its fund-raising strategy from reliance on wealthy donors to foundations, the vice president for development who is expert in "old-boy-network" fund raising may need retraining in corporate grantsmanship or may have to be replaced with a foundation-oriented person. If a college wants to attract adult students, admissions personnel must be trained to counsel them effectively, and/or new personnel must be added.

In adopting a new strategic posture, the school may also have to develop a plan for changing the culture of the institution. Every institution has a culture or, more often, several subcultures, within which a group of people have a particular way of looking at things. The academic culture is often an outspoken critic of the business culture (profit as a worthwhile end) and of the marketing culture (that institutions have to serve and satisfy their markets). College presidents who attempt to persuade faculty to improve their teaching, spend more time with students, develop new courses for nontraditional markets, and so on, may encounter tremendous resistance. For institutions seeking to attract students, the challenge is to develop a marketing orientation in which all members of the institution see their jobs as serving and satisfying markets. Accomplishing this change can be a major task, but it is essential if the institution is to be successful.

Finally, the institution must design or upgrade systems needed to support the new strategies, including procedures, staff, and technology. Procedures may be added for new tasks or streamlined to carry out existing tasks more efficiently. The institution needs to review its staffing plans to make sure that it has the right number and mix of administrators, faculty, and staff to carry out the school's strategic and tactical plans. For example, the school may need a director of financial planning, additional admissions staff, or faculty to replace those about to retire. The school may need to invest in such telecommunications capabilities as voice mail, information lines, and 800 numbers, and in computing for classroom presentations, student use, and faculty and administrative purposes.

Upgrading systems also means assuring that *internal* functions of the institution reflect a culture of service. For example, most schools understand the importance of treating students and their families with care and respect, and urge faculty and front-line staff to extend themselves to serve them. Yet many of these same institutions continue to tolerate officious administrators and staff who hobble the effectiveness of other functions *within* the institution.

Functional areas with little or no student contact should still reflect a marketing orientation toward their *internal* customers within the institution. For example, the personnel (or human resources) department may be slow to respond to faculty and staff questions; or the accounting office may be so rule-bound and the accounting system so complex that other areas of the institution set up their own parallel accounting systems. These and similar cases illustrate unpleasant and wasteful activities that can be reduced or eliminated by proper focus on serving the internal customer.

## THE FORMAT OF A MARKETING PLAN

Tactical marketing planning should follow strategic planning. Strategic planning indicates the particular programs and markets the institution should emphasize. For each selected program or market, the institution must develop a marketing strategy. The formal marketing plan summarizes the information and analysis underlying a proposed strategy and spells out the details of how the strategy will be carried out.

A marketing plan should contain the following major sections: *executive summary, situation analysis, goals and objectives, marketing strategy, action programs, budgets,* and *controls* (see Table 4-1). These sections will be discussed in the context of a hypothetical university.

TABLE 4-1    Contents of a marketing plan

| SECTION | PURPOSE |
| --- | --- |
| I. Executive summary | Presents a brief overview of the proposed plan for quick management skimming. |
| II. Current marketing situation | Presents relevant background data on the market, publics, competition, distribution, and macroenvironment. |
| III. Opportunity and issue analysis | Identifies the main opportunities/threats, strengths/weaknesses, and issues facing the institution/program. |
| IV. Objectives | Defines the goals the plan wants to reach in the areas of enrollment, donations, quality improvement, etc. |
| V. Marketing strategy | Presents the broad marketing approach that will be used to achieve the plan's objectives. |
| VI. Action programs | Answers: *What* will be done? *Who* will do it? *When* will it be done? *How much* will it cost? |
| VII. Budget | Specifies costs and forecasts the expected financial and other outcomes from the plan. |
| VIII. Controls | Indicates how the implementation and effectiveness of the plan will be monitored. |

The board of trustees and the admissions office have agreed on an increase in undergraduate enrollment from 5,000 to 5,500 over the next three years. The director of admissions has been asked to develop a plan for accomplishing this goal.

## Executive Summary

The planning document should open with a summary of the main objectives and recommendations presented in the plan. Here is an abbreviated example:

- The admissions marketing plan for the 1996–97 academic year calls for increasing new student enrollment for fall 1996 by 200 over fall 1995. Assuming an average tuition cost of $11,000 per additional student, this step, if successful, will add $2.2 million to university revenue. (Some of this additional revenue will be allocated for financial aid.) Assuming that 150 decide to live in university residence halls, the university would receive $5,000 per student, or a total of $750,000 while using otherwise underutilized facilities.

- To accomplish this, the plan calls for marketing expenditures of $180,000. Of this, $50,000 will be used to add a community college liaison person to the admissions office staff, $25,000 will be spent on marketing research to measure the present image of the university held by high school and community college students in the region; $30,000 will be spent to buy appropriate mailing lists; $50,000 will be spent to develop awareness of the university's undergraduate program in community colleges and area firms with employee tuition-reimbursement plans; and $25,000 will be spent to produce new brochures on the undergraduate experience at the university.

The purpose of the executive summary is to permit higher-level administrators to preview the major direction of the plan before reading the document for supporting data and analysis. To guide the reader who wants to focus on a certain aspect of the plan, a table of contents typically follows the executive summary.

## Situation Analysis

The first major section of the plan is the *situation analysis*. Here the administrator describes the major features of the situation affecting his or her operation. Whereas the strategic planning process revealed the situation facing the university, the director of admissions must examine those factors that affect the admissions operation over the specified time frame, the first year of a three-year plan. The situation analysis consists of four subsections—background, normal forecast, opportunities and threats, and strengths and weaknesses.

TABLE 4-2    Background data

|  | FALL 1992–93 | FALL 1993–94 | FALL 1994–95 | FALL 1995–96 |
|---|---|---|---|---|
| Number of applications received for fall | 3,000 | 3,000 | 3,300 | 3,500 |
| Number of applications accepted for fall | 2,700 | 2,700 | 2,800 | 2,900 |
| Number of new undergraduate students enrolled | 2,000 | 1,900 | 1,800 | 1,750 |
| Academic year full-time tuition | $9,400 | $9,800 | $10,200 | $10,500 |
| Total tuition revenue from new students for academic year | $18.8 million | $18.62 million | $18.36 million | $18.55 million |

**Background.** This section starts with a summary of performance over the last few years. An abbreviated hypothetical example is shown in Table 4-2 for the undergraduate admissions office.

The number of new students enrolling each year has declined slightly over the past three years. (We are not even considering the institution's retention rate—the percentage of new students who continue to attend after the first term.) These data should be followed by a description of major developments that would bear on the admissions office's strategy—macroenvironmental trends (such as population growth in the region) and changes in competing institutions, for example.

**Normal Forecast.** The background information should be followed by a forecast of the number of new students enrolling in Fall 1996–97 under "normal" conditions—that is, assuming no major changes in the *marketing environment* or *marketing strategies*. The director of admissions could ask, "How many new students are likely to enroll next fall if our admissions operation continues the way it has in the past?" The forecast could be derived by assuming that present trends will continue. In this example, the director might forecast that if no marketing changes are made, about 1,725 new students will enroll. (Institutions with other backgrounds might forecast a stable enrollment level or an increase.) Or the director might use more advanced statistical techniques to predict enrollment from data from previous years, or perhaps survey a sample of applicants about intentions to enroll to make the normal forecast. The normal forecast must then be adjusted if the director expects significant changes in the macroenvironment or in the institution's strategies.

**Opportunities and Threats.** In this section, the director identifies the main opportunities and threats facing the undergraduate admissions office (see Table 4-3, A). Although the director may already have these in mind, they should be put in writing and discussed in admissions staff meetings. Top administration can review the list and raise questions about threats and opportunities that are listed or missing. They may also ask the director to rate the opportunities and threats on their potential effects and probability to indicate which deserve the most planning attention. Also, the director and other administrators can later see how many opportunities were acted on and what threats actually occurred.

**Strengths and Weaknesses.** The director should next list the main internal strengths and weaknesses of the undergraduate admissions office (see Table 4-3, B). Of course, the ultimate success of the undergraduate admissions office depends in large measure on other parts of the university—such as the quality of instruction, the attractiveness of residence facilities, and the availability of certain majors—but in the short term, the admissions office cannot significantly influence changes in these.

TABLE 4-3    An example of oportunities, threats, strengths, and weaknesses

A. Opportunites and Threats Facing the Admissions Office

OPPORTUNITIES

1. The population of the region is growing rapidly, increasing the population base we can attract and serve.
2. Large employers in the metropolitan area are adopting tuition-reimbursement plans for their employees. We could attact some of these employees to our evening courses.
3. Graduates of area community colleges tend to remain here and might be attracted to transfer to the university to complete bachelor's degrees.

THREATS

1. A downturn in the economy may discourage students from applying to private universities.
2. The increasing cost of tuition may discourage applicants.
3. Community colleges offer low-cost vocational training to prepare for well-paying technical jobs in local industry, and may attract students who would otherwise attend a four-year institution.

B. Strengths and Weaknesses of the Admissions Office

STRENGTHS

1. The undergraduate students attracted in the past five years have been of higher quality than before.
2. The admissions staff is well-trained and client-oriented. Even applicants who decide to go elsewhere report favorably on the admissions staff.
3. The applicant pool has grown slowly but surely over the past six years.

WEAKNESSES

1. The admissions office is open weekdays only from 9 to 5, so potential applicants who work or attend college at a distance cannot easily see an admissions counselor.
2. Mailing lists are out of date, making the office dependent on applicant inquiries.
3. The admissions counselors have little experience working with adult applicants.

## Goals and Objectives

The situation analysis section describes where the institution stands and what its likely future will be if no changes are made. Now the director must propose where the undergraduate admissions office should head. Specific goals and objectives need to be set.

The director of admissions starts with the enrollment objective stated by the board of trustees—to increase undergraduate enrollment from 5,000 to 5,500 over the next three years. The director then must develop specific objectives for the undergraduate admissions office to achieve this overall objective. The director decides on the following specific objectives: to increase new student enrollment for the following fall term by 200 (that is, from 1,800 to 2,000), and to spend $180,000 to accomplish this. Other supporting objectives would also be listed in this section—for example, quality levels based on high school grade-point average and test scores.

## Marketing Strategy

The director then outlines a marketing strategy for attaining the specified goals and objectives—the steps admissions-office personnel will carry out to achieve the increase in new students. Marketing strategy consists of a coordinated set of decisions on (1) *target markets*, (2) *marketing mix*, and (3) *marketing expenditure level*.

**Target Markets.**  The director should develop a list of criteria to identify the most attractive potential student markets. Criteria might include age, sex, income, place of residence, and other variables. The director, along with the appropriate admissions staff, should rate each market on these criteria to select the most promising potential student markets, those from which the university can attract a reasonable number of students who meet its admissions criteria. The director might conclude that area community college students are likely to be a more promising pool of students for the university than, for example, high school seniors who live more than 500 miles away.

**Marketing Mix.**  The director should plan a *strategic marketing mix* that answers such basic questions as whether to emphasize personal or mail contacts with community college counselors or to rely upon direct mail or mass media to contact community college students individually. The director should then develop a *tactical marketing mix*. The admissions director may decide to hire or designate a staff person to make personal visits to reach community college counselors in the metropolitan area, but rely on an informational mailing to community college counselors based farther away. To increase applications from high school students, the director would need to select a different marketing mix.

**Marketing Expenditure Level.** Marketing strategy also requires deciding on the marketing expenditure level. When an admissions office takes on a marketing approach to prospective students, it will usually need to increase its budget. The increased expenditure is generally warranted to the extent that it results in more enrolled students; however, if competition exists, the institution may find over time that it must spend more money per enrolled student. In this example, the total admissions office budget will be far more than the $180,000 allocated for attracting additional students.

### Action Plan

Each strategy element must be translated into appropriate actions. For example, the strategy element "attract more community college students" could lead to the following actions:

1. Hire a community college liaison person to visit community college campuses.
2. Hold a conference for community college counselors on helping community college students make the transfer decision (not specific to this university).
3. Send a letter and brochure on the university to second-year community college students.
4. Hold a series of open houses for area community college students.
5. Advertise the college's programs in area community college catalogs.
6. Set up and publicize a 24-hour "transfer line" 800 number where callers can obtain recorded information on how to transfer to the university.

Once the most cost-effective actions have been selected, implementation becomes paramount. In some institutions, the planning process may be hamstrung by institutional structures and overreliance on multiple layers of committees, so that the plan doesn't get put into action. The designated actions should be assigned to specific individuals with specified completion times. To integrate the various actions, they should be charted on a calendar or, even better, with PC-based project management software, to indicate the start/finish dates for each activity and who will do them. These detailed plans can then be reviewed in an iterative "reality check" process, to assure that the final plans are reasonable. This action plan can be revised as new problems and opportunities arise.

### Budget

The objectives, strategies, and planned actions form the basis for preparing the budget. For institutions and programs that must match revenues and expenditures, the budget is essentially a projected profit-and-loss statement. On the revenue side, it shows the forecasted unit enrollment and the expected net realized revenue. On the expense side, it shows the costs of providing the service as well as marketing and administration. The difference is the projected profit or loss. The administration reviews the budget and either approves or modifies it. Once approved, the budget guides the marketing operations, financial planning, and personnel recruitment.

The undergraduate admissions office performs a service to the university, but it is not a profit-making operation. The budget will reflect the admissions director's appraisal of how much money will be required to carry out the required tasks and top administration's willingness to support them. The administration will usually be interested in whether the plan, if successful, is likely to generate tuition revenues that will match or exceed educational costs and the additional marketing costs, but this is not the sole criterion for approval. For example, if the university's objective is to increase minority enrollment, this will probably require additional financial aid, which must come from endowment income or other sources. The administration will look at the appropriateness of the plan, its likelihood of success, and the reasonableness of the costs involved, rather than an evaluation of profit and loss.

## Controls

The last section of the plan describes the controls that will be used to monitor the plan's progress. The objectives and budgets can be spelled out for each month or quarter; then top administration can review the results each period. Where objectives are not being met or budgets are being exceeded, the administrator can request plans for corrective action.

This completes the description of the contents of a marketing plan. We now turn to formal planning systems.

## MARKETING PLANNING SYSTEMS

We have described strategic marketing planning and the tactical marketing plans that guide action. Some institutions prepare such plans from time to time but shun adopting formal planning systems. They see the value of having a plan but reject formal procedures as unnecessary or too demanding. For example, a university president offered the following justification:

1. The deans and department chairs do not have the time to write formal plans, nor does top administration have the time to read them.
2. Most department heads would not be able to plan even if they were asked. They head their departments because they are scholars or leaders in their fields, not because they are managers. They might refuse to plan, or plan poorly, and this would be tolerated as long as they were performing well in other respects.

3. The department chairs would not use their plans. The plans would be mere window dressing, prepared and then filed away. The plans might even be obsolete the day they were written, given the rapid changes in higher education.
4. The administration has plans that are best kept secret from the department chairs, since they might feel threatened. The department chairs should not be encouraged to come up with unrealistic expectations that the president would then have to reject.
5. Installing a formal planning system and making it work would cost too much in money and time.

Although we grant some validity to these arguments, the experience of a growing number of schools and colleges demonstrates that formal planning and control systems are usually beneficial and improve institutional performance. Formal planning also helps the institution communicate with its publics and maintain their support.

All Hallows School, an eight-room parochial elementary school in rural Connecticut, faced closing at the end of the term. The school's enrollment had declined from 260 to 177 students in five years. Persistent rumors of closing brought further declines. In addition, the parish carried a long-term debt on which nothing had been paid for five years. All Hallows' financial problems grew as enrollment and tuition revenue declined.

A marketing consultant worked with school administrators, parents, and parishioners to establish a school board to develop a formal, written long-range plan. With a clear grasp of its resources, problems, and opportunities, the school first took steps to reassure the parish of the school's long-term stability. In this case formal planning helped guide the institution and meet the needs of the school's markets and publics as well. The planning process gave the school a sense of increased confidence, and reports on the plan promoted stability by counteracting rumors. Parents could anticipate the school's performance from year to year. The school then moved ahead to add preschool classes to meet an expressed need and to establish a "feeder system" into the elementary grades. With its well-founded image of stability and action, the school was able to build its enrollment in every grade to full capacity, and the parish debt was repaid.[4]

The relationship between marketing planning and control is shown in Figure 4-2. The planning step calls upon the institution to identify attractive marketing opportunities, develop effective marketing strategies, and develop detailed action programs. The second step involves implementing the action programs in the marketing plan. The third step calls for marketing control activity to ensure that the objectives are being achieved. Marketing control involves measuring results, analyzing the causes of poor results, and taking corrective actions—adjustments in the plan, its implementation, or both.

Educational institutions move toward strategic planning when the administration realizes that annual plans make sense only in the context of a *long-range plan*. In fact, the long-range plan should come first, with the an-

FIGURE 4-2    The marketing planning and control system

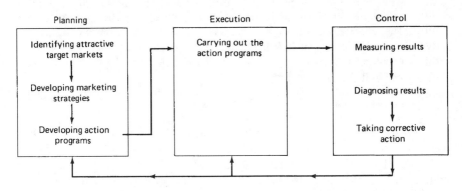

nual plan being a detailed version of the first year of the long-range plan. The long-range plan is based on assumptions about how the institution and its environment will change over time. Therefore, a long-range plan cannot be static and must be reworked each year (called *rolling planning*).

At this stage, the various plans begin to take on a more *strategic character*. An institution beginning long-range planning often assumes that the future will be a continuation of the present and that present strategies, institutional structure, and procedures will remain appropriate. Eventually, the administration sees that the environment is full of probabilities, not certainties, and that broader strategic thinking is required. The planning format is then redesigned to stimulate administrators to contemplate and evaluate alternative strategies that will improve the institution's performance.

Administrators are then asked to develop *contingency plans* showing how they would respond to specific major threats and opportunities. The institution needs to take these contingencies seriously and be prepared to take action if the marketing control system signals a problem.[5] Heights University has experienced some setbacks in its enrollment and fund-raising efforts and will need to adapt its plans to changed circumstances. The development of contingency plans to help the institution respond and adapt to its environment marks the emergence of a true strategic planning culture in the institution.

As the institution gains experience with planning, plan formats are often standardized to permit more meaningful comparisons among similar units. As the planning culture takes hold in the institution, further improvements are introduced. Administrators receive training in financial analysis and are required to justify their recommendations not only in terms of enrollment, donations, and so on, but also in terms of financial measures such as cost-benefit or cost-effectiveness of an activity. Where clear financial measures don't exist, educational administrators can develop substitute measures, including "shadow prices," to guide them in allocating the institution's resources.[6]

*Computer-based planning models* can be developed to help administrators examine the results of alternative marketing plans and environments.[7] Some institutions have developed sophisticated computer models. A growing number of schools use spreadsheets on personal computers to consider alternative courses of action and to evaluate trade-offs among various policies within user-specified constraints on resources and options. To be useful, a model must reflect the institution's policies and practices—its institutional theory—in its set of assumptions.[8]

## Designing the Marketing Planning Process

A planning system doesn't just happen. According to Michael Townsley, approximately one-sixth of America's institutions of higher education are in constant financial trouble. Many of the 500 to 600 smaller, tuition-dependent private colleges don't do much if any planning. Instead, they "live by their wits, battling bankruptcy, improvising, and groping in the darkness."[9] Such institutions often lack the basic financial information to know whether the college is solvent, let alone how resources are being allocated and spent. Such institutions need to quickly establish the basic systems to monitor their use of institutional resources against expenses.

The effective institution needs to adopt or design a planning system that is acceptable to those who will do the planning, clear to those who will review and approve the plans, and suitable for meeting the institution's needs. The following criteria, proposed by John Edgar Miller specifically for small colleges, are useful reminders:

- There must be support from the top. The board of trustees and president must determine if they want a formal planning process and, if so, how they will show evidence of their support.
- There must be involvement of representatives from appropriate constituencies. Faculty, administration, staff, students, trustees, alumni, and community representatives should have an opportunity for input.
- The objectives of the process must be set and agreed upon.
- The process must be defined in specific, discrete steps that produce results to be used in subsequent tasks.
- The process must not be dominated by one person or committee.
- The process must not be allowed to become isolated functionally, politically, or geographically.
- The process must include periodic needs assessments.
- The process must include feedback to involved constituencies after each stage of their involvement.
- Evaluation criteria and techniques must be identified before implementation.[10]

Usually, the initial planning system is established by top administration, often with the advice of a committee and/or an outside consultant with broad experience in designing management planning systems. The outside consultant can provide valuable perspectives on planning as well as specific procedures and forms. Some institutions then hire or designate a director of planning to take responsibility for designing the final system and to manage the planning process.

The planning director's job is not to write the plans but to educate and assist administrators and others in writing their plans. Planning should involve those who must carry out the plans. In this way, they are stimulated to think out their goals and strategies and are motivated to achieve their objectives.

Since planning is a continuous process, the institution needs to develop a calendar of the planning process. The normal calendar steps for a director of planning are these:

1. Develop a set of relevant environmental facts and trends to distribute to administrators as part of their planning.
2. Work with top administration to develop overall institutional objectives for the coming year as a basis for subsequent planning.
3. Work with individual administrators to complete their plans, including marketing plans, by a certain date.
4. Work with top administration to review, approve, or modify the various plans.
5. Develop a consolidated official plan for the institution for the coming year.

Establishing a planning calendar sequence underscores the critical role of marketing planning in the overall planning process. Individual administrators examine environmental trends and institutional objectives. They then set marketing objectives (for enrollment, donations, and so forth) for their programs for the coming period, along with proposed strategies and marketing budgets. Once these are approved by top administration, decisions can be made on needed personnel and other resources to implement them.

## MONITORING THE MARKETING PROCESS

Marketing control is an early-warning system. After a marketing plan is implemented, many surprises are possible that can require adjustments—a change in federal government funding, an earthquake, staff departures, and so on. The marketing control system includes techniques for determining when plan goals are being met and for making adjustments when they are not.

Table 4-4 shows three types of marketing control. Each type has its place in an educational institution. *Annual-plan control* refers to the steps taken during the year to monitor and correct performance deviations from the plan. *Financial control* consists of efforts to determine the actual financial impacts of different programs, services, market segments, or locations. *Stra-

TABLE 4-4   Types of marketing control

| TYPE OF CONTROL | PRIME RESPONSIBILITY | PURPOSE OF CONTROL | APPROACHES |
|---|---|---|---|
| I. Annual-plan control | Top administration<br>Middle management | To examine whether the planned results are being achieved | Performance analysis<br>Market-share analysis<br>Marketing expense-to-performance ratios<br>Market-attitude tracking |
| II. Revenue/cost control | Marketing controller | To examine where the organization is making and losing money | Profitability by:<br>  Program or service<br>  Location<br>  Market segment |
| III. Strategic control | Top administration<br>Marketing auditor | To examine whether the institution is pursuing its best opportunities. | Marketing audit |

*tegic control* consists of a systematic evaluation of the institution's marketing performance in relation to its market opportunities. We describe each form of marketing control in the following section.

## Annual-Plan Control

Annual-plan control is designed to monitor the effects of carrying out the annual plan. The four steps are shown in Figure 4-3. First, the various administrators—deans, department chairpersons, director of admissions, and so on—set well-defined objectives for each month, quarter, academic year, or other period during the plan year. Second, monitoring techniques and checkpoints are established to track achievement of the objectives. Third, administrators seek to diagnose the causes of serious deviations in performance. Fourth, the administrators choose corrective actions that they hope will close the gap between objectives and performance. This system is an example of management by objectives.

FIGURE 4-3   The control process

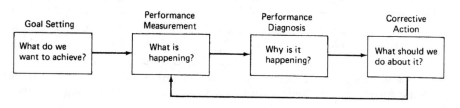

Four main control tools are commonly used: performance analysis, market-share analysis, marketing expense-to-performance analysis, and market-attitude tracking.

**Performance Analysis.** *Performance analysis* is the measurement and evaluation of actual performance, measured by enrollment, tuition revenues, and/or donations in relation to performance objectives. Thus, the director of admissions would compare the actual number of new students enrolled to the expected number, and the director of development could compare the number and amount of donations received with fund-raising goals by donor type (alumnus, parent, and the like), gift size, and so on. If too few alumni are donating, if certain categories of alumni are underrepresented, or if the average gift size in certain categories is down from previous years, the causes should be carefully researched and corrective action taken.

**Market-Share Analysis.** Institutions should periodically review whether they are losing ground relative to their competition. For example, a private school may see its applications grow 5 percent per year while competitor's applications have been increasing by 15 percent. Market share is a much better indicator of marketing effectiveness, but market share must be used cautiously. The institution must identify its real competitors. Heights University, for example, should not measure its enrollment performance against the large state universities or the elite private universities. Instead, it should compare its enrollment performance with other institutions to which its applicants also apply. A close competitor would be another institution that students applying to Heights University see as equally desirable.

**Marketing Expense-to-Performance Analysis.** Annual-plan control also requires evaluating various marketing expenses as a ratio to performance (typically measured by revenue) to ensure that the institution is not overspending to achieve its objectives. An educational institution may want to track the ratio between enrollment marketing (admissions) *expenditures and enrollment*, and the ratio between *fund-raising expenditures and gifts received*. In addition to tracking expenses, the institution should keep track of other ratios that compare effort and results. For example, an experienced development director may periodically check the following ratios: revenue per fund raiser, number of contacts per fund raiser per period, percentage of potential contributors contacted, and percentage of repeat donors.

**Market-Attitude Tracking.** Institutions should periodically check client attitudes toward the institution. The erosion of attitudes can contribute to later declines in enrollment and donations. Students may drop out or discourage potential applicants, donors may reduce the size or frequency of their gifts or quit giving, and certain academic programs may be abandoned by disgruntled majors. Knowing of these attitude shifts early can lead to precautionary changes. Market attitudes can be measured through complaint and suggestion boxes, consumer panels, and consumer satisfaction surveys.

### Revenue/Cost Control

Besides annual-plan control, institutions may periodically determine the actual financial returns for their various programs, consumer groups, territories, or locations. *Revenue/cost analysis* requires identifying all revenues generated by a particular unit (department, program, office) or service and all the costs associated with it, then comparing revenues and costs to determine the financial status of the unit. For small educational institutions with only one or two programs, this task is reasonably straightforward. But isolating the revenues and costs of a college career center from the total college budget would be much more difficult, since a highly effective career center may attract more and better students to the college, increasing tuition revenue, and may attract more donations from employing companies. Furthermore, the assigning of administrative overhead costs to programs is often somewhat arbitrary.

Revenue/cost analysis can be used to provide information on the relative profitability of various programs, services, branches, and other marketing entities. But it does not imply that "unprofitable" marketing entities should be dropped, nor does it measure the likely profit improvement if marginal units are dropped. The institution needs to consider whether each entity should be expected to match revenues and costs. The president of a respected graduate school of education protested a recommendation that each unit of the college be economically self-sufficient: "The library doesn't pay its own way, but we must have a library!" A business school may justify conducting continuing education courses for area businesspeople on the grounds that it encourages donations, improves job prospects for the school's graduates, or provides a service to the community, even if revenue from such courses doesn't contribute much toward overhead.

Most educational institutions have some programs that are expected to pay their own way—or even return a surplus. For private institutions, continuing education is usually intended as a profitmaker. Academic departments, on the other hand, are often viewed as part of a portfolio: The classics department may break even or lose money, whereas the business school will generate a profit. Regardless of whether the entity is expected to make a profit, the comparison of revenues and costs can encourage thinking about possible ways of improving the revenue or reducing the costs of the entity, while preserving or enhancing its quality and functioning.

### Strategic Control

From time to time, institutions should critically examine their overall marketing performance. Marketing is one of the major areas where rapid obsolescence of objectives, policies, strategies, and programs is a constant possibility. The marketing audit is a major diagnostic tool to assess the institution's marketing opportunities and operations. The marketing audit will be presented in Chapter 17.

## SUMMARY

Marketing planning and control guide the institution's operations in the marketplace. Educational institutions have planning systems of various degrees of sophistication, from simple budgeting systems to formal long-range planning systems. Although educators often resist formal planning, sophisticated formal planning systems can contribute to institutional effectiveness.

Educational institutions should carry out strategic planning and tactical marketing planning. Strategic planning consists of several steps that may be carried out for institutional units as well as for the institution as a whole. The first is environmental analysis, in which the institution examines its internal environment, markets, publics, competitors, and macroenvironment. Threats and opportunities are identified so that the institution can prepare contingency plans and monitor trends. The institution then examines its major strengths and weaknesses in personnel, funds, facilities, systems, and other resources. In the goal-formulation step, the institution reviews and revises its basic mission, and formulates its major goals and its specific quantifiable objectives.

Strategy formulation requires analyzing the institution's current portfolio of programs to determine which it should build, maintain, or drop. The resulting strategy includes decisions about the institution's current and future programs and markets, and about needed changes in the institution's structure, people, and culture. Finally, the institution examines its systems of information, planning, and control to be sure they are adequate to carry out the strategy successfully.

Tactical marketing planning is the process of developing the specific plans that will implement the overall strategy. The tactical marketing plan contains the following sections: executive summary, situation analysis, goals and objectives, marketing strategy, action program, budget, and controls. The marketing strategy section of the plan defines the target markets, marketing mix, and marketing expenditures that will be used to achieve the marketing objectives.

Marketing control is an intrinsic part of marketing planning. Institutions can exercise three types of marketing control. Annual-plan control consists of monitoring current marketing performance to ensure that annual goals are being achieved. The main tools are performance analysis, market-share analysis, marketing expense-to-performance analysis, and market-attitude analysis. If underperformance is detected, the institution can take corrective action. Revenue/cost control consists of determining the profit or loss for various programs, customer groups, territories, or locations. Revenue/cost analysis does not indicate whether an entity should be bolstered or phased out. Strategic control consists of ensuring that the institution's marketing objectives, strategies, and systems are optimally adapted to the current and anticipated marketing environment.

## Notes

1. James Gyure and Thomas J. Wonders, "Planning With the Enemy: Gaining Acceptance for Your Marketing Strategies," *Proceedings of the 1993 Symposium for the Marketing of Higher Education* (Chicago, IL: American Marketing Association, 1993), pp. 167–174.

2. Gyure and Wonders, "Planning With the Enemy," pp. 172–173.

3. Peter Drucker, *Management: Tasks, Responsibilities, Practices* (New York: Harper & Row, 1973), Chap. 7.

4. Richard J. Burke, "Can Formal Long-Range Planning Solve Your School's Problems?" *Momentum* (May 1978), pp. 38–41.

5. Andrew H. Lupton, "Nine Ways Toward Better Management," *Educational Record* (Summer 1980), pp. 19–23.

6. Karl A. Fox, ed. *Economic Analysis for Educational Planning: Resource Allocation in Nonmarket Systems* (Baltimore: The Johns Hopkins University Press, 1972).

7. David S.P. Hopkins and William F. Massy, *Planning Models for Colleges and Universities* (Stanford, CA: Stanford University Press, 1981).

8. See Charles Wiseman, "New Foundations for Planning Models," *Journal of Higher Education* (November–December 1979), pp. 726–744.

9. Michael Townsley, "Brinkmanship, Planning, Smoke, and Mirrors," *Planning for Higher Education*, 19 (Summer 1991), p. 27.

10. John Edgar Miller, "Planning in Small Colleges," *Planning for Higher Education* (November 1980), pp. 25–26.

# 5

# Analyzing and Adapting to the Environment

*A blue-ribbon panel on issues affecting American higher educa-*
*tion summarized its conclusions in a letter to trustees and other*
*leaders:*

*"We write as friends of higher education to convey our sense of*
*urgency that great changes are afoot in the United States and the*
*world, and our colleges and universities are not prepared to cope*
*with them. We write as optimists, confident that higher educa-*
*tion's leaders, effectively engaged, will do what is best for their*
*institutions and for the nation. But we write also as realists: The*
*difficulties ahead for our institutions are real. They are sober-*
*ing. They cannot be wished away.*

*Our central conclusion is that the world Americans thought they*
*knew no longer exists. Powerful changes in recent decades have*
*swept aside business as usual in corporations, in the world of*
*work, in the nation's schools, and in foreign policy. Colleges and*
*universities will find no special shelter from these winds of*
*change.*

*The hard fact is that the illusion of the permanence of American*
*institutions is rapidly being shattered amid global change. The*
*harder question is: What will we create to replace the America*
*most of us carry around in our mind's eye? . . . .*

*[T]he outlines of the American future can already be discerned,*
*occasionally with great clarity. In many ways, the future we an-*
*ticipate represents the present come back to haunt us.*

*We rest our convictions on five propositions:*

- *Economic pressures can be expected to grow in the next generation, both domestically and internationally.*
- *Demographic change will continue to remake the face of the nation and the world.*
- *Racial and cultural tension in the United States will continue to mount as the pressures of diversity intensify.*
- *Scientific advances in the next generation will dwarf the changes of the last 25 years.*
- *The nation's crisis of values and ethics will deepen the difficulty of creating a sense of community in a new age.*

*Three statistical trends stand out against a gray background of confusing data. Between 1893 and 1970, the United States never experienced a merchandise trade deficit with the rest of the world; since 1975, it has never experienced a trade surplus. In the next 20 years, America will add 4.4 million minority youth (African-American, Asian, Latino, Native American, and Middle Eastern); in that same period, the number of white youth will drop by 3.8 million. The United States is aging. . . .*

*We believe that every college and university in the United States will feel the force of the changes. The financial shoe is going to pinch. Low rates of economic growth inevitably will hit higher education, increasing tuition dependence of both public and private institutions, with the greatest pressure in the public sector. . . . Higher education will be forced to dance to the economic music of the times.*

*Demographics are destiny for institutions of higher education. Colleges and universities are faced with two possibilities: Diversify the campus or shrink. . . .*

*The demands of science may, and in the panel's view should, force the restructuring of education in science from a process of the survival of the fittest to a commitment to provide all young people with the capability to function effectively in an increasingly technological world.*

*Finally, as Americans sort out their values in this new age of uncertainty, higher education has a profound obligation to light the road ahead."*

**Source:** Excerpted from *Trustees & Troubled Times in Higher Education: Invitation to a Continuing Conversation,*

Report of the Higher Education Issues Panel (Washington, DC: Association of Governing Boards of Universities and Colleges, 1992), pp. vi–vii.

---

To succeed, educational institutions must make timely and appropriate adaptations to a complex and ever-changing environment. Just as "no man is an island," no educational institution is separate and complete unto itself. Every school and college depends on receiving new students, faculty, staff, and funding to continue fulfilling its educational mission. Fulfillment of this mission is reflected in capable, loyal alumni, the community and national reputation of the institution, faculty output of research and publications, and other measures of achievement.

All the institution's activities take place within, and are dependent upon, the external environment. The character of an institution's environment may determine its survival as much as the quality of its programs or leadership. The institution's leaders need to recognize the importance of understanding this environment and of tracking changes over time that could affect the institution's survival and success. Knowing the current state of affairs is useful, but inadequate: Forecasting potential developments in the macroenvironment will give the institution some time to plan effective responses to them.

The institution's environment may be changing quickly or slowly. With a *stable environment*, the major forces of demographics, the economy, ecology, technology, government regulation and law, and culture remain stable from year to year. In a *slowly evolving environment*, smooth and fairly predictable changes take place. The individual institution survives in this type of environment to the extent that it foresees change and takes intelligent steps to adapt. For example, major changes in overall school enrollment can often be predicted far in advance and planned for. In a *turbulent environment*, major and unpredictable changes occur often.

Most educational institutions find themselves operating in turbulent environments. They must carry out four tasks: (1) to understand the nature of the macroenvironment, (2) to systematically scan the institution's environment, (3) to identify the most significant environmental threats and opportunities, and (4) to make intelligent adaptations to the changing environment.

## UNDERSTANDING THE INSTITUTION'S MACROENVIRONMENT

Every institution is aware that it exists in a *physical* environment—a region, a state, a city, a place with a typical weather pattern and a certain terrain—that confronts the institution with certain opportunities and threats. A college near the coast can offer programs in marine biology; a school near an earth-quake fault line will need to spend more to construct safe buildings; a college in a cold-weather area must budget for heating costs.

Institutions tend to be less aware of the wide range of other forces that shape opportunities for and pose threats to the institution. The *macroenvironment* consists of large-scale fundamental forces which are often categorized as *demographic, economic, ecological, technological, political/legal/regulatory,* and *sociocultural forces.*

Two attributes of the macroenvironment are particularly important. First, the macroenvironment is *constantly changing.* The decade of the 1980s, for example, was marked in different periods by runaway inflation, high unemployment, economic expansion, soaring stock values, government budget deficits, and rapid change in computer technology. All these forces created problems and opportunities for educational institutions, and the 1990s and beyond will continue to bring more changes.

Second, macroenvironmental forces are *largely outside the control and influence of educational institutions* or any other organization or group of organizations. No educational institution created the floods, hurricanes, and earthquakes of the 1990s that seriously affected state and regional economies, including family incomes and state tax revenues; and no single educational institution created population shifts or influenced the rate of divorce or teen pregnancy. This does not mean that educational institutions have no influence, but only that their effect, if any, is almost always long term rather than short term. Research at Stanford University did lead to the birth-control pill and the transistor, inventions which have had major, long-term impacts on various facets of the macroenvironment.

Since educational institutions have very limited direct influence on the macroenvironment, they must identify and adapt to macroenvironmental trends. An institution's performance depends on the degree of alignment between its environmental opportunities, objectives, marketing strategy, organizational structure, and management systems. In the ideal case:

Environment→Objectives→Strategy→Structure→Systems

This says that the institution first studies the environment in which it is operating, and specifically the opportunities and threats in this environment. It then develops a set of objectives describing what it wants to achieve in this environment. Then it formulates an institutional strategy that promises to achieve these objectives. After that, it builds an organizational structure capable of carrying out the strategy. Finally, it designs various systems of analysis, planning, and control to support the effective implementation of the strategy.

In practice, this optimal alignment is hard to realize because the various components change at different rates. A typical educational institution may operate in the following way:

Environment—Objectives—Strategy—Structure—Systems
1995             1990            1986           1982          1980

The institution is operating in a 1995 environment but with objectives that were set in 1990 for the environment at that time. Its strategy lags even more, since it is the strategy that was successful in 1986. Its organizational structure is not even geared to supporting its 1986 strategy, having been designed earlier in a quite different environment. Finally, its systems are even older and have not been adjusted to the new conditions, including advances in computer, networking, and telecommunications technologies.

Too often, in fact, institutions operate according to a reverse (and perverse) way of thinking:

Structure and Systems→Objectives and Strategy→Environment

The institution believes that its structure and systems are sound because they worked during its most successful years. Employing these, it chooses objectives and strategies that are manageable with the present systems and structure. Then it scans the environment to find the opportunities that are best suited to its objectives and strategy.

An example would be a hospital nursing school that provides R.N. training. Its organization, staffing, and systems are maximally adapted to providing training for would-be nurses. Furthermore, the hospital desperately needs the services the nurses in training provide. As a result, the nursing school sets its objectives in terms of attracting a certain number of students and its strategy as one of appealing to those who want to work in a hospital setting and who are not interested in college. Then the nursing school searches the environment broadly for this type of student.

The irony is that there are fewer such candidates around, since many states are beginning to require at least an associate degree in nursing to become a registered nurse, and the most able students are selecting community college or baccalaureate programs in nursing. To attract the best candidates, the hospital nursing school should probably be seeking to affiliate with a college-based program so that students can get their academic courses in the academic setting and their clinical training at the hospital.

The environment is the fastest-changing element in the picture, but educational institutions traditionally do not change rapidly. Even when they can spot coming tends, they tend to respond slowly. Even within a rapidly changing environment, some institutions continue to wait until events are upon them before mobilizing. In the 1960s, many school district superintendents and boards of education were preoccupied with constructing school buildings and expanding programs. At that time, the decline in the number of pupils was already predictable (the children were already born), and the effects were felt in the elementary schools in the early 1970s. Only then did elementary schools begin to consider how to cope with this change in demand. Some districts tore down elementary schools and sold the land for private development. In the 1980s, some of these same school districts were caught up short by the "baby boomlet" and had to scramble to build new classrooms.

The optimal approach is to attempt to forecast what the environment will be like in, say, five to ten years. Given this environmental forecast, the institution's leaders will set objectives that will describe where they want to be. Then they will formulate a strategy that will accomplish those objectives in the five- to ten-year time frame. They will begin to alter the institution and its systems so that these will support the new strategy rather than impede its fulfillment. This forward-looking thinking is depicted as follows:

Environment→Objectives→Strategy→Structure→Systems
1999                1999           1999          1999          1999

The institution will have to work diligently on each area to assure the optimal alignment within the planning timeline.


## SCANNING THE ENVIRONMENT

Most educational institutions engage in *environmental scanning* in an informal manner. For example, the president and other administrators of a college will read local newspapers, national magazines, journals, and publications such as *The Chronicle of Higher Education*. Administrators may note a development in other parts of the country and consider the likely effect if it happened in their area. Some of the ideas sparked by reading or talking with counterparts at other colleges may be carefully scrutinized and incorporated into the college's planning. But many ideas either will not appear in print or may be missed, or their relevance may be unclear. The result of such informal environmental scanning may be that a threat or opportunity may materialize before the college recognizes it and too late to plan a response.

In contrast, a university engaged in formal environmental scanning will have a high interest in monitoring legislative thinking, among other things. The university may hire—or join with other universities to hire—one or more intelligence officers, locate them in a Washington office, and give them a budget for initiating and maintaining contacts with knowledgeable people in Congress and relevant government agencies. These officers will assemble information on possible shifts in research funding, financial assistance programs, interest rates, and congressional attitudes toward higher education and relay this information to university administrators for action.

Some institutions have highly formalized processes for environmental scanning. Cardinal Stritch College in Milwaukee, Wisconsin, regularly scans 129 publications, while the Georgia Center for Continuing Education has 65 people from four operational divisions who engage in environmental scanning, along with two committees who review all the scanning data to develop policy and recommend changes based on the data.[1]

From this environmental scanning, the institution aims to spot the macroenvironmental forces with the greatest import for future strategy. These forces can be classified as either threats or opportunities facing the institution. We briefly described these in Chapter 4 with reference to Beloit College. We define an *environmental threat* as follows:

> An environmental threat is a challenge posed by an unfavorable trend or specific disturbance in the environment that would lead, in the absence of purposeful action, to the stagnation or demise of the institution or one of its programs.

A major threat is one that (1) would cause substantial damage to the institution's or program's ability to function, and (2) has a moderate to high probability of occurring. No institution is free of such threats, and every administrator should be able to identify them. For example, a state university in California might face the following threats:

1. Declining demand for undergraduate study in business.
2. Increasing applications from students with academic deficiencies and/or high need for financial aid.
3. State budget short-falls which will lead to continuing reductions in funding for higher education.

An institution facing several major macroenvironmental threats is highly vulnerable, and should prepare contingency plans and consider new opportunities.

We define an *institutional marketing opportunity* as follows:

> An *institutional marketing opportunity* is an attractive area for relevant marketing action in which a particular institution is likely to enjoy a competitive advantage.

A major institutional marketing opportunity is one that (1) has strong potential for contributing to the institution's financial strength and reputation, and (2) carries a moderate to high probability that the institution would have success with it. For example, a college might identify the following marketing opportunities:

1. Establish a bachelor's degree program in nursing.
2. Launch a continuing education program of liberal arts courses.
3. Attract a famous author to head the school's creative writing program.

To the extent that there are strong opportunities facing that institution, we simply say that the institution faces high opportunity. Other tools for identifying and testing new-program ideas are presented in Chapter 11.

FIGURE 5-1   Threat and opportunity matrices

Probability of Occurrence
High         Low

| | 1 | 3 |
| High | 2 | |

Potential
Severity

| | 4 | 6 |
| Low | | 5 |
| | | 7 |

Probability of Success
High         Low

| | 8 | 9 |
| High | | |

Potential
Attractiveness

| | 10 | 12 |
| Low | 11 | 13 |

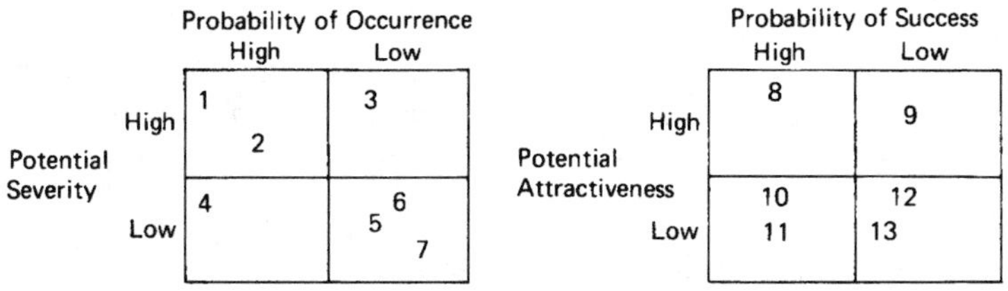

(a) Threat matrix                    (b) Opportunity matrix

Administrators and other managers of an educational institution should periodically identify the major threats and opportunities facing the institution and each of its units (schools or colleges, departments, branches, and so on). This should be done as part of preparing annual and long-range plans. Each threat and opportunity is assigned a number and then evaluated according to its probable effect and occurrence. The threats and opportunities can then be plotted in the *threat and opportunity matrices* shown in Figure 5-1.

The *threat matrix* shows seven identifiable threats. Management should give the greatest attention to threats 1 and 2 because they would have a strong effect on the institution and have a high probability of occurrence. Threat 3 can also hurt the institution substantially, but it has a low probability of occurrence; threat 4 would not hurt much but is highly likely to occur. Management can safely ignore threats 5, 6, and 7.

The *opportunity matrix* shows six identifiable opportunities. The best is opportunity 8, which would have a high positive effect if the institution is successful at developing it, and the institution is highly likely to be successful. Opportunity 9 is attractive, but the likelihood that this school could "pull it off" is not high. Opportunities 10 and 11 are minor in their effect although easy to carry off successfully. Opportunities 12 and 13 can be ignored.

Four outcomes are possible with this analysis, shown in the opportunity-threat matrix in Figure 5-2. An *ideal position* is one that is high in major opportunities and low in or devoid of major threats. A *speculative position* is

FIGURE 5-2   Opportunity-threat matrix

Threat Level
Low                High

| | | Low | High |
| Opportunity Level | High | Ideal position | Speculative position |
| | Low | Mature position | Troubled position |

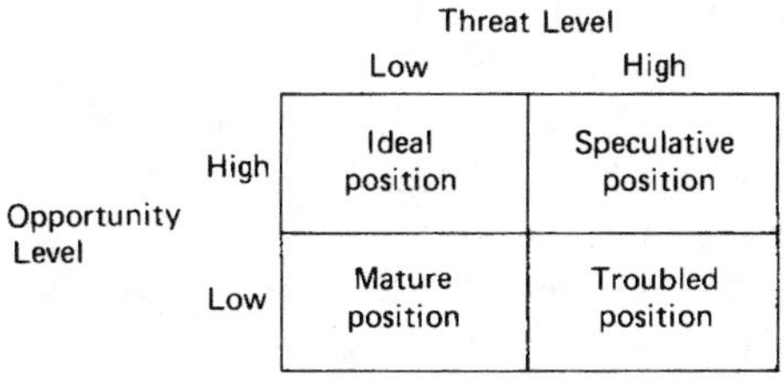

high in both major opportunities and threats. A *mature position* is low in major opportunities and threats. Finally, a *troubled position* is low in opportunities and high in threats.

Each institution should seek to move toward its major opportunities and away from its major threats. The institution must carefully appraise the nature of its opportunities. Theodore Levitt cautions:

> There can be a need, but no market; or a market, but no customer; or a customer, but no salesman. For instance, there is a great need for massive pollution control, but not really a market at present. And there is a market for new technology in education, but no customer really large enough to buy the products. Market forecasters who fail to understand these concepts have made spectacular miscalculations about the apparent opportunities in these and other fields.[2]

## THE NATURE OF ENVIRONMENTAL FORECASTING

Decisions about expansion, programs, and recruitment depend on judgments about the future environment. Making these decisions would be far simpler if the institution could correctly anticipate the character of that environment. To assist in this task, a growing number of large companies—and some educational institutions—are turning to formal *environmental forecasting*. Environmental forecasting aims to identify emerging trends and predict impacts. It goes beyond knowing "what's happening," to trying to predict "what *will happen.*"

No one disputes that environmental forecasting is still more art than science. Despite improvements in forecasting economic and technological developments, forecasting political and cultural developments remains difficult because they interact so much with economics and technology. Some people question the value of environmental forecasting, yet the risk of missing a major threat or opportunity can be so great that many companies continue to invest in it. Our position is that long-range forecasting can contribute greatly to the identification of opportunities and assessment of risks, and that educational institutions should engage in environmental forecasting insofar as they can.

Educational institutions often make two types of mistakes. First, many institutions wait for events or trends to fully emerge before incorporating them in their planning. They feel hard-pressed to scan the present environment for threats and opportunities and respond to them, let alone to try to imagine what the future may bring. They may also conclude that environmental forecasting techniques are too difficult to implement and that the institution cannot afford professional forecasting services.

Second, many institutions rely on *trend extrapolation*, which assumes that trends established in recent history will continue, because the *forces* that created the trend are assumed to continue in the future. Figure 5-3 shows one such forecast. The annual number of U.S. high school graduates for 1969 through 1992 are actual counts; the numbers for 1993 to 2009 are extrapolations based on analysis of birth statistics (most of the high school class of 2009 were already born when the forecast was made) and historical grade-by-grade enrollment data. The graph assumes that *current trends* in migration and dropout rates will remain unchanged.[3]

Trend extrapolation has several limitations. It can be useful in forecasting over a relatively short period of time, but fails for most long-range forecasting or for predicting single events. Thus, trend extrapolation may be useful in predicting enrollment over the next few years, but not in predicting a major catastrophe that would destroy a portion of the institution's facilities. Also, trends can be reversed. The fact that interest in undergraduate and grad-

FIGURE 5-3    U.S. high school graduates, 1969–2009

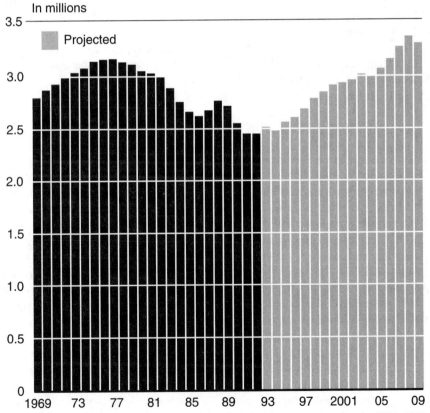

Sources: Data for 1969–1991 from U.S. Department of Education (1992); data for 1992–2009 from Western Interstate Commission for Higher Education (1993).

uate business programs rose in the 1980s certainly does not guarantee that such preferences will continue in subsequent decades.

Trend extrapolation can be very useful for looking at *internal* trends, especially when it calls on the institution to organize existing data on important trends (applications, enrollment, dropouts, donations, costs, and so on) and to examine them thoroughly and thoughtfully. As administrators consider alternative future trends (increase, stable, decrease), they can identify the most substantial and relevant threats and opportunities for further study.

Institutions that cannot afford elaborate forecasting procedures should not forego forecasting altogether. William Ascher reviewed dozens of forecasts of population, economic, energy, transportation, and technology trends and concluded that the accuracy of a given forecast depended primarily on the underlying core assumptions, "which represent the forecaster's basic outlook on the context within which the specific forecasted trend develops."[4] When the core assumptions are valid, the sophistication of the specific forecasting method used is often of secondary importance. Conversely, if the core assumptions are faulty, the most sophisticated methodology will not produce a useful forecast. So institutions should do their best to identify and track relevant trends.

Environmental forecasting involves identifying the trends and events, and then assessing each trend and event for its relevance to the institution, its seriousness, and the probability it will occur.

## METHODS FOR IDENTIFYING TRENDS AND EVENTS

The process of environmental forecasting begins by generating a list of trends and possible events. Items for this list can be derived from many sources. Many educational associations and publications report on emerging trends. At some institutions, designated individuals and/or committees review selected publications and use other sources to produce this list. Those responsible for environmental scanning may talk with experts in each field (e.g., economists, technology experts, and so on) and/or with other knowledgeable people. MGT of America, a higher education management consulting firm, provides clients with a workbook that presents macroenvironmental trends in 13 categories. Table 5-1, A shows one of the 13 trend lists and corresponding examples of university responses.

In addition to these more formal, data-based methods, trends and events are occasionally generated by groups using *brainstorming*. Brainstorming techniques were developed by Alex Osborn to stimulate group creativity. The usual brainstorming group consists of six to ten people, and a brainstorming session typically lasts about an hour. The issue should be specific. For example, the chairperson starts with "Think of as many trends or events in the *economy* that could affect our college. Remember, we want as many ideas as possible—the wilder the better—and remember, *no evaluation*." The ideas start flowing, one idea sparks another, and within an hour many possible trends and events are recorded on the tape recorder.

For example, at the University of Pennsylvania at Johnstown, marketing professors Thomas Wonders and James Gyure hold "Popcorn Parties," which are playful brainstorming sessions based on the societal trends identified by marketing analyst Faith Popcorn.[5] Faculty and administrators try to think of possible implications for the institution of these broad trends. For example, Popcorn predicted a trend toward "cocooning," spending more time cooking, eating, relaxing, and being entertained at home, rather than "going out on the town." This might portend a growing desire for televised courses and for courses on cooking.

For a brainstorming session to be maximally productive, Osborn laid down four guidelines:

1. Criticism is ruled out: Negative comments on ideas must be withheld until later.
2. Freewheeling is welcomed: The greater the number of ideas, the better; it is easier to tame down than to think up.
3. Quantity is encouraged: The greater the number of ideas, the more the likelihood of useful ideas.
4. Combining and improving ideas is encouraged: Participants should suggest how ideas of others can be joined into still newer ideas.[6]

## ASSESSING TRENDS AND EVENTS

Once identified, these trends and events must be carefully assessed on three dimensions: their relevance to the institution, their significance (importance or seriousness), and their likelihood of occurrence. When this discussion takes place in a typical face-to-face meeting, the more assertive or high-ranking members of the group may dominate the discussion and win more support for their own views. Strong differences of perspective may not surface, so that the resulting forecast may reflect a limited range of views, uninspired generalizations, or pragmatic conformity. To overcome these tendencies of typical groups or committees, *consensus methods* have been developed to harness the best individual thinking with a set of procedures for coming to actionable conclusions. Two widely used consensus methods are the Delphi technique and the nominal group technique.

**The Delphi Technique.** The *Delphi technique* is a structured method for obtaining and combining opinions of people with particular expertise about the subject at hand, without the potential bias of putting these experts in face-to-face contact. According to its developer, Olaf Helmer:

> Delphi...operates on the principle that several heads are better than one in making subjective conjectures about the future, and that experts ...will make conjectures based upon rational judgment and shared information rather than merely guessing, and will separate hope from likelihood in the process.[7]

TABLE 5-1, A    Analysis of a major trend: a global economy and society

SPECIFIC TRENDS AND POTENTIAL IMPACTS

*The world in which universities operate is shrinking rapidly. Key trends are:*
- emergence of multi-national manufacturing, retail, financial, transportation, and service firms;
- instantaneous and frequent communications around the globe;
- major increases in foreign investment in the United States and U.S. investments in other nations;
- major economic competition among nations and groups of nations with advanced economies;
- rapid economic growth in some third-world nations;
- major structural changes in those nations previously unable to effectively compete in a global economy.

REQUIRED UNIVERSITY RESPONSE

*For a university to maintain and enchance its competitive position, it will need to:*
- assume a leadership position in preparing the population it serves for effective participation in the global economy and society;
- reduce any administrative barriers standing in the way of expanded international activity;
- offer specific academic courses and programs which will prepare graduates to function effectively in a global economy and society;
- significantly expand the geographic horizons of current programs and operations to include cooperative programs with foreign institutions;
- integrate information about foreign languages, cultures, processes, etc., into curricula;
- create and/or expand ability to compete for foreign contracts and grants.

Source: MGT of America, Inc., *A Workbook: University Strategies for the 21st Century* (Tallahassee, FL: MGT of America, August 1991), p. 6.

When the experts live at some distance, they receive questions by mail and return their answers to the coordinator. The questions may concern the likelihood of a future event or when a future event is likely to take place. The coordinator summarizes the opinions and sends them to all participants for further comment, particularly on those opinions that differed significantly from the group median. In the third "round," the participants are invited to reassess their judgments and modify them.

The Delphi technique offers four advantages. First, a Delphi exercise usually yields a "band" of expert opinion which, although not a complete consensus, narrows the range. This narrowing results from the anonymous "debate" that takes place over the several rounds of the exercise, providing each participant with grounds that might warrant shifting an opinion. Second, the Delphi process clarifies areas where opinions differ substantially. Third, participants in a Delphi exercise do not know the identities of other participants. Therefore, Delphi results can be assumed to be unbiased by personalities, reputations, or debating talents. Fourth, the Delphi technique is easy to administer and relatively inexpensive compared to organizing and conducting group meetings.

TABLE 5-1, B   Examples of translating trends into initiatives

*Our institution should respond with the following initiatives:*

### 1. PROGRAM

1. Establish elective courses on foreign cultures to prepare students to function effectively in a global society.
2. Conduct faculty seminars concerning the integration of foreign cultures, processes, etc. into current courses.
3. Expand overseas education program opportunities, including internships.
4. Establish a faculty exchange program with foreign universities.

### 2. ORGANIZATIONAL

1. Change title of current director of international programs to Assistant Vice President position reporting directly to the Vice President for Academic Affairs.
2. Expand the responsibilities of current international program office to include the coordination and promotion of the integration of foreign languages, cultures, etc. into current student programs and courses.

### 3. OPERATIONAL

1. Establish an international program coordination council to coordinate all university international programs.

### 4. BUDGET

1. Eliminate current Assistant for Community Affairs position and secretary position to release budget dollars for expanded international programs office (transfer Community Affairs responsibilities to Division of Continuing Education). Estimated annual cost savings: $82,000.

### 5. SPECIAL PROJECTS/STUDIES

1. Conduct efficiency study of academic administration and support operations to determine if budget dollars can be saved (to support more internal programs) through more efficient work processes. Estimated cost of study: $75,000.

Source: MGT of America, Inc., *A Workbook: University Strategies for the 21st Century,* p. 37.

**The Nominal Group Technique.** Like the Delphi technique, the *nominal group technique* (NGT) relies on independent, individual work to generate ideas. But the NGT brings all the participants together in a face-to-face meeting, at which participants seated around the meeting table begin by privately writing down their own ideas. In the next step, the meeting is "called to order" and each participant in turn reads off one idea from his or her own list in round-robin fashion until all ideas have been recorded on a blackboard or flip chart. The group then discusses, verbally clarifies, and evaluates each of the individual ideas on this list. Finally, the ideas are rated or rank-ordered as a means for the group to aggregate the individual judgments and arrive at a consensus view.[8]

## PRODUCTS OF ENVIRONMENTAL
## SCANNING/FORECASTING

Five types of diagrams can be developed from the environmental scanning/
forecasting process. Threat and opportunity matrices are explained and illustrated at the beginning of this chapter. The remaining four are described in
the following sections.

### The Macroenvironmental Audit

Environmental scanning and environmental forecasting provide the basis for
(1) producing a list of developing trends and possible events that could affect
the institution, and (2) determining plausible threats and opportunities, their
likelihood of occurrence, and their potential severity. The major forces of
the macroenvironment can be classified under the headings of demography;
economy; ecology and natural resources; technology; laws, regulation, and
politics; and social and cultural change.

A written macroenvironmental analysis would include the preceding
categories or a subset of them, if some are inappropriate. Under each category would be listed the *significant trends and possible events* that are relevant to the institution's continued operation and success, followed by *specific implications for the institution.*

Preparing an analysis is much more than a writing task. Each step involves making decisions. For example, some person or group within the institution must decide which environmental forces are potentially relevant. At
this step, the preparers may overlook some important forces. A private elementary school may list "population size" but ignore changes in the age and
family structures of the community. It might overlook changes in the community's employment picture or the closing of a military base.

Once the relevant factors are listed, the preparers must specify the
trends as carefully as possible. The preparers will probably need to turn to
census and other government documents to get data on changes over time.
From the data on trends, they must draw the implications for the institution.
Table 5-1, B shows how one institution might translate the trends in Table 5-1,
A into institution-specific actions. The draft should then be circulated to others within the institution for comment before the final version is prepared.
The "final" version will, however, need to be updated annually or as new
trends emerge.

Table 5-2 presents a partial example of a macroenvironmental analysis.
A university was considering launching a bachelor's degree program in nursing, and was interested in the forces that would affect demand for such a program. The macroenvironmental analysis takes five forces and presents factors under each that might have an influence. For each factor, relevant trends

TABLE 5-2   A partial macroenvironmental analysis for a university considering adding a bachelor's degree program in nursing

| FACTORS | TRENDS | IMPLICATIONS |
|---|---|---|
| 1. Demographic | | |
| A. Marital status | Increase in percentage of married women and single mothers in the work force. | Nursing provides flexibility and substantial incomes. |
| B. Life expectancy | Life expectancy increasing, and larger elderly population. | More opportunities for nurses to care for this group. |
| 2. Economic | | |
| A. Wage levels | Average salaries for B.S.N graduates growing. | Attractive salaries relative to other high-demand jobs. |
| B. Cost containment | Government-mandated health coverage will increase pressure to use health professionals other than M.D.s where possible. | Increased demand for nurses. |
| 3. Technological | | |
| A. Medical equipment | Expanding use of complex diagnostic/treatment equipment. | Requirement for higher levels of training. |
| 4. Political/legal/regulatory | | |
| A. Licensing | Many states raising academic requirements for R.N. licensing. | More demand for college-based programs. |
| B. Health policy | Movement toward larger health-provider organizations. | More positions for nurse practitioners with B.S.N preparation and graduate degrees. |

are noted, along with implications for the university.[9] This example presents very general trends and implications, which focus on the attractiveness of nursing as a profession, rather than on demand for nursing study by prospective students—an issue which would also need to be carefully appraised. Specific data on the various trends can be obtained from the U.S. Census Bureau publications and other published sources. A macroenvironmental analysis needs to be updated periodically, since subsequent events will alter some of the trends and implications.

Starting with the completed macroenvironmental analysis, the institution lists its perceived threats and opportunities and prepares threat and opportunity matrices. The macroenvironmental analysis and the matrices then become part of the strategic planning process. Together with the resource analysis, they provide the institution with the basis for formulating its mission, goals, and objectives.

## The Vulnerability Audit

The *institutional vulnerability audit* is recommended by James Morrison and George Keller as

> a form of environmental probe that is less time-consuming, less labor in-tensive, and less expensive, one that is more institution-specific and more likely to result in swift decisions and constructive changes, and one that involves busy faculty and campus leaders themselves.[10]

The institutional vulnerability audit (IVA) focuses on the aspects of the mac-roenvironment that directly affect the school, college, or university conduct-ing the audit. By reducing the scope of the audit, this process reduces time and effort. At the same time, focusing on vulnerabilities—negative trends and events—helps assure the institution's survival.

The vulnerability audit consists of five steps:

**1.** Identify the "environmental footings" of the institution. These are the tangible and intangible resources from the external environment on which the institution depends for its stability and continuity. For example, schools with a strong religious affiliation rely on having the esteem of members and on at-tracting students from this faith; and state-supported institutions rely on re-ceiving steady funding. The original list can be elicited by using the nominal group technique, followed by group brainstorming to fill in any that may have been overlooked.

**2.** Identify the forces, shifts, trends, and events that could weaken or damage the institution by attacking the environmental footings identified in step 1. This step requires imagination, since the group needs to reach beyond the more prosaic possibilities.

**3.** The IVA team then switches to the Delphi technique to establish the probabilities of the identified threats. The threats must be stated clearly and indicate a time frame in which the threat might occur. For example, "feder-ally funded scholarship grants will decline in effective value by 50 percent within five years." Using a chart like the one in Figure 5-4, each team member indicates a judgment of the probability of each numbered threat on the list. These individual probability judgments for each threat are then pooled for the whole group and charted (not shown here) so that the team can discuss their degree of consensus—or lack of consensus—and determine the consensus lo-cations of all identified threats on the final probability/impact grid, shown in Figure 5-5.

**4.** The team then reviews the overall pattern of threats and discusses each threat. The team will want to focus on the threats in the upper-left-hand quadrant (I) first. These highly likely and damaging threats require immediate

FIGURE 5-4    One individual's probability/impact chart
showing an assessment of ten threats

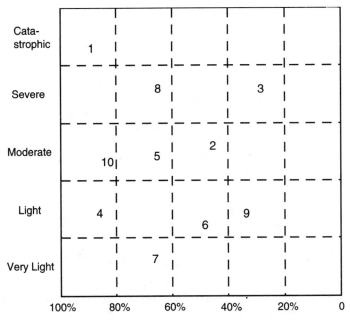

Impact                     Probability That the Threat Will Occur

Sources: James Morrison and George Keller, "Newest Tool: The Institutional
Vulnerability Audit," *Planning for Higher Education*, 21 (Winter 1992–93), 30.

attention. Quadrants II and III are also important, and the team might seek
more information and advice from experts to minimize the possibility that
they have overlooked something that would increase the impact or likelihood
of these threats.

   **5.** The team then designs responses to deal with the most important
threats.

## The Cross-Impact Matrix

*Cross-impact matrix methods* go beyond trend-extrapolation and consensus
methods by asking how future events or trends may be interrelated. If a particular event happens, it may prevent another from taking place or may reduce or increase its effect. For example, a recession may affect government
financial aid assistance and the rate of college attendance. To look at the rate

FIGURE 5-5    A consensus probability/impact grid for the
assesment of 15 threats

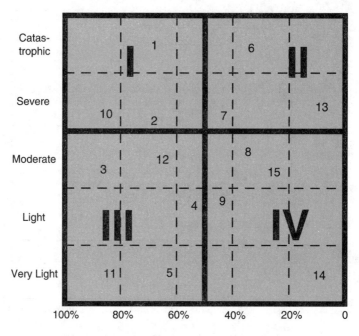

Impact                     Probability That the Threat Will Occur

Sources: James Morrison and George Keller, "Newest Tool: The Institutional
Vulnerability Audit," *Planning for Higher Education*, 21 (Winter 1992–93), 32.

of college attendance, financial aid policies, and economic conditions independently masks their interrelationship and gives a misleading picture of future events.

The analysis of cross-impacts includes judging events or trends. We
speak of a cross-impact effect if the probability of one event occurring varies
positively or negatively as other events occur or don't occur. Several computer simulation models have been developed to analyze the expert judgments and determine the matrix values, but such models are not essential.

As in other forecasting methods that depend on judgment, the usefulness of cross-impact analysis depends upon thoughtful identification of
trends and events and the evaluation of likely effects on the selected situation
or issue. Group members are then asked to consider the events *in pairs* and
indicate for each pair whether the cross-impact would be positive, neutral, or
negative.[11] The resulting ratings are displayed on a cross-impact matrix. The
participants can then discuss the configuration of impacts and plan possible
institutional responses.

## Decision Scenarios

Scenario planning involves identifying the areas of uncertainty in the future environment that are likely to have the most impact on the institution's markets and functioning, and then devising a limited number of *decision scenarios*. The best scenarios organize extensive information from all aspects of the macroenvironment (economic, demographic, technological, ecological, political/legal/regulatory, sociocultural) and translate this information into a framework that helps decision makers to plan ahead and prepare to act.[12]

Decision scenarios are distinct from the previous three approaches in several ways that make this approach particularly valuable in turbulent environments. First, use of scenarios can accommodate discontinuous future events (e.g., a major recession or regulatory change), while trend extrapolation works well only when the environment and relevant trends are stable. Second, scenarios are the product of the intensive and coordinated work of a group of planners, not the compilation and refinement of independent expert opinions.

Third, scenarios aim to describe "different worlds, not just different outcomes in the same world."[13] The scenarios thus go beyond analysis of cross-impacts to creating systems of factors that can be expressed as scenarios. Fourth, decision scenarios focus decision makers' attention on identified areas of uncertainty, rather than presenting an in-depth analysis of all aspects of the macroenvironment.

For example, U.S. colleges can predict the number of high school graduates by state or by the entire nation a decade before these children become prospective applicants. But colleges have uncertainty about sources and levels of scholarship support; the amount and nature of competition from public institutions; desired major fields of study; inflation and interest rates that will affect expenses, returns on endowment, and families' ability to pay tuition; and other key issues.

Experts advise constructing three or at most four scenarios which represent "a few alternative and internally consistent pathways into the future."[14] According to Pierre Wack, the aim is to produce a set of scenarios that illuminate the major forces that will affect the institution's environment, the interrelationships of these forces, and the most important uncertainties. One scenario is typically the "surprise-free" picture of what will happen within the planning horizon (typically five to ten years) if everything evolves as the institution expects at the time the scenarios are developed. The other two (or three) scenarios should describe "other worlds" that could emerge depending on how the critical uncertainties unfold in the future.

Preparing scenarios is a product of rigorous research and analysis. The planners need to understand the decision makers' concerns and prepare scenarios that communicate clearly so that decision makers can plan responsive actions.

## ADAPTING TO THE CHANGING ENVIRONMENT

In the final analysis, environmental scanning and forecasting must be transformed into clear, responsive plans, followed by decisive action. In a turbulent environment, the institution must spend more time and resources to keep abreast of significant macroenvironmental changes. The institution must be prepared to respond and adapt creatively to the changing environment. Only by translating the fruits of macroenvironmental analysis into action can the institution benefit.

## SUMMARY

Educational institutions operate within a complex and rapidly changing environment, which each institution must continuously monitor and adapt to if it is to survive and strengthen. The marketing environment has five components: the internal environment, the market environment, the public environment, the competitive environment, and the macroenvironment. In this chapter, we are concerned with the macroenvironment. The alert institution will set up formal systems for identifying, appraising, and responding to the opportunities and threats posed by the macroenvironment.

The marketing macroenvironment includes demographic, economic, ecological, technological, political/legal/regulatory, and sociocultural forces. These environmental forces affect the institution far more than the institution affects them. Therefore, the institution ignores these forces at its peril. In fact, it should not only scan the environment to determine present opportunities and threats; it should also engage in environmental forecasting to predict what the future will be like in order to set appropriate objectives and develop a strategy to achieve them, supported by an effective institutional structure and systems. Achieving this alignment is difficult because the environment changes rapidly, and educational institutions often wait until events are upon them before taking action.

Environmental scanning calls for identifying the major environmental areas of interest to the institution, assigning responsibility for each area, and developing efficient systems for collecting and disseminating the information. Although many educational institutions leave this task to top administration (who in turn may depend on informal channels of information), a more formal system can help ensure that important information is not overlooked. Environmental scanning helps identify threats and opportunities that may call for a response from the institution. Threats and opportunities are then rated on likelihood of occurrence and extent of impact on the institution.

Environmental forecasting aims to correctly anticipate the character of the institution's future environment. Even though environmental forecasting is still more art than science, many companies routinely carry out or commission forecasts. We expect that educational institutions will try to adapt forecasting techniques to improve their planning. Four types of forecasting methods appear to be most useful: trend extrapolation, consensus methods, cross-impact matrix methods, and decision scenarios. These methods help the institution identify probable trends and events as a basis for preparing an analysis of the macroenvironment.

The macroenvironmental analysis categorizes the significant trends and events facing the institution under the headings of demographics, economic factors, environmental/natural resources, technology, political/legal/regulatory factors, and sociocultural factors. Each trend or event is followed by specific implications for the institution. From the macroenvironmental analysis, the institution can identify and assess threats and opportunities and their likely impact on the institution. The institution must then develop and implement a plan of action to address the identified threats and opportunities.

## Notes

1. James Morrison and George Keller, "Newest Tool: The Institutional Vulnerability Audit," *Planning for Higher Education*, 21 (Winter 1992–93), pp. 27–33.

2. Theodore Levitt, "The New Markets—Think Before You Leap," *Harvard Business Review* (May–June 1969), pp. 53–67, especially pp. 53–54.

3. "Big Increase in High-School Graduates Seen," *The Chronicle of Higher Education*, October 13, 1993, p. A42.

4. See William Ascher, *Forecasting: An Appraisal for Policy-Makers and Planners* (Baltimore, MD: The Johns Hopkins University Press, 1978), p. 199. This book compares the results of a large number of forecasts on population, the economy, energy, transportation, and technology, and analyzes the factors that contribute to forecast accuracy.

5. Faith Popcorn, *The Popcorn Report: Faith Popcorn on the Future of Your Company, Your World, Your Life* (New York: Doubleday, 1991).

6. Alex Osborn, *Applied Imagination*, 3rd ed. (New York: Scribner's, 1963), pp. 286–287.

7. Olaf Helmer, *Analysis of the Future: The Delphi Method* (Santa Monica, CA: Rand Corporation, March 1967). For a report of a study using the Delphi method, see Denny R. Vincent and Kenneth W. Brooks, "A Delphi Projection: Implications for Declining Enrollment," *Planning and Change* (Spring 1982), pp. 24–30.

8. For step-by-step instructions on using the nominal group technique and the Delphi technique, see Andre L. Delbecq, Andrew H. Van de Ven, and David H. Gustafson, *Group Techniques for Program Planning: A Guide to Nominal Group and Delphi Processes* (Middleton, WI: Green Briar Press, 1986).

9. For another example of a macroenvironmental analysis related to education, see "Policy Choices in Vocational Education," Institute for the Future, Menlo Park, CA (December 1979).

10. James Morrison and George Keller, "Newest Tool: The Institutional Vulnerability Audit," p. 28.

11. For a detailed example of cross-impact analysis, see F. Friedrich Neubauer and Norman B. Solomon, "A Managerial Approach to Environmental Assessment," *Long Range Planning* (April 1977), pp. 1–8.

12. Pierre Wack, "Scenarios: Shooting the Rapids," *Harvard Business Review* (November–December 1985), p. 146.

13. Ibid.

14. Ibid.

# 6

# Defining Institutional Resources and Direction

*Eisenhower College opened in 1968 at the crest of the college en-rollment boom and closed 14 years later. The college's local found-ers knew little about higher education but knew that a college could preserve Seneca Falls as a picturesque small town with lit-tle industry. Unfortunately, the college began with little planning and no clear mission and objectives.*

*The boosters of the proposed college did attract a sedate, talented faculty, who developed a unique interdisciplinary world stud-ies program. Less thought was given to attracting able students and establishing a solid financial base. Financial pressures to open the college in 1968 (rather than 1969, as proposed) meant that the admissions director spent the summer of 1968 seeking students for September. Most of the students were marginal; half had dropped out, been suspended, or placed on probation by December.*

*Dwight Eisenhower, for whom the college was named, was a World War II hero and a highly popular U.S. president. The college's founders counted on the Eisenhower name to attract fi-nancial support, particularly important in the early years when the school would have no alumni base.*

*But fund raising was difficult. By 1974, the college was in debt and enrollment was still 800 compared with a projected 1,100. To stay open, the college appealed for funds. Congress took the unprecedented step of awarding the college a $9 million share in* *the profits from the sale of Eisenhower commemorative silver dollars.*

*Although it yielded some much needed financial support, the appeal backfired. As the public became aware of the college's precarious financial situation, enrollment dropped 50 percent over the next three years. In 1979, the college was acquired by Rochester Institute of Technology, which took over its debts and ran it as a unit of the university.*

*But further financial losses close to $6 million and no sign of reversal convinced Rochester Institute of Technology to put the campus up for sale in 1982. Eisenhower faculty began seeking jobs, students other colleges to attend, and townspeople a way to make ends meet with less income.*

*The campus remained on the market for seven years with a price tag of $50 million. Ideas for alternative uses for the campus included a prison or a residential mental health facility. The townspeople, who had supported the original idea of a college campus, were concerned about these proposals. A Seneca Falls resident who served on the board of the New York Chiropractic College urged that it become the new site for that school.*

*Eventually the campus was purchased for $6 million by the New York Chiropractic College, which invested another $20 million to restore deteriorated campus buildings. New York Chiropractic College then relocated its academic programs from Long Island to Seneca Falls, and welcomed students to the new campus in September 1991.*

*The move changed the character of the college from an urban commuter school on Long Island with 600 students to a residential institution in a bucolic area of upstate New York. Many original staff decided against relocating, so new positions were filled by townspeople. By 1993 enrollment had grown to 870, with anticipated maximum enrollment between 945 and 990 within a few years.*

**Sources:** Based on Anne Mackay-Smith, "The Death of a College Underscores the Plight of Private Institutions," *The Wall Street Journal*, December 14, 1982, p. 1; Ira M. Berger, letter to the editor, *The Chronicle of High Education*, July 27, 1983, p. 23; and Brian Mount, Director of Admissions, New York Chiropractic College (November 1993).

Given the same macroenvironmental trends and forces, one institution will succeed and another will fail and close its doors. What is the explanation for such different outcomes? Educational institutions are diverse in their histories, founders, missions, resources, and programs, and no two are affected in the same way by the events around them. An institution that understands its own character, resources, and mission is in a better position to respond by setting goals and objectives and developing an appropriate marketing program.

In this chapter, we consider two steps in the strategic planning process: *resource analysis* and *goal formulation*. We will present ways to define the internal character and identify the strengths and weaknesses of an educational institution. Once the environmental-analysis (discussed in Chapter 5), resource-analysis, and goal-formulation steps are completed, the institution has the necessary framework for developing a marketing strategy.

## ASSESSING INSTITUTIONAL RESOURCES

Institutions have two kinds of resources: *intangible resources*, such as a good reputation, a long history, and traditions; and *tangible resources*, such as facilities, staff, and endowment. Both kinds of resources shape an institution's future success in the marketplace.

An institution engaged in marketing planning needs to consider four resource issues:

1. Its institutional environment and character
2. Its stage in the institutional life cycle
3. Its potential for adaptation
4. Its tangible resources and marketing assets

We will discuss each topic in turn.

### Institutional Environment

Every educational institution has an *environment* or *character* that began to evolve in its earliest days. Educational institutions were often founded to accomplish some societal or religious purpose deeply felt by their founders. Despite many changes over subsequent decades, elements of the founders' direction often remain. Institutional character derives not only from founders and early history, but also from the institution's geographical location, local climate, and size; the success of the founding organization (for example, in the case of church-related colleges); and the match between the institution's offerings and its markets.

An educational institution can often learn a great deal by reviewing its history. What were the educational, economic, social, and other forces that inspired the founding of this institution and that have maintained this institution in the past? Have these forces changed? What has been the institution's distinctive character? Has this changed? For the better? Has something been lost that would be worth reintroducing? These questions may at first appear far removed from the marketing task, but they are not. The institution that knows and reflects the best of its character and values is one that will attract students and supporters.

The institution also needs to determine how it is perceived by students, faculty, staff, alumni, and other constituencies because this information can reveal the extent to which the institution reflects its intended character. An image may linger long after the institution has changed. For example, parents may pass on outdated impressions of schools to their children. The institution can also identify aspects of its current character that are no longer well matched to its markets and the larger environment.

The institution's office of institutional research or some other unit may choose to carry out climate assessments. Many such studies have used the College and University Environment Scales (CUES), which provide a systematic way to determine the environmental characteristics of institutions of higher education. Students respond to 150 statements about college life, including "features and facilities of the campus, rules and regulations, faculty, curricula, instruction and examinations, student life, extracurricular organizations, and other aspects...which help to define the intellectual-social-cultural climate of a college as students perceive it."[1] Students respond "true" or "false" to such items as:

- It is fairly easy to pass most courses without hard work.
- Most courses are a real intellectual challenge.
- There is very little studying here over weekends.

Combining the judgments of a sample of students provides a measure of the institution's environment on five dimensions:

1. Practicality: the degree to which personal status and practical benefit are emphasized in the college environment.
2. Community: the degree to which the campus is friendly, cohesive, and group-oriented.
3. Awareness: the degree to which there is concern with self-understanding, reflectiveness, and the search for personal meaning.
4. Propriety: the degree to which politeness, protocol, and consideration are emphasized.
5. Scholarship: the degree to which serious interest in scholarship and competition for academic achievement are evidenced.[2]

Various other climate assessment measures have been developed. For example, the University Residence Environment Scale can be used to assess the social climate of student living groups (residence halls, fraternities, sororities, and so on), including student/staff perceptions of the way the living group currently is, their conceptions of the ideal living group, and (before students move in) their expectations about the living group they are about to enter.[3]

Many schools also develop their own climate questionnaires, encouraged by the availability of personal computers and user-friendly survey analysis software.

### Institutional Life Cycle and Renewal

While education and learning are perpetual human activities, individual educational institutions may come and go. Through adaptation an educational institution increases its chances for survival, but it will not necessarily enjoy continuous stability or growth. Institutions tend to pass through *life-cycle stages*. In examining its tangible resources, an educational institution should consider its current life-cycle stage and its potential for continued adaptation, since adaptability may help to prolong each stage or produce new life cycles.

Figure 6-1 shows the four main stages in the life cycle of a typical institution. The institution is founded at some point and grows slowly (*introduction stage*). If successful, a period of growth follows (*growth stage*). The growth eventually slows down, and the institution enters maturity (*maturity stage*). If it fails to adapt to new conditions and reestablish its sense of direction, it will enter a period of decline (*decline stage*) unless and until it finds a new mission and resources to redirect its activities.

The duration of the institution's life cycle may be relatively short, as the case of Eisenhower College illustrates, but this is not inevitable. For example, the college might be flourishing today had the college sought participation from key publics, selected a distinctive mission, defined its student market, and so on. In fact, some institutions enjoy a renewed life cycle as a result of new leadership, a major benefactor, a revamped curriculum, or some other development.

FIGURE 6-1 Typical S-shaped life-cycle curve

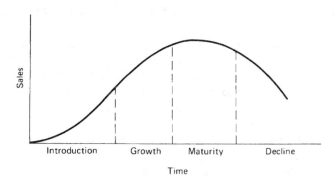

There is nothing inevitable about maturity leading into decline. Many educational institutions currently enjoy a respected maturity, but these institutions must continue to scan their macroenvironment, stay in touch with their key markets, and continue to adapt to new pressures and opportunities.

Institutions that pass through maturity and go into decline are usually those unable to adapt to changing circumstances. The ability to respond to changing circumstances is an important component of the institution's intangible resources. If an educational institution cannot identify a market and serve it well enough to attract the necessary resources, it will probably close and other institutions will take its place. Some educational institutions resist change of any kind. For some, this resistance spells doom. Students go elsewhere, faculty members leave or "retire in place," and alumni lose interest in the school.

One of the major contributions of marketing analysis is to identify new opportunities by which an institution can return to a period of healthy growth or enjoy an extended maturity. An *adaptive institution* is one that operates systems for monitoring and interpreting important environmental changes and shows a readiness to revise its mission, goals, strategies, organization, and systems to be maximally aligned with its opportunities.

For example, consider how Aquinas College in Grand Rapids, Michigan, has changed. The college began as a novitiate normal school where the Grand Rapids Dominican Sisters trained their young members for teaching in the parochial schools of Michigan. Then the sisters invited young laywomen to enroll. In 1931 the school moved to a downtown campus and began to admit men, making Aquinas the first coeducational Catholic liberal arts college in the country. Eventually Aquinas expanded from a junior college into a senior college just before World War II, becoming the first Catholic four-year institution serving Michigan west of Detroit. In the 1970s the college conducted a self-study and implemented several distinctive new programs to better align the college with the unmet educational needs of the community.[4]

Had the college stuck to its original mission to train women for religious life and ignored its emerging opportunities, Aquinas College would have closed decades ago and would not be making a contribution today. But in the process of meeting new educational needs, the college has continued to honor its core values.

Institutions often have to do more than adapt to new market opportunities. Many educational institutions are faced with contracting resources, new financial pressures, and/or declining enrollment. Some institutions accept decline as their fate and may even close; others eventually turn to new ways in which to serve a valid educational purpose, or develop the ability to attract and serve new markets.

Ellen Chaffee studied the strategies adopted by small private colleges which were experiencing declining enrollments and financial difficulties in the mid-1970s. The colleges that later experienced comebacks were those which combined *focused adaptations* to market realities with *actions* by institutional leadership that signaled to the colleges' constituencies that the institutions were "on the move" again.

Introduction of new programs or consolidation of existing ones, changes in the sophistication and extent of efforts to expand enrollments, and other adaptations to the market worked best when they reflected an enhanced sense of institutional mission articulated by the colleges' leadership, and valued and shared by the colleges' constituencies. This leadership action to build a shared sense of purpose for the college improved the constituents' satisfaction and built up the college's credibility in their eyes. For example, rumors that a college was closing were quashed when the college purchased the campus of an adjacent, failing school. Another college was refocused by the trustees' reaffirmation of the college's identity as a liberal-arts institution coupled with a successful fund-raising effort that reinforced this sense of direction.[5]

## Preparing a Resource Analysis

The purpose of a *resource analysis* is to identify the strengths and weaknesses of the institution. An institution should pursue goals, opportunities, and strategies that are suggested by, or are congruent with, its strengths and avoid those where its resources are too weak.

Figure 6-2 shows a resource-analysis checklist suitable for a small school or college. The major resources listed are people, money, facilities, systems, and market assets. Each area should be thoroughly reviewed. Based on this review, the institution indicates a strength (high, medium, low), is neutral, or constitutes a weakness (low, medium, high). The institution then lists the reasons for each evaluation as part of the resource analysis.

For example, suppose the checks in Figure 6-2 reflect a school's evaluation of its resources. The evaluators believe that the school has an adequate number of skilled personnel who, unfortunately, are not very enthusiastic, loyal, or service-minded. As for money, the school has enough for its operations, but most funds are committed, so it does not have the flexibility to take on new projects. The school's facilities are adequate, flexible, and well located. Its management systems for information, planning, and control are quite weak. Finally, it enjoys a strong position with students, alumni, and donors, an excellent faculty, and a good reputation.

Figure 6-3 shows the result of a more extensive analysis of institutional resources, prepared by Thomas Wonders and James Gyure. Note that this analysis looked at more resource areas in greater detail, and then displayed the findings along two dimensions, level of strength/weakness by action needed to increase or maintain that strength. Second, the resulting diagram is very similar to the importance-performance grid introduced in Chapter 2, and provides a clear interpretation of the analysis results as a basis for discussion.

FIGURE 6-2   Institutional resource analysis

(H - high; M - medium; L - low; N - neutral)
(Checks ✔ are illustrative)

| RESOURCE | STRENGTH | | | N | WEAKNESS | | |
|---|---|---|---|---|---|---|---|
| | H | M | L | N | L | M | H |
| **People** | | | | | | | |
| 1. Adequate number? | ✔ | | | | | | |
| 2. Skilled? | ✔ | | | | | | |
| 3. Enthusiastic? | | | | | | ✔ | |
| 4. Loyal? | | | | | | | ✔ |
| 5. Service-minded? | | | | | | ✔ | |
| **Money** (Income and endowment) | | | | | | | |
| 1. Adequate? | | | ✔ | | | | |
| 2. Flexible? | | | | | ✔ | | |
| **Facilities** | | | | | | | |
| 1. Adequate? | ✔ | | | | | | |
| 2. Flexible? | ✔ | | | | | | |
| 3. Location quality? | ✔ | | | | | | |
| **Systems** | | | | | | | |
| 1. Information system quality? | | | | | ✔ | | |
| 2. Planning system quality? | | | | | | ✔ | |
| 3. Control system quality? | | | | | | ✔ | |
| **Market assets** | | | | | | | |
| 1. Student base? | | ✔ | | | | | |
| 2. Alumni and other donors? | | ✔ | | | | | |
| 3. Faculty quality? | ✔ | | | | | | |
| 4. General reputation? | | ✔ | | | | | |

With the results of the resource analysis, the college can consider what opportunities its resources might support. The institution should generally avoid opportunities for which necessary resources are weak or inadequate. For example, if the college is considering establishing a nursing program but its science faculty is weak, it should probably drop the idea, since a good science faculty is important for a successful nursing program. The college lacks a *critical success requirement* for launching a nursing program. On the other hand, a weakness need not be fatal if the institution can acquire the resources it needs. If the college has the funds to build a good science faculty, it might

FIGURE 6-3    A matrix of institutional strengths and weaknesses

| ← EXCEPTIONAL ←    STRENGTH    → HIGH → | |
| --- | --- |
| **AREAS OF PARTICULAR STRENGTH** | **AREAS OF STRENGTH TO MAINTAIN** |
| Uniqueness of "small-comprehensive" | Quality of instruction |
| Commitment to undergraduate education | Quality of advising system |
| Exceptional productivity of faculty/staff | Student, faculty, staff relationships |
| Quality of existing campus/facilities | Quality of "outcomes" from many academic programs |
| Competitive and serious students | |
| Strong enrollment history | General quality of student life |
| Efficient, cost-effective operations | General quality of residence services |
| Private support | Emerging image |
| **AREAS TO BE IMPROVED** | **STRENGTHS: COULD BE ENHANCED** |
| Facilities equal to demands: classrooms, library, student union, athletic | Students, faculty, staff affirmative action resources and programs |
| Programs/services to attract larger number of "highly qualified" students | Academic support services |
| Student aid resources | Variety of student support services |
| Career planning and placement services | Traditional-student recruitment and admissions activities |
| Competitiveness of nontraditional student recruitment/services | Potential for student enrollment growth and control: both qualitative and quantitative |
| Faculty and staff resources equal to demands for courses and services | |
| Budget/pricing: unit management | General service to the community and the region |

Left vertical axis: ↑ L E S S ↑ A C T I O N   N E E D E D ↓ M O R E ↓

Bottom axis: ← SERIOUS ←    WEAKNESS/CONSTRAINT    → MODERATE →

Sources: Thomas J. Wonders and James F. Gyure, "A Marketing Information for Enrollment System," *proceedings of the 1991 Symposium for the Marketing of Higher Education* (Chicago, IL: American Marketing Association, 1990).

consider going ahead with the nursing program if it would be an otherwise attractive program.

As a clue to its best opportunities, the institution should pay attention to its distinctive competencies. *Distinctive competencies* are those resources and abilities in which the institution is especially strong. If a college has a strong foreign language department, it might consider such opportunities as starting an area studies program, an evening noncredit language program, or an immersion language program for business executives being relocated overseas. Institutions often find it easier to work from their strengths than to build up their weaker areas to some average level of strength. At the same time, a distinctive competence may not be enough if the institution's major competitors possess the same distinctive competence. The institution should pay attention to those strengths in which it possesses a *differential advantage*— that is, it can outperform competitors on that dimension. For example, Georgetown University not only has a distinctive competence in international relations, but its location in Washington, DC, gives it a differential advantage in pursuing preeminence in that field.

In evaluating its strengths and weaknesses, the institution must not rely solely on its own perceptions. It must go out and do an *image study* of how it is perceived by its key publics (presented in Chapter 9). For example, the administration may think that the college has a fine reputation in the hard sciences, but an image study might reveal that high school counselors see the college's main strength as the humanities. The administration should study how different key markets and publics—students, parents, business firms, and so on—see its strengths and weaknesses. The findings might indicate certain strengths and weaknesses that the college is not aware of, and others that it exaggerated.

## FORMULATING GOALS AND OBJECTIVES

Goal formulation involves the institution in determining appropriate mission, goals, and objectives for the current or anticipated environment. The three terms are distinguished thus:

- *Mission*: the basic purpose of an institution; that is, what it is trying to accomplish.
- *Goal*: a major variable that the institution will emphasize, such as profitability, enrollment, reputation, market share.
- *Objective*: a goal of the institution that is made specific with respect to magnitude, time, and who is responsible.[6]

We introduced these terms in Chapter 4 and will discuss them in greater detail here.

### Mission

Every organization starts with a mission. In fact, an organization can be defined as a human collectivity that is structured to perform a specific mission through the use of largely rational means. Its specific mission is usually clear at the beginning. Harvard College was founded to prepare young men for the ministry and held to this primary mission for more than 150 years. As the nation industrialized, the traditional classical curriculum was broadened. Harvard established professional schools and added other programs and services that further expanded its mission scope.

From time to time, each institution should reexamine its mission by asking and answering the question, "What is our business?" Educational institutions sometimes get sidetracked by listing the courses or programs they offer, thinking that this is the same as a mission statement. Instead, an educational institution should identify the underlying *need* it is trying to serve. A high school may be in the *preparation-for-college* business. Or it might be in the *keep-teenagers-off-the-street* business, keeping track of young people while their parents work.

Ultimately, the school will benefit by deciding what its mission (at least its primary mission) will be. Otherwise, it will lose sight of its mission and confuse it with the many intermediate goals (meet the payroll, add a French teacher, and so on) it might adopt and services it might provide. Many educational institutions that have struggled to be all things to all people subsequently find that narrowing their mission—deciding what *not* to do—is also a major challenge.

A helpful approach to defining mission is to establish the institution's *scope* along three dimensions. The first is *consumer groups*—namely, who is to be served and satisfied. The second is *consumer needs*—namely, what is to be satisfied. The third is *technologies*—namely, how consumer needs are to be satisfied. For example, consider a traditional junior college for young women. The college's mission scope is represented by the small cube in Figure 6-4, A. Now consider the mission scope of a comprehensive public community college, shown in Figure 6-4, B. This community college serves almost all age groups (with day-care programs and special events for children) and meets at least seven strong needs. It provides credit and noncredit classes, study trips, film and lecture series, and educational and career counseling. Still other colleges will have different mission scopes.

Often educational institutions are eager to broaden their scope to include specialized programs and graduate professional schools, even when such offerings duplicate those available elsewhere. Multicampus state university systems have frequently set limits on the missions that are appropriate for each campus. For example, the University of Wisconsin-Madison offers Ph.D. work and professional schools, whereas the second doctoral institution, the University of Wisconsin-Milwaukee, offers only Ph.D. programs that match the needs of its urban area. The other eleven four-year campuses award bachelor, master, and specialist degrees only.[7] This *mission differentiation* is designed to better serve Wisconsin's educational needs at a reasonable cost.

The mission of the institution must take into account five key elements. The first is the *history* of the institution. Every institution has a history of

FIGURE 6-4    Mission scopes of two colleges

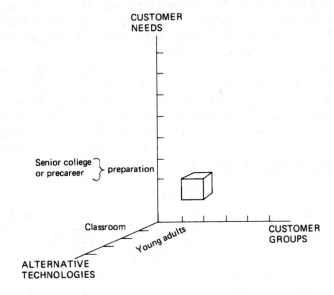

A.  A highly focused junior college

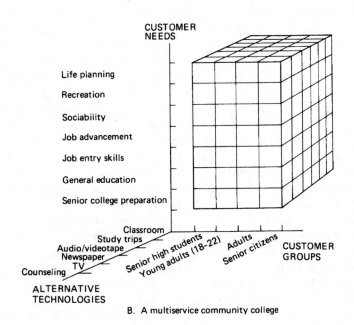

B.  A multiservice community college

aims, policies, and accomplishments. In reaching for a new or expanded mission, the institution must honor the salient characteristics of its past history. Most of the students at Alice Lloyd College come from economically disadvantaged areas of Appalachia; all participate in campus work assignments to meet their expenses. Unless circumstances change dramatically, a decision to become an elite, selective university would violate a founding principle of the college.

Second, the mission statement should take into account the current preferences of the institution's main *constituencies*—trustees, administrators, faculty, alumni, students, and others. Some Catholic schools that took the lead in implementing new religious services and adopting strong positions on social issues have found they have left some alumni supporters behind. Such institutions may continue to innovate, and accept that they cannot please everyone, but they will need to build and strengthen support from other constituencies.

Third, the institution must be prepared to adapt its mission in response to its *environment*. For example, birth and immigration rates indicate that urban-oriented colleges and universities will increasingly serve minority students, some of whom will seek career-oriented preparation and who may need additional remedial programs, in addition to more traditional college programs.

Fourth, the institution's *resources* make certain missions possible and others not. A small private college is unlikely to become the center of high-technology graduate training and research in the United States.

Finally, the institution should base its choice of purpose on its *distinctive competencies*. Although it may be able to accomplish many things, it should aim for what it can do best. A vocational school could probably hire more faculty and become a liberal arts college, but that would not be making use of its main competence—providing vocational skills to recent high school graduates who want to enter the work force as rapidly as possible.

The institution's mission affects everything else. The mission often implies a particular type of student and attracts a certain kind of faculty, and calls for a particular way of rendering value to students. A college whose mission is education in the liberal arts would appeal to students who value the life of the mind. The college would invest in intellectually stimulating professors, a large library, small classes, intellectual events on campus, and so on. This mission would put the college in direct competition with many other colleges. It must believe that the intellectual market is large enough and that it has the resources and potential reputation to compete effectively for a reasonable share of those students seeking intellectual training.

On the other hand, if the college chooses to emphasize the applied liberal arts, it would promote itself to those students who place high value on career preparation. It would select careers to specialize in—law, medicine, business, engineering—and build educational programs to include solid classroom work plus field experience and visiting practitioners. It would build a major network of contacts with businesses and the professions to help place students. Thus, developing a clear definition of its mission will lead the college—and any other institution—to emphasize certain things and de-emphasize others.

An institution should strive for a mission that is *feasible, motivating,* and *distinctive,* and avoid a "mission impossible." The president of a community college might like to add a medical school, but should realize that this is not feasible. An institution should reach high, but not so high as to produce incredulity in its publics.

The mission should motivate those who work for or receive services from the institution to feel they are a part of a worthwhile institution. A school dedicated to academic excellence and service to society will inspire more support than one whose mission is to help relieve the boredom of the over-privileged. The mission should be something that is perceived as significantly enriching people's lives.

A mission works better when it is distinctive. If all educational institutions resembled each other, there would be little basis for pride in and identification with a particular institution. People take pride in working for, donating to, or attending a school that "does it differently" or "does it better." By cultivating a distinctive mission and personality, a school stands out more and attracts more loyalty from its key publics.

A growing number of educational institutions have prepared or revised their formal written *mission statements* to gain the needed clarity. A well-worked-out mission statement provides everyone in the institution with a shared sense of purpose, direction, significance, and achievement. The mission statement acts as a guide to the institution's activities and a touchstone in making sometimes difficult decisions about focus and funding.[8]

Writing a mission statement is hard work. A high-level committee may have to hold many meetings and survey many people before it can prepare a meaningful mission statement. Many schools and colleges undertake to review the institutional mission statement when they face accreditation review or when they are launching a major fund-raising campaign. In the process, the administration, trustees, faculty, and others involved often discover a lot about the institution and about their sometimes divergent perceptions of the institution, its character, and its best opportunities.

For example, at Moreau High School in Hayward, California, the strategic planning committee discussed every word and nuance of its mission statement, including the significance of defining the school as "college preparatory." Did it mean most students would go on to four-year colleges? What about the many students who were selecting convenient and less expensive community colleges? Did that match the school's mission?

Preparing a mission statement can become a seemingly monumental and endless task if the process is unstructured and there are no criteria to deter-

EXHIBIT 6-1    Mission statement for Queen of Peace High School

---

QUEEN OF PEACE HIGH SCHOOL

Queen of Peace is a Catholic Sinsinawa [Wisconsin] Dominican Secondary School educating a diverse adolescent female population. We are committed to preparing women not only for college, but for lifelong learning by empowering intellectual, spiritual, moral and emotional growth. Our mission calls us to encourage collaboration, to instill leadership, to promote dedication to service, and to inspire a passion for peace and justice.

(The original mission statement was printed on recycled paper.)

---

Source: Queen of Peace High School, Burbank, IL 60459.

mine when the mission statement is "done." Some participants in the process will resent the lack of concreteness implicit in most discussions of mission, while others will enjoy abstract discussions and resent pressures for closure. For these reasons, the institution may choose to hire an outside consultant to direct the process and keep a sense of movement. The process is often expedited by establishing agreement on basic principles or assumptions before launching into discussions about wording of the mission statement.

The mission statement is complete when it has passed a series of checkpoints. The mission statement should take into account the five key elements described previously—history, constituencies, environment, resources, and distinctive competencies—as well as the institution's market opportunities. The draft mission statement is often presented to various constituencies for their review and comment. These groups can evaluate whether the mission statement appears feasible, motivating, and distinctive, as well as accurate and in keeping with the institution as they know it. Exhibit 6-1 shows the mission statement for Queen of Peace High School, in Burbank, Illinois.

The final mission statement should be clear and easy to understand, since it will appear in accreditation applications, and most likely will also appear in the institution's brochures, catalogs, annual reports, grant applications, and requests for donations. Some mission statements are—or quickly become—ceremonial verbiage because the committee settled for impressive language that has no clear relevance to the institution, so no one knows what the words really mean. Such mission statements cannot guide decision making and action, which means the effort to prepare them is largely wasted.

The president of Moreau High School, Joseph Connell, set an additional standard for the school's mission statement, the "elevator test": The mission statement, posted in the school's elevator, should be clear and brief enough that a visitor to the president's third-floor office would arrive there with sense of what Moreau High School was and what the school aimed to accomplish.

EXHIBIT 6-2  Guidelines for examining the mission statement

STATEMENT OF PURPOSE OR MISSION STATEMENT
Has the institution a clearly identified purpose?

| AUDIT PROBE/QUESTION | EVIDENCE/PERFORMANCE INDICATIONS |
|---|---|
| Is there a statement of institutional purpose or a mission statement? | Published statement of purpose or mission statement. |
| Who was involved in the creation of the statement of purpose or mission statement? e.g., governors; principal; senior management; academic board; academic staff; nonacademic staff; external agencies; students; employers; local community | Records of the process of evolution of the statement of institutional purpose or mission statement. Documentation of the activities of the participating agencies. |
| Is the influence of the participating agencies reflected in the statement of purpose or mission statement? | Records of debate and recommendations of participating agencies. |
| Is the mission or statement of purpose widely understood? e.g. governors; senior management; academic board; academic staff; nonacademic staff; students; parents; employers; external agencies; local community | Questionnaire; staff handbook; student handbook; governors' briefing pack; prospectus. |
| Is the mission or purpose statement "owned" by those affected by it? | Questionnaires; records of meetings; publicity documentation. |
| How is the mission or purpose statement validated? —external validation? —internal validation? | Procedures established and documented in relation to both internal and external validation. |
| How frequently is the mission or purpose statement reviewed? —annually? —1–3 years? —3–10 years? | Records of review and evaluation of mission or purpose statement. |
| Is there a mechanism for reporting performance in relation to mission or purpose statement? | The existence of appropriate MIS. Records of MIS use for management control and decision taking, including relationship of mission or purpose statment to budgetary/ resource |
| What are the major considerations addressed in the mission or purpose statement? e.g., education; training; community; employment; access; equal opportunities; income generation; external relationships. | Mission or purpose statement details. |
| Are the major considerations addressed in the mission or purpose statement prioritized? | Mission or purpose statement details. |

Source: Adapted from *Towards an Educational Audit* (London, England: Further Education Unit, 1989), pp. 39–40. These guidelines were prepared for colleges of further education (similar to U.S. community colleges).

A mission statement should serve for many years. The mission should not be changed abruptly every few years. The institution should, however, review its mission from time to time and reconsider it if it no longer works or if it no longer defines an optimal course for the institution to follow.[9] In particular, the school should periodically review whether the institution is living up to the mission it set for itself. Exhibit 6-2 presents a set of guidelines for examining the mission statement of an educational institution.

In the case of Queen of Peace High School, the school's key constituencies should monitor the institution's performance regarding empowerment, collaboration, and leadership. If the school was in fact highly regimented and authoritarian, the school would not be living up to its stated mission. If the school's graduates felt that service to others was a waste of time and that "peace and justice" were only words, the school would need to take steps to better fulfill its mission.


## Goals

An institution's mission describes what the institution stands for and whom it will serve. To guide its efforts, each institution also needs to develop major goals and objectives separate from but consistent with its mission statement.

For every type of educational institution, there is a potential set of relevant *goals*. The institution's task is to choose among them. For example, the goals of interest to a college may be increased national reputation, improved classroom teaching, higher enrollment, better-qualified applicants, increased efficiency, larger endowment, improved student social life, improved residence facilities, lower operating deficit, and so on. The college cannot successfully pursue all these goals simultaneously because its budget is limited and because some of the goals may be incompatible.

Formulating institutional goals consists of two steps: determining what the current goals are, and determining what they should be. A review of current goals may reveal that they are inconsistent and even incompatible. For example, a college president may see the primary admissions goal as upgrading the quality of the student body; the director of admissions may see the primary goal as increasing the size of the student body; and the vice president for finance may see the primary goal as increasing the number of nonscholarship students in relation to scholarship students. The faculty may pursue the goal of reduced teaching load to permit more time for research, whereas the administration may adopt the goal of increasing teaching loads to hold down costs.

How does an educational institution determine what its goals are and what they should be? Determining what the goals of an institution should be is a difficult task. In principle, the president and/or the board of trustees can unilaterally set goals for the college. In practice, faculty, alumni, and other publics must be involved in goal formulation to assure that the goals are appropriate, adequate in scope, and worthy of broad support.

One approach involves listing broad goals for the school, and then inviting the school's various constituencies to comment on them. The school may prepare an extensive list of goals, which can then be prioritized as a basis for setting objectives. The goals can be evaluated using a variation of importance-performance analysis (see Chapter 2), in which each goal is rated on its importance and on the institution's current performance on that goal. The responses of various institutional consistencies could be averaged and graphed separately, since an average of all ratings would obscure differences by group.

Alternatively, the institution could ask respondents to rate each goal on (1) how important the goal is at present ("Is") and how important the goal should be ("Should Be"). The partial results of one such study are shown in Figure 6-5. Note that for this institution the trustees' ratings of "Is" and "Should Be" are virtually identical, whereas ratings by faculty, students, and administrators indicate room for improvement for virtually every goal category. This type of analysis is conceptually quite similar to gap analysis (between expected performance and perceived performance), described in Chapter 2.

## Objectives

The institution may select goals based on respondents' overall ratings and/or those with the largest discrepancy between the current situation and the desired state. The chosen goals must be restated in an operational and measurable form called *objectives*. The goal of increased enrollment must be turned into an objective such as "a 15 percent enrollment increase in next year's freshman class." A stated objective permits the institution to think about the planning, programming, and control activities required to achieve that goal. Such questions as these arise: Is a 15 percent enrollment increase feasible? What strategy should be used? What resources would it take? What activities would have to be carried out? Who would be responsible and accountable? All these critical questions must be answered when deciding whether to adopt a proposed objective.

Typically, the institution will be evaluating a large set of potential objectives at the same time and examining their consistency. The institution will probably discover that it cannot simultaneously achieve "a 15 percent enrollment increase," "a 20-point increase in median SAT Verbal scores," and "a 6 percent tuition increase." In this case, those responsible for formulating objectives must make adjustments in the target levels or target dates, or drop certain objectives altogether in order to arrive at an important and achievable set of objectives. Once the objectives are agreed

FIGURE 6-5   Discrepancy ratings on goals for four subgroups

|  | Faculty | Student | Administrators | Trustees |
|---|---|---|---|---|

**Assistance for Faculty and Staff**   1 2 3 4 5   1 2 3 4 5   1 2 3 4 5   1 2 3 4 5

43. Conduct basic or applied research in academic disciplines.

46. Opportunities for the continuing professional development of faculty and staff.

49. Allow faculty and staff to attend scholarly or professional meetings.

53. Provide opportunities for development off-campus.

**Continuing Education**   1 2 3 4 5   1 2 3 4 5   1 2 3 4 5   1 2 3 4 5

54. Help non-college-age adults continue their education.

57. Make available educational, social, and occupational development opportunities for alumni.

60. Admit qualified adults, regardless of age, to regular college programs.

63. Cooperate with local employers in providing in-service training opportunities for employees.

**Democratic Governance and Freedom**   1 2 3 4 5   1 2 3 4 5   1 2 3 4 5   1 2 3 4 5

55. Students, faculty, and staff can be involved significantly in campus governance.

58. Assure that everyone may participate or be represented in making decisions affecting them.

61. Protect the right of faculty and students to present unpopular or controversial ideas in the classroom.

64. To respect individual freedom in matters of personal behavior.

**Campus Community**   1 2 3 4 5   1 2 3 4 5   1 2 3 4 5   1 2 3 4 5

56. Maintain a climate of faculty commitment to the goals and well-being of the institution.

59. Maintain a climate of mutual trust, respect, and concern among students, faculty, and staff.

62. Maintain climate in which differences of opinion can be aired openly and amicably.

65. A climate in which communication throughout the organizational structure is open and candid.

Key:
———— Mean rating on Is
– – – – Mean rating on Should Be

1 = of no importance/not applicable
2 = of low importance
3 = of medium importance

Source: *Goals and Climate: A Manual for Using the Small College Goal Inventory* (Washington, DC: Council for the Advancement of Small Colleges, 1979), p. 40.

upon in the goal-formulation stage, the institution is ready to move on to strategy formulation.

## SUMMARY

Educational institutions require tangible and intangible resources to survive and carry out their missions. Three important intangibles are the institution's environment or character, its stage in the institutional life cycle, and its potential for adaptation.

A resource audit describes the institution's strengths and weaknesses in five areas: people, money, facilities, systems, and market assets. To determine its best opportunities, the institution should strive to identify its distinctive competencies, the resources and abilities it is especially strong in, and its areas of differential advantage in which it can outperform competitors.

Every institution starts with a mission that answers these questions: What is our business? Who is the consumer? What is the value to the consumer? What will our business be? A helpful approach to defining mission is to identify which consumer groups will be served, which of their needs will be addressed, and which technologies will be used to satisfy these needs. A mission works best when it is feasible, motivating, and distinctive. Once the institution has developed or refined its mission statement, it formulates its major goals and its specific objectives. By defining its resources and direction, the institution is better prepared to determine its strategy.

### Notes

1. C. Robert Pace, *CUES: College and University Environment Scales*, Preliminary Technical Manual (Princeton, NJ: Educational Testing Service, 1962), p. 3.

2. Ibid., pp. 3–4.

3. Rudolf H. Moos, *University Residence Environment Scale Manual*, 2nd ed. (Palo Alto, CA: Consulting Psychologists Press, 1988), p. 4. Distributed by Mind Garden, Palo Alto, CA.

4. Norbert J. Hruby, *A Survival Kit for Invisible Colleges*, 2nd ed. (Boulder, CO: National Center for Higher Education Management Systems, 1980).

5. Ellen Earle Chaffee, "Successful Strategic Management in Small Private Colleges," *Journal of Higher Education*, 55, no. 4 (March/April 1984), pp. 212–241.

6. Throughout this book, we use the term *goal* to refer to the broad aim or area of concern, and the word *objective* to refer to the statement of specific outcomes, including when and how the outcome will be determined. Our choice of terminology is based on its greater familiarity to educators. Marketers, on the other hand, tend to reverse the terms, using *objective* to refer to the general area and *goal* to refer to the statement of specific outcomes.

7. Douglas F. Lamont, "Multicampus Systems of Higher Education: A New Organizational Strategy for Knowledge Work," University of Wisconsin, Madison, n.d.

8. R. Duane Ireland and Michael A. Hitt, "Mission Statements: Importance, Challenge, and Recommendations for Development," *Business Horizons*, 35, no. 3 (May/June 1992), pp. 34–42, describes how a small private preparatory school developed its mission statement, and provides an explanation of how and why companies develop mission statements.

9. For an expanded discussion of analyzing institutional mission, see J. Kent Caruthers and Gary B. Lott, *Mission Review: Foundation for Strategic Planning* (Boulder, CO: National Center for Higher Education Management Systems, 1981).

# 7

# Formulating Marketing Strategy

*Metropolis University (name disguised) is a private institution in a region plagued by persistent economic recession that began in the 1980s. The university's evening M.B.A. enrollment has fallen off, since companies have cut back their funding of employee tuition-assistance programs, which previously supported half of Metropolis's M.B.A. students.*

*Metropolis's share of the M.B.A. student market is eroding for a second reason: mounting competition. In one year alone, three new part-time evening M.B.A. programs started up in the city, bringing the total number to six. Metropolis has one quality distinction, as one of only two area M.B.A. programs enjoying the sought-after recognition of American Assembly of Collegiate Schools of Business (AACSB) accreditation. Fifty miles to the south, outside the immediate market area but within commuting distance of Metropolis, are two AACSB-accredited part-time evening/weekend M.B.A. programs.*

*Here are the Metropolis University M.B.A. program director's comments on competitive positioning:*

*"As far as the Metropolis area is concerned, we have attempted to position our M.B.A program as the premier AACSB-accredited part-time evening curriculum. We are the only institution in Metropolis other than State University with a full-time tenure-track graduate business school faculty, and, of course, we view this as one of our major strengths. Almost all of our 500 part-time M.B.A. students are full-time working professionals, more than half with engineering and high-technology backgrounds. Our*

*curriculum is more quantitative than our competitors', owing to our clientele. Thus, we have been able to differentiate our program from our competitors' in terms of the highly quantitative nature of our curriculum, our full-time tenure-track faculty, and our AACSB accreditation.*

*In addition, we emphasize that we have a fine research library and up-to-date computer equipment to support our program, plus all the traditional student services. In contrast, many of our competitors are located in leased office space and offer very little in the way of library and computer support for their programs."*

*Further economic erosion and company "downsizing" in the early 1990s have reduced the appeal of the M.B.A. degree. Applications are down nationwide for almost all but the most elite M.B.A. programs, not only at Metropolis. Metropolis University needs to rethink its strategy for the M.B.A. program in light of these changing circumstances.*

---

Metropolis University has substantial strengths but is buffeted by serious macroenvironmental forces beyond its direct control, and by heavy competition for M.B.A students. The institution is examining its strategy, seeking ways to strengthen its competitive position. Like most educational institutions in the 1990s, Metropolis has to "work smarter" to be successful in attracting students and donors. Virtually all educational institutions are resource-constrained and must use their human and material resources even more effectively. They need to direct their marketing budgets and personnel more productively, by "doing the right things" as well as by "doing things right." This requires having a clear and intelligently planned strategy.

Strategy formulation calls for the institution to develop a strategy for achieving its objectives, discussed in the preceding chapter. For example, Metropolis University may discover that it cannot find a feasible strategy to slow its M.B.A. enrollment slide. If this is so, it may have to revise its enrollment objective. Objectives and strategies must be intertwined, and planners may have to move back and forth in determining a final set of objectives and strategies.

A marketing strategy embodies the ways in which an institution will take advantage of a program/market opportunity. We define *marketing strategy* as follows:

*Marketing strategy* is the selection of a target market, the choice of a competitive position, and the development of an effective marketing mix to reach and serve the chosen market.

Formulation of an institutional marketing strategy includes decisions about:

1. The institution's current programs and markets—whether to maintain, build, or drop them.
2. Future new program and market opportunities.
3. Analysis of competitors.
4. Positioning of the institution in relation to competitors.
5. Selection of target markets and designing of the marketing mix.

This chapter discusses each of these decisions in the strategy-formulation process.

## EVALUATING CURRENT OFFERINGS

Educational institutions often find they have many programs and desires but limited resources. Since they can't support everything equally, such institutions find they must choose which programs will receive emphasis and which may need to be scaled down, combined, or dropped. Financial pressures, including state budget cutbacks, have compelled many institutions to make difficult decisions about investments in programs.

Making decisions about current major programs constitutes an *academic portfolio strategy*. Similar to the periodic review investors give to their

TABLE 7-1    Program evaluation criteria at five universities

| UNIVERSITY | CRITERIA |
|---|---|
| Illinois | Quality |
| | Centrality |
| | Value to society |
| | Potential |
| Washington | Quality |
| | Need |
| | Enrollment |
| | Services |
| Michigan | Quality |
| | Centrality |
| Ohio State | Quality |
| | Value |
| | Resource use |
| SUNY Albany | Quality |
| | Need |
| | Cost |

Source: Robert Cope and George Delaney, "Academic Program Review: A Market Strategy Perspective," *Conference Manual*, 1989 Symposium for the Marketing of Higher Education (Chicago, IL: American Marketing Associations, 1989), p. 140.

FIGURE 7-1    Academic portfolio model

| | Centrality | | |
|---|---|---|---|
| | High | Medium | Low |
| **High** | Psychology  (MV–H) Decision: <br>• Build size <br>• Build quality | | Home Economics (MV – H) Decision: <br>• Build size <br>• Build quality |
| **Medium** | | Geography (MV – M) Decision: <br>• Hold size <br>• Hold quality | |
| **Low** | Philosophy  (MV–L) Decision: <br>• Reduce size <br>• Build quality | | Classical Languages (MV– L) Decision: <br>• Reduce size or terminate |

(Quality — vertical axis label at left)

personal investment portfolios, a college or other educational institution should review its programs from time to time. During decades of expansion, many institutions added courses and programs. With budget contractions, they face the prospect of reducing the number of courses, increasing class size, consolidating programs, making cuts across the board, and/or identifying the stronger programs for full support while drawing funds away from or completely eliminating some programs.[1]

Selecting a course of action can be an exceedingly painful process, despite economic realities which suggest that each institution focus its financial and other resources on programs that further its mission, build on institutional strengths, and meet the needs of identifiable target markets.

Each institution that undertakes a program review needs to establish a set of criteria. Table 7-1 shows the criteria used by five state universities. The academic portfolio model shown in Figure 7-1 illustrates a review of academic departments, which are evaluated on *centrality to the school's mission*, on the *quality* of the program, and on *market viability* (indicated in parentheses). Programs are ranked high, medium, or low on each dimension. In practice, when the criteria are not clearly operationalized, they can become a smoke screen used by decision makers to make expedient rather than strategic decisions. Regardless of how resource reallocation decisions are made, those whose programs (and jobs) are reduced or eliminated are hardly disinterested bystanders.[2]

*Centrality to the school's mission* refers to the extent to which the program is directly related to the current mission that the institution has adopted. For example, clinical training would be central to a hospital school of nursing program, but art history probably is not.

*Quality* is a measure of the features of the program, including its academic depth and rigor and the quality of the faculty. Quality may be measured in terms of national rankings of academic departments, but such ratings are not useful for small, unranked institutions, which must make their own judgments, probably in comparison with other institutions they perceive as competitors. They might turn to accreditation reports and outside consultants for opinions on relative quality.

The decision makers must also weigh the true value of prestige ratings for the institution, since prestige based on faculty research reputations may have little or no direct impact on institutional quality as experienced by students. According to William Massy,

> Unbridled competition for prestige—at least as traditionally defined in terms of research—leads to "mission creep" [where the institution seeks to expand its mission], . . . increases cost per students, . . . [and] deprives undergraduate and professional students of faculty "quality time" that otherwise could be used for the modernization of educational goals, the design of new curricula and teaching methods, and teaching itself.[3]

*Market viability* is the extent to which there is present and future demand for study in this program area. A program may be of high quality and central to a college's mission, but if there is little or no student interest in that area, the program will not survive unless the institution is willing to divert money from other programs to sustain it. Determining market viability may involve examining past experience (enrollment levels, for example) and trends revealed in the environmental analyses, or may require additional marketing research.

The school shown in Figure 7-1 has a strong liberal arts tradition. Psychology and philosophy are judged high on centrality, but philosophy is low in quality and market viability. The philosophy department should probably be reduced in size and its quality enhanced. Although low on centrality, the home economics department scores high on quality and market viability. A plausible strategy would be to hold quality and build size. (The school should also consider whether its students are as committed to liberal arts as the school is; perhaps the school should be adding more applied courses and programs.) Classical languages rank low on all scales. Unless the school will commit the necessary resources to build this major, the school should probably reduce the department, perhaps retaining certain courses as part of another program.

Cope recommends a two-stage process for program review.[4] The first stage aims to decide which programs should be continued, reorganized, or dropped. In this stage, the reviewers evaluate each program on quality and centrality to mission, and decide whether the program should be continued. If the continuation decision is yes, then the reviewers move to the second stage, which leads to a decision about how much of the institution's resources should be allocated to each program. At this stage, the reviewers assess the market demand for the program and the program's comparative advantage. If the comparative advantage is clear and the demand is high, the institution may well decide to invest more in that program. If either comparative advantage or demand is less strong, the institution may decide to maintain the program at current levels. Those programs which do not pass the continuation decision stage are not considered at the second stage, regardless of their comparative advantage or demand.

Table 7-2 presents a decision table for program review that illustrates this two-stage approach. Note that this approach looks at each program individually. In the typical resource-constrained educational institution, the reviewers would ultimately need to weigh the competing value and resource needs of the programs *as a set* to decide how resources will be allocated. Narrowly cost-driven decisions about individual units can have damaging ripple effects on the institution's overall functioning, so the ramifications of each decision need to be reviewed before taking action.

The Boston Consulting Group (BCG) recommends that companies appraise each of their main product lines on the basis of market growth rate (annual growth rate of the market in which the product is sold) and the company's share of the current market relative to its largest competitor. Each product line is then placed in the corresponding quadrant of the BCG matrix, shown in Figure 7-2.

This portfolio approach can be adapted for use by educational institutions.[5] For example, each academic area or program can be rated high or low on two criteria: (1) market growth rate, the growth in full-time-equivalent (FTE) students in that field over the past five years; and (2) market-share dominance, the ratio of FTE students in that field at the largest competing institution to FTE students in that field at the institution doing the analysis.

Newbould defines the four quadrants as follows:

- *Stars* are programs in high-growth fields in which the institution has market-share dominance in terms of relative numbers of students. Star programs are growing rapidly and typically require heavy investment of resources—to add faculty, expand the related library collection, acquire equipment, and so on. If the necessary investment is made and the area proves of enduring interest, the star program will turn into a cash cow and generate cash in excess of expenses in the future.
- *Cash cows* are programs in low-growth fields that attract a high share of the market for such programs. They produce revenues that can be used to support high-growth programs or to underwrite those with problems.
- *Question marks* are programs in high-growth fields but in which the institution has a low market share. The institution faces the decision of whether to increase its investment in the program, hoping to increase its market share and make the program a star, or to reduce or terminate its investment on the grounds that the resources could be better used elsewhere.

TABLE 7-2  A decision table for reviewing programs

| PROGRAM | INSTITUTIONAL VIEW | | | COMPARATIVE ADVANTAGE | STRATEGIC VIEW | |
| | QUALITY | CENTRALITY | DECISION ON CONTINUATION | | DECISION ON DEMAND | BUDGET |
| --- | --- | --- | --- | --- | --- | --- |
| A | High | High | Yes | Clear | High | Invest more |
| B | High | High | Yes | Clear | Moderate | Maintain |
| C | High | High | Yes | Clear | Low | Maintain |
| D | High | High | Yes | Some | High | Invest more |
| E | High | High | Yes | Little | High | Maintain |
| F | High | High | Yes | Little | Moderate | Maintain |
| G | High | High | Yes | Little | Low | Reduce |
| H | Low | High | Yes | None | Low | Invest to improve |
| I | High | Low | Reorganize | Little | High | Maintain |
| X | Moderate | Moderate | Discontinue regardless of comparative advantage or demand | | | |
| Z | Low | Low | | | | |

Source: Robert G. Cope, *Strategic Planning, Management, and Decision Making*, AAHE-ERIC/Higher Education Research Report No. 9, 1981 (Washington, DC: American Association for Higher Education, 1981), p. 44.

- *Dogs* are those programs that have a small market share in slow-growth or declining fields. Dogs usually make little money or lose money for the institution. The institution may decide to drop or shrink dogs. Unless dogs must be offered for other reasons, maintaining them may come at the expense of other opportunities for increasing excellence.[6]

Figure 7-3 presents a BCG-type matrix of the master's degree programs offered by a midwestern state university.

The BCG approach must be adapted for use in making decisions about educational offerings, since most educational institutions have capacity constraints and strive to achieve some balance between programs. They are unable or unwilling to shift significant resources to new programs that may be attractive only for a short time. On the other hand, some educational institutions specialize in meeting emerging educational needs and have the flexibil-

FIGURE 7-2    The BCG matrix

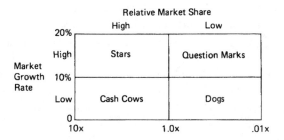

FIGURE 7-3    BCG matrix for all master's programs at a
midwestern university

Market Share

| | | High | | Low | |
|---|---|---|---|---|---|
| | | **Stars** | | **Question Marks** | |
| High | | Art | Physical education | Business | |
| | | Music | Speech; audiology | Chemistry | |
| | | Geology | Languages | Home economics | |
| Market Growth Rate | | Architecture | Geography | | |
| | | **Cash Cows** | | **Dogs** | |
| Low | | Education | Public administration | Engineering | Biology |
| | | English | Journalism | History | Physics |
| | | Philosophy | Library | Political science | Economics |
| | | Sociology | | Psychology | Mathematics |

Source: Based on Gerald D. Newbould, "Product Portfolio diagnosis for U.S. Universities," *Akron Business and Economic Review*, (Spring 1980), p. 44.

ity in acquiring facilities and instructors as needed to pursue such opportunities. For such institutions the BCG approach may prove quite useful in thinking about how to shift the institution's program emphases.

We have presented two portfolio approaches for reviewing existing programs, the academic portfolio method and an adaptation of the BCG product portfolio matrix. Using a portfolio approach offers a major advantage over simply assessing each program individually. Portfolio methods emphasize an institution's academic programs as an interrelated set. Decisions about increasing or reducing investment in particular programs are based on the institution's resources and the relative needs and contributions of each program area. Sound assessment of program strengths and weaknesses lays the groundwork for strategy formulation.

## IDENTIFYING OPPORTUNITIES

After examining its current portfolio of programs, the institution may discover significant gaps in its offerings. There may few stars or cash cows. Market demand may be shifting away from the institution's areas of strength, and the institution must enhance its offerings or search for new programs and markets. Such institutions need a systematic approach to *opportunity identification*. The *program/market opportunity matrix* is a useful framework for undertaking this task. Figure 7-4 shows a program/market opportunity matrix for a college interested in expanding enrollment. (The same matrix format may also be used to identify new donor markets and fund-raising programs.) Starting with a blank nine-cell matrix, the planning group considers existing proposals and brainstorms additional ideas that would fit in each cell. The matrix encourages planners to think in terms of both programs and markets simultaneously.

Each cell in Figure 7-4 has a name. Potential opportunities—in this case, for a college—are listed in small letters. The administration should first consider cell 1, *market penetration*. This cell raises the question of whether the college can maintain or expand its enrollment by deepening its penetration into its existing markets with its existing programs. This strategy is effective only if the current market is not already saturated. A community college may be able to attract more adults to its leisure/fitness courses by increasing advertising and promotion, whereas many private liberal arts colleges seeking to attract more 18-year-old freshmen face a much greater challenge, and a college that wants to increase the number of classics majors may find the greatest challenge.

Cell 2 raises the question of whether the college should consider expanding into *new geographical markets with its existing programs*. The college could open a branch in another part of the city, or in a new city, or even

FIGURE 7-4    Program/market opportunity matrix

| | | PROGRAMS | | |
|---|---|---|---|---|
| | | Existing | Modified | New |
| MARKETS | Existing | 1. Market Penetration<br>Intensify promotion<br>and recruitment of<br>existing markets for<br>existing programs | 4. Program Modification<br>New schedules<br>(weekend,<br>evening)<br>Improvement of<br>facilities | 7. Program Innovation<br>Develop new programs,<br>majors, courses |
| | Geographical | 2. Geographical Expansion<br>Open a branch campus<br>or other site to offer<br>the same programs | 5. Modification for<br>Dispersed Markets<br>Offer programs in<br>distant locations,<br>e.g., overseas | 8. Geographic Innovation<br>Find ways to serve<br>new markets, e.g.,<br>distance learning via<br>teleconferencing,<br>modem, etc. |
| | New | 3. Market development<br>Locate new markets for<br>current programs:<br>• Senior citizens<br>• Homemakers<br>• Local companies | 6. Service Modification<br>for New Markets<br>Special courses for<br>new markets, e.g.,<br>• Elderhostel<br>• Job training for<br>senior citizens | 9. Total Innovation<br>New programs for new<br>markets, e.g.,<br>• "University without<br>walls"<br>• For-profit training<br>company |

start a campus in another country. For example, Southern Methodist University in Dallas offers M.B.A. courses in Houston, and Antioch operates campuses abroad.

The planners then move to cell 3 and consider possibly offering *existing programs to new individual and institutional markets*. Some colleges and universities are successfully attracting senior citizens, homemakers, and full-time employees of local companies.

Next, the planners can consider whether the college should *modify* its *current programs to attract more of the existing market* (cell 4). A school may find that interest and enrollment go up when it improves its residential facilities, upgrades the quality and reputation of its career center, or adopts a more attractive schedule of courses. Standard courses can be shortened or offered in the evening or on weekends. For example, Alverno College, a private women's school in Milwaukee, instituted a weekend college that drew large numbers of homemakers and working women.

Cell 5 is labeled *modification for dispersed markets*. The University of Maryland offers courses and programs for members of the armed forces in the United States and overseas. The University of Pittsburgh has taken leadership in establishing business schools in Central Europe, to train Central European managers, many of whom are subsidized by international companies seeking local managers.

*Program modification for new markets* (cell 6) may be a more realistic growth opportunity for most educational institutions. For example, a college may decide to serve older adults by providing special courses or schedules for them. De Anza Community College in Cupertino, California, offers a job-training workshop for older adults, which includes assessment of financial needs and job skills, plus skill training and paid work experience. Hundreds of colleges and universities host Elderhostel programs each summer for participants over age 60.

*Program innovation* (cell 7) means developing new courses, departments, or programs. Even educational institutions that are not expanding in size need to add new courses and programs or overhaul existing ones to maintain current size and to attract more students. For example, Stanford's Mechanical Engineering Design Division added a master's degree program in product design.

*Geographic innovation* (cell 8) involves finding new ways to serve new geographical areas. For example, with an electronic blackboard, a professor can write something in one location and have the notes transmitted over telephone lines to a distant city. *Distance learning*, often via teleconferencing, is well established in many large companies, which contract with universities to provide specific courses and even whole degree programs. Courses via computer links are now offered, and the evolution of interactive television and other new media will further increase opportunities for geographic innovation.

The final category, *total innovation* (cell 9), refers to offering new programs to new markets. Various "universities without walls" have been established in the past two decades. Empire State College, part of the New York State higher education system, is one example. Some institutions are growing by developing more continuing education programs or starting evening or weekend college degree completion programs.

Rockhurst College, a Catholic college in Kansas City, Missouri, established the Rockhurst College Continuing Education Center as an incorporated commercial business. This division of the college purchased National Seminars Group in 1991. National Seminars presents more than 5,000 seminars annually in the United States, Canada, the United Kingdom, and the Netherlands, and is one of the largest providers of professional/human resource development seminars in the United States. Profits from this venture flow back to Rockhurst College.

Moving from cell 1 opportunities to cell 9 opportunities is a progression from low risk/low return to high risk/high return. Educational institutions are often risk averse, preferring to do more of their familiar activities than to take risks. The program/market opportunity matrix can help planners to imagine new options in a systematic way. The identified opportunities must be evaluated for their centrality, market viability, cost, and other features; the better ones can then be pursued. The results of the program/market opportunity analysis and the preceding portfolio analysis provide the basis for the institution's formulation of its strategic plans.

## ANALYZING COMPETITION

Virtually every educational institution faces competition, yet for decades, few administrators talked openly about it. Educators generally believed that most schools, colleges, and universities were worthy and had something to contribute. They preferred to focus on their own institutions and to believe that they did not compete for students, faculty, and donors. Competition sounded like a concern for business, not for education.

Administrators are now aware that even strong schools cannot afford to ignore competition:

- For students: Academically prestigious institutions compete with each other for the most qualified students, as do less selective institutions.
- For faculty: In some academic areas, there are six or more job openings for each new Ph.D. graduate, and colleges and universities must compete with business and industry for this talent.
- For donors: Educational institutions receive over $10 billion in donations and foundation grants each year, but each must make a case to prospective donors to arouse their interest and obtain their support.
- For favorable public attention: With thousands of other educational institutions, making—and keeping—the public aware of the school and its strengths cannot be left to chance.

Institutional competition for students, faculty, and donations is a fact of life and offers benefits for prospective students, faculty, and donors. The existence of many educational alternatives encourages institutions to offer attractive programs of the best possible quality and, in some cases, to specialize to take advantage of unique strengths and circumstances. Schools and colleges cannot afford to be smug about their faults when other institutions can offer similar or better programs or other features that attract students. Some of Metropolis University's competitors have priced their M.B.A. programs significantly lower, a step they can afford since they do not have Metropolis's fixed overhead costs for physical plant, equipment, and a full-time faculty.

In their competition for resources, educational institutions can use the following marketing assets, among others: program quality, program uniqueness, price, convenience, reputation, and well-qualified students and faculty, who attract others like themselves.

The nature of competition between educational institutions has become more complex over the past decade and calls for more sophisticated analysis than ever. In the sections that follow, we present ways to analyze competitors, and we examine the competitive roles an institution may play and how they relate to institutional survival and growth.

## Analyzing Competitors

Here we will illustrate competitive analysis with the case of competition for students. An educational institution may be interested in knowing the following things about its competition:

- Which institutions do we compete with for students, and how successful are we?

Then, for each competitor:

- What programs does it offer, and how good are they?
- What is its financial situation?
- What are its admissions criteria?
- What is its enrollment? Enrollment trends?
- What are the threats and opportunities facing the institution?
- What are the institution's strengths and weaknesses?
- What competitive strategy is the institution using?

The institution's competitors are anything that might receive the attention of a potential student (faculty member, donor) as an alternative to the institution's offer. Consider the case of Owen, a computer sales representative, whose thought process is shown in Figure 7-5. Owen has spent some time thinking about his goals, which now include running in the Boston Marathon, traveling in Europe, and getting ahead at work. Of these three desires, his practical nature suggests that he should focus on getting ahead at work. He decides that getting an M.B.A. at night would help him most. Since his company will pay all his educational expenses, he decides to attend a private uni-

FIGURE 7-5  Types of competitors facing an M.B.A. program

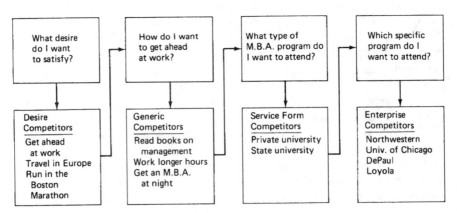

versity M.B.A. program. This example shows that in Owen's mind, there were numerous competitors to getting an M.B.A. at a particular university.

There are two approaches used to answer the question, "Which institutions do we compete with for students, and how successful are we?"

First, M.B.A. programs that require the Graduate Management Admissions Test receive a summary of how many test takers named their M.B.A. program to receive test scores, and how many of these test takers applied to specific competing programs. In effect, the number of test takers applying elsewhere defines the competitive schools from the viewpoint of prospective students. Colleges that require the Scholastic Aptitude Test of the College Board for undergraduate applicants can obtain reports that list the other institutions to which a given college's applicants, admitted students, and matriculants most often send their SAT scores. This information, although very useful as an indicator of competition and easy to obtain, does not allow an assessment of how individual students chose one institution over others.

Second, educational institutions can assess application overlap by comparing totals of shared applications.[7] A study conducted at Boston College illustrates the approach. A questionnaire was sent to more than 2,500 accepted applicants, asking them to list all the schools to which they applied. For each school listed, students indicated whether or not they were accepted. Students who decided against attending Boston College were asked the name of the school they planned to attend. The researchers focused on college choices of students who were accepted at both Boston College and a competitor and who thus had a real choice.

The draw rate was computed for each competing institution by taking the ratio of the number of joint applicants who chose the competitor after having been accepted by both. The top 15 competitors were then categorized by draw rate. Schools in the high category accepted 70 percent of the students Boston College accepted, whereas competitors in the low (highly selective) category accepted 30 percent or less. The middle category of colleges and universities included six institutions: Holy Cross, Tufts, Georgetown, the University of New Hampshire, Notre Dame, and the University of Vermont. At the time of the study, these were Boston College's closest competitors. One implication of such a study is that, where possible, Boston College should strive to improve in areas where competitors are deemed more attractive.

These two approaches—use of data from testing companies and from overlap surveys—are useful ways to identify competitors, but they do not tell the whole story. Perhaps some of the most attractive students don't take the GMAT or SAT tests and instead apply to public institutions that do not require them because they assume that private institutions would be unaffordable. The private institutions "lose out" in the competition on price, with no opportunity to explain their financial aid packages and the advantages they may be able to offer. Or perhaps good prospects never hear about certain colleges because they do not receive good college counseling or because they only consider the colleges nearest their homes. At these early stages of awareness and interest, many traditional elements of competition such as quality and actual cost do not even come into play. So institutions need to think broadly about competition and competitors in order to understand how prospective students, faculty, and donors may appraise them.

In addition to identifying competitors, the institution needs to determine what attributes students use to evaluate the institutions and with what results. We address this issue later in this chapter when we discuss positioning.

Other questions on competitive analysis can often be answered using available data. For example, a competitor's catalog provides information on programs, faculty, costs, and enrollment and may also specify admissions criteria. Faculty quality can be judged by where advanced degrees were obtained, and by consulting faculty elsewhere in the same disciplines. If the competitor is of national stature, its academic programs may be ranked in one of several national polls. Faculty turnover can be assessed by comparing catalogs for several consecutive years. The institution can probably construct a good approximation of the threats, opportunities, strengths, and weaknesses of each competitor. Nonprofit educational institutions must file financial statements, which are available to the public. From these and other sources— news stories, competitor's annual reports, and other publications—the institution can develop a clear picture of each competing institution.

We now turn to the competitive roles educational institutions may play.

## Competitive Roles

An analysis of competing institutions or specific programs within competing institutions often reveals the following competitive roles: the *leader*, the *challenger*, the *follower*, and the *nicher*. The selection of a particular role will depend on the institution's or program's size, stature, and resources, as well as those of its competitors.

The *leader* is the acknowledged dominant institution or program in a particular geographical, disciplinary, or other market. Although leadership could reflect size and/or quality, the leader usually strives to maintain its premier position by increasing the applicant pool to raise the quality of admitted students, and by hiring distinguished faculty. The leader may also take advantage of its strength to increase program or institution size. For example, a large private midwestern university with a nationally ranked law school has 15 applicants for each place, and the quality of applicants has improved each year. The law school could increase revenue without lowering student quality by admitting a certain number of additional law students each year. With this additional revenue, the school can hire additional distinguished faculty who will further enhance the law school's reputation, attracting more and better applicants in the future.

The *challengers* are the runner-up institutions or programs that aspire to match or surpass the leader. They may strive to enhance their reputations by establishing more prestige programs or by adding faculty and other resources to improve on existing ones. Or an institution may compete by introducing innovative programs, by expanding the number of sites where programs are offered, or by advertising its programs more intensively.

The *followers* strive to hold on to their present markets and to be as much as possible like the market leader. Market followers may refine existing programs to meet the needs of their target markets, but typically they are not very innovative.

The *nichers* are those institutions and programs that aim to find and fill one or more niches that are not well served by other educational institutions. Nichers may specialize by serving one type of market (adults over 65), by offering unique program (M.B.A. in telecommunications), by offering a customized program (quality-control seminars customized for specific companies), by providing unique program features (an early morning engineering degree program), or by providing a unique delivery system (tele-conferenced classes). To be successful, nichers should look for niches that are of sufficient size and growth potential to be attractive, that are not well served by other institutions, and that the institution can serve effectively.

Nicher institutions may find that once they have succeeded in a particular niche, they will attract other institutions as competitors. Consider an institution offering a unique program. When other schools see that the program is drawing substantial interest, they may want to set up similar programs. The nicher that initiated the program can often maintain a dominant role as a supplier of that program if it has distinctive competence and differential advantage over competitors, if it controls resources that are in short supply (such as a top expert in the field on the faculty), and if it has marketing advantages—such as a strong institutional and program reputation, good public relations, and satisfied participants and graduates. Even though an institution does not need all these advantages to succeed, the more it has, the better its chances of continuing success.

Educational institutions that understand their markets, analyze their competition, and engage in strategic planning can usually maintain their current strengths and build on them better than can institutions that do not. In the next section, we take up positioning strategy.

## POSITIONING THE INSTITUTION

Every educational institution holds a position in the minds of those who have contact with or know about the institution. A *position* describes how a person or group perceives the institution in relation to other institutions. People often describe schools and colleges in such comparative terms as these: "the

FIGURE 7-6    Steps in positioning strategy development

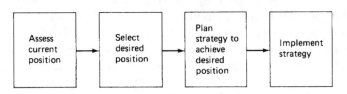

Big Ten school with the best football team," "the Harvard of the West" (Stanford), "the law school if you want to work on Wall Street," and so forth. A position may also describe the institution or program on some dimension that could be used to compare institutions, such as "the M.B.A. program for quant jocks."

The school or college may not be satisfied with its current position. Instead of holding a desirable and distinctive position, it may be considered weak, unfriendly, large and impersonal, "too academic," or "too social" in comparison with other institutions. It may not know what its current position is, or it may be striving to maintain a position that is at odds with the school's reality and performance. The institution may want to adopt a new position more in line with recent changes in its direction and programs, and more attractive to students, donors, and others.

Developing a *positioning strategy* consists of the following steps: (1) assessing the institution's current position in the relevant market, (2) selecting the desired position, (3) planning a strategy to achieve the desired position, and (4) implementing the strategy. Figure 7-6 shows these four steps, which are discussed next.

### Assess Current Position

To find out its current position with respect to its competitors, the institution must survey relevant groups that are qualified to make such a comparison. And although knowing comparative positions is important, it is just as important to find out what *key attributes* people use in comparing institutions, which attributes are most important, and the *relative positions* of the institution and its competitors on the most important attributes. Note that the institution should examine its position in relation to its relevant competitors, not to every school, college, or educational institution in the country or the world.

Consider the example of Yale University. Yale admissions officers were interested in how admitted applicants perceived Yale in relation to competing colleges.[8] Researchers asked 800 admitted students and 800 Yale undergraduates to rate the similarity of 136 possible pairs of 17 colleges. Figure 7-7 presents the results. The lines enclose clusters of colleges rated similar in varying degrees. The researchers did not ask respondents what dimensions they

FIGURE 7-7    Perceptual map of college similarity

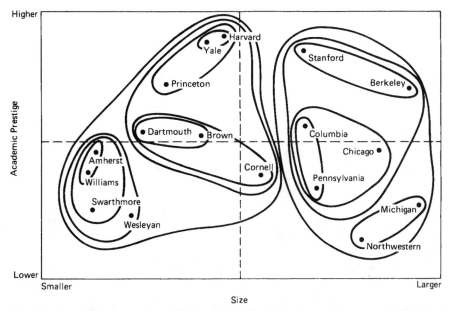

Source: Robert J. Sternberg and Jeanne C. Davis, "Student Perceptions of Yale and Its Competitors," *College and University* (Spring 1978), p. 266.

used to evaluate similarity, but academic prestige and size seemed to explain their ratings.

In a second study, Yale undergraduates rated Yale and 16 competitors using the semantic differential (see example in Exhibit 3-2 and also Chapter 9). Factor analysis revealed three main dimensions: academic prestige, active campus life, and agreeableness. Table 7-3 shows the ratings of the 17 colleges on these three dimensions. The results could be charted on a three-dimensional graph to show positions of each college.

In obtaining and using ratings by current students, the planners must keep in mind that students enrolled in the institution may rate their school or college somewhat higher than those not enrolled, and they are likely to rate Yale higher than those institutions they did not choose to attend. Thus, ratings by admitted students who enrolled elsewhere and, where possible, by qualified students who chose not to apply can be important in positioning studies.

### Select Desired Position

Having assessed its current position, an institution may (1) decide that its present position is strong and desirable and work to emphasize it with poten-

TABLE 7-3    Ratings of Yale and competitors by Yale freshmen

| | ACADEMIC PRESTIGE | ACTIVE CAMPUS LIFE | AGREEABLENESS |
|---|---|---|---|
| Amherst | .39 | −1.04 | .47 |
| Berkeley | −.21 | 1.37 | .59 |
| Brown | −.53 | .05 | .21 |
| Chicago | .11 | .35 | −2.00 |
| Columbia | .01 | .46 | −1.99 |
| Cornell | −.19 | −.12 | .29 |
| Dartmouth | .15 | .28 | .99 |
| Harvard | 1.31 | .40 | −.74 |
| Michigan | −2.01 | 1.63 | .38 |
| Northwestern | −1.21 | .00 | .13 |
| Pennsylvania | −1.18 | −.08 | −.66 |
| Princeton | .72 | −.64 | .18 |
| Stanford | .74 | .93 | 1.99 |
| Swarthmore | .05 | −1.72 | −.54 |
| Wesleyan | -.56 | −1.37 | .54 |
| Williams | .10 | −1.59 | .79 |
| Yale | 2.33 | 1.08 | −.06 |

Note: Scores on some scales have been reversed so that higher values correspond to greater amounts of the attribute used to name the scale.
Source: Adapted from Robert J. Sternberg and Jeanne C. Davis, "Student Perceptions of Yale and its Competitors," *College and University* (Spring 1978), p. 276.

tial students and others; (2) develop a new or clarified position for the school and communicate it; or (3) where appropriate, position the school on a new dimension, one that people may value but that they don't routinely use in evaluating the school.

For example, suppose that Yale administrators were concerned about Yale's position. Note that Yale was rated at the top on academic prestige but low on agreeableness, whereas Stanford was rated high on both. Yale might accept its position as an academically elite university that isn't particularly pleasant for students. (Some educational institutions may even emphasize their spartan atmosphere and the rigors of being a student there, and attract those who feel a school should be tough and unpleasant.)

Before taking action, Yale administrators would want to look at how students rated Yale on the adjective pairs that made up the agreeableness dimension. Yale was judged about average on scales of pleasantness, happiness, fairness, and well-roundness, and slightly below average on beauty. On relaxedness, Yale was considerably below average.

After considering the attributes of greatest importance to its current and potential students, Yale will want to prepare a positioning statement that sets forth how the university wants to be perceived in relation to its competition. This statement by itself is not enough; the university must plan and carry out a strategy to achieve this desired position.

**Plan and Implement Strategy**

Suppose Yale decided it wanted to be perceived as the most pleasant school in the Ivy League. It might attempt to change its position by changing its communications to feature the most beautiful areas of the campus and to show clusters of cheerful students, eating lunch on the lawn, commenting on how little stress there is at Yale.

But communications are not enough. Although such communications may change the opinions of some who read Yale's communications, those who then have direct contact with Yale may find the communications do not match the reality. Instead, Yale would want to consider ways to make campus life more gracious and relaxed, and to make the campus more beautiful. Or the university may decide that such changes are infeasible or unnecessary and continue to strive to attract students who are not only academically able but who are willing to "trade" greater agreeableness elsewhere for what Yale has to offer.

Changing an institution's position in the academic marketplace is difficult. Old perceptions die hard. The institution must select an appropriate position and then support that position by all means available. For example, suppose a moderately strong, financially healthy university wants to increase its academic prestige. It will want to examine its academic portfolio and select areas for investment. The university may seek donations to bring in distinguished faculty in its strongest departments. It may institute an honors program for undergraduates with especially strong high school records. The news director will try to link the university's name with other, academically stronger institutions.

These and other activities must be carefully thought out and orchestrated to obtain the desired effect. All university constituencies need to know and understand what the university is trying to accomplish, so that their efforts can support the desired direction and position. For example, to reinforce the university's academic prestige, alumni events featuring the university's most illustrious faculty would be more in keeping than a program consisting exclusively of football games and barbecues. Even with focused effort, the university must be consistent and patient, since it may be several years before this revised position becomes widely known and held.

## AN EXAMPLE OF STRATEGY FORMULATION

So far in this chapter, we have described the process of reviewing current programs, identifying new program and marketing opportunities, analyzing competitors, and positioning the institution relative to competition. The strategy-formulation process also includes selecting appropriate target markets and designing a marketing mix to serve them. Here we will illustrate target market strategy, competitive positioning strategy, and marketing-mix strategy in terms of the following example:

Desert University (name disguised), located in the Southwest, includes a liberal arts college and several professional schools. One of these, the journalism school, enjoys a good local reputation. Although it has attracted a large number of students in the past, the number of applicants has fallen in recent years because of the growing difficulty of finding journalism jobs for graduates and the low pay. The dean of the journalism school allowed enrollment to decline rather than lower the school's admission standards. The university president, however, is upset with the enrollment decline. The president wants the journalism school to remain at its present size and quality and wants the dean and faculty to develop a marketing strategy that will adapt the school to its best opportunities.

## Target-Market Strategy

The first step in preparing a marketing strategy is to thoroughly understand the market. We define a *market* as follows:

> A *market* is the set of all people who have an actual or potential interest in a product or service and the resources to acquire it.

Thus, the journalism-student market can be defined as the set of all people who have an actual or potential interest in studying journalism and the ability and qualifications to acquire this education. In the commercial marketplace, people must pay—either at the time of purchase or on credit—to acquire the goods and services they want. In contrast, most educational institutions offer some level of financial assistance to deserving, qualified students, to bring the costs of education within their reach. Many educational institutions partially subsidize the cost of education for all students through use of endowment funds for certain purposes that would otherwise have to be covered by tuition revenues.

At the outset, it becomes clear that the national market must be quite large and that Desert University would need only a small share of it to fill its classes. But the administration realizes that not every person in this market would know about Desert University, find it attractive, or be able to attend. Nor would Desert find every person attractive. When looked at closely, every market is heterogeneous; that is, it is made up of quite different types of consumers, or *market segments*. Therefore, the journalism school would benefit from constructing a market segmentation scheme that would reveal the major groups making up the market. Then it could decide whether to try to serve all these segments (*mass marketing*) or concentrate on a few of the more promising segments (*target marketing*).

There are many ways to segment a market. A market could be segmented by age, sex, income, geography, lifestyle, and many other variables. The market analyst tries different approaches until a useful one is found. Sup-

FIGURE 7-8    Segmentation of the journalism
program/market

MARKETS

|  | College-Age<br>Learner | Adult<br>Learner | Practicing<br>Journalist |
|---|---|---|---|
| Broadcast<br>Journalism |  |  |  |
| Print<br>Journalism |  |  |  |
| Public<br>Relations |  |  |  |

PROGRAMS

pose the administration settles on the *program/market segmentation* scheme shown in Figure 7-8. Three student *markets* for journalism are shown: college-age learners, adult learners, and practicing journalists. Three *program* types are shown: broadcast journalism (radio and television), print journalism (newspapers and magazines), and public relations (a program found in most schools of journalism). Suppose the journalism school at Desert University at present caters to all nine market segments but is not doing a distinguished job in any. At the same time, competitors are beginning to concentrate on certain market segments and doing a first-class job: the University of Texas in training college-age students for broadcast journalism, Northwestern University in training college-age students for print journalism, and so on. The dean is wondering whether to pursue target marketing and, if so, what pattern of target marketing to choose.

The school will recognize that there are five basic patterns of market coverage possible with a program/market segmentation scheme. They are shown in Figure 7-9 and are described thus:

1. *Program/market concentration* consists of concentrating on only one market segment—here, teaching print journalism to adult learners.
2. *Program specialization* consists of deciding to offer only one program (here, print journalism) for all three markets.
3. *Market specialization* consists of deciding to serve only one market segment (adult learners) with all the journalism programs.
4. *Selective specialization* consists of working in several program markets that have no relation to each other except that each individually constitutes an attractive opportunity.
5. *Full coverage* consists of undertaking the full range of programs to serve all the market segments.

After researching these alternatives, the school decides that the most attractive one for the school is program specialization—here, print journalism. The journalism school does not have the funds to buy expensive television

FIGURE 7-9    Five patterns of market coverage

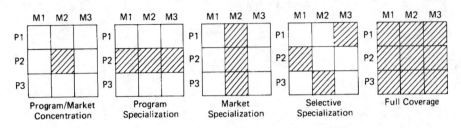

and radio equipment and sound rooms for student training, and it would be doing only a second-rate job compared to the University of Texas, with its excellent facilities for teaching broadcast journalism. The school's program in public relations is quite weak and cannot be the basis for building a distinguished journalism school. The region lacks a good print-journalism school, which happens to be Desert University's strong suit. The school decides to develop print-journalism programs for all three markets because the number of college-age students is not large enough to be the sole market focus.

Having decided on program specialization, the school should now proceed in developing a finer segmentation of the market for print-journalism education. Figure 7-10 shows one possible subsegmentation of the print-journalism market. The columns show different geographical areas from which the journalism school can try to actively recruit students. The school can concentrate on attracting journalism majors from the local area, using easy admission standards since the market is quite small. Or it can try to compete for students in the southwestern region, which will require a larger recruiting budget and contacts with a larger number of newspapers and magazines to place students. Or it can try to develop national eminence and attract students from all over the nation. The rows show that journalism majors have

FIGURE 7-10    Subsegmentation of the print-journalism
market

| | | GEOGRAPHY | | |
|---|---|---|---|---|
| | | Local | Regional | National |
| CAREER OBJECTIVES | News writing | | | |
| | Feature Writing | | | |
| | Advertising | | | |
| | Media Management | | | |

different career objectives—some seeking training in news writing, others in feature writing, still others in advertising, and some in managing media organizations. Looking at the subsegmentation, the dean may decide to cultivate the regional market and emphasize careers in news writing and feature writing. Although the school will also teach advertising and media management, it will seek to build its reputation as a writer's training school.

## Competitive Positioning Strategy

Having selected its target market, the journalism school will now have to develop its competitive positioning strategy vis-à-vis other journalism schools serving the same target market. Suppose there are three other journalism schools in the Southwest that do a good job of training students in print journalism. If the four schools are similar, then high school students going into journalism would not have much basis for choice among the four. The schools' respective market shares would be left to chance. The solution is *competitive positioning*, defined as follows:

> *Competitive positioning* is the art of developing and communicating meaningful differences between one's offer and those of competitors serving the same target market.

The key to competitive positioning is to identify the major attributes used by the target market to evaluate and choose among competitive institutions. Suppose the target market judges journalism schools by their perceived quality (high versus low) and perceived orientation (liberal arts versus vocational). Figure 7-11 shows the perceived competitive positions of the other three journalism schools. Schools A and B are liberal-arts-oriented journalism schools of low quality, B being somewhat larger and slightly better in quality than A. They are locked in competition for the same students, since their differentiation is negligible. School C is seen as a high-quality vocationally oriented journalism school and draws those students seeking this type of school. Desert University's journalism school, shown as D, comes closest to being perceived as a high-quality, liberal-arts-oriented school. Fortunately, it has no competition in this preference segment. The only question is whether there are enough students seeking a high-quality, liberal-arts-oriented journalism school. If not, then D is not a viable competitive position, and the administration has to think about repositioning the school toward a part of the market in which the demand is larger.

## Marketing-Mix Strategy

The next step in marketing strategy is to develop a *marketing mix* and a *marketing expenditure level* that supports the school's ability to compete in its

FIGURE 7-11    Competitive positioning of four
journalism schools

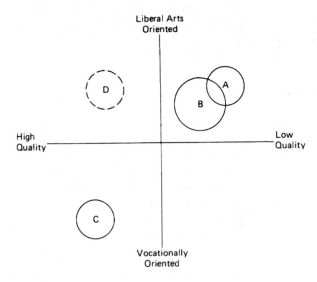

target market. The marketing mix for educational institutions includes 7 "Ps": programs, price, place (location and delivery systems), promotion (including advertising, public relations, personal contact, and other activities), processes, physical facilities, and people.

The institution chooses a marketing mix that will support and reinforce its chosen competitive position. Since the journalism school wants to maintain and project a reputation as a high-quality, liberal-arts-oriented journalism school, it will hire high-quality faculty, require students to take many liberal arts courses, develop high-quality school catalogs and brochures, send them to potential students seeking this type of school, and so on. In other words, the chosen competitive position dictates the elements of the marketing mix that will be emphasized. The marketing mix is presented in detail in Chapters 11 through 14.

As for marketing expenditure level, this depends on estimating how much money is needed to accomplish the school's enrollment objectives. After projecting the recruiting activities needed, the admissions director can estimate the costs associated with each activity. Another estimate can be derived from past experience. If the school has typically spent about $1,200 per student recruited and it wants to recruit 100 students, it may need a marketing budget of $120,000. Of course, the school may find the per-student cost to be greater if the market is shrinking, or if competitive schools increase their marketing budgets. If the school institutes programs that are in high demand, the cost per student may decrease.

Of course, the school's task does not end with attracting and admitting the best possible students to its program. The school must fulfill its promises to its new students by providing orientation, instruction, support services, career development, and other appropriate services so that these students will become satisfied alumni and productive representatives of what the university offers.

## SUMMARY

Before the institution plans its marketing strategy, it needs to formulate an institutional strategy. Strategy formulation is the institution's effort to figure out its broad strategy for achieving its objectives. First, the institution examines its present offerings using portfolio analysis, rating each program on quality, market viability, and centrality to the institution's mission. Based on this assessment, the institution determines which programs to build, maintain, or drop.

Second, the institution examines potential new or modified programs and markets by using a program/market expansion matrix. This analysis helps to identify systematically the range of options the institution could explore.

Before developing its marketing strategy, the institution also needs to analyze its competition. Prospective students and donors have many options. The prospective student could choose another college or could decide to skip college and go to work. The prospective donor could donate to another worthy cause, or spend the money for some personal purpose. Educational institutions need to think broadly in identifying their competition. Once identified, the various competitors should be carefully studied to understand what they do well and how the institution should direct its efforts to maintain its attractiveness.

Once the institution determines the programs and markets it wants to emphasize, the institution proceeds to develop marketing strategies for each program market. Marketing strategy is the selection of one or more target-market segments, the choice of a competitive position, and the development of an effective marketing mix to reach and serve the chosen consumers.

Segmenting the market permits the institution to select and focus its efforts on the best segment or segments. The institution then positions itself to appeal to the desired segments. Positioning involves assessing the institution's current position, selecting the desired position, planning a strategy for achieving the desired position, and then implementing the strategy.

The institution develops an appropriate marketing mix to appeal to and serve its desired target markets. The marketing mix consists of the particular blend of programs, price, place, promotion, processes, physical facilities, and people that the institution uses to achieve its objectives in the target market.

## Notes

1. While academic institutions are often inclined to cut whole programs, in many instances the first and most appropriate action is to review the curriculum and make deliberate decisions about which courses are central, how the curriculum can be consolidated, and how the quality of these offerings can be improved. By offering the "right" number of sections of the "right" courses, optimally staffed, the institution may be able to maintain quality *and* programs. See William F. Massy, "Measuring Performance: How Colleges and Universities Can Set Meaningful Goals and Be Accountable," paper presented at the Second Annual Conference of the Forum for Higher Education Futures (October 1992); and Robert Zemsky, William F. Massy, and Penney Oedel, "On Reversing the Ratchet," *Change* (May/June 1993), pp. 56–62.

2. See Patricia J. Gumport, "The Contested Terrain of Academic Program Reduction," *Journal of Higher Education*, 64 (May/June 1993), pp. 283–311.

3. Robert Zemsky, William F. Massy, and Penney Oedel, "On Reversing the Ratchet," pp. 56–62.

4. Robert G. Cope, *Strategic Planning, Management, and Decision Making*, AAHE-ERIC/Higher Education Research Report No. 9, 1981 (Washington, DC: American Association for Higher Education, 1981), pp. 41–46.

5. See Gerald D. Newbould, "Product Portfolio Diagnosis for U.S. Universities," *Akron Business and Economic Review* (Spring 1980), p. 70.

6. These definitions differ somewhat from the definitions used by the Boston Consulting Group.

7. Robert Lay and John Maguire, "Identifying the Competition in Higher Education—Two Approaches," *College and University* (Fall 1980), pp. 53–65.

8. The discussion of Yale University draws on Robert J. Sternberg and Jeanne C. Davis, "Student Perceptions of Yale and Its Competitors," *College and University* (Spring 1978), pp. 262–279.

# III

# Understanding Markets

# 8

# Measuring and Forecasting Market Size

*Northwestern University enrolls 7,000 undergraduate students on its main campus on Lake Michigan in Evanston, Illinois. Most undergraduates live on or near campus. Full-time attendance is the norm, reinforced by the set tuition fee per quarter regardless of the number of courses taken. To attract top students and enable them to attend, the university has developed financial aid policies and resources that assist almost 60 percent of undergraduates.*

*The university's vice president for institutional relations,[1] who oversees the admissions office, became interested in easing access for older students, particularly women, to come to Northwestern as undergraduates. Historically, older students, even those who had once been undergraduates at Northwestern, had been discouraged from enrolling in undergraduate programs on the Evanston campus.*

*Instead, they were referred to classes offered in downtown Chicago under the Division of Continuing Education, which was renamed University College. University College offered evening courses and part-time schedules and tuition, but the downtown location was perceived as less safe and certainly less convenient for adults who lived close to the main campus in Evanston.*

*The vice president for institutional relations approved a study to determine how many women might be eligible for and interested in completing undergraduate degrees at Northwestern, and to determine their characteristics and preferences. His goal was to use this information to decide whether the number of potential applicants warranted a special program and staff, and what would be the most effective ways to attract and serve this group.*

---

When an educational institution wants to launch a new program, take steps to build enrollment, estimate the future need for more facilities, or determine appropriate goals for a fund-raising campaign, the question of estimating market demand arises. How many students would be interested in enrolling in the new program? In our institution? How many new students should we plan to accommodate? How many prospective donors are likely to give to the school?

Analyzing the marketplace includes three major tasks:

1. *Market measurement and forecasting*: determining the current and future size of the available market for the institution's programs and services
2. *Market segmentation*: determining the main groups making up a market in order to choose the best target groups to serve
3. *Consumer analysis*: determining the characteristics of consumers—specifically, their needs, perceptions, preferences, and behavior—in order to adapt the offer to these consumer characteristics

This chapter will address market measurement and forecasting. Chapter 9 deals with segmentation and targeting, and Chapter 10 with consumer analysis.

Market measurement consists of determining reasonably accurate, quantitative estimates of market demand. Arriving at such estimates calls for a combination of science, art, and luck, but the effort is worthwhile. An institution that has sound estimates can analyze market opportunities, plan the marketing effort, and evaluate marketing performance with greater accuracy. Educational institutions have excellent records of *past* demand in their admissions, registration, and development office files. They often rely on records of past demand or on the experience of other similar institutions to estimate future demand for their programs and services. For example, a school that received 1,000 applications each year for the past five years would anticipate receiving about the same number of applications this year. The development office may expect donations to consistently equal or surpass those of previous years as long as the staff carries out the same activities. These are examples of *trend extrapolation* (discussed in Chapter 5).

Although keeping and reviewing these data about the past is important, the institution cannot rely on the past to predict the future. Such estimates can prove faulty if underlying forces affecting demand should change. For example, in the early 1990s fewer students were selecting undergraduate majors in business and there was a decline in interest in M.B.A. degrees, after strong student demand in the 1980s. Only by monitoring trends in the institution's own data, national trends, and underlying factors influencing the marketplace can the institution make good estimates of future demand and make decisions about how to attract more students or adjust to smaller enrollments.

Some schools err by looking at the success of other schools in attracting students to new programs and concluding that, by offering the same programs, they could attract equal numbers of students. This conclusion may be accurate or faulty, depending on how prospective students perceive the competing institutions and on the total number of prospects. If the total demand is very small, perhaps one institution can adequately meet the demand, leaving the other institutions to divide up a very small number of students, making the new program unattractive. If the institution could determine the maximum number of potentially interested students, it could evaluate its probability of success in entering this new area.

Educational institutions vary in the level of demand they can serve or wish to serve. The institution's resources (faculty, residence halls, library, and so on) may limit the number of students that can be served. The typical institution wants to enroll a specific number of students, neither more than can be well served nor less than required to ensure that resources are effectively utilized. A highly selective school usually wants to generate a large number of applicants to permit selection of those who best match the school's desired characteristics. Such a school will want estimates of how many students have these characteristics and are potentially interested in attending. Or an educational institution plans to launch a new program or service and wants to be sure that an adequate number of participants exists and can be induced to enroll.

In contrast, public elementary and secondary schools and many community colleges are obligated to serve all those who enroll. Such institutions don't need to generate more demand, but they must be able to predict demand in order to determine the number of teachers, classrooms, and other resources that will be required.

Other institutions want to maximize participation and will expand facilities and offerings to meet whatever level of demand materializes. Such institutions often would like to know the maximum market potential for their programs, so they can assess how much of the market they are attracting and can anticipate likely expansion needs. The institution's development office will want to develop good estimates of potential annual giving to assess the effectiveness of its efforts. A successful capital campaign depends on sound estimates of giving potential from major donors in order to establish the overall campaign goal and to assure a strong start to fund raising.

Market measurement and forecasting can be used by educational institutions to answer three key questions:

1. *Who is the market?* Defining who is "in the market" assists in determining market size and in designing and promoting programs for them.

2. *How large is the current market?* Measuring the current market demand for a program or service helps the institution set realistic expectations for enrollment or participation.

3. *What is the likely future size of the market?* Market forecasting permits the institution to plan ahead. For example, if market demand is likely to drop, a school may prepare to cut back staff or may strive to develop programs that will attract more students. If demand is growing, the institution can plan a response.

These three questions are examined in the following sections.

## DEFINING THE MARKET

Every institution faces the task of defining who is "in its market." A college realizes that not everyone is in the market for a college education. Of those who do want a college education, some will not attend at all or will attend another institution. Therefore, each institution must distinguish between its potential customers and noncustomers.

An institution's market depends on what the institution has to offer. Consider the case of a small private college. We can talk about the market for the college's bachelor's degree, or for its sociology major, or for its specific course on the sociology of religion. The definition of the market will vary in each of the three situations. The more precisely we can define the offer, the more explicitly we can determine the market's boundaries and size.

A market is the set of actual and potential customers for a market offer. The *customers* could be applicants, students, participants, donors, or any other appropriate category. The term *market offer* represents a service, program, idea, product—in fact, anything that might be offered to a market.

When we say that individuals are "in the market" for something, we mean that they are interested in acquiring a particular good or service, that they have the money (or credit) to pay for it, and that they have access to what they want to buy—they know where to go and they are able to get there. These three characteristics—*interest, income,* and *access*—define who is in the market. To illustrate this, we return to the situation described at the beginning of this chapter.

Northwestern University is thinking of establishing a program for returning students to attract women over 25 to attend the university to complete undergraduate degrees. The vice president wants to determine whether enough women in the community would be in the market to justify establishing a special admissions program.

Who is in the over-25 female market for an undergraduate degree at Northwestern University? Two market research studies were carried out to answer this question: (1) derivation of an estimate of the potential market based on available secondary data;[2] and (2) a survey of members of area women's organizations to determine the characteristics, preferences, and requirements of members of such groups who might consider attending Northwestern to complete undergraduate degrees.[3] Some of the examples in this chapter draw on these studies.

The first task is to estimate the total potential market. A first estimate of market size would be the number of women over 25 in the community with a potential interest in completing an undergraduate degree. We define the *potential market* as follows:

> The *potential market* is the set of consumers who have some level of interest in a defined market offer.

Now, interest alone is not enough to define the market. If people have to pay something, potential consumers must have adequate income (or loans or other financial aid) to afford the purchase. They must be able as well as willing to buy. Furthermore, the higher the price, the fewer people will remain in the market. The total market size is further reduced if there are barriers that prevent prospects from taking advantage of the opportunity. For example, a survey of women interested in attending college found that attending daytime classes was a problem for 77 percent; for 42 percent, commuting to the campus was a problem. These access problems will make the market smaller. The market that now remains is called the *available market*:

> The *available market* is the set of consumers who have interest, income, and access to a particular market offer.

In some instances, the institution may establish restrictions on whom it will serve. A college may sell football tickets to everyone who wishes to attend a game, but may be unwilling to accept everyone who applies for admission as a student. Northwestern was particularly interested in attracting women over 25 years of age, with strong academic potential. These women constitute the Northwestern's *qualified available market*:

> The *qualified available market* is the set of consumers who have interest, income, access, and qualifications for the particular market offer.

Now the university has the choice of going after the whole qualified available market or of concentrating its efforts on certain segments. We define the *served market* as follows:

> The *served market* is the part of the qualified available market that the institution puts effort into attracting and serving.

Suppose the university has very limited residence hall space and financial aid. It would then want to attract women who live within commuting distance of the campus who can afford to attend with little or no financial aid.

As a result, it might choose to promote the program primarily through local women's organizations whose members are primarily upper-middle and upper class. In this example, the served market is smaller than the qualified available market.

After the program was established, the program attracted an actual number of women, who represent a part of the served market. Those who actually enroll are called the *penetrated market*:

> The *penetrated market* is the set of consumers that are actually consuming the market offer.

Figure 8-1 brings all the preceding concepts together. The bar on the left illustrates the ratio of the potential market—all interested persons—to the total population, here 10 percent. The bar on the right shows several breakdowns of the potential market. In the figure, the available market—those who have interest, income, and access—constitutes 40 percent of the potential consumers. The qualified available market—those who would meet the institution's admissions requirements—is 20 percent of the potential market, or 50 percent of the available market. Suppose the institution is actively trying to attract half of these; that would be 10 percent of the potential market. Finally, the figure shows that the institution is actually enrolling 5 percent of the potential market.

FIGURE 8-1    Levels of market definition

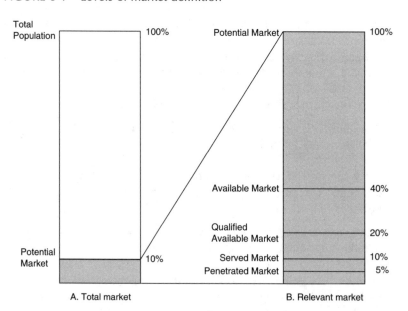

FIGURE 8-2    An admissions funnel

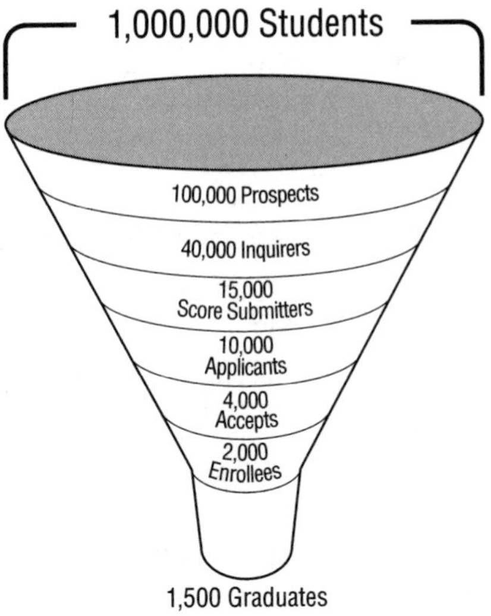

1,000,000 Students

100,000 Prospects

40,000 Inquirers

15,000
Score Submitters

10,000
Applicants

4,000
Accepts

2,000
Enrollees

1,500 Graduates

These concepts are directly comparable to an *admissions funnel* (Figure 8-2), which illustrates the fact that a school has a large number of prospects, some of whom become interested and apply. Of this group, the school admits some smaller number, some of whom actually decide to enroll. The majority of these students ultimately graduate and become alumni of the school.

These definitions of a market are useful in marketing planning. If the institution is dissatisfied with the size of its penetrated market, it can consider several actions, some described in Chapter 7. First, it could try to attract a larger percentage of people from its served market (market penetration). If it finds, however, that the nonenrolling part of the served market has decided to attend college elsewhere, the institution may seek to widen its served market by promoting the program in other nearby communities (geographical expansion). Some institutions may choose to relax the qualifications for admission in order to expand the qualified available market.

The next step would be to consider expanding the available market by lowering tuition or giving more financial aid, improving the convenience of the location and time of course offerings, and doing other things to reduce cost and make the program more accessible. Ultimately, the institution could try to expand the potential market by launching a campaign to persuade women uninterested in attending college that they should consider attending college, expecting that some of the women would consider attending the institution sponsoring the campaign.

## MEASURING CURRENT MARKET DEMAND

We are now ready to examine practical methods of estimating current market demand. A typical educational institution will want to make three types of estimates: *total market demand, area market demand,* and *institution market share.*

## ESTIMATING TOTAL MARKET DEMAND

*Total market demand* is defined as follows:

*Total market demand* for a given product, program, or service is the total volume that would be bought by a defined consumer group in a defined geographical area in a defined time period in a defined marketing environment under a defined marketing program.

Note that total market demand is not one fixed number but depends upon what is being offered, to whom, where, and in what time period. A change in one of these could change the demand. For example, some educational institutions and programs attract more applicants and students during periods of recession than during prosperous times. Students may decide to go to a local community college to study technical and other vocational subjects. Adults may take more leisure courses because the cost of other entertainment is harder to justify. At the same time, prestigious institutions often find that their applications increase as students decide that a top-quality degree may help them stay ahead during future hard times.

The institution's marketing program also can influence demand. The marketing program includes the programs and services offered, their prices and financial aid, the level of expenditures on promotion, and other factors. In most instances, increasing promotional expenditures will yield higher levels of demand—at an increasing rate at first, then slowing down. Beyond a certain level, raising promotional expenditures will not stimulate much further demand, which suggests that market demand has an upper limit, the *market potential.*

We can think of two extreme types of markets. The size of an *expansible market,* such as the market for leisure courses, is likely to be strongly affected by the level of promotional expenditures. On the other hand, a *nonexpansible market,* such as the market for doctoral studies in astronomy, will not be much affected by the level of promotional expenditures. If an institution finds that a market is nonexpansible, it may choose to enter another market and offer different programs, or it may decide to concentrate its efforts on getting a desired share of the existing market. For example, a university offering a doctoral program in astronomy may accept the fact that the number of people who want to study for doctorates in astronomy is stable, that the level of *primary demand* is fixed. The astronomy department may then concentrate on getting a desired percentage of those students who do want to do graduate work in astronomy to enroll in the department rather than to go to another institution. The department thus strives to create *selective demand* for its own program rather than for studying astronomy in general. Creating selective demand is often much more complex that simply increasing promotional efforts. For the university's astronomy department to increase its share of the market for doctoral study in astronomy, the department typically must have some competitive advantage over other astronomy departments.

Once an institution has defined its product, consumer group, geographical area, time period, environment, and basic marketing program, it can then develop a *market forecast*, the expected market demand associated with a defined set of factors.

One straightforward approach to estimating demand is the *chain-ratio method*. The chain-ratio method is conceptually similar to the earlier example (in Figure 8-1) and the admissions funnel (Figure 8-2), which show how the market can be progressively narrowed until the market definition includes the subset of the total market that the institution wants to attract. The chain-ratio method involves multiplying a base number by a succession of percentages that lead to the defined consumer set.

To illustrate the method, we will return to the question facing the vice president for institutional relations: How many women over 25 living near the Evanston campus are likely to have the time, money, and ability to complete undergraduate degrees at Northwestern, yet have not already completed college? This question is rather complex, but existing data were located that permitted a useful estimate of market size.[4] Table 8-1 shows the calculations.

Census and other population data indicated that approximately 10,300 upper-income women between the ages of 25 and 44 lived in the vicinity of Northwestern. This number was multiplied by 0.5, an estimate of the percentage who would have the intellectual ability to succeed at Northwestern, to give 5,150.[5]

But census data do not provide the most crucial information: the prevalence of college noncompletion by upper-socioeconomic-status women with high intellectual ability. A large-scale national longitudinal survey, Project TALENT, found that 29 percent of the high-ability, high-income women in their study had not completed college five years after high school graduation.[6] Multiplying 0.29 by 5,150 yielded an estimate of 1,493 women.

This number probably underestimates the total potential market, since it includes only five of the several nearby communities and only includes women living in census tracts with quite high family incomes. At the same time, it is important to remember that these women may or may not be inter-

TABLE 8-1    Estimating the market potential for an undergraduate education at Northwestern University among North Shore women between ages 25 and 45

|  | TOTAL FORECASTED POPULATION, 1980 |
|---|---|
| 1. *Base market (demographic)* | |
| North Shore communities | |
| (Evanston, Glencoe, Kenilworth, Wilmette, and Winnetka) | 138,000 |
| 2. *Population of census tracts with median 1970 income* | |
| *over $15,000 (demographic)* | 87,400 |
| 3. *Females 25 to 44 (demographic)* | 10,300 |
| 4. *% upper quartile on IQ* | |
| Given the strong relationship between IQ and SES, | |
| probably close to 50% | |
| 50% x 10,300 | 5,150 |
| 5. *% females 25 to 44 in top quartile on SES, in top quartile* | |
| *of age cohort on academic aptitude, and who did not complete* | |
| *college within five years after high school graduation* | |
| Probability of a female (top quartile on SES and academic | |
| aptitudes) graduating from a four-year college within five | |
| years after high school is 0.71. Thus, probability of | |
| noncompletion is 0.29 | |
| 0.29 x 5,150 | 1,493 |
| 6. *% interested in attending college (stage of readiness)* | |
| (Some will decide to continue working, doing volunteer work, etc.) | ? |
| 7. *% interested in attending Northwestern (loyalty status)* | ? |
| 8. *Further corrections must be made for:* | |
| % able to arrange for household help, transportation, family agreement | |
| % willing to cope with application process | |

Source: Karen F. A. Fox, *Attracting a New Market to Northwestern's Undergraduate Programs: Older Women Living on the North Shore* (Evanston, IL: Northwestern University Program on Women, 1979).

ested in completing college. Many of these women may be busy with family responsibilities, community activities, or careers, and see no advantage in returning for a college degree. Those who are interested in college may prefer to go to another institution. Even a highly motivated applicant may be discouraged by the application process, the unavailability of a particular major, or some other act or omission by the university.

The chain-ratio method indicated that at least 1,500 women were potential students for Northwestern. The university decided to develop a special program to encourage them to enroll, including a special admissions counselor, a streamlined admissions process, and a more flexible tuition pricing system since many did not want to attend full-time and pay full tuition. The program subsequently broadened to become the Returning Adult

Program, for women and men who have been out of high school for seven or more years.

### Estimating Demand in a Geographical Area

The market for a particular program or service will vary from one geographical area to another. Women who live within commuting distance of Northwestern would be the most interested in attending, while those who would have to relocate might decide to attend another college or not attend at all. Most institutions want to determine which geographical areas deserve the most attention—usually those having the highest market demand.

There are several ways to estimate the relative attractiveness of different geographical areas. We will illustrate these in connection with the following situation:

St. Clare's School is a Catholic elementary school in Easton. The principal believes that the school is not reaching all the Catholic children in the area, and that additional students might come from nearby communities, including Spencer and Dobbs. The principal wants to identify the areas that have the highest potential for providing additional students.

Four methods of estimating area market demand in a geographical area will be described in the following paragraphs.

**Analysis of Current Enrollment.** A common approach is to study the geographical areas that current students come from. The principal can obtain a large wall map of the surrounding area and have pins or dots placed to show the location of homes of current students. It may be found that of the 15 percent who live outside Easton, 6 percent come from Spencer, 3 percent come from Dobbs, and 6 percent come from other communities.

The conclusion may be that Spencer is a better market than Dobbs and that the school should focus recruiting efforts on Spencer. This conclusion would be premature. Current area enrollment figures reflect not only differences in market potential but also differences in market cultivation. The school may be better known in Spencer, or the pastor of the Catholic parish in Spencer may encourage parents to send their children to the school. Spencer may have a larger population or a higher percentage of children than Dobbs. Perhaps the principal should be impressed that any Dobbs parents send their children to St. Clare's, since they have not received as much school publicity and encouragement as have parents in Spencer.

Furthermore, even if Spencer has twice as much market potential as Dobbs, it does not follow that Spencer should get twice as much marketing effort. It may deserve three times the effort, equal effort, or less effort. The decision should be based on estimates of how much response would occur in each community as a result of additional promotional effort.

**One-Factor Index.** Here the principal would try to discover a single measurable factor that would reflect the market potential of different communities. Suppose the principal believes that the best single indicator of market potential for Catholic school attendance is the number of Catholic families in the community. Using this criterion, if Spencer has 400 Catholic families and Dobbs has 200, we could argue that Spencer deserves more marketing effort—indeed, twice the effort given to Dobbs. Or the principal might choose a different single-factor index: the total number of children in Catholic families in the town.

**Multiple-Factor Index.** The principal may decide that it would be unwise to rely entirely on a single factor. Instead, two or more factors may better indicate each community's market potential. The problem is to form an index that combines these factors. Suppose the principal believes that two factors are highly associated with interest in attending St. Clare's: (1) the number of Catholic families, and (2) the number of families with incomes over $30,000. Suppose the principal cannot obtain the statistics on two variables combined. Table 8-2 shows how a multiple-factor index can be formed.

The rows list the communities within commuting distance of St. Clare's School. The first two columns list the two factors. The third and fourth columns convert these two factors into percentages expressing each community's share of the total of each column. Thus, Spencer has 20 percent of the Catholic families in the area and 10 percent of the families earning over $30,000. We can take a simple average of the two percentage figures for each community and call this the multiple-factor index number. Spencer can be said to have about 15 percent of the market potential, whereas Dobbs has 25

TABLE 8-2    Multiple-factor index

|  | (1)  NUMBER OF  CATHOLIC  FAMILIES | (2)  NUMBER OF  FAMILIES  EARNING MORE  THAN $80,000 | (3)  PERCENT OF  CATHOLIC  FAMILIES[a] | (4)  PERCENT  EARNING MORE  THAN $30,000[b] | (5)  MULTIPLE-  FACTOR  INDEX[c] |
|---|---|---|---|---|---|
| Spencer | 400 | 200 | 20% | 10% | 15 |
| Dobbs | 200 | 800 | 10% | 40% | 25 |
| . | . | . | . | . | . |
| . | . | . | . | . | . |
| . | . | . | . | . | . |
| Total | 2,000 | 2,000 | | | |

[a] This value for Spencer is calculated by dividing 400 by 2,000 (the total number of Catholic families in the region) to yield 20 percent.
[b] This value is calculated for Spencer by dividing 200 by 2,000 to yield 10 percent.
[c] This value is calculated for Spencer by adding the percentages in columns 3 and 4, and then dividing by 2 ((20% + 10%)/2 = 15).

percent. These numbers can be used to guide the percentage of the promotion budget and effort to expend in each community.

The multiple-factor index can be refined in several ways. First, the principal may want to use more than two factors, which would require additional columns. Second, perhaps unequal weights should be assigned to the factors instead of taking a simple average. For example, the percentage of Catholic families might be weighted double because the principal feels it is a much more important factor than level of family income. Third, some of the factors may be impossible to express in percentage terms, and it may be necessary to convert all the row numbers using standard scales (say, 1 to 10 on a ten-point scale), which are then weighted. The general approach described here is the same one used to determine the *index of consumer buying power* that businesses use to assess the market potential of various geographical areas.[7]

**Distance-Adjusted Index.** A potential consumer's interest in a program or service is likely to vary depending on how far he or she must travel to obtain it. Most people view travel as a cost—in time and money—and will choose sources nearer their homes when possible. Studies confirm that market potential drops with distance from the site of the offer.[8] For example, over 90 percent of first-time college students attend an institution within 500 miles of their homes.[9]

One simple way to make an adjustment for distance would be to arbitrarily reduce the multiple-factor index value by a fixed number of percentage points for every unit of distance. For example, most of the residents of Spencer are about seven miles from St. Clare's, whereas Dobbs is about four miles from the school. The principal might deduct one percentage point for every mile of distance between the community and the school. Spencer's multiple-factor index would drop from 15 to 8, and Dobbs' index would be reduced from 25 to 21. Thus, Dobbs has 2.6 times greater potential for enrolling children in St. Clare's than does Spencer (21 ÷ 8).

## Estimating the Institution's Share of the Market

Knowing the level of one institution's enrollment or endowment does not tell the whole story. Institutions may want to compare their performance with that of competitors to determine how well they are doing.

An institution can estimate at least three different measures of its market share. Ideally, the institution should determine its (1) share of the total market, (2) share of the served market, and (3) share relative to the leading competitor or leading three competitors. Each of these market-share figures yields useful information about the institution's market performance and potential. The data from the Enrollment Planning Service provide some useful estimates of the first measure, while the other two can be determined from published enrollment statistics and/or from questionnaires to admitted students, both those who enroll at the college and those who decide to attend elsewhere. Development officers can obtain published statistics on fundraising levels at other institutions as a basis for comparison, as well as internal statistics on what percentage of prospects in each donor category (alumni, parents, and so on) actually gave.

## FORECASTING FUTURE MARKET DEMAND

Having looked at estimating current demand, we are now ready to examine the problem of forecasting future demand. The ease of accurate forecasting varies widely from one educational service or program to another. For example, the number of first graders in a school district can often be estimated quite accurately two or three years ahead of time, since the eligible children have already been born. The forecasts must take into account migration in and out of the area and possible competition from other schools with first-grade classes.

Many public school districts have computer-based models—some are straightforward spreadsheet programs—to forecast projected enrollment, types of instructional programs needed, and costs. These models can consider population shifts in various parts of the district, teacher salary distributions, and other factors, and can determine whether a certain school should be closed, new facilities built, or how many teachers and classrooms will be needed and when.[10]

Other educational institutions find that the total market demand and specific institution demand for educational services change significantly from one year to the next, making good forecasting much more challenging and more important. Poor forecasting may mean that too many teachers and staff have been hired and excess capacity is wasted, or, on the other hand, that there is not enough of either. The more unstable the demand, the more critical is forecast accuracy.

The process of forecasting begins with listing all the factors that might affect future demand, then predicting each factor's likely future level and effect on demand. Three broad categories are (1) *noncontrollable macroenvironmental factors*, such as the state of the economy, new technologies, and changes in regulations; (2) *competitive factors*, such as tuition levels at other institutions, new programs, and promotional expenditures; and (3) *institutional factors*, such as the institution's own tuition level, programs, and promotional expenditures.

A forecast of future demand is always an approximation. A forecast can be based on *what people say, what people do,* or *what people have done in the past.* Determining what people say involves conducting *consumer intentions surveys* or getting estimates from people who are likely to know about market trends (*intermediary estimates*). Building a forecast on what people do involves *market testing*, promoting the institution or program and measuring the response. Determining what people have done involves using statistical tools to analyze records of past buying behavior, using either *time-series analysis* or *statistical demand analysis*. Descriptions of these five methods follow.

## Surveying Consumers About Their Plans

Demand can be estimated by asking a sample of prospective consumers (students, parents, donors, and so on) to state their relevant plans. Asking about these plans can be done in several ways. A "yes-or-no" form of the question requires a definite response. Some researchers prefer to give a range of responses: "Will you (a) definitely enroll, (b) probably enroll, (c) probably not enroll, (d) definitely not enroll in classes here next year?" These researchers feel that the "definitely enrolls" would be a fairly dependable minimum estimate, and some fraction of the "probably enrolls" could be added to arrive at a forecast.

More recently, some researchers have recommended using a full purchase probability scale:

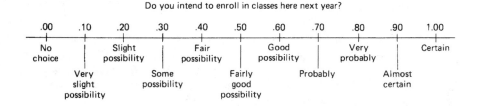

The researcher uses various fractions of the positive responders to form an estimate of the total demand. Afterwards the forecasted enrollment should be compared to actual enrollment to determine what weights would have improved the forecast. These weights can then be applied in subsequent years.

## Asking People Close to Consumers

A forecast can be developed by asking people who are close to the consumers what those consumers are likely to do. For example, the public school district trying to estimate first-grade enrollment for the following year may ask each elementary school principal for an estimate for the school. The principal is likely to know of plans for new construction, population shifts, parental attitudes, and other factors affecting enrollment.

Asking people close to consumers for their estimates is called *grass-roots forecasting*. The grass-roots forecasters should be given a set of basic assumptions about the upcoming year, such as the state of the economy and the institution's anticipated marketing plans, rather than allowing each forecaster to make his or her own assumptions about influences on demand.

## Testing the Market

A direct *market test* can help forecast the attractiveness of a new program or service, or the probable attractiveness of an established one that will be offered in a new format or location. A market test consists of setting up a new program on a small scale (or in one or a few locations) as a test of the program's feasibility and attractiveness before enlarging the program's scale or extending it to additional locations. Market tests are especially valuable when consumer intentions surveys or intermediary estimates are unreliable, for example, when a college wants to launch a new program that is expected to appeal to a broad market. In this instance, the college does not need to know the total market size, but does want to assure that there are "enough" people to launch the program. Methods for conducting a market test are discussed in Chapter 11.

## Predicting Future Demand from Statistics on Consumers' Past Behavior

**Time-Series Analysis.** Instead of surveys or market tests, some institutions forecast market demand using *time-series analysis*. This approach uses statistical analysis of data from past time periods to reveal trends that can be used to predict future demand. Time-series analysis is an extension of trend extrapolation, presented in Chapter 5.

A time series of past enrollment in a program can be analyzed into four major components: The first component, *trend* ($T$), reflects the basic level and rate of change in the size of the market, and is determined by fitting a straight or curved line through the time-series data. The past trend line can be extrapolated to estimate next year's trend level.

A second component, *cycle* ($C$), might also be observed in a time series. Enrollment and donations may be affected by periodic swings in general economic activity. If economic conditions can be predicted for the next period, they can be used to adjust the trend value up or down.

A third component, *season* ($S$), reflects any consistent pattern of applications, enrollments, or donations within a particular time period. The term *season* refers to any recurrent hourly, daily, weekly, monthly, or quarterly pattern. The seasonal component may be related to weather factors, holidays, and so on. The researcher would adjust the estimate for, say, a particular month by the known seasonal level for that month. For example, people are more likely to make donations in certain months due to tax considerations.

The fourth component, *erratic events* $(E)$, includes strikes, blizzards, fads, riots, fire, war scares or wars, entry of new competitors, and other non-recurring events. This erratic component represents everything that remains unanalyzed in the time series and that cannot be predicted. Therefore, it shows the average size of the error that is likely to persist in time-series forecasting. If the error due to erratic events is large, then time-series analysis will probably not provide useful estimates and some other method should be used.

Here is an example of how time-series analysis works:

The alumni director wants to estimate how many people to expect for an alumni weekend next year. Last year 2,300 alumni, family members, and guests participated. The long-term trend, going back several years, shows that attendance has grown about 5 percent per year. This implies that attendance next year would be 2,415 (=2,300 x 1.05). But the economy has been in a downturn, which has typically reduced attendance by 20 percent. This means attendance next year will likely be 1,932 (=2,415 x 0.80). If there is an airline strike, this could reduce the number of out-of-state attendees, which could lower the total by another 15 percent, so the anticipated number of attendees would be between 1,932 (if no strike) and 1,642. Therefore, the alumni director decides to plan for 1,932 and to monitor the airline situation in order to anticipate any likelihood of a strike. Of course, if there is a significant earthquake in the vicinity of the university shortly before the alumni weekend, then the entire event would have to be canceled because virtually no one would attend.

**Statistical Demand Analysis.**   Numerous factors affect the number of consumers of a program or service. *Statistical demand analysis* is a set of statistical procedures designed to discover the most important factors affecting enrollment (or donations) and their relative influence. The factors most commonly analyzed in the case of enrollment are academic ability, family income, age, and promotional expenditures.

Statistical demand analysis consists of expressing enrollment $(E)$ as a dependent variable and trying to explain variation in enrollment as a result of variation in a number of independent demand variables. Multiple regression analysis can be used to statistically fit various equation forms to the data to determine the factors and equations that give the best prediction.[11]

Louisiana State University has used the number of score reports it receives from the American College Testing Program (ACT) as an indicator of the level of student commitment to enroll.[12] Since the typical applicant requests that scores be sent to one or more colleges, the student is indicating something about his or her college intentions. Louisiana State used the following equation to predict how many new freshman students would enroll in a given year:

$$E = (0.4775)SR1 + (0.1022)SR2 + (0.0720)SR3$$
$$+ (0.0756)(SR4 + SR5 + SR6) + (0.4196)SR7$$

where $E$ represents the projected enrollment, SR1 through SR6 are the number of test score reports received that indicate Louisiana State as first through sixth choice, and SR7 is the number of supplemental reports. The coefficients equal the percentage of each choice category that has enrolled at Louisiana State in past years. This particular equation is unique to Louisiana State; other institutions would have to calculate their own coefficients based on several years of tracking reports.

## SUMMARY

Marketing managers need measures of current and future market size in order to plan. A market is the set of actual and potential consumers of a market offer. To be "in the market," a person must have interest, income, and access to the market offer. The marketer's task is to analyze the various levels of the market, including the potential market, available market, qualified available market, served market, and penetrated market.

The next step is to estimate the size of the current demand. Total current demand can be estimated using the chain-ratio method, multiplying a base number by a succession of appropriate percentages to arrive at the defined market. Market demand for a geographical area can be estimated in four ways: area analysis of current enrollment (or applications or donations), one-factor indexes, multiple-factor indexes, or distance-adjusted indexes. Finally, the institution should compare its performance to similar educational institutions to determine whether its market share is improving or declining.

To estimate future demand, the institution can use one or any combination of five forecasting methods: surveys of consumer plans, estimates by people close to consumers, tests of the market, time-series analysis, or statistical demand analysis.

Determining present demand and estimating future demand permit the institution to assess current performance, test the viability of proposed new programs, and plan for needed resources to support future activities.

## Notes

1. William I. Ihlanfeldt.
2. Karen F. A. Fox, *Attracting a New Market to Northwestern's Undergraduate Programs: Older Women Living on the North Shore* (Evanston, IL: Northwestern University Program on Women, 1979).
3. Yvonne Johns, *A Survey of Older Women as Candidates for Re-Entry at Northwestern University* (Evanston, IL: Northwestern University Program on Women, 1979).
4. Fox, *Attracting a New Market.*
5. Personal communication from Dr. Lauress Wise of Project TALENT.

6. John G. Claudy, "Educational Outcomes Five Years after High School," paper presented at the Annual Meeting of the American Educational Research Association, 1971.

7. See "Putting the Four to Work," *Sales Management*, October 28, 1974, pp. 13ff.

8. See George Schwartz, *Development of Marketing Theory* (Cincinnati, OH: Southwestern, 1963), pp. 9–63.

9. Alexander W. Astin, M. R. King, and G. T. Richardson, *The American Freshman: National Norms for Fall 1977* (Los Angeles, CA: Higher Education Research Institute, Graduate School of Education, University of California, and the Cooperative Institutional Research Program, American Council on Education, December 1993), p. 11.

10. Janet Weiner, "Enrollment Projections: Plan the Future," *The Executive Educator* (December 1980), pp. 34, 39.

11. See William F. Massy, "Statistical Analysis of Relations between Variables," in David A. Aaker, ed., *Multivariate Analysis in Marketing: Theory and Applications* (Belmont, CA: Wadsworth, 1971), pp. 5–35.

12. James H. Wharton, Jerry L. Baudin, and Ordel Griffith, "The Importance of Accurate Enrollment Projections for Planning," *Phi Delta Kappan* (May 1981), pp. 652–655.

# 9

# Segmenting, Selecting, and Appealing to Markets

*What are you doing tomorrow morning before breakfast—or after midnight?*

*If the answer is "sleeping," you're out of step with a growing number of busy, very eager learners who are snatching a little more education during odd hours of the day and night.*

*Officials of Triton College and Technical Institute, a public community college in a western suburb of Chicago, noticed that their daytime computer-operator courses were overflowing. They decided to launch an experimental series of technical courses running from 11:30 P.M. to 3:30 A.M. to meet the schedule needs of second-shift factory workers, but the college found the appeal was broader than they first imagined. Triton has more recently begun a 7 A.M. "breakfast college" of 50-minute courses in every field from yoga and algebra to philosophy and investing. Its pitch, with apologies to American Express, is: "Education— don't leave for work without it."*

*Sandwiching education into odd hours has advantages, but it usually calls for adjustments. Jim Jenkins, who signed up for Triton's nighttime machine-tool course earlier this year, reports that the choice of parking places near the class at that hour was superb—"no more of that driving around, waiting for someone to leave a space." But he says he had his regrets about leaving his wife with the chore of getting up every few hours to tend their infant son.*

*The hardest part, says Mr. Jenkins, was getting up after only three hours of post-class sleep to get to his 7 A.M. first-shift job. But between having an "excellent teacher who kept us awake" and catnaps at other hours of the day, he says he now is eager to sign up for an advanced machine-tool course on the same "night owl" schedule.*

**Source:** Lucia Mouat, "When Night School Means College Courses at 2 A.M.," *The Christian Science Monitor*, July 21, 1981, p. 2. Reprinted by permission from *The Christian Science Monitor* © 1981. The Christian Science Publishing Society. All Rights Reserved.

---

Instead of trying to serve everyone, most schools should identify the most attractive parts of the market that they could effectively serve. Triton College provides special courses to serve the "middle-of-the-night" and "breakfast" segments of the community college student market, as well as day students.

Not all institutions segment the market and focus their efforts on a specific segment or segments. Three styles are possible:

**One-Size-Fits-All (Mass) Marketing.** A school could offer one curriculum and try to convince all potential students that this curriculum is best. This is an example of mass marketing, where the institution produces and distributes one market offer and attempts to attract every eligible person to use it. The mass marketer pays little or no attention to potential differences in consumer preferences, but assumes that they are all alike. This approach is more typical of precollegiate institutions, where there may be more agreement about what students should learn.

**Program-Differentiated Marketing.** An institution using program-differentiated marketing offers two or more programs and, like a cafeteria, invites people to select what they want. The programs might differ in quality, content, or other features. In fact, almost all colleges and universities employ program-differentiated marketing by offering different major fields of study. The institution with differentiated programs hopes that each potential consumer will find something suitable among its varied offerings. Many large public educational institutions are committed to this approach, since their mandates are to meet a broad range of educational interests and needs.

**Focused (Target) Marketing.** The most tailored approach to satisfying a market comes from focusing the institution's efforts on identifying and serving a particular *target market*. The institution distinguishes among the different segments that make up the market, chooses one or more of these segments to focus on, and develops market offers specifically to meet the

FIGURE 9-1   Steps in market segmentation, targeting, and positioning

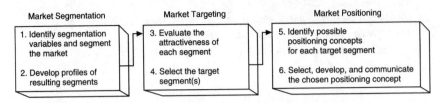

needs of each selected target market. For example, the school could develop a program specifically for talented young musicians, emphasizing performance skills and including attendance at musical events in the United States and Europe. The college could focus on providing a classical education centered around the Great Books.

Educational needs and preferences are so varied that many educational institutions adopt either a mass-marketing or a program-differentiated marketing approach. Educators should, however, seriously consider the potential contribution of target marketing. Target marketing can provide at least three benefits:

1. *The institution can spot market opportunities better when it is aware of different segments and their needs.* By monitoring these segments, the institution can note those whose needs are not fully met by existing offers.
2. *The institution can make finer adjustments of its programs to match the desires of the market.* It can interview members of the target market to determine their specific needs and desires and how the existing programs should be changed.
3. *The institution can make finer adjustments of its prices, distribution channels, and promotional mix.* Instead of trying to reach all potential consumers with a single approach, the institution can create separate marketing programs aimed at each distinct target market.

To use target marketing, the institution must complete three major steps, shown in Figure 9-1. The first is *segmenting the market*, identifying and profiling distinct meaningful groups of consumers which might require or prefer marketing mixes. The second step is *market targeting*, selecting one or more market segments to serve. The third step is *market positioning*, the act of establishing and communicating the institution's key benefits to its various constituencies. This chapter describes the major concepts and tools for market segmentation, targeting, and positioning.

## SEGMENT THE MARKET

Educational institutions segment their markets, often without conscious reflection. The markets of an educational institution typically consist of current students, alumni, donors, faculty, and people the institution hopes to add to these categories. Institutions of higher education are organized to address these groups: for students, the dean of students and/or the vice-president for student services and staff; for alumni, the alumni association; for donors, the development office; for the staff, the staff committee and the human resources department; and, for the faculty, the provost or vice-president for academic affairs and the faculty senate. This is a basic example of market segmentation, dividing the school's internal and external markets into relatively homogeneous subgroups, and designating marketing managers to serve them.

People differ in age, income, preferences, academic ability, geographical location, and other characteristics. Market segmentation makes sense when we can identify common interests and preferences, and then respond in valued ways to identifiable groups of people. Colleges already segment students by their academic interests into majors, and faculty are divided into departments by their fields of specialization.

Suppose a college is particularly interested in prospective students' preferences for two attributes, academic rigor and active social life, in order to identify *preference segments*. Three possible patterns could emerge:

*Shared preferences.* Figure 9-2, A depicts the case where all the students have roughly the same preferences. The market shows no natural segments, at least as far as the two attributes are concerned. We would predict that if students in general had the same preference, colleges would closely resemble each other, because they would all have to please the same kind of student.

*Scattered preferences.* At the other extreme, individual student preferences may be so different that they would be scattered fairly evenly throughout the space with no area of concentration (Figure 9-2, B). We would predict that many different types of colleges would be needed to satisfy the diverse student market.

*Clustered preferences.* An intermediate possibility is the appearance of distinct preference clusters, called *natural market segments* (Figure 9-2, C).

FIGURE 9-2    Examples of market preference patterns

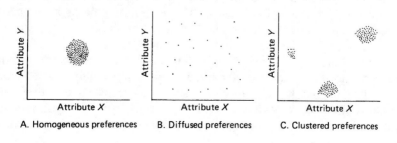

A. Homogeneous preferences    B. Diffused preferences    C. Clustered preferences

In this case, we would predict that three basic clusters of colleges would cater to the three types of students.

Thus, segmentation procedures could reveal the existence of natural market segments, or could be used to construct market segments, or could reveal the lack of any market segments. We now turn to examples of specific variables that can be used in segmenting consumer markets.

## Ways to Segment Markets

There is rarely only one way to segment a market. A market can be segmented using several different variables, singly and in combination, to see which suggest the most useful marketing opportunities. The decision maker's task is to use the best available research to determine which combination of variables yields the best segmentation approach. Some schools rely on intuition, which could be sound or simply rigid, traditional, and misleading. Faulty assumptions at the segmentation step can lead to bad decisions at the targeting and positioning steps that follow. For example, a private school might assume that working-class parents have lower aspirations for their children than do middle-class parents, when the reality may be that working-class parents have the same concerns about school discipline and achievement levels as do white middle-class parents.

Suppose a Catholic high school considered how to segment the potential student market, and identified the following attributes:

- *Religious affiliation*: Catholic, non-Catholic
- *Place of residence*: Inside the diocese, outside the diocese; or within three miles of the school, within three to ten miles, farther
- *Previous education*: Attended Catholic grade school, did not attend
- *Academic ability*: Top 20 percent, second 20 percent, middle 20 percent, bottom 40 percent
- *Ability to pay*: Full, some, none
- *Sex*: Female, male

If the high school is supported by the diocese, the school will probably have policies that give preference to Catholic residents of the diocese. Perhaps only in-diocese students who are in the top 60 percent in academic ability would receive preferential admission. The tuition may be kept moderately low, with scholarships for those unable to pay. Preference may be given to those students who attended Catholic elementary schools.

In contrast, a highly selective, independent Catholic boarding school may admit only girls in the top 20 percent in academic ability whose families can pay the full cost. If the school has vacant places, it may give preference to non-Catholic girls whose families can pay, rather than to Catholic girls who would need financial aid. Although both schools have segmented the market, each has selected different values of these variables to define the market segments they will serve.

Here we review the major geographical, demographic, psychographic, and behavioristic variables typically used in segmenting consumer markets, shown in Table 9-1. The choice of segmentation variables will, of course, depend upon the problem the institution seeks to clarify. The director of admissions will be interested in understanding the characteristics of applicants and enrollees, the director of development will be interested in the characteristics of current and prospective donors, and the director of alumni relations will be interested in the characteristics of alumni that might indicate the need for different types of alumni events and programs.

Most marketers are interested in segmenting a market on a *combination* of several segmentation variables, not just one. This approach is called *multivariable segmentation*. For example, the admissions director using the College Board's Enrollment Planning Service can look at prospective student segments defined by geographic location, ethnic background, family income, academic ability, and preferred major field of study to identify regions and specific high schools where their desired student segments are located. The development office will segment prospects for a major-gifts solicitation on loyalty status, net worth, and past donation history.

The alumni office will segment alumni based on age (year of graduation), region of the country, area of study, and other variables. For example, the Stanford University Alumni Association has over 100 clubs, designated by metropolitan area (e.g., Seattle), country (Indonesia), sex (San Joaquin County Women), sexual orientation (Gay and Lesbian Alumni), age (Bay Area Juniors), ethnic background (American Indian Alumni), and occupation (Alumni in Entertainment, a Los Angeles-based club)—and their list does not even include the alumni clubs from the Graduate School of Business, the School of Education, and other graduate schools of the university.

While most schools find that multivariate segmentation is ultimately the most useful approach, here we describe and illustrate the major types of segmentation variables for clarity.

**Geographic Segmentation.** In geographic segmentation, the market is divided by location—which may be as large as a nation or as small as a neighborhood—based on the notion that consumers' needs and preferences may vary by where they live. Geographic segmentation may be appropriate when a college wants to develop differentiated brochures and student recruitment plans for various regions of the country (or when the development and/or alumni offices want to arrange regional events for alumni). Knowing where prospects live may tell the college some useful things about what the students are seeking in a college and what aspects of the college would be most appealing to them. Community colleges, on the other hand, are char-

TABLE 9-1   Major segmentation variables for consumer markets

| VARIABLE | TYPICAL BREAKDOWNS |
| --- | --- |
| **Geographic** | |
| Country | United States, other specific countries |
| Region | Pacific, Mountain, West North Central, West South Central, East North Central, East South Central, South Atlantic, Middle Atlantic, New England |
| State | Specific state, in-state, out-of-state |
| County size | A, B, C, D |
| City or SMSA size | Under 5,000; 5,000–20,000; 20,000–50,000; 50,000–100,000; 100,000–250,000; 250,000–500,000; 500,000–1,000,000; 1,000,000–4,000,000; 4,000,000 or over |
| Density | Urban, suburban, rural |
| **Demographic** | |
| Age | Under 6, 6–11, 12–17, 18–23, 24–34 |
| School grade | Sophomore, junior, senior in high school |
| Sex | Male, female |
| Family size | 1–2, 3–4, 5+ |
| Family life cycle | Young, single; young, married, no children; young, married, youngest child under 6; young, married, youngest child 6 or over; older, married, with children; older, married, no children under 18; older, single; other |
| Income | Under $2,500; $2,500–$5,000; $5,000–$7,500; $7,500–$10,000; $10,000–$15,000; $15,000–$20,000; $20,000–$30,000; $30,000–$50,000; $50,000 and over |
| Occupation | Professional and technical; managers, officials, and proprietors; clerical, sales; craftspeople, foremen; operatives; farmers; retired; students; homemakers; unemployed |
| Education | Grade school or less; some high school; high school graduate; some college; college graduate |
| Religion | Catholic, Protestant, Jewish, Muslim, other |
| Ethnicity | White, African-American, Hispanic, Latino, Asian-American, Native American, etc. |
| Nationality | American, British, French, German, Swedish, Italian, Mexican, Japanese, etc. |
| **Psychographic** | |
| Social class | Lower lowers, upper lowers, lower middles, upper middles, lower uppers, uppers uppers |
| Lifestyle | Conservative, yuppie, etc. |
| Personality | Compulsive, gregarious, authoritarian, ambitious |
| **Behavioral** | |
| Benefits sought | Academic quality, job skills, social life |
| User status | Nonuser, ex-user, potential user, first-time user, regular user |
| Usage rate | Light user, medium user, heavy user |
| Loyalty status | None, medium, strong, absolute |
| Readiness stage | Unaware, aware, informed, interested, desirous, intending to apply/donate |
| Attitude toward program or institution | Enthusiastic, positive, indifferent, negative, hostile |

tered to meet the educational needs of those who live within their districts. They thus serve one major geographic segment.

The smallest practical unit of geographic segmentation is the 9-digit postal zip code, since that defines targets for direct-mail campaigns. The marketing research firm Claritas used U.S. census data and market data from commercial data services to divide U.S. households into 62 clusters.[1] These clusters were assigned distinctive, descriptive names such as "Money and Brains," "Shotguns and Pickups," and "Urban Gold Coast." They then identified the representation of these segments in each postal zip code in the country, so that marketers can select the most promising areas to which to send direct-mail promotions. For example, Table 9-2 shows the profile for the "American Dreams" cluster.

**Demographic Segmentation.** Demographic segmentation involves dividing the market into groups based on demographic variables such as age, sex, family size, family life cycle, income, occupation, education completed, religion, ethnicity, and nationality. Demographic variables are the most frequently used segmentation variables for three reasons. First, consumer wants, preferences, and usage rates are often highly associated with demographic variables. Second, demographic variables are easier to define and measure than are most other segmentation variables. Third, even when the target market is described in terms of other, nondemographic variables, reaching the desired target market depends upon determining key demographic characteristics of the target market that influence what media they use.

Here are two illustrations of segmentation based on demographic variables:

*Age and life-cycle stage.* Consumer wants and capacities change with age and life circumstances. A college may offer special summer programs to acquaint high school students with college, a regular curriculum for college students, a continuing education program for adults who wish to get their degrees in the evening, and a summer Elderhostel program to provide educational enrichment programs for adults 60 and over.

*Sex.* For centuries, sex segmentation was the norm in education. Separate schools and colleges for males and females often had distinct curricula—such as engineering and agriculture at men's colleges and home economics at women's colleges. Most single-sex institutions have broadened or merged with others to serve both sexes.

**Psychographic Segmentation.** People with similar demographic characteristics may exhibit very different psychographic profiles. In psychographic segmentation, prospects are divided into groups on the basis of their social class, lifestyle, or personality characteristics.

*Social class.* Social classes are relatively homogenous and enduring hierarchical divisions in a society. Social scientists distinguish seven social

TABLE 9-2   Characteristics of the "American Dreams" Cluster

---

AMERICAN DREAMS

---

If any Cluster typifies the dream of success in America, it is Cluster 9. These are multi-racial, multi-lingual neighborhoods populated by immigrants and descendants of many ancestries. Unique in Group U1, they tend to big families. Multiple incomes from trade and public service have raised them to the 2nd decile of affluence.

| | |
|---|---|
| Households (% U.S.): | 1,333,600 (1.4%) |
| Population (% U.S.): | 4,170,600 |
| Demographic Caption: | Established Urban Immigrant Families |
| Ethnic Diversity: | Mixed |
| Family Type: | Married Couples with Children |
| Predominant Age Ranges: | 35–54 |
| Education: | Some College |
| Employment level: | White-Collar |
| Housing Type: | Owners/Single Unit |
| Density Centile: | 88 (1 = Sparse, 99 = Dense) |
| Social Group: | U1—Urban Uptown |

MORE LIKELY TO...

---

**Lifestyle**

| | |
|---|---|
| Rent foreign videos | Join health club/gym |
| Have a passport | Go to Walt Disney World |
| Travel to Japan, Asia | Spend $150+ on weekly groceries |
| Belong to an auto club | Use call forwarding |
| Rent car for personal use | Go to the movies |

**Radio/TV**

| | |
|---|---|
| Listen to news/talk radio | Watch Arsenio Hall |
| Watch Arts & Entertainment | Watch Star Trek-TNG |
| Listen to golden oldies radio | Watch Disney Channel |
| Watch Showtime | Watch Siskel & Ebert |
| Listen to urban contemp radio | Watch Saturday Night Live |

**Print**

| | |
|---|---|
| Read *Home* | Read *Business Week* |
| Read *Motor Trend* | Read *People* |
| Read *Tennis* | Read *Time* |
| Read *Working Mother* | Read *Vogue* |
| Read newspaper entertainment section | Read *Life* |

---

Source: Claritas Inc., Arlington, VA.

classes: (1) upper uppers (less than 1 percent of the population); (2) lower uppers (about 2 percent); (3) upper middles (12 percent); (4) middle class (32 percent); (5) working class (38 percent); (6) upper lowers (9 percent); and (6) lower lowers (7 percent), based on measures of income, occupation, educational attainment, and type of residence.[2]

People within each class division tend to share similar values, interests, and behavior. Individuals can move from one social class to another—up or down—during their lifetime, and education has traditionally been viewed as one mechanism by which people can move up. Social classes may show distinct preferences for certain educational institutions. Upper-middle-class students may, for example, prefer elite colleges where they will have the opportunity to socialize with higher-status peers.

*Lifestyle.* Different consumer lifestyles exist between and even within social classes. Researchers have found that people's interest in various educational institutions and programs is influenced by their lifestyles, and, in fact, the educational choices they make express their lifestyles. Sun City, Arizona, is a leisure-oriented planned community with golf courses. Most residents are retired with comfortable incomes. Arizona State University has opened a branch campus there to serve the educational interests of this group, and most of the faculty are retired professors who live in Sun City.

*Personality.* Marketers also use personality variables to segment markets. They strive to endow their products with brand personalities (brand images) that will match and appeal to corresponding consumer personalities (self-images, self-concepts). An educational program with a successful brand personality will prompt potential students or participants to say, "That's my kind of program." A conservative school with a dress code and other rules of student conduct will appeal to students who value social conformity and a familiar and safe environment. Schools that offer students many choices about curriculum and living arrangements will appeal to students who value their independence and who do not feel uncomfortable making decisions.

**Behavioristic Segmentation.** Sometimes marketers are particularly interested in how consumers respond to an actual program or service, rather than their general lifestyle or personality. Many marketers believe that behavioristic variables are the best starting point for constructing useful market segments because behavior has direct implications for what institutions and programs consumer segments will choose. Some specific examples follow.

*Benefits sought.* Consumers can be segmented according to the particular benefit(s) they are seeking through participation in the program. Some consumers look for one dominant benefit; others seek a particular combination of benefits, a *benefit bundle.*[3]

For example, Goodnow surveyed students attending the College of DuPage, a large community college in Illinois, and found five benefit segments: (1) *social/improvement learners,* (2) *learning/career learners,* (3) *leisure/status learners,* (4) *submissive learners,* and (5) *ambivalent learners.* She matched these desired benefits with demographic characteristics and recommended a separate marketing strategy for each benefit segment. The leisure/status learners were typically middle-aged women seeking leisure activities and prestige. They attended noncredit physical education and creative arts programs, which met informally in small groups on weekday evenings. These programs could appeal to this group's desire for a "night out" and be promoted through a mailed college brochure, the suburban newspaper, and women's clubs. The other four segments would each call for separate marketing strategies based on the benefit(s) sought and other characteristics of each segment.[4]

*User status.* Many markets can be segmented into nonusers, ex-users, potential users, first-time users, and regular users of the product. For example, a development office may segment donors into those who have never given, those who gave in the past but have not given for several years, students who are about to graduate, first-time donors, and long-time consistent donors. Each segment might receive different appeals or types of contact to encourage their participation.

*Usage rate.* Many markets can be segmented into light-, medium-, and heavy-user groups of the product, an approach called *volume segmentation.* Volume segmentation is important because although heavy users may constitute only a small percentage of the market in numbers, they may account for a major percentage of the services used. For example, certain segments of the enrolled student population may need more services than others, in which case the school may want to charge more for these segments or find increasingly efficient ways to meet these needs. For example, if all enrolled students are eligible to use the library and health services, educational institutions whose tuition charge is based on units taken may decide to charge a uniform fee to cover these costs.

Some educational institutions, including most community colleges, are mandated to identify and address the educational needs of their communities. A recent report on continuing education for the elderly noted that "the vast majority of those most in need are still unreached," and those who do avail themselves of educational offerings "tend to be those who are already advantaged educationally and economically."[5]

An educational institution interested in meeting the needs of the underserved can use volume segmentation to identify the groups that make the *least* use of educational services, and then develop programs to bring them in and serve them. Sometimes these underserved groups have the same needs as the currently served groups, but need more encouragement to enroll and perhaps more support services as they begin their studies. On the other hand, some of the underserved are quite different from the institution's current students and could be described as *niches.* A niche is smaller than a segment and represents a group that seeks a special, narrowly defined combination of benefits. For example, Foothill Community College in Los Altos Hills, California, has a special program for (often well-educated) adults who have sustained brain injuries, and who need to learn to read, write, recall their own names, and care for their basic needs all over again.

*Loyalty status.* Loyalty status describes the strength of a consumer's preference for a particular entity. The degree of loyalty can range from zero to absolute. We find consumers who are absolutely loyal to a brand (Budweiser beer, Crest toothpaste, Cadillac automobiles); an organization (the University of Texas, the Republican Party); a place (New England, Southern California); and so on. Being loyal means maintaining a preference despite incentives to switch to something else.

A school or college may want to analyze alumni loyalty. Four groups can be distinguished: (1) *hard-core loyals*, who are exclusively devoted to the institution; (2) *soft-core loyals*, who are devoted to two or three institutions; (3) *shifting loyals*, who are gradually moving from favoring this institution to favoring another; and (4) *switchers*, who show no loyalty to any institution.

Alumni tend to lavish most of their attention and contributions on their undergraduate college, with institutions where they acquired professional certification—law, business, and medical schools—running a close second. Schools also compete for attention with the many other organizations in which alumni may become active. If most of the school's alumni are hard-core loyals or even soft-core loyals, the institution probably has a basically healthy alumni base. The school may want to study its loyals to find out the basic satisfactions that contributed to their feelings about the school and then work to create these satisfactions for current students and for other alumni.

*Stage of readiness.* At any one time, some members of the potential market for a product or service are *unaware* of its existence; some are *aware*; some are *informed*; some are *interested*; some are *desirous*; and some *intend to buy*. The distribution of people over stages of readiness makes a big difference in designing the marketing program. When an educational institution launches a new program, most of the potential student market will be unaware of it (see Figure 9-3, A). At this stage, the marketing effort should go into advertising and publicity directed to those most likely to find the program attractive.

If this campaign is successful, more of the market will be aware of the program but will still need more information (see Figure 9-3, B). After knowl-

FIGURE 9-3    Stages of market readiness

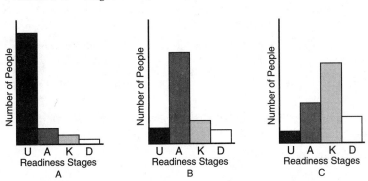

Note: U = unaware,  A = aware only,  K = knowledgeable,  D = desirous

edge is built up, the advertising should feature the benefits of the program, perhaps including testimonials from program participants, in order to move people into a stage of desire (see Figure 9-3, C). As more people become interested in participating in the program, the institution will need to expand the capacity of the program or refine application procedures to handle the demand.

*Attitude.* Markets can be segmented according to consumer attitudes toward adopting the program or institution. For example, members of a chapter of Sigma Chi fraternity at an eastern college interviewed incoming freshmen about their attitudes toward fraternities. They found that 10 percent were *enthusiasts*, 20 percent *positives*, 30 percent *indifferents*, 25 percent *negatives*, and 15 percent *hostiles*. Each segment had a distinct consumer profile. Enthusiasts generally came from higher-income, better-educated families living in cities. The fraternity developed a better picture of its natural market and saw some opportunities for converting indifferent people to be more favorable toward fraternity membership. (See Exhibit 9-1.)

EXHIBIT 9-1    An approach to segmenting prospective students

---

CORE MARKETS—Student types we are currently attracting

1. Primary Core Market: Students we are most pleased about attracting

2. Secondary Core Market: Students we find acceptable

3. Tertiary Core Market: Students we find barely acceptable

WISH MARKETS—Student types we would like to attract

1. Primary Wish Market: Students we would most like to attract but who prefer other programs to ours (students with high academic and financial ability)

2. Secondary Wish Market: Students we would like to attract but who prefer other programs to ours (students with high academic ability but low financial ability)

SAFETY MARKETS—Student types we tend to reject but would be willing to accept if our core and wish markets dry up

1. Primary Safety Market: Students with low academic ability and high financial ability

2. Secondary Safety Market: Students with low academic ability and low financial ability

SPECIAL TEST MARKETS—Student types we might reach and serve through special programs

1. Continuing Education Market

2. Summer School Market

**Bases for Segmenting Organizational Markets**

Educational institutions may market to other organizations as well as to individuals. A college may want to identify appropriate foundations and corporations to approach for financial support. A business school may want to identify companies interested in sending managers to its training programs. In both cases, the educational institution wants to get other organizations to buy something. The process by which organizations buy things is discussed in the next chapter. Here we will consider how a market of organizations can be segmented.

Consider the example of a business school interested in providing training programs to company employees. The business school would need a clear understanding of the concerns of potential customer companies. In the 1990s companies are demanding that executive education and other training programs—whether provided by business schools, consulting and training firms, or others—be linked to the companies' most pressing business needs. More companies are interested in courses that are tailored to their own circumstances, rather than in "off-the- shelf" courses.[6]

The business school might segment companies in the following ways:

*Organization size.* The companies can be divided into large, medium, and small companies. The business school might find that large companies have "in-house" programs and would be less likely prospects than medium- and small-sized companies that recognize the value of training but have no training staffs. Or the business school might focus on the larger companies, since such companies would have the resources and the significant number of prospective participants to justify a customized program.

*Geographical location.* Companies can be grouped by their distance from the school—whether they are in the same city as the school, within commuting distance, or beyond commuting distance. The business school may focus on local companies for programs that meet in the late afternoon, or on commuting-area companies for Saturday programs, and may develop telecourses, teleconferencing courses, or residential short courses for those who cannot conveniently commute to the campus.

*Interest profile.* Companies can differ tremendously in their interest in contracting with educational institutions for company training. Companies in certain industries place great value on collaborative relationships with academic institutions and emphasize additional education and training for employees. Other industry groups, including those characterized by high employee turnover, may not be interested in employee training involving universities, preferring to provide essential training on the job.

*Resource level.* Companies differ in the resources they have and are willing to budget for training. Even a committed company will be less interested when it faces difficult economic conditions. The business school will be more successful if it can identify those companies that are likely to have the necessary resources.

*Buying criteria.* Companies differ in the qualities they look for in schools that supply training. Some companies emphasize the prestige level of the business school, others the qualifications of the professors who will conduct the specific program, and still others will consider the ties that have developed between the company and the business school over time. If the business school does not have a prestigious reputation, the school should focus on attracting companies that will value the strengths the school does possess, rather than the national reputation it lacks.

*Buying process.* Companies tend to differ in how much detail they require in training proposals and how long the decision process usually takes. Some companies expect detailed proposals and then take a long time to review, discuss, and evaluate them. The business school may prefer to identify companies that have a good relationship with the school and can make quick decisions based on relatively short proposals.

Each of these segmentation approaches is designed to identify the types of companies that the business school can best serve and those it can most effectively attract.

## Developing the Customer Segment Profile

After considering the range of segmentation variables, the decision makers need to decide which variables will be most relevant to the current project. For example, the bases for segmenting the donor market will differ for a capital campaign and an alumni-giving campaign because the capital campaign will want to focus (at least initially) on the enthusiastic large-giver segment, while the alumni-giving campaign will employ a variety of approaches to reach all subsegments of the alumni market, with the goal of getting the largest number of alumni to participate, even if their contributions are relatively small.

After identifying the relevant variables, the decision makers will need to profile each segment in more detail. Describing the segments by their demographics, psychographics, attitudes, behavior, and their media preferences will yield more insights into how to reach and influence each segment.

## Requirements for Effective Segmentation

Although markets can often be segmented in several ways, the most useful segmentation approach will have the following characteristics:

- The segments will be *measurable*; the size and characteristics of the resulting segments can be readily determined. A school offering an extremely specialized program may find it very challenging to identify what kind of people will find the program attractive and how many there are.

- The segments will be *accessible*, so that they can be reached and served effectively. Certain segments are more difficult to reach than others. Consider trying to reach elderly shut-ins interested in taking tape-recorded courses at home. An educational institution may still attempt to locate members of this segment even though they are not easily accessible, but its job is harder.

- The segments will be *substantial*, large enough to warrant a special marketing effort. Educational institutions typically offer programs that they believe will appeal to one or more large segments of the population. On the other hand, some educational institutions are responsible for serving unmet educational needs and will make a point of seeking out those smaller segments that are not served by existing educational programs. The institution needs to determine how large a segment must be to warrant the additional effort to serve it. (The example of Northwestern's program for returning women students in Chapter 8 illustrated this.)

- The segments will be *durable*, likely to persist over time. Designing educational programs often requires extensive planning time, money, and commitments to teachers and other staff. Educational institutions need to consider whether identified segments will persist long enough to justify these efforts.

## TARGET SELECTED SEGMENTS

Segmentation reveals the market segment opportunities facing the institution. Next, the institution has to decide among three broad market coverage strategies, shown in Figure 9-4.

1. *Undifferentiated marketing.* The institution can decide to go after the whole market with one offer and marketing mix, trying to attract as many consumers as possible. (This is another name for mass marketing.)
2. *Differentiated marketing.* The institution can decide to go after several market segments, developing an offer and marketing mix for each segment.
3. *Concentrated marketing.* The institution can decide to go after one market segment and develop the ideal offer and marketing mix.

Here we will describe the logic and merits of each of these strategies.

### Undifferentiated Marketing

In undifferentiated marketing, the institution chooses to ignore the different market segments and instead focuses on the common needs of consumers.[7] It designs one program that will appeal to the largest number of consumers. Undifferentiated marketing is exemplified by a school that offers one program for all students, such as a school or college with a fixed curriculum for all students.

FIGURE 9-4   Three alternative market coverage strategies

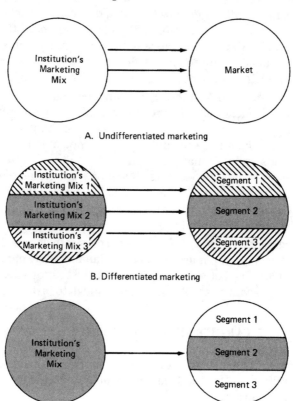

A. Undifferentiated marketing

B. Differentiated marketing

C. Concentrated marketing

Undifferentiated marketing is comparable to mass production in manufacturing. This marketing approach enables the costs of developing, offering, and marketing educational programs to be kept low through limiting efforts to one program. Lower costs, however, are accompanied by reduced consumer satisfaction, since the institution fails to meet varying individual needs. Other institutions may already meet the needs of these "neglected" segments, or competing institutions may step in to serve these segments.

## Differentiated Marketing

An institution using differentiated marketing operates in two or more segments of the market but designs separate programs for each segment. For example, many institutions of higher education have both graduate and undergraduate programs, and may offer a range of programs at each level. A business school may offer both undergraduate and master's degree programs, and perhaps doctoral study. The same university may have specialized development programs for alumni giving and for corporation donations.

Through the use of differentiated marketing, the institution hopes to realize the following benefits:

- To attract more prospective students and donors and to have a bigger effect on each selected market segment.
- To strengthen consumers' perceptions of the institution as a specialist in those programs it offers.
- To create greater consumer loyalty, since the institution's offerings have been bent to the consumer's desires rather than the other way around.

The institution using differentiated marketing can anticipate more success than one using undifferentiated marketing. Differentiated marketing is usually more costly, however, since the institution has to spend more on marketing research, program development, communication, and other tasks. Before deciding whether to adopt differentiated marketing, the institution needs to balance the likelihood of better results against higher costs. Some institutions push differentiated marketing too far by offering more segmented programs than are economically feasible, while others fail to recognize real opportunities to serve selected market segments better. Some institutions meet the needs and expectations of diverse segments cost-effectively by devising customized programs which integrate a number of standardized modules.

**Concentrated Marketing**

Concentrated marketing is a special case of differentiated marketing, in which the institution segments the market and then selects one segment as the focus of its marketing efforts. The institution concentrates on serving that one segment well, hoping to achieve the following benefits:

- A strong following and standing in a particular market segment
- Greater knowledge of the market segment's needs and behavior
- Operating economies in production, distribution, and promotion

For example, Gallaudet College provides a liberal arts education for deaf students, and the National Technical Institute for the Deaf at Rochester Institute of Technology offers preparation in technical and related areas.

Concentrated marketing may involve higher than normal risks, in that the selected market segment may decline or disappear. In the early 1900s, National College of Education was the National Kindergarten and Elementary College. By the late 1970s, National College of Education faced severe economic difficulties when elementary school enrollments dropped, along with the number of prospective students interested in teaching careers. Fortunately, National College successfully launched additional programs to reduce its dependence on its earlier market segments. The college had moved from concentrated marketing to differentiated marketing.

## Choosing a Market Coverage Strategy

The choice of a market coverage strategy depends on several factors. If the institution has *limited resources*, it will probably choose concentrated marketing because it lacks the resources to serve the whole market or to tailor special programs for more than one segment. If the market is fairly *homogeneous* in its needs and desires, the institution will probably choose undifferentiated marketing, since little would be gained by differentiated offerings.

When the institution aspires to be a *leader* in several segments of the market, it will choose differentiated marketing. When *competitors* have established dominance in all but a few segments of the market, the institution might try to concentrate its marketing in one of the remaining segments.

## Identifying Attractive Market Segments

Educational institutions usually start out with a strategy of undifferentiated marketing or concentrated marketing, and, if they are successful, they may evolve into a strategy of differentiated marketing. For example, a school may start as a strong academic school but then develop an enhanced reputation for its offerings in the performing arts and seek more students interested in music and drama. Whether an institution elects to use a concentrated or differentiated marketing strategy, it must identify the best segment(s) to serve. A market segment is worth further consideration when it satisfies two criteria: (1) The segment is attractive in its own right, and (2) the institution possesses the factors required to succeed in that segment. We will consider each in turn.

Several factors generally contribute to making a market or market segment attractive, independent of the institution that seeks to serve it. The following are the major features:[8]

- *Market size.* Large markets are more attractive than small markets.
- *Market growth rate.* Markets with high growth rates are more attractive than markets with low growth rates.
- *Ability to pay.* Markets that can make larger donations or can pay a higher percentage of educational costs are more attractive than those that cannot.
- *Competitive intensity.* Markets that are served by few competitors or substitute services are more attractive than markets that are served by many and/or strong competitors.
- *Variability.* Markets that fluctuate in size are less attractive than those that are stable or growing.

- *Scale economies.* Markets that can be served at lower unit cost as size increases are more attractive than constant-cost markets.
- *Learning curve.* Markets are more attractive when the institution serving them experiences lower unit costs as it gains more experience serving their needs than where no learning curve exists.

The second issue is whether the institution possesses the necessary success factors to make a strong showing in this market segment:

- *Relative market share.* The higher the institution's relative share of the market it serves, the greater the institution's strength.
- *Price competitiveness.* The lower the institution's costs relative to competitors, the greater its strength.
- *Program quality.* The higher the quality of the institution's offerings relative to competitors, the greater its strength.
- *Knowledge of consumer/market.* The deeper the institution's knowledge of consumers and their needs and wants, the greater its strength.
- *Marketing effectiveness.* The greater the institution's relevant marketing effectiveness, the greater its strength.
- *Geography.* The greater the institution's geographical presence and advantages in the market, the greater its strength.

When an institution evaluates possible segments, both market segment characteristics and institutional success requirements must be carefully weighed. An attractive segment for one school or educational program might be unattractive or inappropriate for another. For example, the adult-learner market (or a subsegment of it) might exhibit most of the key factors listed earlier and be an appropriate match for an urban college or university but be an inaccessible market for a rural institution. Of course, the selected segments must also be a good match with the institution's mission.

## DEVELOP AND IMPLEMENT A POSITIONING STRATEGY

The institution must give considerable thought to how it will appeal to its selected segments and, in particular, how the institution will stand out from other schools. Many institutions assume that if they have good programs and students and "do a good job," they will receive accolades from all who come in contact with them. They assume that most people know about them and know why they are worthy institutions. It therefore comes as a surprise to learn that many people haven't heard of them or consider them to be "just like" most other such institutions.

In some cases, this is a fair judgment. Many schools and institutions of higher education are fundamentally good and worthy, but they have done little to forge strong, individual identities for themselves. The institution should strive to have a clear, positive image and a distinctive, memorable identity. This state is reached by paying attention to *positioning*:

> Positioning is the process of establishing and maintaining a distinctive position—in terms of image and offerings—so that the institution (or program) occupies a distinct and valued place in the target customers' minds.

For many institutions, the issue is not so much positioning as *repositioning*. The institutions and/or programs have been in operation for years but want to change their positions in the marketplace. Positioning is easier to accomplish when done as a new program or service is first introduced, but the principles are the same in the either case.

Successful positioning consists of four steps:

**1.** *Determine the images held by the institution's key markets and publics, and how key constituencies "position" the institution in relation to competing institutions.* Note that different constituencies/segments may have different images of the institution. Chapter 7 introduced the idea of positioning and competitive analysis, using the case of Yale University. The following section presents image measurement.

**2.** *Select the desired feasible position for the institution.* This may vary by segment. For example, the institution may wish to position its undergraduate liberal-arts college as a center for intellectual growth, its M.B.A. program as entrepreneurial preparation for a fast-track management career, and its evening division as a place where members of the local community can improve their work-related skills. Thus, the institution will want an overall institutional position of quality and responsiveness, but it will want to develop auxiliary positioning plans for its various schools. The selection needs to be based on what positions are realistic, attractive (to key constituencies), and distinctive in positive ways.

**3.** *Carry out carefully selected actions to achieve the desired position.* The last section of this chapter discusses how to differentiate the institution.

**4.** *Evaluate and monitor the effectiveness of these positioning efforts.* Positioning and repositioning strategies require constant monitoring since new constituencies (including new prospective students and donors) are always emerging, and their preferences are changing. Other competing schools are—or should be—changing with the times, so their positioning and institutional attractiveness will undergo changes too.

## The Institution's Image

We will look first at how the institution's image is formed. People often respond to the institution's image, not necessarily its reality. Publics holding a negative image of a school will avoid or disparage it, even if the institution is of high quality, and those holding a positive image will be drawn to it. The same school will be viewed as responsive by some groups and unresponsive by other groups. People tend to form images of schools based on very limited and even inaccurate information, yet these images will affect their likelihood of attending, recommending the school to a relative, donating, or joining the faculty or staff.

Every educational institution has a vital interest in learning about its various images in the marketplace and making sure that these images accurately and favorably reflect the institution. According to David Garvin,

> An institution's actual quality is often less important than its prestige, or reputation for quality, because it is the university's perceived excellence which, in fact, guides the decisions of prospective students and scholars considering offers of employment, and federal agencies awarding grants.[9]

An institution's present image is usually based on its past record. Therefore, an institution cannot change its image through a quick change in public relations strategy. Its image is a function of its deeds and its communications. A strong favorable image comes about when the school performs well and generates real satisfaction, then lets others know about its success.

Institutions need to know the following things about image: (1) what image is; (2) how image is measured; (3) how image can be changed; and (4) the relationship between image and a person's behavior toward the object.

**Defining Image.** The term *image* came into popular use in the 1950s and is currently used in a variety of contexts: institutional image, corporate image, national image, brand image, public image, self-image, and so on. Its wide use has tended to blur its meanings. Our definition of *image* is as follows:

> An image is the sum of beliefs, ideas, and impressions that a person has of an object.

This definition enables us to distinguish an image from similar sounding concepts such as *beliefs, attitudes,* and *stereotypes.*

An image is more than a simple belief. The belief that it is difficult to get admitted to Harvard University would be only one element in a larger image that might be held about Harvard University. An image is a whole set of beliefs about an object.

On the other hand, people's images of an object do not necessarily reveal their attitudes toward that object. Two people may hold the same image of Harvard and yet have different attitudes toward it. An attitude is a disposition toward an object that includes cognitive, affective, and behavioral components.

How does an image differ from a stereotype? A stereotype suggests a widely held image that is highly distorted and simplistic and that carries a favorable or unfavorable attitude toward the object. An image, on the other hand, is a more personal perception of an object that can vary greatly from person to person.

**Image Measurement.** Many methods have been proposed for measuring images. We will describe a two-step approach: (1) measuring how familiar and favorable the institution's image is, and (2) measuring the location of the institution's image along major relevant dimensions (called the semantic differential).

*Familiarity-favorability measurement.* The first step is to establish, for each public or segment being studied, how familiar it is with the institution and how favorable it feels toward it. To determine level of familiarity, each respondent is asked to indicate one of the following:

| Never heard of | Heard of | Know a little about | Know a fair amount | Know very well |
| --- | --- | --- | --- | --- |

The results indicate the public's awareness of the institution. If most of the respondents place it in the first two or three categories, then the institution has an awareness problem.

Those respondents who have some familiarity with the institution are then asked to describe how favorable they feel toward it by indicating one of the following:

| Very unfavorable | Somewhat unfavorable | Indifferent | Somewhat favorable | Very favorable |
| --- | --- | --- | --- | --- |

If most of the respondents check the first two or three categories, then the institution has a serious image problem.

To illustrate these scales, suppose that parents are asked to rate four local schools—Adams, Barclay, Carson, and Donner. Their responses are averaged and the results are displayed in Figure 9-5. Adams School has the strongest image: Most people know it and like it. Barclay School is less familiar to most people, but those who know it like it. Carson School is negatively viewed by the people who know it, but fortunately, not too many people are familiar with it. Donner School is in the weakest position: It is seen as a weak school, and everyone knows it.

Clearly, each school faces a different task. Adams School must work at maintaining its good reputation and high community awareness. Barclay School must bring itself to the attention of more parents, since those who know it find it to be a good school. Carson School needs to find out why people dislike it and take steps to improve, while keeping a low profile. Donner

FIGURE 9-5    Familiarity-favorability analysis

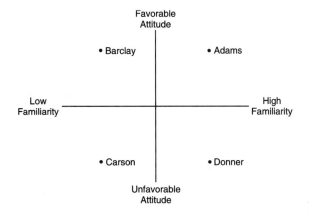

School would be well advised to lower its profile (avoid news), mend its ways, and, when it is a better school, start seeking public attention again.

*Semantic differential.* Each school needs to go further and research the content of its image. One of the most popular tools for this is the *semantic differential.*[10] It involves the following steps:

**1.** *Develop a set of relevant dimensions.* The research first identifies the dimensions that people normally use to reflect the object. People could be asked, "What things do you think of when you consider a school?" If someone suggests "well-trained teachers," this would be turned into a bipolar adjective scale-say, "inferior teachers" at one end and "superior teachers" at the other. This could be rendered as a five- or seven-point scale, such as the ones shown in Figure 9-6.

**2.** *Reduce the set of relevant dimensions.* The number of dimensions should be kept small so that respondents don't get tired and bored. Osgood, Suci, and Tannenbaum feel that there are essentially three types of scales:[11]
- Evaluation scales (good-bad qualities)
- Potency scales (strong-weak qualities)
- Activity scales (active-passive qualities)

By using these scales as a guide (or by performing a factor analysis on the dimensions), the researcher can remove dimensions that don't prove useful.

**3.** *Administer the instrument to a sample of respondents.* The respondents are asked to rate one institution at a time. The bipolar adjectives should be arranged so as not to load all the poor adjectives on one side.

**4.** *Average the results.* Figure 9-6 shows the results of averaging the respondents' pictures of Adams, Barclay, and Carson Schools. Each school's image is represented by a vertical "line of means" that summarizes how the

FIGURE 9-6    Images of three schools (semantic differentials)

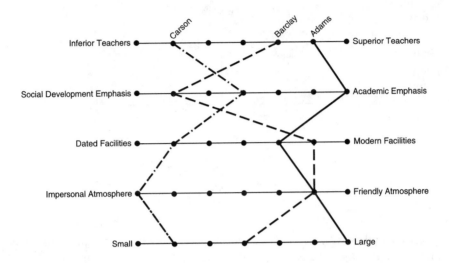

average respondent sees that institution. Thus, Adams School is seen as a large, modern, friendly, and superior school; Carson School, on the other hand, is seen as small, impersonal, and inferior.

**5.** *Check on the image variance.* Since each image profile is a line of means, it does not reveal how variable the image actually is. If there were 100 respondents, did they all see Barclay School, for example, exactly as shown, or was there considerable variation? In the first case, we would say that the image is highly *specific*, and in the second case that the image is highly *diffused*. An institution may or may not want a very specific image. Some institutions prefer a diffused image so that different groups can project their needs onto this institution. The institution will want to analyze whether a variable image is really the result of different subgroups rating it, with each subgroup having a different but highly specific image.

The semantic differential is a flexible image-measuring tool that can provide the following useful information:

**1.** *The institution can discover how a particular public views it and its major competitors.* It can learn its image strengths and weaknesses along with those of its competitors and take remedial steps that may be warranted.

**2.** *The institution can discover how different publics and market segments view it.* Suppose the image profiles in Figure 9-6 represented the images of *one* school held by three different *publics* (rather than three different schools evaluated by one public). The school would then consider taking steps to improve its image among those publics who view it most unfavorably or among those publics whose image is likely to have the most influence on the school's effectiveness.

**3.** *The institution can monitor changes in its image over time.* By repeating the image study periodically, the institution can detect any significant image slippage or improvement. Image slippage signals that the institution is doing something wrong. Image improvement, on the other hand, verifies that it is performing better as a result of some steps it has taken.

**Image Modification.** The administrators of an educational institution are often surprised and disturbed by the measured image. Thus, the principal of Carson School (see Figure 9-6) might be upset that the public sees the school as dated, impersonal, and of low quality. The administrator's immediate reaction is to disbelieve the results by complaining that the sample is too small or unrepresentative. But if the results can be defended as reliable, the administrator must consider what ought to be done about this image problem.

The first step is for the school's administrators and board to develop a picture of a *desired image* that they want to have in the general public's mind, in contrast to the *current image.* Suppose Carson School would like the public to have a more favorable view of the quality of its teachers, facilities, friendliness, and so on (shown in Figure 9-7 as the desired image). It is not aiming for perfection because the school recognizes its limitations. The desired image must be feasible in terms of the school's present reality and resources.

The second step is for the school to decide which image gaps it wants to work on initially. Is it more desirable to improve the school's image of

FIGURE 9-7    Current and desired image of Carson School

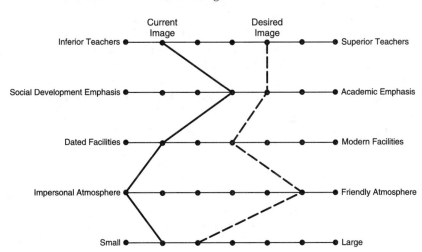

friendliness (through programs for parents, staff training, and so on) or the look of its facilities (through renovation)? Each image dimension should be reviewed in terms of the following questions:

1. What contribution to the school's overall favorable image would be made by closing that particular image gap to the extent shown?
2. What strategy (combination of real changes and communication changes) would be used to close the particular image gap?
3. What would be the cost of closing that image gap?
4. How long would it take to close that image gap?

For example, the school might decide that it would be more effective and less costly to improve the school's image of friendliness than to improve its physical facilities. An overall image-modification plan would involve planning the sequence of steps through which the school would go to transform its current image into its desired image.

An institution seeking to change its image must have great patience. Images, negative and positive, tend to last long after the reality of the institution has changed. Thus, the quality of teachers may have deteriorated at a well-known school, and yet it continues to be highly regarded in the public mind. Image persistence is explained by the fact that once people have a certain image of an object, they tend to be selective perceivers of further data. Their perceptions are oriented toward seeing what they expect to see. It will take highly disconfirming stimuli to raise doubts and open them to new information. An image can enjoy a life of its own for a while, especially when people are not likely to have new firsthand experiences with the changed object.

**The Relation Between Image and Behavior.** Institutions are interested in image measurement and modification because they assume that there is a close relationship between the public's image of the institution and the public's behavior toward it. The institution feels that it can obtain better public response by acquiring a better image.

Unfortunately, the connection between image and behavior is not as close as many schools and colleges believe. Images are only one component of attitudes. Two people may view a school as small and yet have opposite attitudes toward a small school. Furthermore, the connection between attitudes and behavior is also tenuous. Parents might prefer a small school to a large one and yet end up enrolling their child in the large one because it is closer to their home or neighbors recommended it.

Nevertheless, one should not dismiss image measurement and planning simply because images are hard to change and their effects on behavior are unclear. Quite the contrary. Measuring a school's image is a very useful step in understanding what is happening to the school and in pointing to some possible desirable changes in its image. Furthermore, although the connection between image and behavior is not strong, it does exist. The connection should be neither overrated nor underrated. The institution should attempt to make an investment in developing the best image it can for the advantages it might bring.

## Differentiation

*Differentiation* is the process of designing a set of meaningful differences to distinguish the school's offer from competing institutions' offers. A school can differentiate itself in many ways. Here is a partial list, with examples:

- By location—part of the country, "in Washington, DC," near skiing
- By quality, number, and/or type of faculty
- By the nature of the curriculum—broad, "something for everyone," or focused on preparation for a maritime career
- By special features, such as a three-year curriculum, a co-op program, and so on
- By performance quality
- By the achievements of graduates ("Sixty percent go on to graduate school.")
- By the technologies used or available ("All students use computers.")
- By program requirements (requiring music or religion or ethics)
- By the campus atmosphere—traditional, "fun in the sun," lots of friends, and so on
- By the price charged
- By the caring manner of faculty and staff

Note that these differentiating factors are a result of the school's actions and assets, *not* a result of advertising. These are factors which will appeal to some students more than others, and these students will pick the school because it is different and it appeals to their own tastes and preferences.

On which specific features should the school differentiate itself? Some differences will be more valued by consumers; some will be easier for the school to implement successfully. The selected features should meet the following criteria:

- *Important:* The difference delivers a highly valued benefit to a sufficient number of students, alumni, donors, and so on.
- *Distinctive:* The difference should be one that isn't offered by (many) other schools, or which the school can offer in a more distinctive or convenient way.
- *Superior:* The difference is superior to other ways to achieve the same goal or benefit.
- *Communicable:* The difference is one the school can demonstrate—and preferably show—to customers.
- *Preemptive:* The difference ideally cannot be copied by other schools—at least in the short term.
- *Affordable:* The school can afford to provide or the student can afford to pay for the difference.
- *Profitable:* The school will be able to charge enough—or get financial support through grants or donations—to make implementing the difference worthwhile.

Successful differentiation need not be extreme or complex. One new private day school differentiated itself from the budget-constrained public schools by providing art and music classes—and then further differentiated itself by *requiring* that all students take art and music. The school quickly became known as a school that was "strong in art and music." In fact the school was reasonably strong in all areas of the curriculum, but not especially so in art and music.

Differentiating on price is more complex. While students and their families are concerned about price, they also care about quality. An urban Catholic girls' high school once promoted itself as "affordable for all" and set its tuition at several hundred dollars a year less than its major—and more upscale—competitor. Instead of increasing applications, the urban school's enrollment dropped, in part because the focus on low price implied that the school wasn't as good or prestigious as the other school.

Differentiating on value is another story. The school can point to the success of its graduates and their attainment of interesting, significant positions. Or the school can point to its graduates' success in professional or other graduate schools.

Clearly each institution and program will have several different potential positions from which to select the best one to implement. Whatever the final selection of features, they must ultimately be of value to the institution's constituents. The chosen position is expressed through the institution's—or program's—marketing mix: its programs, its value and pricing, its facilities and accessibility, and its advertising and other communications. These are considered in detail in subsequent chapters.

## SUMMARY

Educational institutions recognize that various groups expect and need different things from them. Even small schools approach their students, alumni, and other donors in different ways. They intuitively segment their constituents—their markets and publics—into relatively homogeneous subgroups, and then design offers to appeal to each key group or subgroup.

Educational institutions can take three different approaches to a market. Mass marketing consists of mass-producing and mass-distributing one program, or service and attempting to attract everyone to it. Product differentiation consists of producing two or more programs differentiated in style, features, quality, and so on, to offer variety to the market and to distinguish the institution's offerings from those of competitors. Target marketing consists of segmentation, distinguishing the different groups that make up a market; targeting, selecting the most attractive segments; and positioning, developing an appropriate program and marketing mix for each target market.

The first step in target marketing is market segmentation, dividing a market into distinct and meaningful groups of consumers which might merit separate programs and/or marketing mixes. Market segmentation is a creative act. The investigator tries different variables to see which reveal the best segmentation opportunities. The major consumer segmentation variables are broadly classified as geographical, demographic, psychographic, and behavioristic. Organizational markets can be segmented by variables such as organization size, geographical location, interest profile, resource level, buying criteria, and buying process. The effectiveness of a segmentation approach depends upon the extent to which the resulting segments are measurable, accessible, substantial, and durable.

The institution then has to choose a market coverage strategy, either ignoring segment differences (undifferentiated marketing), developing differentiated programs for several segments (differentiated marketing), or striving to serve only one or a few segments (concentrated marketing). No one strategy is superior in all circumstances. The institution needs to consider the inherent attractiveness of potential market segments in relation to the institution's strengths and its mission.

The next step is to consider how to position the school and what it offers, to make it appealing to the segments the institution wishes to attract. Positioning involves identifying possible positioning concepts for each target market, and then selecting, developing, and communicating the chosen positioning concept through a carefully designed marketing mix.

A significant aspect of the institution's positioning is often referred to as its image. Educational institutions have a strong interest in how they are perceived by their publics and markets. The "image" an institution possesses can be more influential than its reality. Ideally, the image held by its key constituencies accurately and favorably reflects the institution.

An image is the sum of beliefs, ideas, and impressions that a person has of an object. The researcher will want to measure how familiar and favorable the institution's image is and how various groups evaluate the institution on relevant attributes. After determining how the institution is perceived, the administration must decide whether the image is positive and appropriate, or whether the institution needs to undertake changes and take steps to correct a negative or faulty image.

## Notes

1. Michael J. Weiss, *The Clustering of America* (New York: Harper & Row, 1988).
2. Richard P. Coleman, "The Continuing Significance of Social Class to Marketing," *Journal of Consumer Research* (December 1983), pp. 265–280; and Richard P. Coleman and Lee P. Rainwater, *Social Standing in America: New Dimension of Class* (New York: Basic Books, 1978).

3. See Paul E. Green, Yoram Wind, and Arun K. Jain, "Benefit Bundle Analysis," *Journal of Advertising Research* (April 1972), pp. 31–36.

4. See Wilma E. Goodnow, "Benefit Segmentation: A Technique for Developing Program and Promotion Strategies for Adults in a Community College," unpublished Ed.D. dissertation, Northern Illinois University, DeKalb, Illinois, 1980.

5. "Education Found Unused by Adults Who Need It Most," *The Chronicle of Higher Education,* December 15, 1980, p. 6.

6. See *The Wall Street Journal Reports* special section "Executive Education," September 10, 1993.

7. See Wendell R. Smith, "Product Differentiation and Market Segmentation as Alternative Marketing Strategies," *Journal of Marketing* (July 1965), pp. 3–8; and Alan A. Roberts, "Applying the Strategy of Market Segmentation," *Business Horizons* (Fall 1961), pp. 65–72. Both articles are included in James F. Engel, Henry F. Fiorillo, and Murray A. Cayley, eds., *Market Segmentation: Concepts and Applications* (New York: Holt, Rinehart & Winston, 1972).

8. The criteria for market attractiveness and the institutional success factors are based on the General Electric strategic business planning grid.

9. David Garvin, *Economics of University Behavior* (New York: Academic Press, 1980).

10. C. E. Osgood, G. J. Suci, and P. H. Tannenbaum, *The Measurement of Meaning* (Urbana, IL: University of Illinois Press, 1957).

11. Ibid.

# 10

# Understanding Consumers

*Ross Lenhart, former director of admissions at a small liberal arts college, describes his perceptions of his son's college-choice process:*

*It's finally here. After I've spent a twenty-five-year career in and around college admission, it hits home. My son, Scott, is seventeen, in the spring of his junior year, and looking. With a decent set of SATs, a class ranking far exceeding that of his old man's, a student body officer, and varsity status in several sports, Scott is ready to choose his college.*

*As his father, my first task is to divorce myself from my own prejudices and opinions. After years of looking at colleges and universities from both sides of my desk, I do have my own ideas. But it's Scott who'll be packing up for college, not me.*

*Yet, as a parent, this is serious stuff, one that calls for a "positive family decision," as they say. Besides, if we join together in this quest for the perfect match of good student to good school, it can be fun for both of us. Who knows, maybe I'll learn a thing or two myself.*

*The routine is familiar to me, of course. It begins in the spring of Scott's junior year with a slow trickle of publications. Then the search kicks in along about April. With some good information in hand, we sit down together and make a list, included are thirteen private and three public institutions. It's my impression that Scott is avoiding the social and athletic favorites of so many of his peers. He doesn't seem to mind if his friends or even his guidance counselor haven't heard of most of the schools on his wish list. I get the idea that he wants to find the perfect match, that special campus that's right for him. In all these points we are in total agreement.*

*The next step is the visit. For both of us, location plays an important role and the colleges and universities on his list are so spread out that we decided on three separate trips—two in the spring and one in the summer. We begin during vacation with a family trip from Atlanta up I-85 to Davidson, Duke, Chapel Hill, Guilford, and Furman. Side visits over several weekends take us to Princeton, Georgetown, Berry, and the University of the South. The summer trip is a marathon crisscrossing of Virginia, with stops at William and Mary, Richmond, University of Virginia, Washington & Lee, Roanoke, and, on the way home, Wake Forest.*

*I am conscious during these forays that my so-called "expertise" may prejudice Scott in his selection process. I will find out that my concerns are unfounded.*

*Suddenly, Scott is about to become a high school senior. He tells me he has trimmed his choices to three schools: Davidson, Washington & Lee, and Sewanee. Those of you who know these schools must agree that although there are distinct differences between them, there are common links as well. I am pleased with his choices; they seem suited to him, no matter what yardstick he uses. His mother and younger brother, Clay, agree. We four breathe a partial sigh of relief.*

*As we enter the fall, Scott seems to want to end his search as soon as he can; I concur, worn down by the process almost as much as he. On Saturday, December 15, 1990, my son receives an early Christmas present: early decision acceptance by Davidson College. The choice is made. A positive family decision has been reached. Scott will enter Davidson College with the class of 1995.*

> **Source:** Ross W. Lenhart, "Travels with Scott: A Parent's Odyssey in Search of the Right College," *The Journal of College Admission*, No. 132 (Summer 1991), pp. 7–8.

---

Scott Lenhart struggled through a process familiar to hundreds of thousands of young (and older) adults each year: selecting, applying to, and getting accepted by one or more colleges, and then deciding which one to attend.

Consumers' decisions directly affect the institution. Students decide whether to apply and enroll. Alumni support affects the institution's financial well-being. A foundation reviews a college's request for funds for a library addition. These and similar decisions have crucial implications for the school or college because they influence who the institution's clients will be and what resources it will have to carry out its mission.

## CHOICE, SELECTIVITY, AND CAPACITY

Commercial enterprises often aim to create the maximum possible level of demand. If demand grows rapidly, the company will expand to serve the new, higher level of demand since greater demand typically means higher profits. A for-profit technical-vocational school would quickly hire additional instructors, lease additional instructional space, and continue advertising for additional students. For such institutions the total level of demand is determined by student interest and school marketing effort.

Most U.S. educational institutions are not-for-profit entities that have a desired level of demand and either can't or don't want to expand very much. Their aim is to attract "enough" well-qualified students and they use higher student demand to increase institutional selectivity.

Thus, educational institutions also make choices, based on the institution's mission and the level of demand the institution can and wishes to serve. As we pointed out in Chapter 8, some educational programs serve anyone who wants to participate (noncredit telecourse broadcasts), some programs serve all those who are willing to pay (most athletic and cultural events), others serve all those who meet certain qualifications (many community colleges), and still others select only a subset of all those who apply and are qualified (most colleges and universities).

The most prestigious schools often experience *overdemand*. They have limited facilities and faculties, and a set level of desired enrollment. So many prospects apply that these schools could fill their entering classes several times over with academically able students whose families could afford to pay the entire cost. These schools must winnow the applicants—usually by applying highly demanding academic and other selection criteria—to arrive at the groups they can and will admit. Students' ability to pay is typically less important than academic criteria, since these institutions use financial aid to enroll a more economically and ethnically diverse class than would otherwise be the case. To attract the strongest prospects, these highly selective institutions need to understand how the best students evaluate and select the schools they will attend.

A second group of schools is experiencing overdemand: some state universities. For more than three decades, the University of California was committed to serving the brightest 12.5 percent of the state's high school graduates. But the number of high school graduates is expected to almost double by 2010, which would mean a 70 percent increase in undergraduate enrollment. But the State of California doesn't have the money to build additional campuses, so the University of California System may reduce eligibility to the top 10 percent or even 7.5 percent of high school graduates.[1]

Some public elementary and secondary schools experience overdemand as well. School districts try to predict demand several years in advance because they do not have the option to tell eligible students to go somewhere else. They must stretch their resources to serve all these students, hiring additional teachers and staff and adding classroom space as needed.

Some schools experience *underdemand*. Perhaps they once had a clear identity and attracted certain types of students. With population shifts and/or the expansion of educational opportunities, their natural constituencies have moved away or found more attractive alternatives. These schools need to review their strengths and weaknesses as part of a strategic planning process. They need to conduct research to find out what their current students find attractive and what would attract additional qualified students, and then make the appropriate changes to attract and serve them.

Many other schools have a substantial level of demand, but the schools want to attract more academically able, committed students than those they are currently serving. These schools have a choice: They can make efforts to attract more and stronger students, they can continue to accept students like the ones they currently serve, or they can reduce their overall enrollment to become more selective. Most schools become committed to a certain level of enrollment and prefer to try to increase selectivity by raising the school's stature and increasing awareness of what it offers to able students.

The institution's task in each case is to determine how current and prospective customers make their decisions, including what factors they consider, how they weigh the relative importance of these factors, the process by which they arrive at a decision, and the influences that operate on that process. By understanding these dimensions of decision making and choice, the institution can be more effective in attracting and satisfying its constituents.

Knowledge of the consumer is the basis for effective program development and other marketing activities. No wonder then that so many admissions officers and fund raisers wish they had a clearer understanding of what influences the decision to apply, attend, or donate.

We will deal with *individual* consumers in the first part of the chapter and *organizational* consumers in the second part. In both cases, we will seek to understand the choice and decision-making process from the consumer's perspective.

## INDIVIDUAL CONSUMER BEHAVIOR: THE SCHOOL-CHOICE PROCESS

The choice of which school to attend is often considered one of the most important decisions young people and their families make. The process often starts years before applying and enrolling (Exhibit 10-1). In this section we discuss the following features of this process:

- Why the school-choice process is so complex.
- The interrelationship between the choice process by the school and by the prospect.
- The steps in highly complex decision making.
- Ways students narrow their choices and weigh their alternatives to come to a decision.
- Factors that can come into play after the decision has been made.

### The Role of Involvement and Experience in Decision Making

The level of personal involvement and prior experience a person brings to a decision will influence how complex and time-consuming the decision process will be. Table 10-1 shows a taxonomy of three decision-making approaches: *routinized, simplified, and extensive decision making.*

People make choices every day, but most of those choices are *low-involvement* decisions. Which brand of cereal, milk, or bread to buy is usually a trivial choice, taking at most a few seconds. Even the decision of deodorant or toothpaste brand rarely takes much time or creates much anxiety, despite advertisements that attempt to make these decisions more salient. Low-involvement decisions are those which have low personal importance or relevance. Frequently purchased, low-cost goods usually fall into this category.

Many decisions about educational choices (and about making significant donations) are *high-involvement* decisions. High personal involvement usually is present when one or more of the following conditions exist:

1. The consumer's decision will reflect upon his or her self-image and could have long-term consequences.
2. The cost to carry out the decision involves major personal or economic sacrifices.
3. The personal and social risks of making a "wrong" decision are perceived as high.
4. There is considerable reference-group pressure to make a particular choice or to act in a particular way, and the target consumer is strongly motivated to meet the expectations of these reference groups.

The decision about which school or college to attend is a process that starts long before the final enrollment decision is made and may have consequences long afterward. The school one attends may well affect one's future career, friendships, choice of marriage partner, location of future residence, and life satisfaction. Also, depending on where the prospective student lives, how mobile the student is, and the type of school sought, the number of op-

EXHIBIT 10-1    The timing of educational purchase decisions

**Elementary school.** Research suggests that in the majority of cases the decision as to where a child is going to elementary school is made by the time the child is three and one-half years of age. Moreover, the research suggests that in a majority of cases the decision is made by the child's mother. The most important influences on the mother's decision typically include:

1. friends, neighbors, other mothers

2. the mother's mother, sisters, and/or extended family members

3. kindergarten and/or primary-grade teachers, especially if they are well known to the family

4. nursery school teachers and day-care providers

This research leads to the conclusion that if elementary schools could design and implement plans to reach mothers of two-year-olds, enrollment at the entry level would improve. Such plans might include introducing kindergarten and first-grade teachers to day-care providers and nursery school teachers, and scheduling activities that bring day-care and nursery school children in contact with the school.

**Secondary schools.** In a majority of cases the decision as to where the child is going to high school is made when the child is in sixth grade. In a majority of cases, the decision is made by the preteens themselves. The major influences on this decision include

1. friends, peers

2. parents, with a larger role played by the father than in the elementary school decision

3. elementary school teachers

4. secondary school teachers

5. the availability of cocurricular and extracurricular activities

Attracting these students could be improved by inviting fifth and sixth graders to high school activities and events, and by bringing secondary school teachers into the elementary schools.

**Higher education.** Students planning to attend even somewhat competitive colleges typically begin their search process during their junior or even sophomore year in high school.

Colleges seeking a diverse student body face an important challenge: Many high school students, particularly minority students, either do not complete high school or do not imagine college or other higher education as an option for themselves. Young people in either of these two categories do not apply to college and do not prepare academically to qualify for admission. Colleges or groups of colleges that want to increase college attendance by minority students can help increase the number of prospects by working with high schools and/or individual students to increase students' academic abilities, motivation, and self-confidence, and by exposing them to what college is like.

Source: Information on the timing of elementary and high school decisions comes from *Catholic School Management Letter*, XII, no. 4 (February 1991), 24 Cornfield Lane, Madison, CT 06443.

TABLE 10-1  A taxonomy of decision-making approaches

| EXPERIENCE | DEGREE OF PERSONAL INVOLVEMENT | |
|---|---|---|
| | HIGH | LOW |
| None | Extensive decision making | Extensive decision making |
| Some | Simplified decision making | No observable decision making |
| Much | Routinized decision making | No observable decision making |

tions to consider can be extensive, making the sorting process even more involving. The decision-making process can be time-consuming. Based on estimates that a typical prospect spends 40 to 50 hours investigating colleges, Larry Litten estimates that total financial cost would be approximately $1,400, not including any commercial test-preparation courses or private counseling.[2] Litten's estimate, shown in Table 10-2, includes foregone salary at the rate of $5 per hour, and does not reflect the psychological costs of test anxiety, parental pressure, and stress.

We can imagine circumstances under which any one of three levels of decision complexity could exist—routinized, simplified, or extensive decision making. Here are three examples:

Andy Janeway lived in a town that had grown up around a highly regarded state university. In fact, his home was one mile from the university. From early childhood he had attended fairs, athletic events, concerts, and other activities at "The University," and from junior high age he had attended the annual open houses when students in each academic field presented exhibits of their work. He had participated in summer programs for high school students and even enrolled for credit in a Japanese course during his senior

TABLE 10-2  The cost of the college-decision process

| | |
|---|---|
| Time spent in college investigation and self-examination (45 hrs.) | $225 |
| College guidebooks | $ 25 |
| Application fees ($30) | $120 |
| Admission tests (two sittings at $13 each) | $ 26 |
| Achievement tests (three at one time) | 21 |
| Study/review for tests (10 hours)[a] | $ 50 |
| Preenrollment visits (assuming three trips at $300/trip, which is low if parents are also involved or more than one distant college is explored)[b] | $900 |

[a]Commericial test-preparation courses are not assumed.
[b]No private admission counseling is assumed. Such counseling may cost between $200 and $1,000.
Source: Larry H. Litten, *Ivy Bound: High-Ability Students and College Choice* (New York, NY: The College Entrance Examination Board, 1991), p. 52.

year in high school. The in-state tuition at the university was a few hundred dollars a year, which Andy's family could easily afford. Andy's older brothers had graduated from the university, and many of Andy's high school friends were planning to go to the university. The only requirement for admission was a C average from one of the state's high schools, and he could apply and be admitted a day before registration. For Andy, this was probably a case of routinized decision making.

Joseph Sullivan grew up in a medium-sized city where the majority of the population, like his family, was Catholic. There were three private colleges in the city, one Protestant and two Catholic—one for men, one for women. There were no public colleges. Coming from a devout Catholic family and having attended Catholic schools, it was always assumed that he would attend a Catholic college. When he graduated from high school, he went to the "obvious choice"—the local Catholic men's college. Joseph Sullivan's decision was probably an example of simplified decision making.

Elizabeth Morris was named a National Merit finalist. Her parents had both graduated from elite colleges, and both had graduate degrees and professional careers. While their mailbox was stuffed daily with direct mail from colleges and universities around the country, Elizabeth's parents wanted "the best" for Elizabeth and encouraged her to look at the most academically elite, selective colleges and universities. Elizabeth herself recognized that the college she attended would help determine her prospects for graduate school and her future career. She spent many hours reading about the most selective colleges, made two lengthy trips to visit several campuses, and spent many hours preparing her application essays. Elizabeth clearly engaged in extensive decision making.

These three examples do not mean there are only three possible scenarios. Students with weak academic records may engage in extensive decision making, and some very strong students may spend little time and effort selecting a college to attend.[3] A major study found that 30 percent of first-time, full-time college freshmen applied only to the college in which they later enrolled, 18 percent applied to one other, 17 percent to two others, 14 percent to three others, and 20 percent applied to four or more schools beside the one attended.[4]

The extensiveness of the decision-making process depends not only on prior experience and the extent of personal involvement, but also on the range of available and feasible choices, the decision maker's awareness of these choices (and the information available about them), and the time available for making the decision, among other considerations. For example, if a parent's choice for a young child is between the neighborhood public school and the area's only Catholic school, the information-gathering phase—and perhaps the final decision—will probably be easier than for the capable high school senior with family resources who is sorting through a large number of possible colleges.

### The Parallel Decision Process

In many instances both prospective students and educational institutions have the opportunity to choose. In Chapter 8 we introduced the admissions funnel concept. But just as the institution narrows its selection, so too do prospective students. The individual student's decision is probably the more difficult because the eventual decision is to attend one specific institution. The school, on the other hand, is selecting a mix of various students, of whom some may prove to be less attractive than the school prefers, but others will be stronger. The distinction can be expressed in investment terms: The prospective student can only invest in a single "stock," while the school is investing in a diversified and therefore less risky "mutual fund."

Figure 10-1 shows two funnels. On the left is the typical recruitment funnel, which shows the choice-narrowing process an educational institution goes through in selecting a class. On the right is a hypothetical student's decision funnel to select a college. Each party's decision affects the other party's decision, so college marketers need to examine and understand both decision processes.

The college (or other educational institution) can only accept students who apply, and students only apply to schools they have heard of. So the college wants to make sure to reach the most attractive students, make them aware of the college, and tell them what the college has to offer. We will have much more to say about this in subsequent chapters on programs, pricing and financial aid, communications and advertising, and enrollment management. Here we will focus on choice and the decision-making process.

The school aims to "convert" leads into applicants, and then goes through a screening and selection process in which it tries to determine which

FIGURE 10-1    An institution's recruitment funnel and a prospect's decision funnel

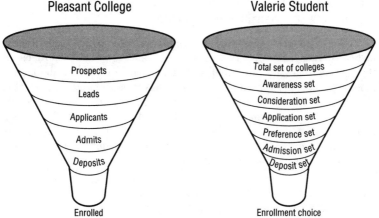

are the strongest students who will be a good match with the college. Some schools have so few applicants that they accept and then try to enroll every possible applicant. This approach is not a decision process. These schools need to increase their number of leads and applicants.

Most schools are able to apply some selection criteria. What they need is to formulate a decision framework and philosophy to guide the selection process. Thomas Vance Sturgeon proposes the following steps.[5]

1. *Define the ideal applicant.* The school should be able to explain why it selected a particular student, and why another student was not admitted.
2. *Establish an admissions philosophy.* How will the school determine which applicants are best suited to succeed academically and in other ways? How will the school establish criteria for predicting success?
3. *Determine the rating variables to be used and prioritize them.* Typical rating variables—such as high school grade-point average, SAT verbal scores, SAT mathematics scores, recommendations, essays, and so on—need to be prioritized based on their weight in the final selection process.
4. *Create a selection framework that incorporates the variables and weights.*
5. *Apply the selection framework* to prepare a profile of each applicant, and then select those students whose profiles best match the school's ideal applicant.

There is considerable debate whether a school's student-selection process is based on science or art, and the extent to which "hard" indicators such as grades and test scores alone are as good or better predictors of success than such "soft" indicators as motivation. Most institutions don't have the luxury of making such fine-grained distinctions, as long as they have relatively few applicants per place, but the basic review and decision process remains the same.

Now let's consider the decision process for the college applicant. A hypothetical student who wants to attend college in the United States has over 3,000 possibilities but can attend only one. Admissions professionals are convinced that for each student there are several prospective colleges at which the student will be happy and well served. Yet many students and their parents don't believe it. According to Fred Zuker,

> Choosing the "right" college has become an individual and family process highly charged with anxiety. . . . Students place inordinate burdens on themselves to get into the "right" college. Parents of a student bound for a prestigious college often perceive themselves as giving the student the ultimate "good" of American society. Some parents live vicariously through the student's triumph in the college admissions "game" . . . . Such parents are fixated on attendance at a college that will gain—for them—the highest approval rating in their social circle, where such things are used as a measure of parental success.[6]

No wonder, then, that for many applicants the process of applying and deciding often exemplifies highly complex decision making.

### Steps in Highly-Complex Decision Making

Figure 10-2 shows the steps in highly complex decision making, which elaborate the steps shown in the preceding decision funnel for the student's decision process. The heart of the process involves narrowing down the range of choices by identifying alternatives, determining evaluation criteria, and then applying the criteria to the alternatives to come to a choice.

**Forming the Choice Set.** Figure 10-3 shows the specifics of Valerie's successive sets of schools as she moves from the top to the bottom of the decision funnel. Of course, we can't list the total set of over 3,000 schools. The total set can be divided into Valerie's *awareness* set—the schools she has heard of—and her *unawareness* set. The schools in her unawareness set will never be considered unless somehow they make their way into her awareness set. Since Valerie has read widely about colleges, she is aware of several dozen colleges. We give a somewhat truncated list of schools in Valerie's awareness set.

Of all the schools she is aware of, Valerie narrows the list down to her *consideration* set consisting of eight schools. She quickly decides that three of the schools she knows of are not feasible for her to consider further, either because she feels her academic record isn't strong enough, or because they don't offer her preferred major, or for some other reason. She then moves to examine each of the five remaining colleges in detail to decide where to apply. As she continues to gather information, a few colleges remain very appealing

FIGURE 10-2    The steps in highly-complex decision making

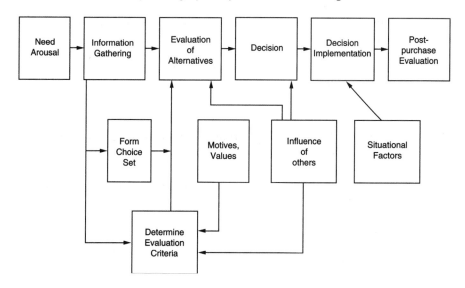

FIGURE 10-3   Successive sets in decision making

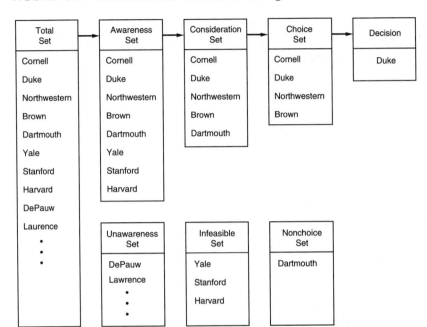

and these become her *choice* set. Valerie then applies to the four schools in her choice set and is fortunate enough to be accepted at three of them.

**Information Gathering.** Students considering college undertake varying degrees of information gathering, depending on their own level of need for information. The marketer is interested in the following two questions at this stage:

- How much information are consumers likely to gather before making a decision in this product class? (*information neediness*)
- What information sources will consumers use, and what will be their relative influence? (*information sources*)

*Information neediness.* Some students jump right into making a decision, while others take months and months, weighing every piece of information. We can distinguish between two broad levels of information gathering. The milder level is called *heightened attention.* Thus, Valerie may simply become more attentive to information about colleges, noticing news about colleges and listening to friends discuss them. On the other hand, she may undertake an active *information search*, seeking books on the subject, writing for catalogs, attending college fairs, and meeting several times with her high school counselor. How extensive the search she undertakes depends upon the strength of her motivation, the amount of information she initially has, the ease of obtaining additional information, the value she places on additional information, and the satisfaction she gets from the search process.

The college marketer must understand the information gathering and evaluation activities of prospective consumers. The marketer's task is to help students learn about the key attributes of colleges, their relative importance, and the standing of the particular college on the more important attributes.

**Establishing Selection Criteria.** Throughout the narrowing process, Valerie has been applying some criteria. She will seek to make her criteria more explicit as she goes along, since she will have some hard decisions to make as she forms her choice and application sets. Some students turn to college-selection software to help them narrow down the range of possible schools. These software packages typically begin by asking the respondent to state preferences for certain school and location attributes. For example, Valerie might be asked to respond to questions about which state or states she would prefer to study in, private versus public, religious sponsorship versus none, student body size, size of the surrounding community, majors offered, cost, presence or absence of sororities and fraternities, and athletic programs. The software then screens its database of schools and presents Valerie with the schools that came closest to matching her criteria.[7]

Of course, Valerie could choose her own criteria and do some screening without the software. She will want to determine what factors to consider— her *criteria*—in making her decision, and the relative values—*importance weights*—she will use to assess each school on each of the criteria.

Valerie's criteria and her importance weights will be shaped by her needs. One useful typology of basic needs is Maslow's *hierarchy of needs*, shown in Figure 10-4.[8] Maslow held that people act to satisfy their lower needs first before satisfying their high needs. A starving man, for example, first devotes his energy to finding food. If this basic need is satisfied, he can spend more time on his safety needs, such as eating the right foods and breathing fresh air. When he feels safe, he can take the time to deepen his social affiliations and friendships. Still later, he can develop pursuits that will meet his need for self-esteem and for winning the esteem of others. Once this need is satisfied, he is free to actualize his potential in other ways. As each lower-level need is satisfied, it ceases to be a motivator, and a higher need takes on more importance in motivating the person's actions and choices.

We can ask what basic needs are stimulated by the aroused interest in college. Some high school seniors will become concerned about whether they can afford college and meet their basic needs for food and adequate housing. Others will wonder how safe they will be away from home. Still others will be concerned with whether they can find people they like and who like them. And others will be concerned with self-esteem and self-actualization. A college will not be able to give attention to all these needs. Thus, we find colleges

FIGURE 10-4    Maslow's hierarchy of needs

Source: Based on Hierarchy of Needs in "A Theory of Human Motivation" in *Motivation and Personality,* Second Edition, by Abraham H. Maslow. Copyright © 1970 by Abraham H. Maslow. By permission of Harper & Row, Publishers, Inc.

that cater primarily to the need for belonging (small schools with small classes, a caring faculty, and a good social life), others to the students' need for esteem (many "name" schools), and still others to the students' need for self-actualization (schools that emphasize exploring one's values).

Students often want to satisfy several sometimes-conflicting needs with one decision. Thus, a student may have a high need for both achieving and belonging. This can create internal conflict, which the person could try to handle by treating one need as more important than the other, or by fluctuating between the two needs at different time. Resolving this conflict is the role of the person's values—namely, the principles the person employs to weigh the various consequences that might follow from a particular choice.

**Evaluation of Alternatives.** Through the process of gathering information, the consumer forms a clearer picture of the major available choices. He or she eliminates certain alternatives and moves toward making a choice among the few remaining alternatives.

Now we turn to the question, How do consumers make a choice among the colleges in the choice set? The simple answer is that they form a set of preferences by some process and choose their first preference, assuming they are admitted. Here we shall want to explore the process by which consumers form their preferences.

We return to Valerie trying to make a choice among a set of colleges. We

FIGURE 10-5    A high school student's beliefs
about three colleges

Attribute

|  | Academic Quality | Social Life | Location | Cost |
|---|---|---|---|---|
| A | 10 | 8 | 6 | 4 |
| B | 8 | 9 | 8 | 3 |
| C | 6 | 8 | 7 | 5 |

College

Note: Ten represents the highest desirable score on that attribute. In the case of tuition, a high number means a low tuition, which makes the college more desirable.

shall assume that her choice set consists of three colleges, to be identified as A, B, and C, rather than using the specific colleges mentioned earlier. We will assume that Valerie has provided the information shown in Figure 10-5. Six basic concepts are necessary to analyze the consumer evaluation process.

The first concept is the notion of a *choice set*, which we already described as consisting of colleges A, B, and C.

The second concept is that of *school attributes*. We assume that each consumer sees a given school as consisting of one or more attributes. Where do attributes "come from"? One direct approach is to ask consumers to name the factors they consider when thinking about schools to attend. In Valerie's case, she named four attributes as most important: academic quality, social life, location, and cost.

Third, the consumer is assumed to have a set of *perceptions* about where each specific school stands on each attribute. The set of perceptions about a particular school is the school image. Each row of Figure 10-5 represents Valerie's image of the corresponding college. A number from 1 to 10 is assigned to represent how much of each attribute Valerie sees the college as possessing.

Fourth, the consumer is assumed to have a *utility function* for each attribute. The utility function describes the consumer's varying level of satisfaction with varying levels of an attribute. For example, Valerie believes that her satisfaction will rise with higher levels of academic quality and social life; she would most prefer a college in the South and least in the West; and her satisfaction falls as the cost rises. If we combine Valerie's preferred attribute levels, they make up her ideal college.

Fifth, the consumer is assumed to value some school attributes more than others, attaching different *importance weights* to the various attributes.[9] The relative importance of each attribute is specific to each prospective student, although considerable research has been conducted to try to understand patterns of importance weights for selected student categories.

A student might consider four school attributes important: academic quality, social life, location, and cost. Few students would rate all four attributes to be *equally* important. A student admitted to a school high in academic quality in the most preferred location at a very reasonable effective cost might decide that a dull or nonexistent social life can be compensated for during holidays and summer.

The consumer's importance weights can be elicited in at least three ways: (1) the consumer can be asked to rank the attributes in order of their importance (*ranking method*); (2) the consumer can be asked to distribute 100 points among the attributes to indicate their relative importance (*constant-sum method*); (3) the consumer can be asked to rate the importance of each attribute on a scale going from 0 to 1 (*rating method*).

Sixth, the consumer arrives at preferences about the school alternatives through some *evaluation procedure*. Unfortunately, there is no one decision evaluation process used by all consumers, or even by one consumer in all situations.[10] The major decision models are described in Exhibit 10-2, with numbers referring to Figure 10-5.

EXHIBIT 10-2    Different ways to come to a decision

1. *Jump-the-Hurdles Model.* Here the consumer sets minimum attribute levels that he or she will consider, then drops from consideration those schools that fall short on any attribute. Valerie might decide that she will consider only colleges with an academic quality greater than 7 *and* a social life greater than 8. Only college B will satisfy her in this case.

2. *Either-Or Model.* Here the consumer will consider schools that meet at least one minimum attribute level. Valerie might decide that she will consider only colleges with an academic quality greater than 7 *or* a social life greater than 8. Here, colleges A or B will remain in the choice set.

3. *Tie-Breaking Model.* Here the consumer will rank the attributes in order of importance. Valerie will compare all the schools on the most important attribute and choose the superior one. If two schools are tied, she repeats the process with the second attribute. Valerie might decide that academic quality is the most important attribute. In this case, she will choose college A.

4. *Consumer Reports Model.* Here the consumer lines up the major alternatives, rates each alternative from high to low, multiplies each attribute rating by the importance weight of that attribute, and then selects the alternative that gets the best (highest) total rating. The underlying decision principle is that the consumer is looking for the "best deal" and so will buy the product, service, or school experience that offers the highest value.

EXHIBIT 10-2    (continued)

This decision-making approach is called the *expectancy-value* model because it aims to identify the choice that will yield the highest anticipated value.

Suppose Valerie assigned the following importance weights to the four respective attributes: 0.4, 0.3, 0.2, and 0.1. That is, she assigns 40 percent of the importance to the college's academic quality, 30 percent to its social life, 20 percent to its location, and 10 percent to its tuition cost. To find the expectancy value for each college, these weights are multiplied by the perceptions about the college, and the products are added to give the expectancy value for each college:

College A = 0.4(10) + 0.3(8) + 0.2(6) + 0.1(4) = 8.0

College B = 0.4(8) + 0.3(9) + 0.2(8) + 0.1(3) = 7.8

College C = 0.4(6) + 0.3(8) + 0.2(7) + 0.1(5) = 6.7

We would predict that Valerie will favor college A, since it has the largest expectancy value, 8.0. Note that there is not much difference between colleges A and B on total expected value. With this result, *Consumer Reports*—and our hypothetical students—would probably look again at the components of the model —the attribute ratings and importance weights—to see whether these should be reexamined. In the case of a real student, the student would probably want to visit each school to break what is, in this case, essentially a tie. (*Consumer Reports* would typically look at cost and rate the less costly product a "best buy.")

5. *My-Ideal Model.* Here the consumer decides on the idea level of each attribute. Suppose Valerie would prefer a college with the levels of 9, 9, 10, and 4 on the respective attributes. The further a college is from these levels, the more likely Valerie would reject it, assuming that she assigns the same importance weights as shown earlier. We multiply the weighted differences of each college from the ideal levels and take the sum. The lower the resulting sum, the closer the college is to Valerie's ideal. The vertical bars mean that we are interested only in the absolute distance and not the relative distance. The results follow:

College A = 0.4|10–9| + 0.3|8–9| + 0.2|6–10| + 0.1|4–4| = 1.5

College B = 0.4|8–9| + 0.3|9–9| + 0.2|8–10| + 0.1|3–4| = 0.9

College C = 0.4|6–9| + 0.3|8–9| + 0.2|7–10| + 0.1|5–4| = 2.2

We would predict that Valerie will favor college B, because it is the smallest weighted difference from her ideal college.

6. *Standout Model.* A consumer might ignore attributes that may be important but are pretty much at the same level for all colleges. Suppose the three colleges all have excellent music programs. In spite of the fact that Valerie may attach high importance to a music program, it will have no determinance on her college choice, since all colleges in her set are equal on this attribute. *Determinant attributes* are those that are both important and highly variable in the product class.

FIGURE 10-6    Influences on the college-bound student

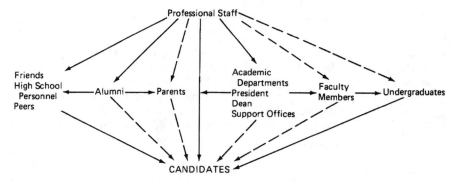

Note: Solid lines imply direct influence in the college-choice process; dashed lines indirect influence.

Source: William Ihlanfeldt, *Achieving Optimal Enrollments and Tuition Revenues* (San Francisco: Jossey-Bass, 1980), p. 129.

**Influences on the Decision Process.** Many people have an influence on the school-choice decision. The college marketer should be keenly interested in knowing the major information sources that prospective students will turn to and the relative influence each will have. One way to understand the role of personal influence is within the context of roles in the decision process. We can identify up to five roles:

- *Initiator.* The initiator is the person who first suggests or thinks of the idea of enrolling in college or choosing a particular school.
- *Influencer.* An influencer is a person whose views or advice carries some influence on the final decision, and who expresses his or her opinions or presents information.
- *Decider.* The decider is a person who ultimately determines any part of the whole decision: whether to enroll, where to enroll, or when to enroll.
- *Purchaser.* The purchaser is the person who makes the actual purchase.
- *User.* The user is the person who enrolls.

William Ihlanfeldt identified the major influences on the college-choice decision, shown in Figure 10-6. The relative influence of these sources can be found by asking prospective students to describe the type and amount of influence that different persons had on their decision making.

Valerie might report that her uncle initiated her interest in college by asking a year ago where Valerie planned to go to college. Her school counselor provided considerable information and influenced her thinking about the types of colleges she should consider. Her parents were both influencers and purchasers, since they would be paying for her education. Valerie, however, made the final decision and will enroll in college.

*How schools can influence choice.* Marketers can gain useful insights by interviewing consumers to find out how they form their evaluations of schools—what factors they consider and the processes they use to narrow their choice. Maguire Associates interviewed nearly 10,000 high school students, and then used a statistical analysis procedure called CHAID to determine what college characteristics were most important to respondents who reported they were in the top 10 percent of their high school class (Exhibit 10-3).

Suppose the admissions director discovers that most prospective students form their preferences by comparing actual colleges to their ideal college. College A, which would be the second choice to people like Valerie (ac-

EXHIBIT 10-3 What do high-ability high school students want?

What do high-ability high school students care about in a college? Most studies seeking to answer this question can tell you which factors were most frequently mentioned, or which factors students said were most important, but we know that high-ability students are not all alike. Can we get a closer look?

CHAID (CHi-square Automatic Interaction Detector) is a systematic exploratory technique that can sucessfully identify market segments by uncovering interactions between attitudes toward several *different* factors, and the relationship between identified patterns of attitudes and such decisions as which college to attend. In admissions CHAID can be used to identify differences—patterns of differences—of a school's inquirers, to determine what factors will most influence their decision to attend.

The figure shows one part of a CHAID analysis from a national database of almost 10,000 high school students, revealing the priorities of high-ability students. Of the students sampled, 54 percent said they ranked in the top 10 percent of their high school class. The first subgrouping distinguishing the top 10 percent from lower-ranked students, is on students' concern about the academic challenge of college coursework.

To determine which combinations of factors are most appealing, we can follow each "path" on the diagram to see which paths lead to higher percentages—the middle number in each box—of high-ability students. For example, of students who rated challenge of coursework to be extremely important (a value of 5), employment opportunities after graduation important (value of 4), and advising and counseling to be neutral or unimportant (values of 1, 2, or no answer), 72 percent were in the top 10 percent of their high school class.

## EXHIBIT 10-3 (continued)

Advising and Counseling Program

| 3-5 | 58% | n = 143 |
| 1,2,6 | 72% | n = 384 |

Employment Opportunities after Graduation

| 6 | 86% | n = 270 |
| 5 | 60% | n = 1504 |
| 4 | 68% | n = 527 |
| 3 | 62% | n = 195 |
| 2 | 60% | n = 85 |
| 1 | 55% | n = 51 |

Advising and Counseling Program

| 4,5 | 28% | n = 303 |
| 1–3,6 | 42% | n = 1092 |

Merit-Based Financial Aid

| 5 | 67% | n = 698 |
| 1–4,6 | 52% | n = 3532 |

Merit-Based Financial Aid

| 5 | 61% | n = 228 |
| 4 | 48% | n = 259 |
| 1–3,6 | 39% | n = 1395 |

Challenge of Coursework

| 5 | 64% | n = 2632 |
| 4 | 55% | n = 4230 |
| 2,3 | 43% | n = 1882 |
| 1,6 | 47% | n = 997 |

Total Sample
n = 9741
(54% are in top 10% of high school class)

1 = Not at all important
2
3
4
5 = Extremely important
6 = Missing value

Source: Maguire Associates, 2352 Main Street, Concord, MA 01742.

cording to the ideal-product model), wants to strengthen its chances of attracting students like Valerie. The school can consider at least six alternative strategies.[11]

**1.** *Modifying the school.* The college could alter its attributes to bring it closer to this segment's ideal college. For example, college A could improve its social life so it gets a higher rating. This is called *real repositioning*.

**2.** *Altering perceptions of the school.* The college could try to alter students' perceptions of where it actually stands on key attributes. Thus, Valerie may believe the effective cost is higher than it actually is, and information about financial aid and work opportunities can correct her perception. This is called *psychological repositioning*.

**3.** *Altering perceptions of other schools.* The college could try to alter students' perceptions of where a leading competitor stands on different attributes. This is called *competitive repositioning*. While common in commercial marketing, in the world of school admissions and marketing this approach is often unethical at worst, and ineffective at best.

**4.** *Altering the attribute-importance weights.* The college could encourage students to attach more importance to those attributes that the college excels in. For example, college A can attempt to persuade students that academic quality is the most important aspect of any college—more important than social life, palm trees, and winning athletic teams.

**5.** *Calling attention to neglected attributes.* The college could encourage students to pay attention to an attribute that they are normally unaware of or indifferent to. If college A offers unusually good career-preparation and placement services, the college can present these as a benefit of attending college there, and communicate this through publications on its career services counseling and workshops, meet-the-employers events, and its job placement record and alumni testimonials.

**6.** *Shifting the ideal school.* The college could try to persuade students to change their ideal levels for one or more attributes. College A might try to convince students that a location in a cold climate is ideal, since they can get more studying done.

The college will need to carefully evaluate these alternative strategies according to their importance, feasibility, and cost. The difficulty of implementing each strategy, such as repositioning the college or shifting importance weights, should not be minimized. If a school wants to present itself as technologically up to date, it would provide computer access for all students, wire residence-hall rooms for access to the computer network, make the library catalog available on-line, and provide cable-television connections to campus resources. This costs money in equipment, installation, training, and other support.

**Moving from Decision to Action.** The evaluation stage leads the consumer to form a ranked set of preferences among the alternative schools in the choice set. Normally, the consumer will move toward enrolling in the most preferred school. He or she will then form an enrollment intention, contingent on receiving the school's acceptance. However, other factors can intercede between forming an enrollment intention and actually enrolling. These factors are shown in Figure 10-7.[12]

*The attitudes of others.* Suppose Valerie prefers college B but her father prefers college C because it will cost less. As a result, Valerie's *enrollment probability* for college B will be somewhat reduced. The extent to which a preference will shift depends upon two things: (1) the intensity of the other person's negative attitude toward the consumer's preferred alternative, and (2) the consumer's motivation to comply with the other person's wishes. The more intense the other person's negativism and the closer the other person is to the consumer, the more the consumer will revise downward his or her purchase intention.[13]

Of course, two other factors play a role in the school-decision case: First, Valerie is the one who will attend the college, but her father expects to pay all or some significant part of her expenses there. The "power of the purse" goes beyond simple differences of opinion. Second, "an education" is a composite of so many services and experiences that it is hard—or impossible—to determine the impact of academic quality or even social life in advance of actually attending. (In fact, the true value of attending a particular school may become apparent only many years after graduation.) Valerie's father may feel that college B does in fact have a higher reputation for academic quality than college C, but that the offerings in Valerie's intended major are almost as good at college C, so she will not "miss" much.

*Situational factors.* The student forms an enrollment intention on the basis of such factors as expected family income, expected total cost of the attendance, and expected benefits of attending. But when the consumer is about to act, something may happen that prevents carrying out the enrollment intention. Her father may lose his job and be unable to contribute to-

FIGURE 10-7    Situational factors that affect action

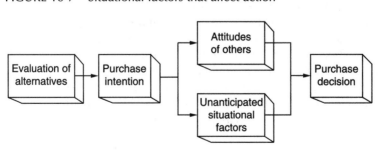

ward her education. Valerie may learn that she cannot get a college loan to attend college. She may not like the looks of the campus when she visits it. Some failing in the *critical contact situation* could influence the final decision. She may be turned off by some of the students or professors she meets. She may decide to go to a different college because her friends are going there.

Thus, preferences and even enrollment intentions are not completely reliable predictors of actual behavior. They give direction to behavior but fail to include a number of additional factors that may intervene.

When a person modifies, postpones, or avoids making a decision, he or she is probably perceiving that the decision involves considerable risk. Marketers term this feeling *perceived risk*. Marketers have devoted considerable effort to understanding buying behavior as risk taking.[14] Consumers cannot be certain about the performance and psychological consequences of their purchase decisions, which produces anxiety. The amount of perceived risk varies with the amount of money at stake, the amount of uncertainty about school attributes and importance weights, and the degree of consumer self-confidence. Often consumers have certain routines for reducing risks, such as procrastination, asking friends for information, and selecting well-known institutions. The marketer must understand the factors that provoke a feeling of risk in the consumer and must attempt to provide information and support that will help reduce this risk in order to help the consumer arrive at a decision.

**Postenrollment Assessment.** After making the decision and enrolling, the student will experience some level of satisfaction or dissatisfaction that will influence his or her behavior. Valerie's satisfaction with her decision has important implications for the college and for her college career. While waiting for her acceptance letters, Valerie has already started to think about which school she most wants to attend—her *preference set*. She has decided that if she is accepted by Brown, she will definitely go there. But if she is not accepted by Brown but is accepted by Northwestern and Duke, she would have a harder time deciding which she would accept.

The letters arrive. Brown has sent regrets, and Northwestern and Duke have said yes. By this time Valerie has decided that she is no longer interested in Cornell, so when Cornell's acceptance letter arrives, she quickly responds that she will not be attending.

When the notification date arrives, Valerie still has not made up her mind. She urges her parents to send deposits to both Northwestern and Duke. The deposits are nonrefundable, but the amounts are relatively modest and will "buy her time" to figure out which one she really wants to attend.[15]

When September arrives she appears at Duke and enrolls. She is still not completely sure of her decision, but she can't be two places at once. Her decision process is over—until she starts thinking about whether she made the right decision and should consider transferring to Northwestern!

A satisfied student will keep enrolling each term and will also tend to say good things about the school to others. A marketing truism is "Our best advertisement is a satisfied customer." On the other hand, a dissatisfied student will probably drop out or, at any rate, bad-mouth the college.

Educational institutions can take positive steps to help students feel good about their choice. A college can send a warm congratulatory letter to recently admitted students. The college can develop effective communications describing its philosophy and aspirations to reinforce the students' reasons for coming. Such postpurchase communications can reduce the amount of consumer postpurchase anxiety.[16] Of course, the college must do more than communicate a positive image; it must deliver the quality and attributes that attracted students in the first place. We discussed satisfaction in Chapter 2 and will discuss student retention in Chapter 15.

We have now completed our review of the steps in the consumer decision process. To illustrate the process we deliberately chose an example involving extensive problem solving, which features important aspects of decision making, but this does not imply that all prospects in all situations move smoothly and deliberately through each stage in the order shown. The purpose of the model is to provide clues on how to understand and better attract, serve, and satisfy a given group of consumers.

We have focused on similarities among consumers as they go through the buying process, rather than on their differences, but differences there are. Each consumer will be uniquely influenced by *cultural factors* (subculture and social class), *social factors* (reference groups, family roles, and statuses), *personal factors* (age and life cycle, occupation, economic circumstances, lifestyle, personality, and self-concept), and *psychological factors* (motivation, perception, learning, beliefs, and attitudes).[17] Many of these factors have been discussed in the preceding chapter on market segmentation, and the most significant factors need to be taken into account in the student-recruitment process.

## ORGANIZATIONAL BUYER BEHAVIOR

Organizations buy programs and services from educational institutions to train employees in specific skills, to develop employee and management talent through longer educational programs, and to obtain consulting and other services to improve the organization's functioning and/or profitability.

Most educational institutions are most comfortable thinking about their customers as individuals and their families, and have a harder time understanding the mindset of companies and their needs, resources, policies, and buying procedures.

Institutions dealing with organization buyers need to take into account several considerations not normally found in consumer marketing:

- Organizations buy goods and services in order to make profits, reduce costs, serve their internal clientele's needs, and meet societal and legal obligations.
- More people tend to participate in organizational buying decisions than in consumer buying decisions. The participants in an organizational buying decision usually vary in their organizational responsibilities and in the criteria they apply to the purchase decision, making the decision process more lengthy and complex.
- Organizational buyers operate under formal policies, constraints, and requirements established by their organizations.
- Selling to organizations tends to involve more personal contact and negotiation than does consumer marketing.

To illustrate the process, we will examine how a large corporation might go about contracting for educational services for its employees.

### Need Arousal

Corporations need well-trained, up-to-date employees. The more rapid the pace of technological change facing the company, the more important is an ongoing program of training and education. Evidence on the "half-life" of knowledge in many fields, particularly technology fields, suggests that most employees should be "replacing" 20 percent of their knowledge every year!

Some companies have been passive about filling this gap, relying on occasional on-site training programs and on eager employees' own efforts to keep up with new developments through reading or courses. A company may set up a tuition-reimbursement program, paying for employees' tuition and books as long as the employee contributes his or her own time and enrolls in courses relevant to job responsibilities. (Despite the ostensible educational purpose of such programs, a 1985 study of large Silicon Valley technology companies found that an equally strong motive was to match the employee educational benefits offered by direct competitors, who might otherwise lure away employees.) Companies often set up rather loose guidelines on institutional acceptability, leaving the decision up to employees.

As such programs have grown in popularity with employees—and thus in cost—companies have begun to look for ways to maximize company benefits without unduly discouraging employee participation. One approach has been to limit reimbursement to schools meeting certain standards and to offer differential levels of reimbursement to guide employees to the more reasonably priced options. Some companies have begun the practice of tracking the company's educational investment in terms of individual employees, rather than simply by the total annual company expenditure on education.[18] In addition, companies are becoming increasingly sophisticated purchasers of educational services.

Suppose a corporation decided to examine its purchase of educational services in preparation for altering its educational reimbursement program. This reexamination was inspired by lower company (and industry) profits and pressure for cost-cutting, as well as tuition costs increasing faster than inflation and profits. These circumstances produce the need arousal stage.

### Information Gathering

The company has several possibilities that merit consideration, among them:

- Reimbursement could be limited to a small number of schools, only for courses passed with a certain grade, and only for employees who have been with the company for at least five years.
- The company could offer company-specific training programs on-site, and discontinue purchase of educational services from educational institutions.
- The company could set an upper limit on the annual educational reimbursement level, but the leave the decision of where to attend to the employee.

The company seeks information to help determine the most productive way to provide educational programs for its employees. After reviewing its options with the assistance of an educational consultant, the company decides to continue its internal company training programs, but to modify its educational-benefits program which pays employees' tuition for courses and degree programs offered by area colleges and universities.

The company decides to offer educational reimbursement to all employees with at least one year of service, but the company planning group decides to contract with specific nearby institutions, which will give the company "preferred tuition" rates and other advantages.

To obtain uniform, directly comparable data, the company sends each candidate school a set of forms—a request for proposal (RFP)—on which each school will present a formal bid. The request for proposal will detail the courses, programs, and approximate numbers of employees to be served in a given time period, and each school's response will detail what the school will provide and the "best price" the institution will charge for these educational services.[19]

This is a new approach for the company. Robinson, Faris, and Wind distinguish among three types of buying situations that they called "buy classes":[20]

**1.** *Straight rebuy* refers to the situation when an organization is buying something similar to what it has bought in the past. For example, if the company and the supplying educational institutions were fully satisfied with the existing contracts, the company could simply renew them with—perhaps—readily negotiated increases in price based on inflation. A straight rebuy is analogous to routinized decision making by individual consumers.

**2.** *Modified rebuy* refers to the situation when the company is considering some change from its past purchases. The task calls for gathering more information than in the case of a straight rebuy. The company may find that its educational needs have changed significantly because it has hired more young workers who need specialized skill training, because it will be greatly increasing the number of employees in a particular location, and/or because it will be implementing new processes that require that more employees get master's degrees. The company will need to do a reassessment of its educational needs, determine an expanded list of potential suppliers (colleges and universities), and prepare a new request for proposals. It will then need to apply its criteria and select the best provider(s).

**3.** *New task* calls for more information gathering and extensive decision making because the company is faced with buying a new program or service. The first time a company goes through an educational assessment/RFP cycle will probably be a new-task situation because it is so different from the way most companies obtain educational services.

The task will be new because for the first time the company will be buying educational services "in bulk" directly from educational institutions. The planning group will probably send the RFP only to area institutions that already meet some identifiable standards of quality, such as accreditation. The consultant can prescreen local institutions and help the company to identify institution-selection criteria. For example, the company may ask institutions for the following:

- Reduced tuition for multiple employees attending one college.
- Elimination of "nuisance" fees such as application and student activities fees.
- Scheduling of elective courses on the company's site on a lower per-course, rather than per-student, basis.
- Academic credit for life/work experience and assistance in transferring credits from one college to another.
- Acceptance of standard reimbursement rates for introductory-level courses, based upon comparable courses at similar institutions.

## Evaluation of Alternatives

The planning group will then appraise the proposals. Companies that carefully screen potential suppliers of raw materials, parts, and services will find that the process is quite similar. The company's planning group will need to sift through them to assess how well each proposal meets the company's objectives (as spelled out in the RFP) and the cost of buying educational services under each institution's proposal.

## Decision Making and Implementation

The planning group will then select the best provider or set of providers and accept—or conduct more negotiations—with the institutions offering the best combination of programs and terms. Since the company can select multiple providers, not just one, the planning group will want to weigh the cost advantages of concentrating its purchases with one or two institutions versus spreading out its purchases among many. The company will eventually sign agreements with providing institutions, and then publicize the educational benefits program to its employees.

Informing employees will probably start with briefing sessions for managers, so they can understand and communicate the program to others. Publications with guidelines for applying and participating in the educational benefits program need to be prepared, explaining the terms of participation. The company's human resources/benefits managers will administer the program and maintain liaisons with the supplying institutions.

## Postpurchase Evaluation

The company's human resources/benefits managers should have a keen interest in how well each institution is living up to its contract. The company may require copies of course syllabi, teacher-evaluation results, and other documentation. Employee-participants would be asked to provide qualitative evaluations of individual professors and courses. The company should also try to ascertain improvements in employee performance—in range and/or level of skills—as a result of participation in the program. Results of this monitoring of programs and employee-participants will be used in reviewing the next cycle of proposals.

## Institutional Response

Educational institutions seeking to meet the needs of company "buyers" need to understand the company's motivations and objectives. The first company request for proposal will probably create some turmoil, as the school will have to calculate the institutional advantages and costs of offering tuition discounts and other special features to this company and—in the future—to other companies that adopt this approach to paying for educational benefits.

By understanding the company, the institution is more likely to design an attractive set of benefits. Of course the college can't afford to "give away" its services at a loss. By agreeing to give tuition discounts, the institution initially reduces its revenue, with the expectation that an increased level of employee participation will increase the number of enrollments and the total revenue. If the college decides not to offer these discounts and features, the college may face the loss of a portion of its part-time enrollment.

## SUMMARY

Choice is at the heart of marketing, and marketers strive to understand the processes consumers use to decide what and when to buy. And while prospects decide where to apply, educational institutions must decide which prospects to appeal to and which to admit.

Individual buyers tend to pass through several stages in connection with a school decision. The first stage is need arousal. Understanding this stage involves determining what factors triggered the interest, and what needs and wants became activated. In the second stage, information gathering, the prospective student seeks out information from both personal and impersonal sources, including institutional sources.

In the third stage, the prospect evaluates alternatives and develops a preference for one of them. Models of how this evaluation process takes place can help schools understand how they can work more effectively with prospects. The fourth stage is making the decision, and the fifth is the implementation of that decision. After implementing the decision the consumer often goes through a stage of post-purchase evaluation, feeling satisfied or dissatisfied.

Organization purchasers are motivated by the need to increase productivity, retain good employees, and meet societal and legal obligations. The educational institution that seeks to provide services to these organizations needs to understand their needs, wants, and decision processes.

### Notes

1. Ben Wildavsky, "UC May Narrow Eligibility for Top Students," *San Francisco Chronicle*, February 12, 1994, pp. A17–18.

2. Larry H. Litten, *Ivy Bound: High-Ability Students and College Choice* (New York: College Entrance Examination Board, 1991), p. 52.

3. An outstanding Native American student at a Bureau of Indian Affairs boarding school reputedly did not want to attend college at all in part because she did not want to leave her extended family. The counselor pressured her to go to college and finally the young woman acquiesced, agreeing to attend what she thought from its name—Leland Stanford Junior University—was a "junior college."

4. Alexander W. Astin, William S. Korn, and Ellyne R. Riggs, *The American Freshman: National Norms for Fall 1993*, Cooperative Institutional Research Program (Los Angeles, CA: The Higher Education Research Institute, University of California at Los Angeles, December 1993), p. 50.

5. Thomas Vance Sturgeon, "Creating a Standardized, Systematic, and Testable Rating Framework for Competitive Admission," *The Journal of College Admission*, no. 142 (Winter 1994), pp. 6–13.

6. R. Fred Zuker, "Admissions Anxiety in the 1990s," *The College Board Review*, no. 164 (Forum Issue 1992), pp. 8–10.

7. PC-based software by the College Board, titled *The College Explorer*, performs this sorting and then presents selected facts for each identified school. Similar choice-narrowing software is the *U.S. News College Planner*. Both software packages assume that prospective students form profiles of preferred colleges based on location, cost, availability of majors, and similar objective criteria.

8. Abraham H. Maslow, *Motivation and Personality* (New York: Harper & Row, 1954), pp. 80–106.

9. The importance of an attribute should be distinguished from its salience. The attributes that come to a consumer's mind when asked to name a product's attributes are called the salient attributes. They may be salient because the consumer was just exposed to a commercial message mentioning them or had a problem involving them, hence making these attributes "top of the mind." The consumer, when prompted, may recall other attributes that are equally important. We are more interested here in attribute importance than attribute salience. See James M. Myers and Mark I. Alpert, "Semantic Confusion in Attitude Research: Salience vs. Importance vs. Determinance," *Advances in Consumer Research*, 1976, pp. 106–10.

10. See Paul E. Green and Yoram Wind, *Multiattribute Decisions in Marketing: A Measurement Approach* (Hinsdale, IL: Dryden Press, 1973), Chap. 2.

11. See Harper W. Boyd, Jr., Michael L. Ray, and Edward C. Strong, "An Attitudinal Framework for Advertising Strategy," *Journal of Marketing* (April 1972), pp. 27–33.

12. See Jagdish N. Sheth, "An Investigation of Relationships among Evaluative Beliefs, Affect, Behavioral Intention, and Behavior," in *Consumer Behavior: Theory and Application*, John A. Howard, and L. Winston Rind, eds. (Boston: Allyn & Bacon, 1974), pp. 89–114.

13. See Martin Fishbein, "Attitude and Prediction of Behavior," in *Readings in Attitude Theory and Measurement*, Martin Fishbein, ed. (New York: John Wiley, 1967), pp. 477–92.

14. See James W. Taylor, "The Role of Risk in Consumer Behavior," *Journal of Marketing* (April 1974), pp. 54–60.

15. The practice of sending multiple deposits plays havoc with colleges' efforts to predict enrollment and offer vacancies to wait-listed students, and it raises ethical questions, but nonetheless it is a growing phenomenon that colleges cope with.

16. See James H. Donnelly, Jr., and John M. Ivancevich, "Post-Purchase Reinforcement and Back-Out Behavior," *Journal of Marketing Research* (August 1970), pp. 399–400.

17. For a discussion of these factors, see Philip Kotler, *Marketing Management: Analysis, Planning and Control*, 8th ed. (Englewood Cliffs, NJ: Prentice-Hall, 1994), pp. 173–189.

18. Silton-Bookman of Cupertino, CA, pioneered in designing and selling software for companies to use to track their educational investment by individual employee.

19. This example is based on the work of James B. Johnson, President of Educational Advisory Services International of Philadelphia, PA, an innovator in this field.

20. Patrick J. Robinson, Charles W. Faris, and Yoram Wind, *Industrial Buying and Creative Marketing* (Boston: Allyn & Bacon, 1967).

# IV

# Designing
# Marketing Programs

# 11

# Designing Educational Programs

*Everywhere business schools are reinventing—or "reengineering"—the M.B.A. Business schools across the country are engaged in a dramatic transformation. They are infusing their master's-degree programs in business administration with all sorts of innovative courses and practical experiences. They are integrating new subjects, such as ethnic diversity, into the curriculum, and they are paying more attention to teaching, especially team teaching.*

*Business education's current plunge into self-analysis is the deepest in 30 years, prompted by, among other things, an end to the exploding demand for the M.B.A degree by college graduates, increasing complaints from companies about the usefulness of M.B.As, and new rankings of schools that appear every few years.*

*These claimed transformations typically begin by reflecting on what exactly it is that an M.B.A—or anybody else—will need to know or do to be effective in business a decade from now. Every B-school dean knows what to promise: The ideal executive of the future—and every one of his school's graduates—will be a leader, not a mere manager. Global in outlook. Facile with information systems and technology. Able to capitalize on adversity. A visionary. A master of teamwork and a coach. Walks on water too.*

*Even when business schools know what to do, it's difficult for them to stay up with, let alone get ahead of, what fast-changing companies need. Schools nonetheless are trying to respond and the upheaval at some is enormous. At some places, the barriers to change are formidable. Business schools are often as badly or-*

*ganized as the worst corporations, with tenured faculties that refuse to do anything differently. Other institutions cannot afford the high cost of developing new teaching methods.*

*Still the pressure on the nation's 700-plus business schools to improve their product is high. Many, especially some of the 400 or so that sprang up in response to the big demand for MBAs in the 1970s and 1980s, may eventually be forced to close for lack of students.*

*The prestigious business schools have either engaged in continuous innovation or are moving program-development efforts into high gear to retain their appeal to prospective students and their future employers. In searching for ideas to rejuvenate Columbia University's program, "we took some of the advice we give our students," says Professor Linda Green at the Graduate School of Business, who headed the curriculum review committee there. "Do this in consultation with your customers." Columbia embarked on a research program of surveys, focus groups, and interviews with faculty, students, 2,000 alumni, and senior executives in successful companies to find out where to improve its program.*

*At the same time that the bloom is off the M.B.A degree in the United States, the M.B.A degree is growing in popularity in Europe. An estimated 200 M.B.A programs now operate in Western Europe. The degree is also enjoying a surge of popularity in the former Communist countries of Central and Eastern Europe, now home to a growing number of programs. An estimated 9,000 M.B.A degrees were awarded in Europe in 1993, up from 4,000 just six years earlier.*

**Source:** Based on Robert L. Jacobson, "Shaking Up the MBA," *The Chronicle of Higher Education*, December 15, 1993, pp. A18–A19; Brian O'Reilly, "Reengineering the MBA," *Fortune*, January 24, 1994, pp. 38–46.; David C. Walters, "B-Schools Adapt to Meet Demand," *The Christian Science Monitor*, November 16, 1992, p. 13; and Kirsten Gallagher, "In Europe, MBA Fever," *The Chronicle of Higher Education*, December 1, 1993, pp. A41, A44.

---

The educational marketer is typically offering a service and has a marketing mix of seven marketing tools, the 7 Ps: program, price, place (delivery system), promotion, processes, physical facilities, and people. In this chapter, the first of four addressing the marketing mix, we discuss programs, including processes, program development, and enhancement. In Chapter 12 we discuss price, in Chapter 13 delivery systems and physical facilities, and in Chapter 14 communication. We address the issue of people, their importance as service providers, and training throughout this book.

The most basic decision an educational institution makes is what programs and services it will offer to its students, alumni, donors, and other markets and publics. An institution's mix of offerings establishes its identity, positions the institution vis-a-vis other educational institutions in the minds of consumers, and determines how consumers will respond. We have only to compare a maritime academy and a liberal arts college. Each school will attract a distinct clientele and be in competition with a distinct set of other institutions. Institutions with similar programs will find their markets and publics differentiating between them on the basis of their programs and their quality.

Most educational institutions offer several programs and many services. An institution's *program/service mix* consists of all the programs and services that the institution makes available. A *product line* is a group of offerings that are closely related in some way—because they either function in a similar manner, are made available to the same customers, or are marketed through the same outlets. For example, many colleges offer educational programs (classes, library and information services, computer laboratory, campus lectures, and so on), recreational programs (athletic facilities and clubs, film series, dances, and the like), personal-growth programs and services (counseling center, religious organizations, advisors), curative services (health center), and future-planning programs and services (career counseling, placement service, and so on). Each of these categories can be considered a product line. Or the institution might think of all its undergraduate academic majors as a product line and all its graduate professional programs as another product line.

## THE NATURE OF EDUCATIONAL OFFERINGS

We have frequently referred to educational offerings as programs and services. Most for-profit companies selling manufactured goods offer product items that can be seen, touched, and examined. Customers can inspect them carefully before purchase. Customers can also assume that goods produced on the same manufacturing line will be essentially identical, regardless of which workers staffed that line. The products can be stored in inventory in a warehouse until customers want to buy them and, if stored appropriately, they will last for quite a while. In short, physical goods are tangible, consistent, storable, and exist quite independent of the persons who made them.

Offering services involves special challenges because most services are intangible, inseparable, variable, and perishable. Most services don't exist until the service provider performs the service, usually in the presence of the customer. A student can check out a course by sitting in for a few sessions, but probably can't judge the professor's teaching effectiveness by reading the course syllabus. Besides, if the student's roommate "loved" the course the year before, this year's course may not be quite so good. The professor may be preoccupied with family problems or be serving on a time-consuming committee, and may not put as much energy as previously into teaching the course. And if the student enrolls but misses many classes, the student may borrow another student's class notes, but that's not the same thing as being in class.

The limitations of services vis-à-vis products also comprise the strengths of services. The professor can look for responses from students—their puzzled looks during a lecture or their fuzzy answers on a quiz—and modify the course content and explanations. During office hours, the informal instruction may be tailored to the specific student. The immediacy of the teaching/learning encounter can increase its impact and value for the student, aiding his or her learning.

Most educational services combine both tangible and intangible elements—they aren't "pure" services. In fact, most services involve some physical elements. The physics class takes place in a room equipped with tables and chairs or desks, and probably a blackboard and a screen for projecting slides or overhead transparencies. Students use books and notebooks, and the professor probably uses some apparatus to illustrate various physics concepts. Each service thus requires or benefits from equipment and other physical objects.

We can analyze a service on three levels—the *core, tangible,* and *augmented* levels. By understanding these levels the marketer can fine-tune the service to be most attractive to consumers.

## Core Offer

At the most fundamental level stands the *core offer*, which answers the questions, What is the consumer really seeking? What need is the program or service really satisfying? The marketer's task is to understand the program's benefit from the consumer's perspective. By uncovering the want-satisfying potential that underlies every program, the marketer can describe program benefits, not just program features. The core benefit stands at the center of the total offering, as illustrated in Figure 11-1.

The desired core offering may differ from one consumer to another. Consider Avon cosmetics. The company's representatives sell cosmetics, but many of its customers are buying hope—for beauty, admiration, and romance. Other customers buy the Avon products to collect the distinctive bottles and jars they come in. Still others buy the products because the Avon repre-

FIGURE 11-1   Three levels of an offer

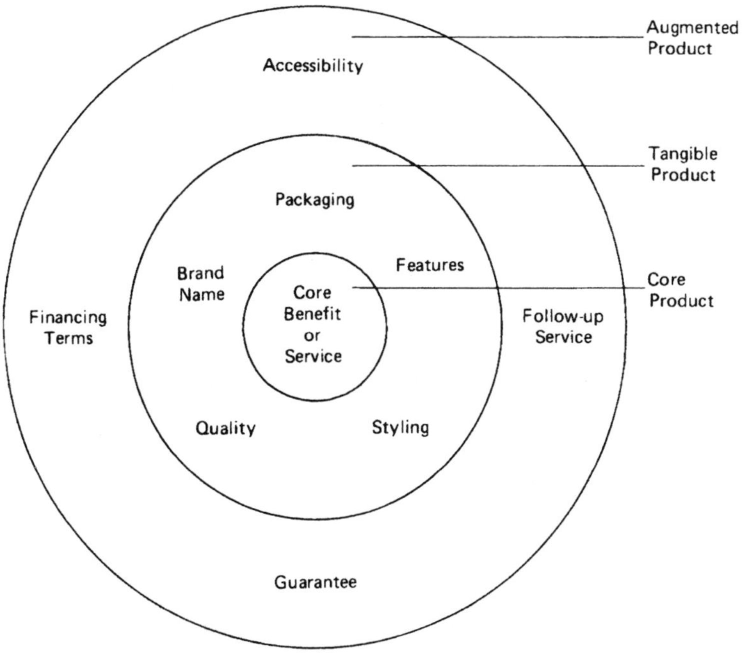

Accessibility

Augmented
Product

Packaging

Tangible
Product

Brand
Name

Features

Core
Benefit
or
Service

Core
Product

Financing
Terms

Follow-up
Service

Quality

Styling

Guarantee

sentative's visit alleviates their loneliness.[1] The same is true of educational services. A college provides instruction, but some students are seeking marketability, and others are seeking a good time before going to work. A Sunday school may offer religious instruction, but some participants are seeking peace of mind or salvation.

### Tangible Offer

The core offer is almost always embodied in some tangible form, even in the case of a largely intangible service.[2] Consider a student in a classroom. The core benefit that the student may seek is information. The *tangible offer* may take the form of a classroom where the student sits at a desk facing the blackboard, and the instructor stands at a podium and reads from notes, occasionally making diagrams on the board. Clearly, this is not the only form that the tangible product can take. We could imagine the same student sitting in front of a computer work station, seated in a carrel designed for comfort by a specialist in ergonomics. The student can access thousands of photographs and pages of text, as well as audio recordings of speeches and even newsreel footage, while studying history.

The tangible offer can be described as having up to four characteristics: *features, quality level, packaging,* and a *brand name.* We will examine each of these four characteristics of the tangible offer in more detail because each can be modified to make the offer more attractive to consumers.

**Features.** Features are individual components of the offer that could be easily added or subtracted without changing the service's style or quality. Consider an elementary school that is seeking to expand enrollment. There are many feature improvements it could offer, for instance:

- Offering before- and after-school day care
- Adding more playground equipment
- Offering a free course in effective parenting

The use of features has many advantages. The institution can go after specific market segments by selecting those features that would most strongly appeal to them. Features are also a tool for differentiating the institution's products from those of competitors. Features often have the advantage of being easy to add or drop quickly, and they can be made optional at little expense. Novel features are often newsworthy and can be used to get media publicity.

**Quality.** Quality represents the perceived level of performance of a service. (This is discussed in detail in Chapter 2.) The quality of a service is particularly important precisely because quality can vary so much, depending on the provider's skills, motivation, and mood—and on how much control the institution can exercise over service providers. Consider the case of colleges A and B. College A is a publish-or-perish institution where professors are judged primarily by their research output, not by their classroom performance. College B, on the other hand, insists on high-quality teaching and drops instructors who do not meet this standard. Whether college A will continue to attract enough students depends upon the extent to which prospective students get information about this quality difference and care enough about quality teaching—or quality research—to have it determine their college choice.

**Packaging.** Packaging is the container or wrapper surrounding the specific product or service. We know that good packaging can add value beyond that perceived in the product itself; consider the fancy perfume bottle and its contribution to the aura of the perfume. In the case of a service, packaging is the contribution of the larger context in which the service is obtained. Thus, a college campus's environment serves as the packaging of the academic product:

> The architecture, topography, and landscaping of a campus should support the educational function of the university. . . . The campus should evoke the feeling of a tone poem, a festival, a composition that washes over the inhabitants. It should combine all the senses—sight, sound,

touch, taste, and scent—becoming a street scene, a block party, a family gathering, a tactile encounter, a tribute to the intermeshing of the sights and sounds of human beings.[3]

Of course, not every school's campus can be a "tone poem," but reflecting on how the campus is experienced may at least suggest priorities for improvement.

**Branding.** The products and services of an educational institution can be branded—that is, given a name, term, sign, symbol, or design, or some combination, that identifies them with the institution and differentiates them from competitors' offerings. Branding can add value to the institution's offer and more satisfaction for the consumer. College football teams, for example, generate loyalty and enthusiasm in part because they carry the brand name of the school and the team. Likewise, a well-titled program or idea will attract more favorable attention than one with a name that is dull or a turnoff. For example, people are apt to think better of a program called "individualized learning" than one called "programmed instruction" because the first name suggests personal attention, whereas the latter suggests a rigid process.

Some academic institutions change their names to match their actual or hoped-for stature. Iowa State College of Agriculture and Mechanic Arts became Iowa State University of Science and Technology. Southwestern College in Memphis, Tennessee, took a new name, Rhodes College, as part of its repositioning plan to improve its academic quality and reputation. The name "Rhodes" evokes the memory of the British explorer Cecil Rhodes and, in particular, the very prestigious academic scholarships he established.

### Augmented Offer

The marketer can offer the target market additional services and benefits that go beyond the core offer and the tangible offer, thus making up the augmented offer. Of the thousands of educational institutions, many are seeking or will seek ways to augment their services to attract more customers. To paraphrase Theodore Levitt, the new competition is not between what educational institutions offer in the classroom but between what they add to their standard offerings in the form of packaging, services, advertising, financing, delivery arrangements, and other things that people value.[4] A college can offer lifetime use of the career-placement center, membership in the alumni organization, and perhaps access to college classes to update skills in the future.

We see that a service (or other product form) is not a simple thing but a complex offer consisting of a core need-satisfying service, a set of tangible characteristics, and a set of augmenting benefits. The institution should examine each of its services and design them in a way that will serve customers' needs and wants, distinguish the institution's offer from competitors' offers, and convey the intended qualities to the target market.

In the rest of this chapter we consider the fundamental program and service decisions faced by educational institutions:

- What is our current mix of offerings—programs and services? How well aligned are our offerings with the institution's strategic plan? With customer expectations and preferences? How does this alignment change over time and how do we adapt?
- What are the steps in planning and implementing new programs?
- What are the considerations in adding or modifying auxiliary services?

## THE ALIGNMENT OF CURRENT PROGRAMS AND SERVICES

The institution should begin by understanding its current program/service mix. In discussing segmentation and targeting, we pointed out that some institutions engage in concentrated marketing. They have one program and offer it to a clearly defined target market. St. John's University, with campuses in Maryland and New Mexico, offers one curriculum based on the Great Books. This focused offering enables St. John's to plan its sequencing of course offerings, library needs, registration process, and faculty hiring around delivering this curriculum in the best possible way. Students selecting St. John's want the specific program it offers.

For institutions with many offerings, thinking in terms of product lines as well as of individual program and services can reveal several options. Suppose the college is thinking of expanding its program/service mix. The college could add more product lines; for example, a commuter college could add residential services by building or acquiring residence halls. Or it could add more programs to an existing product line; for example, it might add a new degree program or lecture series. If the college needs to reduce the number of programs to bring down its costs or to attain a more specialized position in the marketplace, it might drop an entire product line—say, by closing its health center and sending students to local doctors—or drop one offering from one or more product lines, such as dropping an academic major that is no longer in demand.

Making decisions about current offerings should be based on information and analysis. An educational institution should evaluate its program/service mix periodically, and particularly when considering modifications. Some programs and services are more central than others. For this reason, educational institutions should use the academic portfolio model (presented in Chapter 7) to assess the quality, centrality, and market viability of various offerings before adjusting the program/service mix.

They will find that some—specifically, educational offerings—are *essential programs* that they cannot do without. Others may be easier to modify.

For example, recreational activities are usually *ancillary programs*. Furthermore, certain programs will play a major role in attracting consumers; these are called *flagship programs*. For example, students and donors will be attracted to a college with a strong reputation in at least one academic field. Often an institution will seek to add a *crown jewel* to its mix, and then showcase that in its literature and promotion. The crown jewel is often some program that establishes or reinforces the institution's quality or uniqueness. For example, Tufts University is a well-respected university, but its Fletcher School of Law and Diplomacy is particularly famous.

Programs and services can be examined one by one, but decisions about changes must consider the interrelationships among various programs and services. Just as the strategic planner looks at the school's programs as part of a portfolio, so too do the school's constituencies see it as a collection—an interrelated collection—of offerings. Student preferences, faculty morale, and alumni/donor loyalty are typically based on blends—or "bundles"—of the school's offerings.

Students may select the school because it has the desired major, an active athletic program, and a top-notch career center. Dropping any one of these programs/services would reduce the student's interest in attending. Auxiliary services such as residence halls may also play a role. If residence-hall living diminishes in attractiveness due to program cutbacks, the student contented with every other aspect of the school may have second thoughts about staying.

## THE PROGRAM/SERVICE LIFE CYCLE

We can think about programs and services as passing through a life cycle of introduction, growth, maturity, and decline. Few programs and services remain optimal forever. Some were probably not very well conceived when they were first implemented and have just lurched along. Others were optimal at one time but no longer match what the institution's markets and publics now want. Other programs and services are now available from many sources, so that only the best providers are succeeding at attracting students and support.

Broad changes in the macroenvironment, in consumer needs and interests, and in competitors' offers usually call for significant adjustments in the program and its marketing strategy over time. The nature of the appropriate adjustments can be conveyed through the concept of the *product life cycle*.

Many programs and services are well received at their introduction, later grow, and then eventually move into a period of maturity and then decline. The American M.B.A degree is a program at the mature—or even the declining—stage of its life cycle, after decades of rapid growth, while in Europe the M.B.A degree continues to grow in popularity. For American business schools to breathe new life into the traditional M.B.A curriculum will require substantial curriculum updating and even redesign of entire programs.

Figure 11-2 shows the life cycle for classical liberal-arts programs such as those based on the Great Books. The introduction of this curriculum dates back many centuries (the introduction stage). At one time, this was the one and only university curriculum and the growing number of university students were studying this (the growth and maturity stages). Eventually the expansion of knowledge and increased specialization led to the rise of other fields of study, including highly technical fields and the emerging social science disciplines. The traditional Great Books curriculum went into decline, to the point that very few institutions offer it.

The life cycle of a typical program or service often goes through the following four stages (sometimes called an S-shaped curve):

- *Introduction* is a period of slow growth as the program is introduced in the market.
- *Growth* is a period of rapid market acceptance.
- *Maturity* is a period of slowdown in growth because the program has received acceptance by most of the potential consumers.
- *Decline* is the period when consumer interest shows a strong downward drift.

We can see that the concept of a product-life cycle can be applied to a *program class* (educational services), a *program form* (Great Books curriculum), or a *brand* (the Great Books curriculum at St. John's College). Program classes have the longest life cycles: Educational services can be expected to be around indefinitely. Program forms tend to exhibit more standard life-cycle histories. As for brands—specific institutions or programs—they are the most

FIGURE 11-2    The program life cycle for classical liberal-arts programs

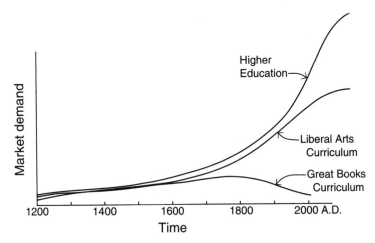

FIGURE 11-3    Two nonstandard life-cycle patterns

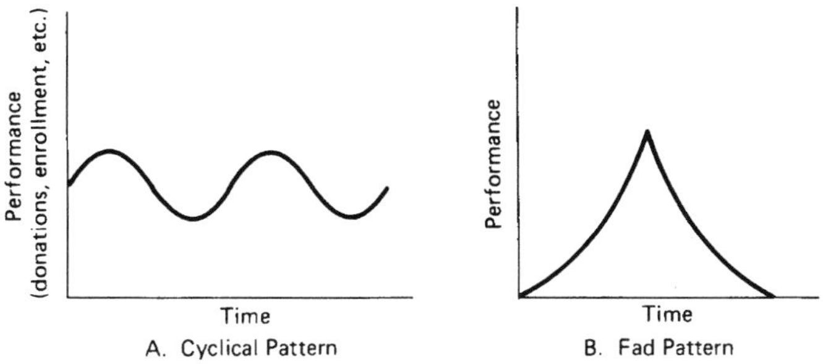

A. Cyclical Pattern          B. Fad Pattern

likely to show finite histories. For example, St. John's College launched its Great Books Curriculum in 1937.

Not all programs and services exhibit an S-shaped life cycle. Two other common patterns are these:

- *Cyclical pattern.* Some programs show a cyclical pattern (Figure 11-3, A). For example, engineering schools go through alternating periods of high enrollment and low enrollment, reflecting changes in the demand for and supply of engineers. Programs with a cyclical pattern should not be eliminated during the decline stage but should be maintained as much as possible, awaiting the next boom.
- *Fad pattern.* Here a new program appears, quickly attracts attention, is adopted with great zeal, peaks early, and declines rapidly (Figure 11-3, B.) The acceptance cycle is short, and the program tends to attract only a limited following of people who are looking for excitement or diversion. Some community colleges offer a constantly changing list of leisure offerings to meet public interest in short-lived topics that are not part of the regular curriculum.

We will now return to the S-shaped product life cycle and examine the characteristics and appropriate marketing strategies at each stage.

## Introduction Stage

The introduction stage of the product life cycle takes place when the new program is first made available in the marketplace. The introduction into one or more markets takes time; growth is apt to be slow. The institution needs time to expand its capacity—to locate more classroom space or hire more instructors, for example—and to work out "bugs" in the design. Potential consumers may be reluctant to try something new, and if the new program or service is expensive, only a few consumers may be interested enough to spend the money when it is first introduced.

Costs are often high during the introduction stage because the institution must invest in the new endeavor and in advertising while there are few consumers. Heavy promotional expenditures are often necessary to inform potential consumers of the new and unknown program, and to induce them to try the program. At this stage, there are few if any competitors. All the providing institutions strive to attract the early adopters—those people who tend to be the first to try new programs and services.

## Growth Stage

If the new program satisfies the market, many consumers will be attracted to it. Other consumers will follow the lead of the early adopters, especially if there is favorable word of mouth. New competitors may enter the market, attracted by the institution's success. They may introduce feature, style, and packaging variations in order to expand the market. During this stage, the institution tries to sustain rapid market growth as long as possible in several ways:

1. It undertakes to improve program quality and add features.
2. It vigorously searches out new market segments to enter.
3. It keeps its eyes open for new ways to gain additional attention for its program or service.
4. It shifts its promotion from building awareness of the program or service to trying to bring about a decision to purchase.

## Maturity Stage

At some point, a program's rate of growth will slow down, and the program will enter a stage of relative maturity. Most educational programs are in the maturity stage of the life cycle. This stage normally lasts much longer than the previous stages, and it poses some of the most formidable marketing challenges.

The school needs to "refurbish" or even reconceptualize the curriculum/program for two reasons. First, the beginnings of a slowdown in the rate of growth usually produce overcapacity with too many institutions providing a certain program while demand is falling. This overcapacity leads to intensified competition among the institutions. Competitors engage more frequently in price-cutting (through scholarships, credit for life experience, and so on) and increase their promotional budgets. Some institutions focus attention on improving their programs. Still others resort to modifying their consumer mix or program/service mix—for example, by admitting less qualified students or adding new programs. These steps often result in higher costs, and some of the weaker competitors start dropping out. What remains eventually is a set of well-entrenched competitors striving to maintain or gain a competitive advantage that will help them survive.

Second, the institution should keep reviewing and updating its offerings because the institution should aim to provide the best possible education and other services to its target markets. The school shouldn't fail to attend to its offerings just because it knows that students won't abruptly "take a hike." Proactive institutions try to sense emerging needs and take steps to address them.

## Decline Stage

Programs may eventually enter a stage of declining demand. The decline may be slow or rapid. Enrollments and donations may plunge. More typically in education, enrollment or other indicators of consumer interest may petrify at a low level for many years.

Commonly, interest declines for several reasons. The market may lose interest because a particular program or major is no longer "in fashion" or does not meet consumer needs. Changes in technology or the economy may affect what educational services people seek. No matter what the reason, some changes must be made or the institution will suffer.

As interest declines, some programs will be eliminated. Responding to funding cuts, one state university made plans to eliminate many degree programs, including urban planning, Near Eastern languages, kinesthesiology, nutrition, children's drama, textiles, art education, and dance. To other programs, the university planned to admit fewer students—dentistry, medicine, education, social work, architecture, and public administration.[5]

Remaining programs may reduce their number of offerings, withdraw from smaller market segments, or close satellite facilities. They may cut their promotion budgets and perhaps reduce their tuition price for certain programs (usually by giving financial aid as a "discount" on tuition price). On the other hand, some educational institutions faced with declining programs will increase their promotion budgets, add new courses, and keep raising prices to cover higher costs. In general, this strategy works only when the institution has successfully identified an opportunity in which it has distinctive competence and a differential advantage, along with a growing market.

Unless strong retention reasons exist, carrying a weak program is very costly. The cost of maintaining a weak program can be more than the financial loss. The weak program tends to consume a disproportionate amount of administrative time and requires both advertising and other attention that might be better spent making the "healthy" programs more successful. The program's weakness can create consumer misgivings and cast a shadow on the institution's image. The biggest cost may lie in the future. When not eliminated at the proper time, these programs delay the aggressive search for replacements that offer more to students and other constituents. They create a lopsided program mix, and they depress current cash and weaken the institution's foothold on the future.

In the face of declining interest, some institutions will abandon the market earlier than others. Those that remain often enjoy a temporary increase in consumers as they pick up those of the withdrawing institutions. For example, as several universities dropped Master of Arts in Teaching (M.A.T.) programs in the 1970s, the remaining programs received more applicants. But each institution faces the issue of whether it should be the one to stay in the market until the end.

If it stays in the market, the institution faces further strategic choices. It could adopt a *continuation strategy*, in which case it continues its past marketing strategy: same market segments, channels, pricing, and promotion. In this case, the number of consumers will probably shrink. Or it could follow a *concentration strategy*, concentrating its resources in the strongest markets while phasing out its efforts elsewhere. Thus, an M.A.T. program could prepare only science and mathematics teachers, since teaching positions in those fields are plentiful. Finally, it could follow a *harvesting strategy*, in which case it sharply reduces its expenses to increase its positive (or decrease its negative) cash flow, knowing that these cuts will accelerate the rate of decline and the ultimate demise of the program.

When a program has been singled out for elimination, the institution faces some decisions. First, it might decide to move the program to another institution or simply drop it. Second, the institution has to decide whether to drop the program quickly or slowly. Third, it must decide what level of service to maintain to cover existing students or customers. Educational programs often require several years of study; therefore, an educational institution usually cannot in good faith drop a program without transition plans to allow currently enrolled students to complete it.

Dropping a program has internal as well as external consequences for the institution. Ending a program may lead to reductions in staff and faculty, or to their transfer to other positions. Some of the best faculty, staff, and administrators may lose faith in the institution and leave for positions elsewhere. Alumni of the program may protest its demise. While the institution probably cannot retain all its programs in order to prevent these outcomes, plausible outcomes should be considered in advance, along with institutional approaches to reduce their impact.

While dropping a program can be painful, it presents the institution with the opportunity to redirect its resources to improve existing programs or provide a more valued new program or service.

## THE STEPS IN NEW-PROGRAM DEVELOPMENT

Educational institutions differ in their need for and interest in ideas for new programs and services. Some are fully occupied in providing their current services; others are looking for new courses or programs to meet the changing interests of the public. Some hope that a new program or service can keep them from sliding into oblivion.

Educational institutions often assume that designing and launching a new program is a simple task. The following actual case is typical of many efforts to develop new educational programs.

A major university's school of education had seen its undergraduate enrollment dive and was concerned about keeping viable graduate programs as educational-administration and college-teaching positions dwindled.

The faculty held a meeting to decide how to restructure the school's graduate programs into four specialties. After existing graduate courses were listed on the blackboard, faculty in each proposed specialty met to consider what new courses to add. The faculty group then completed the diagram of courses and discussed how to recruit prospective students. Faculty members called out names of nearby colleges that might have students interested in graduate programs in education. The colleges were listed on the blackboard, and each faculty member selected two campuses to visit.

The meeting closed with the decision to place ads in college newspapers announcing when faculty members would be available to discuss the programs. The whole process took about *three hours*.

This approach is unlikely to be successful. The faculty planners ignored important considerations in planning for new programs and services. They never considered what would be the best program ideas based on innovations in the field, career possibilities, or student interests. They did not analyze past trends·in graduate enrollment at the university and its competitors for clues about which programs would be most interesting to students and future employers. Finally, the recruiting "plan" used a shotgun approach of highly doubtful effectiveness.

Most educational institutions think that new-program planning must be informal because they lack the time and money to do the job right or they are inclined to "try something and see if it works." On the contrary, precisely because they have scarce resources, educational institutions cannot afford to waste them on thrown-together programs. Consumer-products companies can launch many new products that fail because they can recoup their losses and make a profit on those that succeed. Even then, effective consumer-products companies invest heavily in developing and testing each new product.

Figure 11-4 shows the development process for new programs and services. *Opportunity identification* involves selecting the best program areas, generating ideas, and screening these ideas to identify the best ones to turn into new programs. *Design* includes several activities. Consumer measurement involves studying how consumers make their decisions about this type of program, what program features will attract them, and what alternatives they know about. Concept development entails preparing descriptions of program alternatives. The remainder of the design phase includes designing the program and the marketing strategy to be used. If the resulting design looks promising, *testing* begins—testing of the course or program, its market potential, its appeal to consumers, and the proposed marketing strategy. Only then is the program introduced. After *introduction*, the new program must be monitored (*management*) to ensure that it will continue to be successful.

This section describes each step in the context of De Paul University's interest in launching a new program. The same process is applicable to any new program or service.

## Opportunity Identification

De Paul University wanted to expand its educational services in the greater Chicago area. De Paul needed to determine what types of educational programs seemed most promising and what specific ideas merited further consideration.

FIGURE 11-4    New-program and service
development process

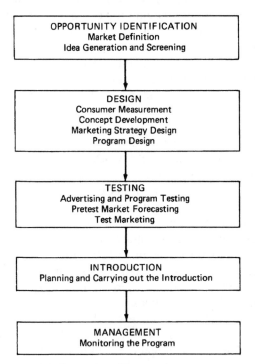

Source: Adapted from Glen L. Urban and John R. Hauser, *Design and Marketing of New Products* (Englewood Cliffs, NJ: Prentice-Hall, 1980), p. 33.

**Market Definition.** De Paul is already in the education business and is looking for new educational programs it could provide. The university will want to find unmet educational needs or wants and then consider whether De Paul has the resources and interest to provide programs to meet them.

The De Paul planning group identified the following potential program areas it might enter: women's studies, black studies, dentistry, evening degree programs for adults, and weekend graduate business programs. De Paul did not have the resources to provide all these programs and had to identify the most attractive one. An attractive opportunity should be attractive both in itself and in relation to the institution. Table 11-1 lists factors to consider in each step. De Paul can evaluate each of the five program areas in terms of its market size, growth rate in demand, absence of competition, and other characteristics. The planning group will then want to consider how well each program area matches the university's capabilities. A particular program area— say, animal husbandry—may be a good opportunity for one institution, an agricultural college, but not for De Paul, an urban institution.

At this stage, the institution also needs to consider what consumers it wants to appeal to because this will affect which program area will ultimately be chosen and how the particular program will be designed and promoted. The planning group needs to segment the consumer markets for each program and identify the segments that have the most potential—in size and interest. Here the planners can use the market measurement tools presented in Chapter 8. For example, the chain-ratio method was used to determine the size of the potential market for a special recruiting program for returning women students.

The result will be an evaluation of the characteristics of each new-program area and a clearer picture of which segments each might address. De

TABLE 11-1   Factors to consider in determining attractive markets

Program Characteristics
   Size of market demand for this program area
   Growth rate of market demand
   Cost to enter this program area
   Time needed to become established
   Likelihood of competition
   Investment required
   Availability of required resources
Match to Institution's Capabilities
   Have financial resources required
   Match to present location(s) and delivery system
   Match to marketing capabilities
   Utilize existing personnel and facilities
   Compatible with existing programs and services
   Management skills and experience with this program area or closely related program areas

Source: Adapted from Glen L. Urban and John R. Hauser, *Design and Marketing of New Products* (Englewood Cliffs, NJ: Prentice-Hall, 1980), p. 88.

Paul University decided that a degree program for adults presented its best opportunity.

**Idea Generation.** Once the institution has identified the broad program area it wants to enter, the planning group develops ideas to take advantage of the identified opportunity. Defining the program area does not automatically imply a particular curriculum, format, or delivery system. The planners should generate several alternatives before testing and settling on the best one.

Ideas come from many sources. Current or potential consumers may have ideas about new programs or modifications of existing ones. Their ideas can be gathered through direct surveys, projective tests, focus groups, and suggestions and complaints. The institution should also watch its competitors to see what new services they launch and with what success. The institution's administrators, faculty, and staff are other good sources of ideas, along with outside consultants, educational associations, and others who are familiar with the field. Educational publications and academic journals may contain critiques of current programs and curricula in certain disciplines.

When the University of the Pacific started planning for a new M.B.A program, the planning team carefully examined the new accreditation guidelines of the American Assembly of Collegiate Schools of Business, did a thorough analysis of what nationally known scholars were writing about the flaws of existing M.B.A curricula, and surveyed local business people about what they felt a new M.B.A curriculum should accomplish.[6]

We recommend also using the program/market opportunity matrix, described in Chapter 7, as a systematic way to generate new-program ideas. The planners can examine each cell, considering new possibilities for each one. For example, an existing program might be modified to serve a new market, or a new program might be developed for the school's traditional market. Then the planners can search for specific ideas in the most attractive cells.

New-program ideas are sometimes prompted by *inspiration, serendipity, consumer requests*, or *formal creativity techniques*. Institutions have little influence in the first two processes, other than maintaining an open atmosphere and encouraging creativity. They should carefully study customer requests—and seek them out—in search of good ideas. They can also employ creativity techniques to encourage group members to come up with promising ideas.[7] Of the many such techniques, three widely used ones are these:

**1.** *Brainstorming.* In this approach, a group of six to eight people is told to come up with as many solutions as possible for a broad problem. The brainstorming may start with a task, such as, "Think of as many ways as you can to provide degree programs to working adults." No criticism is allowed while ideas are being generated, and group members are encouraged to propose wild ideas—the wilder the better—and to build on other people's ideas. After the group runs out of ideas, the members discuss and evaluate the ideas that have been listed.

**2.** *Synectics.* This group approach begins with stating the problem, describing its background, and reviewing past solutions. Goals and statement of the characteristics of the ideal solution are formulated. The group then generates a large number of ideas. One promising idea is selected, developed, and—if acceptable—added to a list of possible solutions. The group then considers the other ideas it has generated, using the same process.

**3.** *Attribute lists.* The purpose of attribute listing is to think of new features and approaches that might otherwise be overlooked. For instance, American colleges and universities have long assumed that earning the bachelor's degree "should" take a full-time student four academic years. Now this standard program attribute (which Harvard College put in place in 1636) is being challenged by several university presidents. They point out that a three-year baccalaureate program would reduce the cost of college by one-fourth. Supporters say that colleges should think hard about what students should learn, and then redesign the curriculum to make the process more efficient.[8]

The planners start by listing the attributes of the proposed program area. De Paul's planners might make the following attribute list:

Time of day
Class size
Theoretical/practical
Location
Course length
Meeting frequency
Tests and grades

The group would then consider each attribute to see whether the attribute could be adapted, increased, minimized, reversed, rearranged, substituted, or combined.

For example, De Paul's planners might list several ideas to broaden the idea of "time of day": early morning "breakfast" courses, late evening (after dinner), noon, weekends only, and so forth. Under "tests and grades," the planners could list daily testing, testing only at the end of each module or year, testing solely by examination of the student's portfolio of best work, testing only at the end of the entire program, testing by external examiners, and so on.

**Idea Screening.** The resulting ideas must be screened and winnowed to identify the most promising ones and to eliminate the ones that are not worthy of further consideration.

The planning group (or the university) needs to develop screening criteria. For example, De Paul has already considered the factors in Table 11-1 at the opportunity-identification stage. The planners could subject each new-program idea to the same or similar criteria to determine if the university has the *success requirements* to carry out the idea.

Some institutions use very formal criteria and apply weights for each criterion. For example, the institution could attach weights to each factor in Table 11-1. The six criteria under "Program Characteristics" might be weighted to add up to 1, but "Size of market demand" would count 35 percent (0.35), while "Availability of required resources" would count 25 percent (0.25), and other four criteria would each count 10 percent (0.1). The six criteria under "Match to Institution's Capabilities" would also be weighted to sum to 1. If the institution planned to use a new delivery system, "Match to present location/delivery system" would not be an important criterion (and could even be weighted zero), but "Have financial resources required" might count 40 percent (0.4).

The screening may take place at several levels. First, the planning committee may be able to eliminate the more obvious "clunkers." Then the planning group could prepare descriptions of each idea as a basis for discussion and review. Next, the descriptions could be read and discussed by the planning group and/or other committees. Each idea should then be rated, either by individual group members or by collective opinion, based on its attractiveness and its match to the institution's capabilities. An example of opportunity analysis is presented in Chapter 4.

### Program Design

Designing the new program involves more than preparing a list of courses or program features. The ideas that survive the screening process must be developed into program design concepts. These concepts must be tested by gaining a clear understanding of what consumers want. The information from consumer testing then guides the design of the program and the marketing mix.

**Concept Development.** The institution needs to be able to describe its proposed program ideas to consumers to get their reactions. An educational institution usually cannot "show" the proposed program to potential customers, so it must prepare a verbal description. De Paul began with a product idea, a possible program described in objective and functional terms, that the university could offer to the market. The next step was to convert this program *idea* into a program *concept*. A program idea can be embodied in a variety of different program concepts. For example, starting with the product idea, an adult degree program, the following program concepts could be created:

**Concept 1.** An evening program with a liberal-arts orientation, mostly required courses, and no credit for past experience.

**Concept 2.** An evening program with a career-development orientation, much latitude in course selection, and credit for past experience.

**Concept 3.** An evening program with a general-education orientation primarily for people over 50 years of age who want a bachelor's degree.

Each concept should then be prepared in written form in enough detail to allow consumers to understand it and express their reactions. Here is an example of concept 2 in more elaborate form:

> An evening program, called the School for New Learning, with a career-development orientation and much latitude in the courses that can be taken. The program would be open to people over 24 years of age, lead to a bachelor's degree, give course credit for past experiences and skills that the person has acquired, give only pass-fail grades; and involve a "learning contract" between the student and the school.

Target consumers are identified and asked for their reaction to this and other concepts. Table 11-2 shows the type of questions that might be asked. The last question in Table 11-2 addresses the consumer's intention to act and reads: "Would you definitely, probably, probably not, definitely not enroll in this program?" Suppose 10 percent of the target consumers said "definitely" and another 5 percent said "probably." De Paul could apply these percentages (or slightly lower ones) to the size of the entire target market to estimate whether the estimated number of enrollees would be sufficient.

Even then, the estimate is at best tentative because people often do not carry out their stated intentions. Nevertheless, by testing the alternative concepts with target consumers in this way, De Paul would learn which program concept has the best market potential and would get ideas for improvements.

An alternative approach to developing and testing program concepts is the use of conjoint analysis, described in Chapter 3. Suppose De Paul identified five program dimensions and "levels" of each dimension:

1. Emphasis: (a) liberal arts, (b) general education, (c) career development
2. Credit for life experience: (a) yes, (b) no
3. Age range of students: (a) mostly under 35, (b) mostly 35 to 50, (c) mostly over 50
4. Tuition cost per course: (a) $800, (b) $1,000, (c) $1,200
5. Frequency of class meetings: (a) four times weekly, (b) two times weekly, (a) once a week.

TABLE 11-2    Factors to use in determining attractive program areas

Major questions in a concept for a new education program
1. Is the concept of this adult degree evening program with its various features clear to you?
2. What do you see as reasons why you migh enroll in this program?
3. What expectation would you have about the program's quality?
4. Does this program meet a real need of yours?
5. What improvements can you suggest in various features of this program?
6. Who would be involved in your decision about whether to enroll in this program?
7. How do you feel about the tuition cost of this program?
8. What competitive programs come to mind, and which appeals to you the most?
9. Would you enroll in this program? (Definitely, probably, probably not, definitely not)

A sample of adult potential students would then be presented with concept descriptions of potential programs. Each concept description would combine one level from each dimension and be described in enough detail that the potential student could picture what the program would be like. Each respondent is asked to rank the concept descriptions from "most preferred" to "least preferred." For the most highly ranked description, the respondent is asked how likely he or she would be to enroll in that program.

The use of conjoint analysis would suggest which alternative is rated highest overall, which dimensions and levels are valued most highly, and how attractive each combination would be to the target market. Exhibit 11-1 shows how MIT used conjoint analysis to design new M.B.A options.

EXHIBIT 11-1     How a university business school applied research to program redesign

---

The MIT Sloan School of Management undertook a study to improve its graduate management programs in 1975. The first step was qualitative research, focus groups, to understand the market and to generate a set of attributes that potential students used to evaluate alternative progams. Questionnaires were then sent to potential students who had indicated an interest in pursuing a career in management.

Factor analysis was used to define and label three dimensions: program outcomes (job prospects, high salary, prestige, and so on), realism (program relevance and real-world orientation), and process (high faculty contact, financial aid, friendly and cooperative fellow students, and so on). Respondents' ratings of Harvard, Northwestern, Wharton, and MIT on these dimensions are shown in the following figures.

On the same questionnaire, potential students evaluated two new-program ideas based on segmenting the market by providing one program for those interested in breadth, and a second program that allowed the student to specialize in a particular functional area of business.

The research showed that these segment-specific programs appeared to fill a gap. Preference regression revealed the relative importance of outcomes (0.65), realism (0.2), and process (0.15). Simulations of consumer preference showed that the addition of the two new master's degree programs improved MIT's preference share from 11 percent to 37 percent. And 87 percent of the respondents preferred the two new concepts—the practical "Young Executives Program" and the process-emphasis "Intensive Program in Management"—to the existing programs.

The new elements for the programs were tested using conjoint analysis to find out which elements contributed to the overall positioning of each program. The planners wanted to know the contribution to "realism" of a proposed two-week trip to visit business leaders in New York and Washington, DC; a computer exercise; and intensive group sessions with individual faculty members. The conjoint analysis

EXHIBIT 11-1    (continued)

indicated that the trip was the most important component contributing to the realism position, followed in importance by the computer game. (A similar analysis was done for components of the second program.)

After filling in the specifics of these two programs, the brochure was revised to describe the new programs. Since MIT graduates commanded high salaries and since outcomes was the most important dimension, the brochure emphasized career advantages and starting salaries. At the same time, the personal nature of the process was better portrayed with pictures and testimonials. Realism was substantiated with a computer game and a trip to visit business leaders. Because conjoint analysis of preferences indicated that students would prefer the features even at a premium tuition, MIT now charges a premium fee to cover the cost of the added features.

The results were significant. Applications rose 250 percent, acceptance rates increased, and in the judgment of the admissions committee, the average quality of the students also increased.

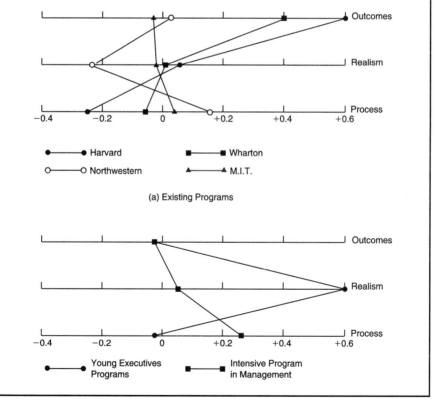

(a) Existing Programs

Source: Based on Glen L. Urban and John R. Hauser, *Design and Marketing of New Products* (Englewood Cliffs, NJ: Prentice-Hall, 1980), pp. 256–259.

**Marketing Strategy Design.** Many educators assume that the marketing strategy is developed *after* the program is ready to offer to the market. In fact, the marketing strategy is as much a part of the success of the new program as the program itself and requires attention during the design stage. The preliminary marketing strategy may, of course, be modified throughout the development process as new information emerges.

The core marketing strategy should be spelled out in a statement consisting of three parts. The first part describes the size, structure, and behavior of the target market, the intended positioning of the new program in this market, and the enrollment and income goals in the first few years. Thus:

> The target market is adults over 24 living in the greater Chicago area who have never obtained a bachelor's degree but have the skills and motivation to seek one. This program will be differentiated from other programs by offering course credit for relevant past experience, as well as by its career-development emphasis. The school will seek a first-year enrollment of 60 students with a net loss not to exceed $150,000. The second-year aim will be an enrollment of 100 students and a net income of at least $40,000.

The second part of the marketing strategy statement outlines the new program's intended price, distribution strategy, and marketing budget for the first year:

> The new program will be offered at the downtown location of De Paul University. All courses will take place once a week in the evening from 6:00 to 9:00. Tuition will be $1,000 per course. The first year's promotion budget will be $160,000, $100,000 of which will be spent on advertising materials and media and the remainder on personal contact activities. Another $20,000 will be spent on marketing research to analyze and monitor the market.

The third part of the marketing strategy statement describes the intended long-run enrollment and profit goals and the marketing-mix strategy over time:

> The university ultimately hopes to achieve a steady enrollment of 400 students in this degree program. When it is built up to this level, a permanent administration will be appointed. Tuition will be raised each year in line with the rate of inflation. The promotion budget will stay at a steady level of $100,000 per year. Marketing research will be budgeted at $20,000 annually. The target long-run income level for this program is $1.2 million a year, and the net income (after salaries, and so on) will be used to support other university programs that are not self-supporting.

These budget figures were derived by estimating the revenues and costs of the program for different possible enrollment levels. Breakeven analysis (see Chapter 13) is the most frequently used approach. Suppose De Paul learns that it needs an enrollment of 260 students to break even. If it manages to attract more than 260 students, this program will produce a net income; otherwise, if there is a shortfall, De Paul will lose money.

**Program Design.** A program concept is not a program. The program elements must be carefully designed to embody the program concept and to reflect the best preliminary marketing strategy. De Paul University's program design will include planning the overall structure of the academic program and setting admissions requirements and procedures. Then each course will need to be designed to fit the purpose of the program and the students who will attend. A planning group, including core faculty, will need to examine individual courses and plan course sequences that will carry out the program concept. Thought will have to be given to how student achievement will be assessed. Faculty training in teaching mature students may be important to the program's success and must then be included in the program design.

## Testing

Testing is part of every phase of the new-program development process. Just as the product concepts were reviewed by potential consumers, the materials, schedules, advertising, and other components of the new program should be consumer-tested before they are printed or distributed. For example, a sample of prospects might be asked to comment on a mockup of the brochure describing the new program. This review usually results in valuable suggestions leading to an improved brochure.

**Market Testing.** When the planning group is satisfied with the initial design, materials, and schedules, it can then set up a market test to see if the proposed program and marketing strategy are likely to be successful. At this stage, the program and marketing strategy are introduced into an authentic consumer setting to learn how many consumers are really interested in the program. Thus, De Paul might decide to mail 10,000 brochures to strong prospects in the Chicago area during the month of April to see whether at least 30 students can be attracted. If more than, say, 30 students sign up, the market test will be regarded as successful, and full-scale promotion can be launched. Otherwise the program can be reformulated or dropped.

**Test Markets.** Test markets are the ultimate form of testing a new program. The institution can measure the viability of the new program without installing it wholesale throughout the system. Test marketing can also reveal which of several marketing strategies is best. Suppose the State University of New York (SUNY) was considering the same program as De Paul. SUNY consists of 64 campuses, not just one. SUNY could develop the program and test it at one of the campuses to see how well it works, or it could test the new program at two or more campuses. Each campus could emphasize a different promotional approach. For example, one campus could use local newspaper advertising, while another could use purchased mailing lists. Promoting the program in different ways permits testing the cost-effectiveness of different promotion approaches. If the new program proved successful in one or both test markets, it could then be launched at other campuses where appropriate.

### Introduction and Management

When the design and testing steps are complete, the institution will be ready to introduce the new program. The timing and skillful management of the program introduction are important. The institution should begin informing potential participants well in advance of the program, but not so early that waiting for it to start dampens their enthusiasm. By the same token, the institution should not wait until the last minute to begin promoting the program; otherwise, interested people will have other commitments and be unable to attend.

The tasks involved in the introduction should be clearly spelled out on a chart that indicates when each task must be completed and who is responsible. There are a number of appropriate scheduling tools, including PERT and CPM, for this task. The purpose of employing scheduling tools is to ensure that all needed tasks are done in the right order and done on schedule. If program materials are delayed or faculty members are unclear about their roles, program participants may question their initial attraction to the program and perhaps drop out, creating "lost business" and bad word of mouth as well.

Those responsible for managing the new program should follow through with planned monitoring activities to ensure that the program is executed as designed and that participants are satisfied. Controls should be established to determine if enrollment, revenue, and costs are within the target ranges.

## ADDING OR MODIFYING OTHER SERVICES

In addition to their academic programs, educational institutions have many supporting and auxiliary services. Supporting services are essential to the core educational activities of the institution. Examples include admissions and financial aid operations, course registration, record keeping (registrar), financial services (tuition payment), and similar functions that are required for the institution to function. Auxiliary services include residence halls and food service, snack bars, entertainment, athletics, book store, and other services which are often highly valued but which are more independent of the institution's core service.

Each of these services can be improved and enhanced in various ways, but not all will get attention. Many institutions wait until complaints pile up before trying to make improvements, while other institutions are constantly on the lookout for "squeaky wheels" to grease or well-functioning systems to improve further. Chapter 2 presents several ways to identify the areas that most need attention, and Exhibit 2-3 shows how one institution reorganized its provision of student administrative services to improve coordination and customer satisfaction. The institution will want to identify the services that most need improvement and identify new services that should be provided.

The planning group can follow the steps described in the section on new-program development to develop new or revised service concepts and to test them for feasibility and attractiveness. Discussion of attribute lists can expand the set of ideas to include novel and more effective ways to perform basic services. For example, registration procedures can be varied in many ways, including:

- registration by touch-tone phone
- registration via fixed terminal or personal computer
- registration via mail
- registration for a full academic year at one time
- registration in the advisor's office as part of the advising process

The best approach will appeal to customers and provide them with excellent results while using the institution's resources effectively.

### Service Design

Once the best approach has been selected, the service-design phase has just begun. The planners—including representatives of those who will manage and/or provide the service—should plan the service carefully. This usually means *blueprinting* the service.

**Service Blueprinting.** Performing a service or implementing a program usually requires a series of steps, and sometimes a very complex set of overlapping activities. Only by mapping—or blueprinting—the steps can the designer verify that the process is likely to work and to be as close to optimal as possible.

According to Shostack and Kingman-Brundage, experts on service blueprinting,

> Service design can be thought of as a form of architecture, but an architecture dealing with processes instead of bricks and mortar. The objective is the creation of a complete blueprint for a service concept that can be translated into a soundly functioning service. What makes service devel-

opment unique is the number and complexity of issues that must be dealt with in order to plan and manage a service concept from conception to realization.[9]

The complete blueprint will show each of the actions in sequence on a flow chart. The blueprint will also show the *line of visibility*, which demarcates the actions observable to the customer from those which, although necessary to the performance of the service, are invisible to the customer. The blueprint shows the *facilitating goods* that are necessary to perform the service, the approximate time each activity takes to perform, and the possible places where problems could surface—the *fail points*—and where special attention is required.

Figure 11-5 shows a simplified blueprint for the course-registration procedure at a college. Such blueprints clearly show the interrelationship of several different functions that must be coordinated to achieve the institution's and the customer's objectives.

**Service Encounters and Scripts.** Once a blueprint has been constructed, the planners can identify the specific instances when customers come in direct contact—in person or by telephone—with the institution's employees. These *service encounters* are important because they create or reinforce customers' judgments about the institution's image and responsiveness, and about its ability to perform the services it promises.

Positive service encounters are not simply the result of hiring service-oriented employees. Employees, particularly those with customer-contact responsibilities, need to have the right information, equipment, and training to perform their tasks at a high level.

If the same employees tend to repeat the same types of encounters over and over—for example, handling students' financial aid questions, they will probably be able to provide better service if they have written *service scripts* that spell out the sequence of questions to ask to obtain key information from the student (student ID number, and so on), as well as the answers to the typical questions that arise. Then, instead of seeking out the basic information each time a question arises, the employee can feel confident about the information in the service script. The employee can then spend more time listening to the student, probing for issues not resolved by the service script, and offering assurance and help.

At the same time, the employees who have the most contact with questions from students, prospects, and others should be encouraged to keep track of these questions and count their frequency. The employees and/or planners can then consider the most effective ways to simplify the process, provide clearer information, spread the information more widely, prepare more or better service scripts, or come up with some other way to reduce uncertainty and communicate information more effectively.

FIGURE 11-5    A simplified example of a service blueprint for course registration

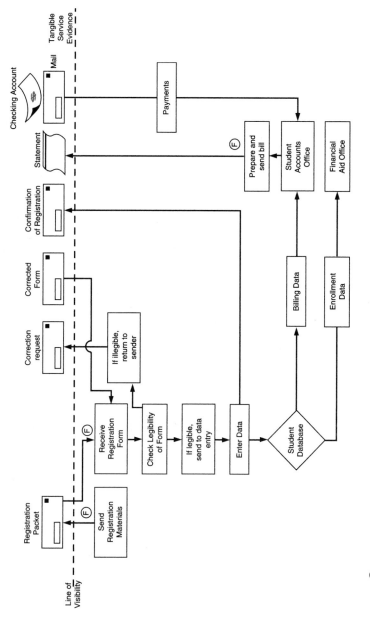

Key: (F) = Fail Point

**303**

## SUMMARY

A school's educational programs and services reflect the school's mission and define the school in the eyes of its markets and publics. Most schools offer several programs and many services, including education, recreation, personal development, and others. These programs and services are *experiences*, not tangible products. Most services are intangible, inseparable, variable, and perishable, existing only when they are "performed" by the service provider (often the instructor) in the presence of the recipient, the student or another person. Educational services usually combine both tangible and intangible components, in that provided services may require classroom space, instructional media, books, desks, and other physical goods.

Each service can be examined as the core offer—the benefit that the customer is really seeking; the tangible offer—the features, quality, packaging, and branding; and the augmented offer—convenience, guarantees, financing, and other advantages.

The institution needs to review its current mix of offerings to see whether they remain well aligned with the institution's strategic plan and with their customers' and society's needs and wants. Services and programs go through a life cycle of introduction, growth, maturity, and (often) decline. Each stage in the life cycle calls for well-considered responses, including adaptation and modernization. Few programs remain optimal forever, yet many institutions assume that programs once launched will remain the same forever.

As certain programs become irrelevant or new needs emerge, the institution will want to consider launching new programs. The new-program development process starts with opportunity identification to select the best program areas and program ideas. The design stage involves consumer measurement, concept development and testing, and design of the actual program and marketing strategy. The testing stage includes testing of program's market potential and appeal, and of the proposed marketing strategy. Decisions at each of these stages should be based on the best possible market information, research, and analytical techniques.

The institution may also need to add new services and programs or modify existing ones. Continuous improvements in service design and performance contribute to customer satisfaction. Service blueprinting can identify better ways to implement new services or improve the functioning of existing ones, through enhancing service encounters and providing service scripts where appropriate.

### Notes

1. See Ben M. Ennis and Kenneth J. Roering, "Services Marketing: Different Products, Similar Strategy," in James H. Donnelly and William R. George, eds., *Marketing of Services* (Chicago: American Marketing Association, 1981), pp. 1–4.

2. See G. Lynn Shostack, "Breaking Free from Product Marketing," *Journal of Marketing* (April 1977), pp. 73–80.

3. William F. Sturner, "Environmental Code: Creating a Sense of Place on the College Campus," *Journal of Higher Education* (February 1972), pp. 97–109.

4. Theodore Levitt, *The Marketing Mode* (New York: McGraw-Hill, 1969), p. 2.

5. Barry Mitzman, "U. of Washington Plans to Drop 24 Degree Programs," *The Chronicle of Higher Education*, November 10, 1982, p. 3.

6. Ronald Hoverstad, Mark Plovnick, Thomas Brierton, and Richard Vargo, "Beginning a New Academic Program: A Case Study of the MBA Program at the University of the Pacific," in the *Proceedings of the 1993 Symposium for the Marketing of Higher Education* (Chicago: American Marketing Association, 1993), pp. 45–52.

7. James L. Adams, *Conceptual Blockbusting*, 3rd ed. (Reading, MA: Addison-Wesley, 1986).

8. Christopher Shea, "Concept of a 3-Year Bachelor's Degree Gains Support Among Campus Leaders," *The Chronicle of Higher Education*, February 10, 1993, pp. A33–A34.

9. Lynn Shostack and Jane Kingman-Brundage, "How to Design a Service," in Carol A. Congram and Margret L. Friedman, eds., *The AMA Handbook of Marketing for the Service Industries* (New York: American Management Association, 1991), p. 243.

# 12

# Pricing Educational Programs

*Richard Moll, long-time admissions director and author of several books on the admissions process, recently reflected on what he termed "the scramble to get the new class":*

*Undergraduate admissions and financial aid directors say they are losing sleep over "meeting enrollment goals," a smooth academic term that means delivering bottom-line revenue from new students after the discounts to lure them and the attrition within last year's student body have been taken into account. Although much of the current talk is about "creative financial aid incentives" to build the new class, admissions directors know they must remain concerned about the old horses of "imaging" and "positioning," not to mention "structuring" first impressions during a family's visit to the campus. There are many parts of this package called "college" to be defined, designed, marketed, and sold. An admissions director hardly knows where to begin these days.*

*Stephen T. Briggs, undergraduate dean of admissions and financial aid at the University of New Haven, tells me about his routine: "I take the 'Money Walk' with the head of buildings and grounds, just to make certain the plantings look fresh, the grass is not worn to the ground, and there is no litter, or, God forbid, graffiti. What's the Money Walk? It's the tour route parents and kids take to see the campus with our student guide. We know initial impressions can be lasting impressions in this don't-miss-a-trick campaign to encourage a potential student and his or her parents to believe that we have something the campus they just visited, or will visit next, doesn't have. Hell, it's easier to dress up the Money Walk than to grind out backing for one more merit scholarship, given the tense financial squeeze at most colleges today. Every player and scene counts as the enrollment drama unfolds through the year."*

*Briggs is a good spokesperson for the current scramble to land a freshman class (and for the related scramble to quickly increase transfer enrollees if anticipated freshman numbers don't hit target). As Briggs says, competing with other private and public institutions to land the class today is "war."*

*"What else can you call it but war when in mid-summer a transfer admittee with an appropriate-to-need financial aid package finds your home number and telephones to say that one of our leading rivals has just countered New Haven's 'offer'—with not only full-grant tuition and full-grant room and board, but also a generous book fund? Rumor has it that this competitor ventured so far out on a limb with killer merit awards last year that it's running a big deficit and can't possibly continue the practice. But they sure beat up on us in the interim. Which of our 'colleague colleges' will try it next?*

*"What's really heartbreaking is to see a family roll into the parking lot by the admissions office for the big appointment, look around briefly, and drive back out. You see why the shrubs and tidy walkways become important—just to get prospects inside the front door! If they come in, I know their review of us later will appropriately turn to the quality of our programs and how our student body and location compare to the competition. But be assured that down the line, their top-of-the-list question—even if they like our shrubs and students and programs and location—will be everybody else's number one question: 'What can you do to help us reduce the cost?'"*

*Probably even at Yale, but certainly at the large majority of colleges and universities in the country that cannot possibly be considered "selective" (including some with prestigious names achieved during healthier times), the driving principle today in enrollment matters is delivering bottom-line net revenue.*

*According to William Pickett, president of St. John Fisher College in Rochester, NY, "Today I expect the admissions/financial aid team to invent and oversee a marketing plan that, by the end of each recruiting year, produces a student body that achieves net tuition revenue targets. Remember: total enrollment can't be up with net tuition revenues down if the admissions/financial aid team attracts new students only by enhanced discounting, which means luring students with unfunded institutional aid. So comparing the student body size from year to year can be deceptive—it's the net revenue collected that allows this place to continue to work," he says.*

*"I hate to say it," he continues, "but we're getting to be like the airlines in creative discounting. United Airlines and Continental have all those planes that have to fly. They prosper and have the means to improve their product only if those planes are full, or nearly full. So they take a reading of the diverse populations they are happy to attract, market creatively to each of them with their eyes glued to the competition, alter pricing among the populations, walk the different groups who've paid very different prices down the red carpet, and lift off."*

**Source:** Richard W. Moll, "The Scramble to Get the New Class," *Change*, 26, no. 2 (March/April 1994), 11–13.

---

Most educational institutions depend heavily on tuition and fees to keep operating and, therefore, pricing issues are very important. Tuition covers most of the operating expenses of many private colleges and universities, with variations from zero to over 100 percent. Cooper Union in New York City is perhaps the only tuition-free private four-year college in the United States. Every student receives a full-tuition scholarship, thanks to its nineteenth-century founder, self-made millionaire Peter Cooper, who declared that "education ought to be as free as air or water"—and who had the financial resources to back up this conviction. At the other end of the spectrum are the for-profit schools (such as proprietary trade/career schools and test-preparation programs) at which tuition exceeds operating expenses.

Tuition at public and not-for-profit educational institutions rarely covers the "true cost of education," but is subsidized by donors and/or taxpayers who have contributed toward buildings, scholarships, and other components of quality education. Many very good schools rely on tuition to cover as much as 80 to 90 percent of the operating budget, the rest covered by endowment income, gifts, and grants. At most state colleges and universities, tuition covers about a third of operating expenses and most of the rest comes from state tax receipts.

For most U.S. educational institutions, the decade of the 1990s is a period of belt-tightening marked by efforts to cut costs, increase productivity, incorporate expensive, up-to-date technology to build capabilities and value, and offer more financial aid. The pressure on both sides of the balance sheet is felt almost everywhere. The most prestigious universities in the United States are just as involved in belt-tightening as are tiny colleges virtually unknown outside their immediate areas.

In this chapter we examine pricing issues in the *marketing* context. (We leave many other financial issues to the finance and accounting fields.) Price plays a role in determining who will apply (since some prospects will experience "sticker shock" and never apply), who will attend, who the institution will serve, what the institution will be able to offer (in programs and personnel), and whether the institution will meet its enrollment objectives and revenue needs.

We will address the following issues:

- The relationship between pricing decisions and institutional mission and goals.
- How customers look at price.
- Institutional responses on price and value.
- Maximizing net tuition revenue.
- Determining cost-recovery prices for educational programs.

## PRICING AND INSTITUTIONAL MISSION AND GOALS

Setting prices for most educational programs should take into account cost-oriented, customer-demand-oriented, and competition-oriented factors. In the past, few institutions viewed tuition pricing from a marketing perspective, but this has changed rapidly.

Here is a simplified example of how tuition used to be set: The chief financial officer determined expected operating expenses for the coming year and projected revenues from endowment, donations, and other sources. Subtracting expenses from revenues determined the amount that must be covered by tuition. That amount would be divided by the expected total enrollment, which yielded a first estimate of the amount needed. The percentage increase in tuition would then be examined for "reasonableness," checked against news (or leaks) of what other similar institutions were planning, and then the resulting number was sent on to the board of trustees for approval.

The difficulty with a cost-based approach to tuition setting is that every educational institution can find good uses for any increase in revenues: There is never "enough money" and, in the past, few incentives to hold down tuition. The benefit of the competition-oriented approach is that each institution can weigh its "value" and establish its price relative to its competitors—in prestige, academic quality, and other factors. But regardless of the measure used by the institution, the final decision on price is always made by the customers—what they can and are willing to pay. The experience of the 1980s, when college tuition grew faster than the rate of inflation and faster than real growth in family incomes, has led to the 1990s concern for "value," "discounting," and pressures on financial-aid budgets.

According to William Ihlanfeldt, the institution should consider (1) the effects of a given pricing policy on the nature and mission of the institution, (2) the effects of a given pricing policy on enrollment, and (3) the degree to which a particular pricing policy may encourage acceleration.[1] In addition, the institution must weigh (4) prices charged by comparable competing institutions, and (5) the effects of its own price level and price changes on the actions of such competitors. These considerations provide a basis for setting prices.

Pricing decisions should reflect the institution's mission, goals, and priorities. Even if the school can't offer "free education to all who want it," the school's pricing policy—and financial policy—should be congruent with good fiscal management and with the institution's mission. John Maguire, a founder of enrollment management, stated the following two goals within a longer list:

> *admissions marketing*—to develop an admissions marketing program in order to attract outstanding students in sufficient numbers during a period of national enrollment declines, and *pricing and financial aid strategies*—to implement pricing and financial strategies that will optimize the institution's ability to attract and retain the desired academic, racial/ethnic, and socioeconomic mix of students.[2]

Of those schools that could fill all their places—some several times over—with full-paying students, most aim to meet diversity objectives by providing financial aid to many applicants who cannot pay the full expense. That is, they are not concerned solely with the size of the entering class but with the composition of the class.[3] Educational institutions have traditionally seen financial aid as a way to "even the playing field" so that worthy applicants can benefit from what the school offers. Growing educational costs and confusing—and conflicting—standards for determining financial need have greatly complicated the prudent allocation of financial aid.[4] The challenge now is how to meet students' financial need in an era of declining government funding and deficit-running institutional budgets.

For some institutions there is a very obvious connection between program, price, and target market. For example, Northeastern University emphasizes the educational and career advantages of its cooperative program, but the paid work experience at intervals throughout the undergraduate years also helps participating students afford tuition at a private university. Berea College in Kentucky was founded to serve the Southern Appalachian region, and admissions preference is given to students whose families would have a difficult time financing a college education without assistance. According to admissions director John Cook, "It doesn't matter how bright a student is, or how high he can jump, or how well he can sing. If he doesn't meet the need criterion, he cannot come to Berea."[5]

Each Berea student receives a labor grant of $2,500, which is applied to the annual tuition of $11,300. The remaining tuition cost of $8,800 is met by federal, state, and other scholarships. Any remaining cost is guaranteed by Berea College. Every student works 10 to 15 hours a week on campus for $2 to $4 an hour. The student and family are expected to contribute the very modest cost of living expenses and books.[6] The college has structured its operations to be able to support its commitment to helping needy students, its mission.

Institutions that once took pride in "need-blind admissions"—admitting students based on their talents, and then allocating sufficient aid to cover their expenses—are now finding it difficult or impossible to continue to meet the full need for their new and continuing students. Some colleges are turning toward what B. Ann Wright of Smith College calls "need-aware admissions," very consciously seeking out full-pay students to counterbalance the students who need financial aid, and giving preferential admission to students who can afford to pay all or most of the cost. We will have more to say about particular approaches to allocating aid and tuition later in this chapter.

## HOW CUSTOMERS LOOK AT PRICE

Educational administrators who set prices often overlook the meaning of price to consumers. For example, the actual charges made by a school or college are not the only cost to the consumer. As Adam Smith noted long ago, "The real price of everything, what everything really costs to the man who wants to acquire it, is the toil and trouble of acquiring it." Figure 12-1 shows the costs and benefits for consumers. In addition to the monetary price, consumers face other costs: effort costs, psychic costs, and time costs.[7] Some high school students avoid applying to colleges that require a long essay as part of the application. Some select a college close to home because they feel living at home will reduce the psychic pressure of going to college away from family and friends.

The money consumers pay to obtain a good or service goes by various names:

> You pay RENT for your apartment, TUITION for your education, and a FEE to your physician or dentist. The airline, railway, taxi, and bus companies charge you a FARE; the local utilities call their price a RATE; and the local bank charges you INTEREST for the money you borrow. The price for driving your car on Florida's Sunshine Parkway is a TOLL, and the company that insures your car charges you a PREMIUM. The guest lecturer charges an HONORARIUM to tell you about a government official who took a BRIBE to help a shady character steal DUES collected by a

FIGURE 12-1    The consumer's costs and benefits.

---

## COSTS

Time and effort
Self/family savings/income
Loans
Work-study jobs
Other concurrent employment
Outside scholarships
School scholarships

---

## BENEFITS

Career prospects
Prestige
Ongoing experience
  during education
Program uniqueness

---

trade association. Clubs or societies to which you belong may make a special ASSESSMENT to pay unusual expenses. Your regular lawyer may ask for a RETAINER to cover her services. The price of an executive is a SALARY; the price of a salesman may be a COMMISSION; and the price of a worker is a WAGE. Finally, although economists would disagree, many of us feel that INCOME TAXES are the price we pay for the privilege of making money![8]

Regardless of the school's *list price* (the official tuition and fees printed in the catalog), prospective students and their families—and reimbursing companies—are interested in the *effective price* (the amount they will actually pay for the educational benefits) and the value received. The effective price is the net amount actually paid after financial assistance and other discounts are subtracted.

Prospective buyers find it impossible to measure *effective price* early in the decision process, since the effective price can be known only after the student has gone through the application process and been accepted, when financial aid awards are announced. And only when all the college replies are in can the prospective students compare the offers of admission. It is no surprise then that some students file large numbers of applications, and that many apply for financial aid despite substantial family incomes—just to make sure they don't miss out on possible institutional largesse. Almost every admissions and financial aid director can now tell stories of families with incomes over $150,000 asking for aid, pleading poverty in the face of paying college expenses.

Assessing the actual *value* of attending a particular school is also nearly impossible in advance of enrollment—and perhaps not until after graduation! Education is an experience that cannot be appraised before experiencing it, and the outcomes of attending a particular schools may not be readily apparent until the graduate seeks employment or begins moving ahead professionally. Even then, the connection may be quite subtle, such as getting a position through a classmate, obtaining a job recommendation from a key professor, or having an opportunity to study abroad that changed the course of a life's work.

In the absence of firsthand experience, people often form judgments based on those aspects they can observe, including the beauty of the campus and adequacy of the facilities—hence, "the Money Walk." Many prospects will engage in comparing prices and expected benefits available from other institutions. They may use the list prices of other comparable schools to form an impression about the appropriate reference price, with which all candidate institutions' prices are compared.

Richard Moll tells the story about a father with a half-million-dollar salary who wrote to Robin Jaycox, Colgate's director of financial aid, "You are asking $18K for a year's tuition at Colgate, but I think you're worth $15K. My son would like to attend Colgate, but we will not pay above $15,000 for tuition. Might he attend? Please respond."[9]

This example highlights a frequently ignored distinction between the ability, the willingness, and the necessity to pay for educational expenses. Some students and/or their families are able to pay all or most of the costs, but are not willing to do so—except under certain circumstances. The more confident the student and family feel about the value of the school and its offerings, the easier it will typically be to justify the price of that school. One family willingly refinanced their home in order to send their son to Stanford, but would not do so to pay for a "lesser" university.

Research confirms that consumers often use the price of a product or service as an indicator of its quality.[10] Consumers tend to rely on price more frequently in making an important decision, especially when they lack self-confidence in making the decision.[11] In practice, consumers seem wary of schools that charge significantly less than comparable schools. They may wonder what is wrong with the school and presume that other, more expensive schools offer a better education.

One Catholic high school promoted the fact that its tuition was "affordable for all"—well below tuition levels at nearby, comparable Catholic schools. Price increases were so modest that the school's tuition lagged way behind that of its principal competitor, and deficits made it impossible for the school to improve its program in areas where it was at a competitive disadvantage. Its altruistic efforts to hold down prices and price increases hurt its image and depressed enrollment rather than enhancing them. Families who could easily afford the tuition began sending their daughters to a more expensive surburban Catholic high school, while the working-class families who stretched their budgets to send their daughters to this school began to feel that this "affordable" school was no longer bestowing the sense of "advantage" the parents sought for their daughters.

A parish elementary school in a wealthy suburb maintained its in-parish tuition at $350 year after year by subsidizing the school from parish contributions. The tuition was one-half to one-third of tuition at nearby parish schools. The school had a long waiting list, but the building and grounds were in disrepair, and the school had depleted the parish resources needlessly.

Both these schools would have been better served by setting realistic prices and making appropriate annual changes.

Acknowledging this price/quality relationship, some few schools tried to substantially raise their tuition charges in the hope of raising institutional prestige and attractiveness, while simultaneously reducing the effective price through generous scholarships. This "high-tuition/high-aid" strategy might work for some institutions, but the focus should be on value—is the school worth what it costs to attend?

Students and families or companies that pay the tuition may have a psychological *price barrier* beyond which they will decide the price is too high and select a lower-priced school. This is analogous to the "sticker shock" automobile shoppers experience when they see the total price, including all accessories, additions, and services, not just the quoted base price. For example, a university developed a specialized training program for high-level executives. To cover the university's costs (including research and development costs, overhead, and contribution to university overhead) and offer the program in an ideal setting and manner, the university would need to price the program at $10,000. Since area companies seemed to consider $7,000 a psychological price barrier for such programs and experienced sticker shock at amounts over that, the university decided to reduce some of the features in order to offer the program at $7,000. If the program is highly successful, its features and price can be increased when it is repeated.

Although some people experience a price barrier, others make less price distinction at high price levels than at low ones. For example, the tuition difference between, say, a state college at $2,000 per year and a private college at $10,000 is sufficiently large that some parents who have adjusted their thinking to accept the higher cost of a private college find the increment from $10,000 to $15,000 for an elite college to be less of a psychological barrier.

Finally, it should be kept in mind that price is just one component of the marketing mix that influences consumers' choices. Prospective students will be interested in the school's program, quality, and features; the location; and communications by and about the institution. Many students will pay more for a high-quality education. If the institution is attractive and conveniently located, this can outweigh some price differences. A college that is well known and well respected will command more attention and attract more applications than one that is a well-kept secret.

Price increases for an educational program should be supported by a communications campaign that indicates the amount and timing of the increases, reasons that necessitate them, and institutional efforts to reduce their effect (such as increases in financial aid and additional fund-raising efforts). Information on the increase should be made well in advance, to help applicants and current students make plans to accommodate the increased cost as well as to minimize resentment that the news of the price increase came "too late to do anything." The institution also needs to keep reminding students (and their parents) of the institution's strengths, so that the increased price is more acceptable.


## INSTITUTIONAL RESPONSES ON PRICE AND VALUE

Customer demand for value, the slow growth of family incomes compared to the rate of tuition increases, the high degree of competition for students, and educational institutions' dependence on tuition revenue have worked together to significantly alter how educational institutions recruit students and how, once admitted, the institution divides up the tuition cost among students.

Each school's recruiting and admissions process is, in principle, a matching process, in which the school seeks out the students attractive to the institution who also see themselves benefiting from their education there. In the matching process, the school also needs to meet its revenue goals, to be able to keep functioning and to continue to enhance quality.


### The Revenue Function

The following function is for a university, but with minor adaptations this model could apply to any school. The basic definition of revenue is price times quantity, but stating the revenue function more completely can reveal ways in which an institution can potentially increase its revenue. The private university in this example gets its revenue from four main sources: student payments for tuition and room and board; payments for other services; sponsored research; and donations and return on endowment.

| Revenue | = | Average annual tuition per student per year | × | Number of students enrolled |
|---|---|---|---|---|
| | + | Average room and board payment per person per year | × | Number of students in residence halls |
| | + | Revenue from other services, conferences, programs, facilities, rentals, sponsored research, and so on | + | Net contribution to overhead from |
| | + | Donations | + | Return on endowment |

Specifying the revenue function helps identify actions that can increase revenue. The university can generally improve its revenue by increasing any one or more of the factors, as long as an increase in price, for example, is not offset by a decrease in quantity. The university can consider raising tuition, which most schools do annually. We will discuss this in greater detail later. It can seek to attract and retain more students. It can increase room and board charges (increases usually pegged to cost increases) or, if rooms are vacant, consider ways to increase the attractiveness of campus living or set policies requiring students to live on campus for at least part of the time they are enrolled.

The institution can use revenues from one source to *cross-subsidize* other programs. For example, summer rentals of residence halls for conferences may cover maintenance and enhancements, and athletic receipts over program costs may subsidize other activities. The same is true of some academic programs, which produce a higher contribution margin than others; that is, they return more in revenue than it costs to provide them.[12] These cross-subsidies between programs give the institution the flexibility to offer and maintain programs that may never pay their own way.

The university will also want to encourage sponsored research, improve the effectiveness of its fund-raising efforts, and arrange for the best possible management of its endowment to maximize the return to the university. If the university can reduce costs, the pressure on revenues is reduced. Implementing energy-conservation measures, eliminating nonessential expenditures, and reducing waste can reduce the cost side of the budget equation.

Most educational administrators are aware of the general principles briefly outlined earlier. But the same schools concerned about raising tuition revenue to avert faculty/staff layoffs may be simultaneously ignoring the dozens or hundreds of empty places in the residence halls. This unused capacity must still be maintained and can't be "laid off," yet few institutions are consciously taking a marketing approach to create residence halls where students would want to live and to promote the advantages of on-campus living. Educational administrators need to be looking comprehensively at the revenue function and the marketing implications of various courses of action, not just at tuition.

As for the instructional program, many institutions have a proliferation of courses and sections, but no clear sense of how well the supply and scheduling of these courses matches (1) student demand and (2) student needs. Many courses are scheduled to meet the preferences of instructors or to balance the number of courses from term to term in a way that "looks" sensible to department chairs. Few institutions have considered optimal sequences of courses toward various majors, then scheduled course sequences accordingly while reducing time overlaps between complementary courses, and advised students of the best path to complete all needed courses. But schools following this model can reduce the total number of sections, lowering costs, while increasing student satisfaction.[13]

The effective price of the total program can be reduced by providing financial aid or by reducing the time spent earning a degree and correspondingly increasing the graduate's years of gainful employment. For example, Boston University (and a number of other schools) offers a six-year B.S./M.D. program for outstanding entering freshmen, who thus save two years of tuition and foregone income. The combined program in effect contains a very attractive financial aid package and attracts top students to the university. Of course, any program that reduces the length of time a student is enrolled will also reduce the institution's per-student revenue. Several university presidents are discussing reducing the time to complete a bachelor's degree from four years to three years, which will mean the universities will need to admit one-third more students each year than they do now.

Some institutions are already reducing the time-to-degree by granting generous amounts of credit based on examinations or life experience. Awarding such credit may increase an applicant's interest in getting more education. Reducing the number of courses the student needs for a degree may decrease the institution's per-student tuition revenue or, on the other hand, it could actually increase tuition revenue if the time reduction means the student needs less institutional financial aid to attend. Offering such programs can provide some benefits to the institution in attracting mature students discouraged at the alternative of many years of formal college courses to get a degree, but the institution should do some deep soul-searching about what the student may be missing in academic experience and rigor by substituting life-experience credits for academic study.

## MAXIMIZING NET TUITION REVENUE

While current and potential customers seek to reduce the effective price, educational institutions need to cover costs and generate some "surplus," a large part of which goes into financial aid. Educational institutions therefore need to be even more concerned about maximizing tuition revenue than maximizing student enrollment. Increasing the number of students without increasing net tuition revenue leaves the institution even poorer than before and unable to meet the added financial aid burden. But as long as the institution has unused capacity—room in classes and/or in residence halls—the institution is better off "selling the seat on the departing plane" for something than having it go unused and bringing in no revenue.

### Setting Tuition Levels

The school must decide how it will price its programs. Here we are referring to list price, and we consider financial aid as a discount off list price. But list price is the starting point, and every school needs to determine—and publish—its list prices. In practice the determination of tuition levels historically has not been done in a particularly sophisticated manner, but rather has reflected a blend of examining costs, considering what close competitors charge, and predicting what students and their families will be willing to pay. The resulting figures often are suboptimal on all three measures because it is difficult to meet three conflicting objectives.

One pricing approach would be to set a moderate tuition level for all students. The limitation is that some students and their families can afford to pay a larger share of the total cost of education and the school would be providing less of a subsidy for the truly needy. A low-tuition strategy, which most public higher education institutions employ, sets an artificially low price, which must then be compensated for by tax receipts. Well-to-do students often have higher grades and test scores and thus have a greater likelihood of admission to the top public institutions, filling places that would otherwise go to less well-off students, while paying the same amount as their low-income, high-need classmates. The third option is a "high-tuition, high-need" strategy that reallocates tuition from the well-to-do to low-income students, so that each student pays relative to ability and need. Each of these three approaches presents both possibilities and pitfalls, and needs to be carefully weighed.[14]

We will look first at how educational institutions can use differential pricing to allocate tuition costs among students and programs, and then we turn to how financial aid can be allocated among students.

### Allocating Tuition Costs Among Students and Programs

The traditional one-price-for-all-students approach is increasingly being replaced by a price schedule with one level of tuition for undergraduates, another for graduate students in arts and sciences, and still another for each professional school. Such variations may be based on differences in costs of instruction, anticipated earnings of graduates, and demand by various market segments, as we have noted previously.

Consider the case of Northeastern University in Boston. Tuition increases were for decades based on adding a flat percentage each year based solely on covering costs. In fact, its overall price structure was significantly below those of such competitors as Boston University and Boston College. Northeastern then instituted differential tuition based on program and year, such that business students pay more than humanities students and upperclassmen pay more than freshmen and sophomores.

A number of basic pricing approaches have been adopted or proposed.[15] Here are several examples. Each pricing approach will have a different effect upon students' educational plans, how total tuition costs are allocated among students, and on the institution's revenues, as we will illustrate.

**Unit Pricing.** Institutions with many part-time students often set tuition on a per-unit or per-course basis. This approach is easy to administer, provides great flexibility for students, and encourages attendance by more part-time students. On the other hand, the institution cannot forecast enrollment and tuition revenue as accurately. The students who took one course last term may take three this term, or vice versa. There are no built-in price incentives for students to take additional courses, so the institution's revenue depends on external forces that might encourage or discourage taking courses, such as the job market. Nor does unit pricing account for the costs associated with recruiting, record keeping, and providing counseling services, which do not vary whether the student takes one course or more.

**Two-Part Pricing.** Two-part pricing addresses the latter two limitations of unit pricing. This approach adds a flat charge for each student to the total tuition based on a per-course or a per-unit formula. The fixed cost might vary from program to program, or be the same for all. Part-time students would have a greater incentive to take more courses per term than under unit pricing.

**Term Pricing.** Under this approach, a student make take as many (or as few) courses as desired for the same fixed tuition each term. This approach encourages students to take a full course load and penalizes part-time students. Term pricing encourages some students to accelerate their programs to complete at least one whole term early, since to take even one course the last term would represent no cost saving. Some colleges discourage acceleration by requiring every student to pay four academic years of tuition.

**Scaled Pricing.** Under scaled pricing, a student would pay a larger tuition charge for the first and second courses, then a smaller charge for additional courses. This approach covers the administrative costs as in two-part and term pricing, while offering the flexibility of unit pricing for part-time students and a price incentive for full-time students. An institution wanting to discourage acceleration could set a higher tuition price for each additional course over the normal course load.

**Differential Pricing.** Educational institutions are giving serious thought to pricing their programs and services in new ways that may better serve potential students and the schools. One form of demand-oriented pricing involves charging different prices for particular programs or services. This practice is termed *price discrimination* or *differential pricing.* Many schools are looking carefully at differential pricing and several already charge differential tuition fees on the following bases:[16]

- By *program*—by student major, for example, business, engineering, arts and sciences, law, medicine, and so on; or by cluster of majors, for example, humanities, social sciences, physical and life sciences
- By *student level*—undergraduate and graduate, lower division and upper division; grad 1 and grad 2; by individual class.
- By *student course load*—by student credit hours or for student credit hour intervals (for example, 10 to 18 hours at a fixed rate).
- By *type of student*—degree versus nondegree (since nondegree students generally require fewer support services)
- By *residency status*—for publicly-supported institutions which distinguish between resident and nonresident students.
- By *course*—each course, or for each course in a cluster of disciplines.
- By *time/place of offering*—differentials for summer session, evening classes, or for classes offered at different sites (for example, at a company).

Differential pricing works only when certain conditions are met.[17] First, the student market must be segmentable by category, and each segment must show different intensities of demand. For example, differential pricing would fail if day students all decided to attend evening classes owing to lower tuition. If courses in the mathematics department cost less than in the quantitative methods department of the business school, students might prefer to enroll in mathematics department courses.

Second, there should be no chance that members of the segment paying the lower price could turn around and resell the product to the segment that would otherwise pay a higher price. For this reason, students are limited in the number of reduced-price tickets they can purchase for school athletic and other events. Third, there should be little chance that competing institutions can attract the higher-paying segment with a lower-priced program or service. Finally, the cost of segmenting and policing the market to verify eligibility for special prices should not exceed the extra revenue derived from differential pricing.

Differential pricing may imply that some people or groups are being treated unfairly, but this is usually not the case. In fact, given the different costs of providing courses in English composition and more expensive courses in mechanical engineering, having students pay the same tuition regardless of major field means that some students are subsidizing the instructional costs of others. Of course, the rejoinder is that no student is paying the full cost, since they benefit from endowment income and other gifts to the school.

Differential pricing has an important policy consequence. When all courses and fields of study cost the same, price is not a factor in student choice. If high-cost and/or high-demand programs are priced significantly higher than others, price-sensitive students may make curricular and thereby career decisions based on tuition-cost differences. The same effect occurs when scholarships and loans are given for study in specific fields.

**Negotiated Tuition.** Some Catholic schools offer parents the option of negotiating the amount of tuition they feel they can pay, ranging from zero to full cost.[18]

**Quantity Discounts.** A college might offer a discount for five, ten, or more registrations for the same course or program, submitted together. This would encourage people to discuss their educational plans with their friends and colleagues and might increase demand for selected programs. This is attractive to companies also, as discussed earlier. Sibling discounts—reduced tuition for siblings enrolled at the same time—are examples of quantity discounts.

**Time-Based Discounts.** An educational program might offer a discount to students who register and pay early, since this gives the school a more accurate basis for planning. Several colleges have offered guaranteed-tuition plans that involve paying the entire four years' tuition in advance at the first year's tuition rate. The college invests the unused portion, yielding interest income equal to the tuition increases for future years.

**Peak-Load Pricing.** An educational institution may find its facilities are full from 9 A.M. to 2 P.M., but underutilized during the rest of the day. The school might charge higher tuition for classes during the peak hours than during the off-peak hours, with the aim of attracting additional students willing and able to pay off-peak rates.[19]

**Work Contribution.** Most colleges and universities participate in the College Work-Study Program and include this as part of students' aid packages. Such work programs, like scholarships, provide ways to reduce the financial cost of attending college.

## Allocating Financial Assistance Among Students

Since every institution's financial aid is limited, the practical question is how to allocate that aid to best serve students and the institution's financial and educational objectives. There are two basic components of allocating tuition assistance. The first is to factor need into the admissions decision, by either giving first preference to applicants meeting institutional academic standards who can afford to pay all or most of the costs; or by reserving a certain number of places at the lower end of the student-quality ranking that are then allocated by the student's ability to pay. That is, the best and better students are admitted on a need-blind basis, while the students less well-qualified who are secondarily ranked according to ability to pay.

The second component is determination of the amounts and types of aid to offer to specific students who are offered admission—called "packaging" financial aid. Here there are several patterns, each reflecting a certain view of price and its impact on consumer decisions.[20]

- *Uniform self-help.* Each student is expected to provide the same dollar amount from borrowing and from employment during the school year.

- *Self-help by ability to borrow.* Students whose overall family resources provide them with a greater capacity to borrow funds will be expected to use loans to cover a larger percentage of college costs. The school may set a lower self-help amount for students whose borrowing capacity is limited.

- *Self-help varied by desirability.* The school will set a low self-help amount for highly desirable students, and a higher level for those who are less attractive candidates. In effect, the "gap" between actual need and covered need will be greater for these less desirable students.

- *Admit/deny.* The school will go down its ranked list of applicants and meet their financial need until the financial-aid budget is exhausted, and then continue down to list to admit other needy students but with no offer of financial aid.

- *Aid-conscious admission.* The school will go down its ranked list of applicants and meet their financial need until the financial aid budget is exhausted, and then continue down the list, admitting students who have no financial need and rejecting all those with financial need.

- *Equity packaging.* All students receive aid that meets the same dollar amount or percentage amount of need.

- *Differential packaging and preferential packaging.* Individual students receive aid, but with different proportions of self-help, loans, grants, and work-study allocations, depending on their desirability to the institution. For example, the more attractive applicants would receive a larger amount of aid in the form of grants rather than loans and work. The school may give better packages to underrepresented groups than to other students.

## Living Within a Fixed Aid Budget Versus
## Maximizing Net Tuition Revenues

Two approaches to the use of financial aid budgets are illustrated in Exhibit 12-1. If an institution is already enrolling the maximum number of students that it can accommodate without significantly adding to fixed costs, the school may wish to cap financial aid as a percentage of tuition income. This

EXHIBIT 12-1    Two institutional approaches to allocating financial aid

Scenario One

In keeping with the dictum that scholarships should represent less than 30 percent of tuition income, which yields the $5 million financial aid budget, the admission and financial aid offices believe they can enroll 290 new students, freshman and transfer, and 870 continuing students for a total of 1,160. Multiplying the 1991–92 tuition of $14,500 by 1,160 produces $16,820,000 of gross revenue. Subtracting $5 million of financial aid expenditure leaves $11,820,000 net tuition revenue. Financial aid therefore represents 29.7 percent of tuition income.

Scenario Two

For an extra $400,000 of institutional aid, the admission and financial aid offices believe they can enroll 300 new students and 900 continuing students for a total of 1,200. That student population times the tuition of $14,500 produces gross tuition revenues of $17,400,000. When the $5.4 million financial aid budget is subtracted, net tution revenues are $12 million, or $180,000 higher than in the first scenario. Because the ideal enrollment has been met there are no additional fixed costs. Thus the $180,000 additional tuition revenue is new net income to the university. The percentage of tuition income going to scholarship aid, however, has grown from 29.7 percent to 31 percent.

There are other ancillary benefits to meeting the ideal enrollment, such as:

a. there are more students on campus, which creates the potential for a better educational environment;

b. there is better utitilization of the residence halls with additional revenue of $90,000 (40 x $2,250);

c. there are fewer withdrawals by continuing students who could not otherwise afford T.M.L.A.U.;

d. there are lower per unit costs for dining; and

e. there is a larger enrollment base to build upon for enrollment in subsequent years.

Source: James J. Scannell, *The Effect of Financial Aid Policies on Admission and Enrollment* (New York: The College Board, 1992), p. 48.

is shown in Scenario One. On the other hand, if the school has excess capacity, then limiting aid to an arbitrary percentage of tuition income is "probably inappropriate and possibly counterproductive."[21] Scenario Two illustrates how the use of additional institutional aid can increase total enrollment and net tuition revenue.

When student financial aid is in fact a price discount (as in Scenario Two), it is not an expenditure but rather a deduction from gross revenue. Deducting such aid from gross revenue yields the institution's net tuition revenue.

James Scannell points out the value of closely examining the effect of different levels of student financial aid on the enrollment yield by the quality and need of the student. The purpose of financial aid is to make it possible— and attractive—for particular students to enroll. The question is, Does it work? He points out that "as (student) quality increases, yield decreases (since these students have many options); as aid increases, yield increases; and as need increases, yield increases."[22] The enrollment manager can experiment by varying the amounts of total aid and of "free aid," to see at what levels the increases translate into higher percent yields from these groups.

## DETERMINING COST-RECOVERY PRICES FOR EDUCATIONAL PROGRAMS

Schools now considering launching new programs—for example, a new master's degree program—often do so to generate additional revenue. If the new program will not at least pay for itself, the school may decide to "stick to its knitting" and not move into new areas. In such instances, the school should carry out a breakeven analysis to determine how much money and how many tuition-paying students the program will need to bring in to pay its way.

### Breakeven Analysis to Determine Program Viability

Breakeven analysis is used to determine, for any proposed price, how many places would have to be sold to fully cover the costs; this is known as the breakeven volume. To illustrate, a business school is considering establishing an "off-site," part-time M.B.A program, but only if it can anticipate attracting enough participants prepared to take the complete program as a group and willing to pay enough to cover the fixed and variable costs of offering the program. The director needs to determine the number of participants necessary to cover these costs and thus make the proposed program viable.

The director would calculate the fixed costs of the program—facilities rental, director's salary, marketing and advertising for the program, professors' salaries and travel expenses, and so on. Estimated fixed costs for the entire program are $300,000, for one cohort of no more than 30 participants. The variable cost per participant—books and materials, food for breaks, computer rental if needed, and so on—will be $3,000. Finally, the program director initially considers charging $25,000 tuition per participant for the entire M.B.A program. The breakeven volume can be directly calculated for any proposed price by using the following formula:

$$\text{Breakeven volume} = \frac{\text{Fixed cost}}{\text{Price} - \text{Variable cost}} = \frac{\$300,000}{\$25,000 - \$3,000}$$

Given fixed costs of $300,000 and variable costs of $3000, the breakeven volume would be 13 to 14 participants at a tuition of $25,000. The director will want to have perhaps 18 participants signed up at the beginning, since a few may drop out during the two-year program.

Suppose the director believed that at a lower tuition more participants would sign up. He considered charging $20,000 instead of $25,000, and calculated that it would take 17–18 participants, or 22 to be "safe" at that tuition level. If the program can serve a maximum class size of 30 without altering the fixed costs, then the director will want to analyze the price elasticity of demand to determine what tuition level will be likely to attract 30 participants while maximizing the revenue to the business school. Here the director will need information about the price sensitivity of the target audience. Will lowering the price by 20 percent encourage more candidates to participate? Thirty candidates? If yes, the director would be better off attracting 30 students at $20,000 each ( = $600,000 gross revenue) versus 14 students at $25,000 ( = $350,000 gross revenue). The class of 30 participants at $20,000 would return a surplus of $210,000 ($600,000 minus fixed costs of $300,000 and variable costs of 20 times $3,000); the class of 14 at $25,000 would return a surplus of only $8,000.

It should be noted that even if the school finds it cannot generate a surplus from a specific course or cohort, it should consider its overall institutional strategy before making a definite decision not to proceed. For example, is the proposed program likely to grow in popularity once it has been implemented? Can the school solidly expect to gain goodwill and donations by virtue of offering the program? Is the program a good fit with the institution's mission, capabilities, and resources?

## How Companies Are Using Breakeven Analysis

Companies have been paying for educational services for their employees for decades, but only recently have some large corporations begun using their buying strength to purchase educational services. While this is a new concept in education, its use will increase since (1) it is a familiar process for companies in purchasing other goods and services, including health-care plans, (2) companies are reducing their costs, and (3) companies understand how to do breakeven analysis and they have a good idea of the costs to use in doing the analysis. They calculate that the combined cost of hiring a part-time instructor and renting facilities is far less than the total of individual per-student tuition payments. They want to pay the actual cost with a modest margin rather than the tuition price.

As described in Chapter 10, companies are issuing requests for proposals for educational providers, seeking the "best price" for a course, a bundle of courses, or whole degree programs, and then concentrating their purchases in one or a few institutions. They may, for example, encourage employers to take courses at designated "preferred provider" institutions at no additional cost to them, or allow employees to attend a higher-priced provider but pay the difference in cost out of their own pockets. Wide adoption of this practice will minimize opportunities for educational institutions to cross-subsidize more expensive courses and programs with revenues from less costly offerings.

## SUMMARY

Pricing decisions are important to educational institutions because they depend on revenues to operate. Price is part of the marketing mix and should be considered as an element in the institution's strategic planning, including the role of price and financial aid in the institution's mission and goals.

When setting or changing prices, educators need to understand how consumers perceive price. In addition to monetary prices, consumers face effort costs, psychic costs, and time costs. They may use price as a measure of quality of a service or program. Customers are particularly interested in the effective price, the net amount they must pay, rather than the list price. They are looking for lower prices and greater value.

With these factors in mind, the institution should consider ways to reduce the nonmonetary costs of its services while enhancing the perceived quality. The institution should examine its revenue function to see where value can be increased while cutting costs and using assets more intensively.

Most schools are now striving to maximize net tuition revenue, not simply fill a certain number of places. They can benefit from examining the rationales for setting tuition levels, and particularly from considering how various tuition decisions allocate tuition costs among students and programs.

Financial aid allocations have been growing to try to meet burgeoning student need, but few schools have enough endowment and other funds to meet the needs of all students. Schools are becoming more creative about how to allocate financial aid to attract, enroll, and serve the number and quality of students they seek.

When considering adding new programs, educational institutions should examine their revenue assumptions by carrying out breakeven analysis. Companies purchasing educational services for their employees are beginning to look closely at the costs of providing educational services and using this information to bargain with educational institutions for lower tuition levels.


## Notes

1. William Ihlanfeldt, *Achieving Optimal Enrollments and Tuition Revenues* (San Francisco: Jossey-Bass, 1980), p. 115. Acceleration—completing the degree in less than the usual time—actually increases institutional revenue if it enables students and their families to pay a larger percentage of their educational costs than would be possible for a full-length program.

2. John Maguire, "To the Organized Go the Students," *Boston College Bridge Magazine*, XXXIX, no. 1 (Fall 1976), p. 17.

3. William G. Bowen and David W. Breneman, "Student Aid: Price Discount or Educational Investment?" *The College Board Review*, no. 167 (Spring 1993), pp. 2–6, 35–36.

4. The Reauthorization of the Higher Education Act in 1992 established a new method for determining students' eligibility for federal financial aid, a method which often yields quite different results than do the methods used by most educational institutions to determine student financial need as a basis for allocating institutional funds.

5. Rudy Abramson, "From the Beginning Berea Nurtured Those Most in Need," *Smithsonian Magazine* (December 1993), pp. 92–104.

6. Data from Director of Admissions John Cook, Berea College (March 1994).

7. For a discussion of how marketers can reduce time and effort costs, see Karen F. A. Fox, "Time as a Component of Price in Social Marketing," in Richard P. Bagozzi et al., *Marketing in the 80s: Changes and Challenges* (Chicago: American Marketing Association, 1980), pp. 464–467.

8. David J. Schwartz, *Marketing Today: A Basic Approach*, 3rd ed. (New York: Harcourt Brace Jovanovich, 1981), p. 271.

9. Richard W. Moll, "The Scramble to Get the New Class," *Change*, 26, no. 2 (March/April 1994), p. 14.

10. See Kent B. Monroe, "Buyers' Subjective Perceptions of Price," *Journal of Marketing Research* (February 1973), pp. 70–80.

11. Benson Shapiro, "Price as a Communicator of Quality: An Experiment," unpublished doctoral dissertation, Harvard University, 1970.

12. A contribution margin of 1.15 means that the program brings in 15 percent more in revenue than it costs to provide it.

13. William F. Massy, "Faculty Discretionary Time: Departments and the Academic Ratchet," *The Journal of Higher Education*, 65, no. 1 (January/February 1994), pp. 1–22.

14. Mike Lopez, "High Tuition, High Aid Won't Work," *The Chronicle of Higher Education*, April 7, 1993, pp. B1–B2.

15. See Ihlanfeldt, *Achieving Optimal Enrollments and Tuition Revenues*, pp. 117–120, for a fuller discussion of these approaches.

16. See Marilyn McCoy, "Differential Tuition at the University of Colorado," University of Colorado Office of Planning and Policy Development (August 1983), for results of a survey of state universities' use of differential tuition and discussion of policy implications.

17. See George Stigler, *The Theory of Price*, rev. ed. (New York: Macmillan, 1952), pp. 215ff.

18. "The Pay-What-You-Can Plan," *Time*, March 29, 1982, p. 61.

19. Susan Lee Taylor, Barry E. Langford, and Danny R. Arnold, "Peak-Load Pricing of College and University Services," *Proceedings of the 1992 Symposium for the Marketing of Higher Education* (Chicago: American Marketing Association, 1992), pp. 145–152.

20. A more detailed discussion of these approaches is presented in James J. Scannell, *The Effect of Financial Aid Policies on Admission and Enrollment* (New York: The College Board, 1992), pp. 40–47.

21. Ibid., p. 47.

22. Ibid., p. 58.

# 13

# Delivering Educational Programs and Services

*When Dima Ponomaryov got an opportunity to earn a master's degree from the State University of New York, he jumped at the chance.*

*But the computer-science student at the Moscow Institute of Electronics and Mathematics won't have to leave Russia to earn the degree. The most he is likely to see of a New York campus will be in a color brochure, and he will meet his professors in person only once a year, when they come to Russia.*

*Mr. Ponomaryov is taking part in a pilot project that is bringing to Russia an innovative system of learning that until now was largely unknown there: distance education. The Moscow Center for Distance Learning, based at the electronics institute, is coordinating the project in Russia.*

*Mr. Ponomaryov is one of eight people who enrolled in a master's-degree program in information systems and computer science offered through the SUNY Institute of Technology at Utica–Rome, New York. The pilot project is supported by a $150,000 grant from the U.S. Information Agency.*

*Their course of study is identical to that followed by students on the New York campus and even uses the same textbooks; the instruction and course work are in English. Students are linked to SUNY through E-mail, video lectures, and annual visits by their U.S. professors, who come to Moscow to administer examinations and introduce special course material. The master's degree that the students receive at the end of the two-year program is the same as the one awarded to their counterparts in the United States. The Russian students are required simultaneously to pursue their five-year undergraduate diplomas at the institute in Moscow.*

*"For the students, this has opened an unexpected window on the world," says Alexander V. Danilin, an associate professor at the institute who is the Moscow coordinator of the pilot project.*

*"The students are getting a new perspective," says Jorge Norillo, a SUNY faculty member who is teaching a course in artificial intelligence to the Russians from his Utica base. "Individually, they're getting training or knowledge that they can't get at all in Russia. They simply don't have the literature or materials."*

*The students agree. "We get the chance to study at an American university," says Mr. Ponomaryov. "To have such a degree would give me a better choice of interesting jobs."*

*If the pilot project succeeds and is broadened, it could offer wide benefits. Russian students who cannot afford to go abroad to study—particularly in subjects that either are not taught at home or are taught inadequately—can enroll in a foreign institution through a distance-education program.*

*"Russian students are in no position to pay $15,000 a year in tuition to study at a U.S. university," he says. Distance education, he says, could enable many Russians to enjoy some of the benefits of study abroad "but at a fraction of the cost."*

**Source:** Adapted from Gregory Gransden, "Distance Education in Russia," *The Chronicle of Higher Education*, January 26, 1994, pp. A41–A42.

---

The basic service-delivery question for an educational institution is, How can we make our programs and services available and accessible to our target consumers? SUNY is delivering one of its master's programs to an eager target group through telecommunication links. While the program would be *available* to these students if each could pay the tuition and other costs and travel to the United States, the classroom program is too expensive and too far away to be truly *accessible* for these students.

Note that availability and accessibility are not the same thing. Suppose a college ran a program to enhance the skills of elementary school teachers, but the college was located an hour away from where most of the teachers lived and worked. Furthermore, suppose, that the program was offered from 9 to 12 on weekday mornings from September to May—precisely the hours when even nearby teachers would be working. The program, although available, was not accessible to those for whom it was planned. For such a program to succeed, the college must increase the program's accessibility, perhaps by offering the program closer to the potential participants and by scheduling it for late afternoons, weekends, or concentrated summer sessions.

The location and scheduling of programs can determine their success. Offering a high-quality, appropriately priced program is not enough. Students may avoid classes in rundown, dangerous urban areas because the surroundings are unpleasant and unsafe. Likewise, they may avoid rural campuses that seem isolated and boring.

Some educational institutions, recognizing these market changes, have adopted new schedules, delivery systems, and locations to retain existing markets and serve new markets. Realistically, few institutions can make fundamental changes in the short term. They can, however, consider how to improve their use of existing resources in making educational offerings available. They can begin planning ways to modify or expand current systems to create more consumer satisfaction.

The typical mode of delivering educational services is for the institution to present courses at one location, with students gathering for classroom instruction. A more comprehensive picture shows a variety of educational programs and services, each of which may be provided in a different way. For example, a university may offer a lecture course in introductory psychology for undergraduates, a correspondence course for armed forces personnel, and a short course on the psychology of personnel administration via teleconferencing for professionals at sites across the country.

Educational institutions often have several different programs, and they need to plan an appropriate strategy for providing each one. How these programs and other outputs are made available constitutes the institution's *delivery system*.

Consider the case of Iowa State University, a 25,000-student land-grant university in Ames. Its product line includes educational programs, extension services, publications, cultural and athletic events, research findings in agriculture and other fields, veterinary care, and, at one time, packaged cheese! The university also "produces" intangible products, such as lasting friendships among students and feelings of pride on the part of the state's residents.

Many services are created and delivered directly by the producer to the consumer—the lawyer advising the client, the doctor treating a patient, the teacher instructing a group of students. The teacher is usually the creator of the instructional plan as well as the performer. (Of course, in many instances, the content of the lesson draws on the research and ideas of other scholars, and may incorporate audiovisual resources prepared by others.)

We can diagram the process by which the course is distributed, as shown in Figure 13-1, A.

Another important instructional program at Iowa State is carried out by home-economics and agricultural-extension directors who inform Iowa homemakers, farmers, and commercial enterprises of research findings that affect their activities. The research is conducted at Iowa State and other centers around the world. The "ag extension" director's task is to inform farmers of new practices, to prepare and send out printed information, and to look for problem areas that might warrant future research. The extension directors may also appear on television or radio or prepare news stories featuring useful information for farmers. The delivery system for Iowa State's extension services is shown in Figure 13-1, B.

The university also produces books. The Iowa State University Press ob-

FIGURE 13-1   Delivery systems for three Iowa State University products and programs

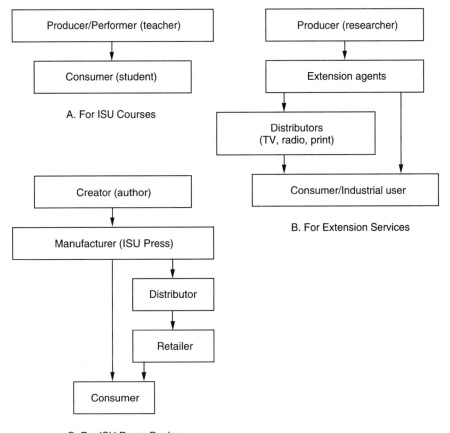

A. For ISU Courses

B. For Extension Services

C. For ISU Press Books

tains manuscripts from authors, and edits and prints them. The books are available for purchase at the press's own book store, by mail order, and through traditional book-distribution channels, shown in Figure 13-1, C.

In deciding how to distribute its programs and products, Iowa State must consider the nature of each as well as the important characteristics of the consumers who will ultimately benefit from it. A workable delivery system successfully provides the desired benefit—product, service, program—to the consumer who wants it, at a cost that both producer and consumer can afford. A superior delivery system accomplishes the same task in a way that makes the process easier, reduces the cost for one or both parties, and/or provides better outcomes.

## THE MEANING OF LOCATION

When we speak of an institution's location, *location* can have four different meanings. First, it can refer to the absolute place in which the institution exists: New York University is located in New York City. Second, it can refer to the character of the area in which the institution is located: New York University is located in an urban area. Third, it can refer to a decision-making area for an educational institution: NYU might consider where to locate off-campus programs.

Finally, location has a relative meaning—that is, location relative to where its actual and prospective students live. Fall 1993 data collected by the Cooperative Institutional Research Program show that 90 percent of entering full-time freshmen attend colleges within 500 miles of their permanent homes, and about 42 percent attend colleges within 50 miles of their homes.[1] Student mobility seems to be greatly influenced by family economic background and the number of colleges located in the geographical area: In a region with many colleges and universities, young people are likely to attend a college within their own region.

Most educational institutions already have facilities at one or more fixed locations. When they begin to consider how to serve their markets more effectively, their thinking about distribution patterns and systems is usually colored by their existing investment in facilities. They consider how to attract people to their current facilities, and often are slow to consider how to bring their offerings closer to their customers.

Often the question of where to locate facilities was answered years ago, for pragmatic reasons:

- The land (and even buildings) may have been donated. Leland and Jane Stanford founded Stanford University on their 8,000-acre farm.
- Centralized facilities were established for administrative convenience and economies, as in the case of many state universities.
- A location may have been selected because a site was available or because the land was relatively inexpensive. Public school sites were designated when the

Northwest Territory was surveyed and platted, along with additional lots to be farmed to provide the teacher's salary. Sites set aside for public schools were often those deemed unsuitable for farming.

The location of facilities can have tremendous symbolic and/or political significance. The Catholic parish school was typically located next to the church building. As for public schools, the "neighborhood school" is such a well-established concept that public outcry is virtually assured whenever a school is closed.

Past decisions about the location of educational facilities may create later imbalances. A number of states founded their land-grant institutions a century ago in small towns, away from what are now major population centers. Liberal arts colleges have often been located in rural areas and small towns, sometimes based on the notion that a bucolic setting is particularly conducive to morality, reflection, and learning. In his speech at the 1965 groundbreaking for Eisenhower College, Dwight D. Eisenhower expounded this view:

> I believe that the liberal arts college should seek its natural habitation in rural areas. Let the universities go to the cities where they have the benefits of great lawyers, great engineers, great people all around them. In this period of maturing in a liberal college, let's have the finest faculty, let's bring in the knowledge lecturers, and let's do it in an atmosphere and an environment where the student's standards of respect for law, his moral standards, his willingness for accommodation with his fellow students will be expanded and strengthened.[2]

Of the institutions located for the preceding reasons, some are flourishing while others are struggling. These educational facilities may once have been well located, but shifts in population, and particularly in their target markets, have reduced the locations' appropriateness. Yet the cost of leaving existing facilities behind and moving to new ones may be prohibitive. Caught in this dilemma, some institutions close, some identify ways to make their location an advantage, and others make strategic alterations to serve new markets.

Decisions about location and delivery systems should be consciously related to the institution's overall strategy. If the strategy is to specialize in offering a particular program or serving a particular target market, this will imply a certain location or delivery system. For example, the School of the Art Institute of Chicago offers a particularly rich program because it is located next to a world-class art museum in a major metropolitan area with many artists and film makers, as well as galleries, theaters, and other enriching opportunities.

Here are the major decisions educational institutions often face in delivering their programs:

- What should be the delivery-system objectives?
- Should new facilities or delivery systems be established?
- What are alternative ways to expand services geographically?

- Where should new facilities be located?
- How can distance learning and new technologies be used?
- How should facilities function and "feel"?
- How can intermediaries be used?

We will explore each question in the sections that follow.

## WHAT SHOULD BE THE INSTITUTION'S DELIVERY-SYSTEM OBJECTIVES?

An educational institution can think of its delivery system on three dimensions: location, including accessibility, atmosphere, and facilities; scheduling, to appeal to participants; and the mode of delivery, including technology as well as traditional instructional forms.

The institution's delivery system should accomplish the institution's objectives while reflecting an understanding of the consumer; the institution's mission and resources; the nature of the program, service, or product to be distributed; and the available alternatives. The school will want to consider the attractiveness and convenience for its customers. The school wants to attract and serve enough customers to meet enrollment and revenue goals.

A very basic question is what level of convenience should be offered to the target market. Obviously, cost will be an issue, but the institution might begin by trying to describe the maximum convenience it could offer. For an educational institution, the maximum level of service might be to provide individual instruction in each student's home upon request. Once the norm for children of the very wealthy, private tutors are no longer practicable. Few consumers could or would pay for the extra convenience, and the supplying institution could not afford the cost of providing this level of service to everyone. But describing "ultimate convenience" may suggest alternative ways to provide services that come closer to the maximum than was formerly thought possible. Thus, although schools may not be able to provide an entire instructional program offered by personal tutors, many schools offer small classes, tutoring for specific courses, and labs with self-instructional software for learning certain subjects.

Educational institutions must usually offer less than the maximum convenience in order to keep down the cost of delivery. Thus, a public school district will have one or more elementary and secondary schools, and students will have to travel to the schools. Schools may have to increase class sizes or eliminate certain courses when qualified instructors or other necessary resources are lacking. Students may have to wait longer for teacher assistance. Since virtually all educational institutions have limited resources, they must base their delivery planning on a clear picture of the level and quality of service they will offer.

Making programs available and accessible involves more than convenient locations or innovative delivery systems. Unlike physical products, which can be purchased and used at the consumer's convenience, educational services often require that the service provider (the teacher) and the consumer (the student) coordinate their activities so they can be available in the same place at the same time.

Many would-be students cannot attend during traditional class hours, and many colleges are beginning to adapt to their time constraints. Evening courses are widely available. Others offer "early-bird" classes so people can attend class on their way to work. Several business schools offer M.B.A. programs to participants able to attend all-day classes on alternate Fridays and Saturdays for two years. Other institutions offer courses on weekends or during lunch hour. Northwestern's Kellogg Graduate School of Management launched a Master of Management program for qualified executives who will come—often fly from out of state—alternate weekends for two days of classes and study. These examples demonstrate how educational institutions can modify locations and schedules to meet their service-delivery objectives.

## SHOULD NEW FACILITIES OR DELIVERY SYSTEMS BE ESTABLISHED?

Educational institutions should consider whether to offer some of their programs in other locations or through different delivery systems. Institutions that provide direct services are like retail stores, where people can come to make their selection and purchase. Like retail businesses, they must decide how many locations to operate. The most economical decision for the school is to operate a single location and have all customers come to it. For example, many small high schools were established in widely separated rural towns. Beginning in the 1950s, most of the small high school districts were consolidated into larger districts that could provide a wider range of subjects, vocational training, and other services.

Educational institutions establish new locations or delivery systems for four major reasons:

1. The local market is saturated. There are many educational options and the school does not stand out in a way that attracts its share of customers. Or the school offers programs that are no longer well aligned with the interests of its local market, yet there are other locations where these offerings are still attractive.
2. The local market has declined in size, or residential and/or employment patterns have changed, so the school needs new locations or delivery systems to continue to have a market for its offerings.
3. The school is doing fine, but knows of strong potential markets in other locations that would value what the institution has to offer.

4. The school is doing well but wants to expand its "institutional presence" to new locations, perhaps to build further demand for its offerings.

The cost of running a state university used to be minimized by operating a single campus. Years ago, the University of California was located in Berkeley, and the University of Wisconsin was in Madison. As populations grew, these universities established branches, often by incorporating existing colleges and universities. The aim was partly to make educational opportunities more accessible to residents (and taxpayers) in other parts of their states and partly to keep a single campus from becoming too large. Now most states have *systems* of state colleges and universities, as well as locally supported community colleges. Once these universities decided to distribute their offerings throughout the state, they encountered all the service-delivery issues faced by business firms: how many branch campuses/locations to establish, how large they should be, where they should be located, and what specializations should be featured at each branch.

Some private institutions have opened satellite branches in areas of strong population growth, sometimes competing directly with public institutions. Satellite branches can make the institution's programs accessible to new markets while relieving space limitations or inadequacies on the main campus, as well as locating the educational programs closer to key supporting facilities. For example, Roosevelt University, a 7,000-student private institution in downtown Chicago, opened three satellite campuses in rented facilities in the more affluent suburbs of Arlington Heights, Waukegan, and Glenview, and offers complete degree programs at each.

A few educational institutions have expanded their facilities by holding classes in unusual classroom settings. The principal value is in increasing accessibility. Indiana University–Purdue University at Indianapolis offers credit courses in the training rooms of department stores in local shopping malls in its Learn & Shop Program. The program offers plenty of free parking space, excellent teaching facilities provided free by the stores, regular faculty, university credit, and the same tuition as on-campus courses. The University of Wisconsin Extension provides volunteer "traveling teachers" to nursing homes, retirement communities, senior centers, and other organizations for the elderly, to offer classes in more than 20 subjects.

## WHAT ARE ALTERNATIVE WAYS TO EXPAND GEOGRAPHICALLY?

Consideration of geographical expansion presents a variety of options. An entire new campus could be established that is a "twin" of the original campus, providing the same offerings. Or just one or a few of the school's current programs could be offered at a different site. For example, Northwestern's Kellogg Graduate School of Management offers its master's programs on the main campus in Evanston and in a location near Chicago's Loop.

The institution could offer a significantly modified program at a different location. For example, Santa Clara University's Leavey School of Business has offered a very flexible evening M.B.A program on its campus since 1959. In 1992 the school started a satellite M.B.A program east of San Francisco, about 40 miles from the main campus. Unlike the main program, all students at the satellite program take a predetermined set of courses together as a cohort in a prescribed sequence, and the group meets for class twice weekly in a corporate conference room.

Some programs combine a portion of the program at the main site and a portion at a different site. Cathay Pacific Airlines has teamed up with the University of Michigan Business School to offer an M.B.A program for its Hong Kong-based managers. The Michigan instructors teach via interactive satellite television, computer networking, and facsimile. Program participants spend a seven-week period studying on the Michigan campus during the three-year program and Michigan faculty come to Hong Kong for a total of four days of intensive instruction.

What do we mean by *different site*? We have already mentioned some examples from the wide range of options: company conference rooms, department-store training rooms, rented facilities, and institution-owned facilities. In these cases, the institution typically "puts the instructor on the road," bringing the teacher to the students instead of the reverse. Penn State faculty members go to Mexico City to teach quality-control short courses, and Santa Clara University faculty members drive to San Ramon to teach M.B.A students.

With computers installed in most companies and many homes, the definition of *different site* for education is increasingly becoming the employee's own desk or home. A growing number of educational institutions are wiring residence halls for computer networking and cable television. Students can watch the news in French, German, Spanish, Russian, Japanese, or some other language they are studying, and they can access instructional videos to review for class. Via the computer network they can send a "paper" to a professor for feedback, along with a message setting up an appointment to discuss the next term's course offerings.

Several universities, including the University of Nebraska, are offering M.B.A courses through electronic bulletin boards and electronic mail. The student's different site may be a desk at work, a home computer in a corner of the bedroom, or a laptop computer at a hotel while on a business trip; and the delivery system includes the telephone network.

## WHERE SHOULD NEW FACILITIES BE LOCATED?

If the program is to offered with students and faculty working together at the same location, the school must decide where new or additional facilities should be located. The institution could use rented or loaned facilities, convert existing ones, or build new ones.

Figure 13-2 shows the steps involved in the decision process.[3] First, the institution evaluates its current delivery pattern to determine whether it adequately meets current and projected needs and matches the institution's resources. Second, if the current pattern has some inadequacies, the institution determines its revised delivery objectives. It may state its objectives in terms of percentage of the community that enrolls in courses, size of enrollment, or some other measurable outcomes.

Third, the institution considers its desired delivery system. For educational programs, this step involves deciding whether to have one facility to serve everyone, or to establish multiple locations. This decision depends on consumers' ability and willingness to travel to facilities. Although some students will travel hundreds of miles to enroll in a high-quality, prestige college, community colleges draw most of their students from a relatively small geographical area. If the institution wishes to maximize enrollment, facilities should be convenient. At the same time, the institution must balance the cost of multiple locations with the state or local funding and consumer revenue that will be generated if the multiple locations succeed in bringing in more students than if the school did not expand.

Fourth, the institution selects the location. At the outset, the institution should identify the location (or locations) that would provide the best access for the target markets and then compromise from that optimum location as little as possible in settling on the final site. Determining appropriate locations will depend on residential and work patterns, commuting routes, demographic characteristics of various areas, and locations of competing and complementary institutions.

Consider how a major public urban university with 20,000 students planned where to locate a satellite campus to consolidate dispersed off-campus courses.[4] The planning task force mapped where current students

FIGURE 13-2    The decision process for locating facilities

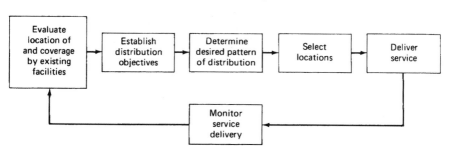

Source: Adapted from Charles W. Lamb, Jr., and John L. Compton, "Distributing Public Services: A Strategic Approach," in Philip Kotler, O.C. Ferrell, and Charles Lamb, *Cases and Readings in Marketing for Nonprofit Organizations* (Englewood Cliffs, NJ: Prentice-Hall, 1983), p. 211.

lived, drawing on data from computerized student-record files, to identify strong and weak attraction areas. Next the planners analyzed population trends and delineated four major growth centers located just outside the perimeter highway around the city, each within 25 minutes of downtown.

The planners then identified five market segments for the satellite campus—traditional students, workers seeking job-skills courses, married re-entry women, remedial-needs students, and people seeking leisure and personal-development courses—and located concentrations of these groups on an area map. The planners assessed the locations and reputations of the university's 18 competitors and determined that the university had high status and a stronger regional and national reputation than all but one of them, a private university with much higher tuition.

The next step was to select the specific sites. Four criteria were used:

1. The sites should be located near population growth areas and defined market segments.
2. The sites must be highly accessible—that is, near major thoroughfares and public transportation.
3. The sites should be located near services for students—restaurants, shops, service stations, and so on.
4. The cost of the potential sites should not be exorbitant.

The planners identified four potential sites within or near regional shopping centers and office parks where leasable space and adequate parking were available. One "best" site was selected after economic feasibility studies of each site. Figure 13-3 shows the perimeter highway and the four growth areas, and the stars mark the four potential sites.

The planners next surveyed four of the five market segments to answer three questions: (1) What is the level of interest among potential students for a satellite campus? (2) What classes would respondents like to take? and (3) What schedules would be most attractive? With this information, the university planners could implement the satellite-campus program.

Although some educational institutions are expanding, most have fixed facilities, and some face declining demand. Buildings cannot be moved as population shifts or surroundings change, but buildings or parts of buildings can be leased, sold, or closed. Some public schools are leasing school facilities to day-care centers, fine-arts programs, and other education-compatible users, and other schools have been sold and converted into shopping centers, apartment buildings, and corporate headquarters buildings.[5] Some educators recommend that high schools with declining enrollments could attract and serve new markets, including adult education programs, and might even take on new functions.[6]

FIGURE 13-3    Locations of proposed satellite campus sites

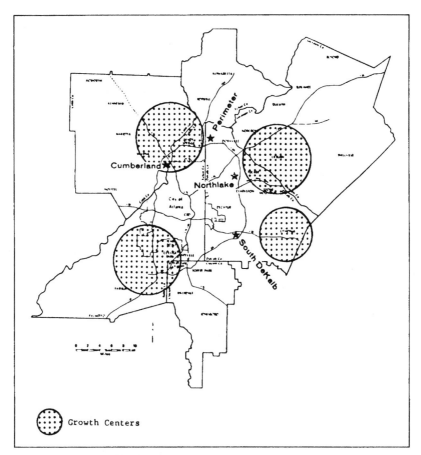

Source: Wayne G. Strickland, "The University and the Community: Planning for an Alternative Form of Educational Service Delivery," *Planning for Higher Education* (Summer 1980), p. 14.

## HOW CAN DISTANCE EDUCATION AND NEW TECHNOLOGIES BE USED?

*Distance education* refers to instruction that occurs while there is a separation in time and/or distance between the learner and the instructor. The critical attributes of distance education are:

- Physical separation of learners from the teacher—short (down the hall) to long (from New York to Moscow).
- An organized, structured instructional program (not just a set of slides with-

out a supporting lesson plan or instructional design).
- Technological media (print, audio, video, or computer).
- Two-way communication via surface mail or telecommunications, such as radio, telephone, television, or computer network.[7]

Many educational institutions are using the telephone, television, radio, newspapers, tape recorders, and the mail to serve their current markets or to attract new ones. In some countries of the world, many students attend classes by radio or television. Hundreds of thousands of Chinese are enrolled in courses given by over 30 "television universities," and many other students take courses by radio. In the United States, these approaches often supplement more traditional learning settings, but their popularity has grown rapidly. Exhibit 13-1 describes the telecourses prepared by Coastline Community College.

Educational institutions considering the use of new instructional technologies need to ask three questions: Is the new technology likely to be more effective than the one it replaces? Is the alternative channel appropriate for the intended market? What will be the additional resource costs and added benefits of adopting the new channel?

## HOW SHOULD FACILITIES FUNCTION AND "FEEL"?

A very important factor in facilities planning is how well the facilities will serve the planned educational activities to be carried out there—their functionality. Educational facilities planning has become increasingly sophisticated, drawing on the talents of the best planners, architects, and designers. Since money for "bricks and mortar" is usually scarce, any investment in new or upgraded instructional space must be well conceived.

Incorporating audiovisual and other instructional technologies requires careful planning for maximum effectiveness. The University of Notre Dame's state-of-the-art DeBartolo Hall, completed in 1992, was especially constructed to incorporate the hardware and software need for computer-aided instruction and electronic communications. Before class the professor, with the educational-media staff in the building's basement command center, lines up the materials he or she wants to use—up to six audio and/or video sources in one class session. The professor can then "punch up" the selections on a console in the classroom, starting, stopping, or moving to any point in the videodisk, videotape, or computer-based presentation.[8]

Educational institutions should also include the right *combination* of facilities to support their programs. The University of Maryland is paying more attention to facilities for commuters, with improved parking, a commuter lounge, better signage, and evening office hours. A school that wants to at-

EXHIBIT 13-1   Telecourses from Coastline Community College

---

Telecourses are complete learning systems that combine video and print components to be used under an instructor's direction, but without classroom instruction. Professionally produced video series—usually comprising 26 half-hour programs, course textbooks and study guides, and a full complement of quizzes, study activities, and examinations—enable students to attain the telecourse goals and learning objectives.

Telecourses are an exceptionally flexible means of providing instruction and training. Not only can they be delivered by broadcast television and such modes of communication as satellite and cable, students can take telecourses using videocassettes in their homes, at training sites, or at learning centers. And telecourse video programs can be effective in meeting the training needs of businesses and institutions as well as serving traditional educational purposes.

Coastline College's Office of Instructional Systems Development (ISD) pinpoints new methods of instruction and identifies new subjects for telecourses. After obtaining (usually outside) funding, ISD provides the expert instructional design that ensures the new course will be academically sound and instructionally effective. Every telecourse produced at Coastline must be approved for transfer credit to California state upper-division institutions.

ISD instructional designers work with instructors, academic authors, consultants, and video producers to create informative and interesting video programs and print materials for each telecourse. To keep all its telecourses up to date, ISD continually revises course materials. Video programs are edited or replaced as necessary to maintain accuracy and timeliness.

Coastline telecourses reach students throughout the world, including Australia, Canada, Germany, Greece, Hong Kong, India, Italy, the Netherlands, New Zealand, Portugal, Saudi Arabia, Singapore, Spain, Sweden, Taiwan, Turkey, and the United Kingdom.

---

Source: Coastline Community College: Developing Instructional Systems for a Changing World of Learning (brochure, n.d.).

tract male students must provide athletic facilities, and an engineering school must have plenty of student access to computer systems and other key equipment.

School should also pay attention to *signage* that helps visitors as well as students and staff to find their way around campus. According to designer Robert Brown,

> Campus signage is often one of the weakest design elements [of a college campus]. Though finding one's way around an unfamiliar campus is essen-

tial..., most college planners and administrators do not seem to understand the importance of wayfinding signs and building identifications. . . . There appears to be an attitude that clearly marked signs are not necessary or appropriate on campus.[9]

As colleges have more adult education and evening programs, more international and part-time students, signage becomes even more important. Signs should be clear, well designed, consistent in style, and appropriately located.

Educational institutions should also consider the "look" and "feel" of their facilities because the atmosphere in which educational services are delivered can affect consumers' attitudes and behavior. Architect Bruce Carmichael believes that "physical resources play a far more important role in recruiting students, and especially retaining students, than is generally recognized":

> Young students may not have the vocabulary or developed sensibility to talk about architecture, horticulture, and campus design. But they do have . . . emotional responses to college campuses and the "feel" of an admissions office, a library, the science laboratories, or the art studios. . . . A college's buildings, interiors, furniture, spaces, landscaping, and equipment make a statement about that institution. They express what the college or university stands for, cares most about, and how it views the intellectual and aesthetic enterprise.[10]

Private colleges and universities are often particularly aware of the value of having an attractive campus. Many have taken pains to maintain their original architectural style and master plan, or at least to integrate newer buildings by using materials that blend with the earlier style.[11] Newer institutions have the opportunity to develop and follow a unified plan from the start.

Some schools are so aware of operating within tight budgets that they completely ignore or give up on the appearance of the facilities and surroundings. In the process they may miss the "communication value" inherent in these visible aspects of the school. For example, a 100-student independent school started operating within a large but rundown school facility that had originally been a preseminary Lutheran high school. The "new" school was not well known in the community, in part because most students commuted from a distance. In fact, some nearby residents thought the school was "closed" because they saw some doors chained shut from the outside (wings that were not in use).

At the main entrance to the school was a large flagpole, which never had a flag on it, since the school's headmaster was more concerned with keeping the school afloat. Yet a flag raised in front of a school communicates that "school is in session" and that the school is a going concern. The headmaster had the flagpole checked out (the company said it was one of the nicest they'd seen, made of a single piece of wood), and then started having the flag raised each day to announce the school was "open." Of course the point is not that every school should have a flagpole and flag, but that features ignored by the school may be communicating to the public a message—favorable or unfavorable—of which the school is unaware.

Marketing planners, working closely with designers and architects, can use atmospherics consciously and skillfully. *Atmospherics* describes the conscious designing of space to create or reinforce specific effects on consumers, such as feelings of well-being, safety, intimacy, or awe.[12]

An educational institution designing a facility for the first time faces four major design decisions. Suppose a university business school is planning a facility to use for its management training programs. Many of the participants will be executives from major corporations. The four decisions are as follows:

1. *What should the building look like on the outside?* The building can look like a villa, a bank, an office building, or another genre. The decision will be influenced by the site where the building will be located, and by the message that the business school wants to convey to potential students and program participants.
2. *What should be the functional and flow characteristics of the building?* The planners have to consider how the building will be used and what types of spaces are needed. In addition to classroom spaces, study areas and areas for meals and social hours will be needed. The rooms and corridors must be designed in a way to handle all those likely to be attending programs in the building at one time. For legal and practical reasons, the building must also meet the specifications provided in the Americans with Disabilities Act.
3. *What should the building feel like on the inside?* Every building conveys a feeling, whether intended or not. In designing the interior, the planners need to consider whether it should be bright and modern, somber and businesslike, or warm and relaxing. Each feeling will have a different effect on the participants and their overall satisfaction with the programs offered there.
4. *What materials would best support the desired feeling of the building?* The feeling of a building is conveyed by visual cues (color, brightness, size, shapes), aural cues (volume, pitch), olfactory cues (scent, freshness), and tactile cues (softness, smoothness, temperature). The planners need to choose colors, fabrics, and furnishings that create or reinforce the desired feeling.

The same questions arise for other educational facilities. In addition to instructional space, schools have other spaces that may need to be upgraded or redesigned to improve their functioning. Each facility will have functional or atmospheric aspects that add or detract from consumer satisfaction and employee performance.

The latter point deserves special emphasis. Since the employees work in the facility all day long, the facility should be designed to support them in performing their work with ease and cheerfulness. But planning work space for employees could result in a layout that is awkward or even unpleasant for the customers (students, faculty, staff, visitors, and others) who come there to receive service. For example, if students must fill out forms and wait in line for service, the area should have standing-height writing areas and perhaps a queuing system or "take-a-number" system to minimize aggravation.[13]

Granted, many educational institutions are financially pressed and cannot provide the most desirable facilities. But they should pay attention to small details of present facilities and take all possible steps to improve their comfort, effectiveness, and communication value.

## HOW CAN INTERMEDIARIES BE USED?

Educational institutions usually produce and deliver their services directly to the consumer, either in person or through other channels. Most businesses rely on *intermediaries*—including *wholesalers, retailers, brokers,* and *agents*—to assist in getting their products and programs to the final consumer and in supplying supplementary services.

While schools rarely rely on intermediaries to deliver *instructional* services, educational institutions often rely on intermediaries in the student-recruitment, career-development, or fund-raising process. For example, a university might call on alumni volunteers to interview prospective students, give career advice to current students, and ask donors—particularly other alumni—to contribute to the school.

Schools also routinely rely on intermediaries to provide assessment data on applicants (The College Board, American College Testing, and so on), to provide scholarship and loan funds (various government and other sources), to process financial aid, loan, and tuition-plan requests (various banks and lending organizations), to provide health insurance to students (insurance companies), and (in some cases) to provide health care to students (by contract with a medical group or hospital).

Even if an institution has the funds to perform all these services internally, intermediaries may be less expensive and more efficient because of their experience, specialization, and contacts. When an educational institution determines that the needed service can be provided as well or better and at lower cost by others, the school should investigate using an intermediary to provide the service.

## SUMMARY

Delivering programs and services is as important as designing them because delivery systems determine who can benefit from the school's programs and services. Since educational services usually cannot be "stored up," educational institutions need to consider how to make their services as convenient as practicable to their target markets in terms of both locations and schedules. Increased convenience and quality may include implementation of distance education and/or the use of new technologies.

To design an efficient delivery system, an institution must first decide on the level of convenience it can and should offer to its target market. Often the institution cannot offer the maximum level of consumer convenience, but it is often possible to make some improvements. The school may open additional facilities and/or use alternative delivery systems to serve its markets.

The school should also pay close attention to its physical facilities, including the quality of design and signage, the functionality and "feel" of the instructional and service spaces, and the messages that the buildings and surroundings convey to visitors, employees, and students about the school.

## Notes

1. Alexander W. Astin, William S. Korn, and Ellyne R. Riggs, *The American Freshman: National Norms for Fall 1993* (Los Angeles, CA: Laboratory for Research in Higher Education, Graduate School of Education, University of California, and the Cooperative Institutional Research Program, American Council on Education, 1993), p. 29.

2. Cited in *Choices*, Eisenhower College Bulletin, 1980–81, p. 1.

3. This section draws on Charles W. Lamb, Jr. and John L. Compton, "Distributing Public Services: A Strategic Approach," in Philip Kotler, O. C. Ferrell, and Charles Lamb, eds., *Cases and Readings in Marketing for Nonprofit Organizations* (Englewood Cliffs, NJ: Prentice-Hall, 1983), pp. 210–221.

4. Wayne G. Srickland, "The University and the Community: Planning for an Alternative Form of Educational Service Delivery," *Planning for Higher Education* (Summer 1980), pp. 7–15.

5. C. William Brubaker, "What to Do With Surplus School Space" *American School & University* (February 1980), pp. 36–41.

6. Terrence E. Deal, "High Schools without Students: Some Thoughts on the Future," *Phi Delta Kappan*, 64 (March 1983), 485–491.

7. Robert Heinich, Michael Molenda, and James D. Russell, *Instructional Media and the New Technologies of Instruction*, 4th ed. (New York: Macmillan, 1993).

8. Peter Monaghan, "Supertech Classrooms: Notre Dame Puts Computer Age at Professors' Fingertips," *The Chronicle of Higher Education*, December 8, 1993, pp. A17–A19.

9. Robert Brown, "Improving Campus Signs," *Planning for Higher Education*, 21 (Winter 1992–93), p. 1.

10. Bruce Carmichael, "Using Campus Facilities for Marketing," *Planning for Higher Education*, 20 (Winter 1991–92), pp. 20, 23.

11. Stanford University not only has a campus master plan (as do many other universities), but it also has an Historic Values Index, assessing each building and open space on age, aesthetic quality, uniqueness, importance to Stanford history and culture, and importance to the external community. Five campus features were designated as "untouchables" including the Quad, which incorporates the Memorial Church, and the Stanford Musuem. These buildings suffered significant damage in the

October 1989 earthquake, but their designation as untouchables means they were priorities for rebuilding and reinforcement. See "Working to Preserve Stanford's Heritage," *Stanford Observer* (June 1988), pp. 14–15.

12. For more details, see Philip Kotler, "Atmospherics as a Marketing Tool," *Journal of Retailing* (Winter 1973-74), pp. 48–64.

13. For an example of how behavior-setting analysis can assist in this design process, see Karen F. A. Fox and Sherry D.F.G. Bender, "A New Approach: Diagnosing Bank Service Environments as Behavior Settings," *Journal of Retail Banking*, 8 (Winter 1986–87), pp. 49–55; David H. Maister, "The Psychology of Waiting Lines," in John A. Czepiel, Michael R. Solomon, and Carol F. Surprenant, eds., *The Service Encounter* (Lexington, MA: Lexington Books, 1985), pp. 113–123; and Karen L. Katz, Blaire M. Larson, and Richard C. Larson, "Prescription for the Waiting-in-Line Blues: Entertain, Enlighten, and Engage," *Sloan Management Review*, 32, no. 2 (Winter 1991), pp. 4–53.

# 14

# Communicating with Markets

Communication Problem: *How do you present a 450-year-old intellectual tradition as both accessible and intriguing for today's students?*

Insight: *Rockhurst College, steeped in the estimable academic tradition of the Jesuits, needed a program targeted to students who would relish Jesuit methodology and would learn well within such a rigorous system. Because the college's professors teach largely through the use of provocative questions, one after another, the marketing communications team decided to use the same tactic.*

Solution: *Rockhurst's direct-mail piece opens with the question,* When do you begin to respect your own mind? *And each panel dovetails into further stimulating questions, such as,* When is the answer not the answer? *and* What if the problems keep changing? *The viewbook, paralleling in structure the core curriculum's six traditional modes of inquiry, introduces Rockhurst with a powerfully differentiating cover line:* Not just what to think. How to think. *To soften the possibly daunting academic standards of Rockhurst, a light-hearted campus visit piece entitled* A Rock Climber's Guide *was prepared, the title inspired by the college president's penchant for coining "rock" words for campus activities. ("The Rock of Gibraltar" is the Learning Assistance Center.) Colorful bookmarks, in a series, reproduce a professor's tips for students who want to achieve a 4.0 GPA.*

Results: *The program began to meet its goals early, attracting students who share the college's values and distinguishing Rock-*

*hurst within the Jesuit pantheon. Within two months of the program's debut in April 1992, Rockhurst's direct-mail yield had doubled. And the outstanding results have continued: The college's 1993 freshman enrollment showed a phenomenal 71 percent increase over the previous year, surpassing Rockhurst's goal by 50 percent. Transfer enrollment, also exceeding the yearly goal, reached a 20 percent increase.*

**Source:** Communicorp, Atlanta, GA.

---

Educational institutions need effective communications with their markets and publics. The three preceding chapters have explained the marketing aspects of program development, pricing, and delivery decisions. But developing good programs and services, pricing them attractively, and making them readily available to target consumers is not enough. The institution must also inform consumers and others about its goals, activities, and offerings and motivate them to take an interest in the institution.

This communication takes many forms. Educators usually think in terms of catalogs and bulletins describing their institution and its programs. Colleges, schools, and other educational institutions communicate about themselves by their very existence, whether or not they have a formal communications program. Many are rethinking their communications efforts, both formal and informal.

The educational communicator must start with a clear picture of the communications tasks facing the institution. The following tasks are typical:

- To maintain or enhance the image of the institution.
- To build alumni loyalty and support.
- To attract donors.
- To provide information about the institution's offerings.
- To attract prospective students and encourage application and enrollment.
- To correct inaccurate or incomplete information about the institution.

In addition, the institution must determine and meet the information needs of faculty, staff, current students, and others in the internal environment.

Communication involves an exchange between the institution and the audience. The communicator must consider the institution's purpose for preparing the communication and the purpose(s) for which the audience will be paying attention to it. Only then can the form, content, and delivery of the message be planned to match the audience and achieve the intended purpose.

Most educational institutions use public relations, marketing publications, and—to a lesser extent—advertising.

*Public relations* consists of efforts to obtain favorable interest in the institution and/or its programs, typically through planting significant news about them in publications; through obtaining favorable unpaid presentation on radio, television, or in other media; or through the institution's own activities and events.

*Marketing publications* consist of the institution's published materials for which the school controls both the content and the context of the message, and which are designed to convey the institution's most important messages to its most important audiences. From this perspective, virtually every institutional publication is a marketing publication, and the most obvious use of marketing publications is in admissions, development/fund raising, and public relations.

*Advertising* consists of paid presentation and promotion of ideas, products, programs, or services—typically through mass media including magazines or newspapers, on television, radio, billboards, or bus cards.

Effective public relations, marketing publications, and advertising call for three distinct sets of skills coming from distinct but interrelated professional fields, each with its own precepts. We discuss each communication area separately, yet the institution will want to draw on each approach and coordinate two or all three of them, depending on the situation and the communication objective.

This chapter is divided into four sections. The first addresses the steps in planning an effective communication, reviewing principles that apply to every communication. The following three sections address public relations, marketing publications, and advertising in turn.

## STEPS IN PLANNING EFFECTIVE COMMUNICATIONS

Communications planning should start with an understanding of eight elements of every communication. The exchange aspect of every effective communication is diagrammed in Figure 14-1. There are two parties—a *sender* and a *receiver*. One or both send a *message* through *media*. To communicate effectively, senders need an understanding of the needs and wants of receivers. The senders must be skillful in *encoding* messages that reflect how the target audience tends to *decode* messages. They must transmit the message over efficient media that reach the target audience. They must develop *feedback* channels so they can know the audience's *response* to the message. Marketing research will be required at each stage: to identify potential audiences, segment them, determine their information needs, develop appropriate messages, and measure audience response.

FIGURE 14-1     Elements in the communications process

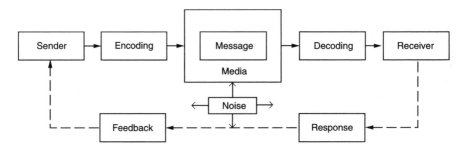

The communications planning flow should begin with considering the target audience and work backward to the communicator. The marketing communicator must make the following decisions: (1) identify the target audience, (2) clarify the response sought, (3) develop a message, (4) choose the medium or media, (5) select source attributes, and (6) collect feedback. These planning steps are essential for effective communications, whether advertising, marketing publications, or public relations is used.

### Identifying the Target Audience

An effective communication speaks directly to the concerns of a specific person or group. A college will want to identify the key audiences and their specific concerns in order to provide information tailored to their needs. For example, parents may be particularly interested in educational costs and faculty quality, whereas high school seniors may be more interested in social activities and students' evaluations of the educational experience.

Potential target audiences include all the institution's publics and markets. The institutions will need to develop a communications program for each target audience, not just the two or three key audiences. For example, a college may identify its main audience as prospective students, but at various times, it will need to communicate with its other publics and markets—including alumni, current students, their parents, donors, and the general public.

### Clarifying the Response Sought

A purposeful communication is designed to obtain a response from the receiver. The response may be a change in awareness of the institution and its programs, or a change in attitude—being favorably impressed by the quality of a program, for example. Or the institution may be seeking a behavioral response—a request for additional information, an application, or a donation.

Only by determining the desired response can the institution shape the best message and later assess its effectiveness.

## Developing the Message

Having defined the response desired from the target audience, the communicator then develops a communication. An ideal communication would manage to *get attention, hold interest, arouse desire,* and *obtain action* (known as the *AIDA model*). In practice, rarely will a single message take the consumer all the way from awareness through action. The institution may need to use different messages and different types of communication at various stages of the communications process.

For example, prospective donors may have first had contact with the college when attending an event there. Impressed by the campus and the college's faculty and staff, the would-be donors take the time to read news stories that tell about events at the college and reinforce their interest. They may meet alumni of the college socially and listen attentively to their reminiscences. If their interest becomes known (and based on their "giving potential"), the prospective donors may be contacted by a representative of the college's development office or even by the college president to discuss the college's plans and needs. In this case, the college is engaging in event creation to get attention, relying on informal personal contact by alumni along with publicity to hold prospective donors' interest, and depending on professional personal contact to arouse desire and obtain action—making a donation.

A message has both *content* and *format.* Preparing the content requires understanding the target audience and what will motivate them to respond. The communicator then needs to select a format that attracts attention, arouses interest, and presents the message clearly.

## Choosing Media

The communicator must select efficient media or channels of communication. Channels of communication are of two broad types, *personal* and *nonpersonal.*

**Personal Communication.** *Personal communication* includes direct communications from representatives of the institution (such as alumni-office representatives, development staff, admissions officers, and telemarketers); and word-of-mouth influence through conversations with neighbors, friends, family members, and associates—a highly persuasive form of communication. Personal influence is often a potent factor in decisions to apply to, attend, or donate money to an institution.

Institutions can stimulate personal-influence channels to work on their behalf. They can (1) identify individuals and groups that are influential and devote extra effort to them; (2) create *opinion leaders* by supplying them with information and asking them to help the institution (say, in fund raising or admissions); (3) work through community influentials, such as club presidents, elected officials, and others; (4) feature influential people in press releases and advertising; and (5) develop advertising that is high in "conversation value."[1]

**Nonpersonal Communication.** *Nonpersonal channels* include all channels of communication that do not involve direct person-to-person contact: newspapers, magazines, radio, television, billboards, events, and most direct mail.

Communication through nonpersonal channels can encourage and reinforce personal communications. After seeing a news story on a new career-planning course at the local community college, a woman may tell her neighbor about the course. A high school student may talk with a college counselor about a number of colleges and then read brochures from those colleges with increased interest. Therefore, educational institutions should strive to combine personal and nonpersonal channels of communication according to their communications objectives.

### Selecting Source Attributes

A communication's effect on an audience will be influenced by how the audience perceives the communicator. Messages delivered by highly credible sources will be more persuasive. Three factors underlie *source credibility*: expertise, trustworthiness, and likability.[2] *Expertise* is the degree to which the communicator is perceived to possess the necessary authority for what is being claimed. Students or recent graduates are usually perceived as experts on the college experience. Professors rank high on expertise when speaking about their areas of specialization. *Trustworthiness* is related to how objective and how honest the source is perceived to be. Audiences tend to put more trust in friends and others like themselves than in strangers or recruiters. *Likability* is related to how attractive the source is to the audience. Qualities such as candor, humor, and naturalness tend to make a source more likable. The most highly credible source, then, would be a person who scored high on all three dimensions. Exhibit 14-1 summarizes the findings of a survey on what sources college-bound seniors and their parents used to obtain information about various features of colleges.

EXHIBIT 14-1    Information sources used during college search

Students and parents have remarkably similar associations between information sources and college attributes. This is generally consistent with other findings in this study. There are apparently few significant differences between students and parents with regard to college search behavior.

A college's literature is viewed as an appropriate means for learning about "institutional hardware" (objective facts about an institution) such as student body composition, majors, costs, facilities, and resources.

College guidebooks provide comparative (and presumably relatively unbiased) information on academic reputation of colleges.

College admissions representatives are seen as useful in providing "institutional hardware" and especially financial aid information. Interestingly, college admissions representatives are not seen as relevant in providing "institutional software" (subjective lifestyle considerations) such as related to on-campus lifestyle.

Current college students are the primary source of "institutional software" such as lifestyle, on-campus housing, campus spirit, and extra-curricular activity possibilities.

Campus visits are seen as further opportunities for students and their parents to learn about "institutional software." As may be noted, campus visits permit students and parents to see and experience for themselves a sampling of a college's campus attractiveness, on-campus housing facilities, social climate and spirit, and campus community setting.

College videos, college graduates, high school guidance counselors, and high school students are apparently not seen by either students or parents as having been of particular value in providing information about any of the 16 specific academic and nonacademic college attributes studied here.

Source: Randall G. Chapman, "College Search Information Sources: How Do High School Seniors and Their Parents Learn About Colleges?" *Proceedings of the 1993 Symposium for the Marketing of Higher Education* (Chicago, IL: American Marketing Association, 1993), pp. 132, 134.

## Collecting Feedback

The communicator should test the communication before it is used and should research the message's effects on the target audience. This may involve keeping records of requests for further information, applications or donations received, or other measures of attention and interest. The communicator may survey target-audience members and ask them whether they recognize or recall the message, how they felt about the message, their previous and current attitudes toward the institution that sponsored the message, and their intentions to apply, enroll, or donate.

## PUBLIC RELATIONS

Every school, college, or other educational institution is involved with public relations in some way, since each must deal with a variety of publics. The local community, politicians, the news media, and others—all may take an active or reactive interest in the institution's activities. In many instances, the institution's top administrator plays a major role in public relations. Arnold points out that the first two letters in *president* and *principal* are PR.[3] A national sample of community college presidents reported that they have as much influence on institutional image as do more formal public relations activities, through their relationships with other community leaders and external publics, and through activities directly connected with their colleges.[4]

Of course, every other member of the institution is also, to a degree, a representative whose words and actions can influence public opinion about it. But institutions usually recognize the advantages of a more formal public relations operation. In fact, many public relations activities date back to the first two decades of this century: Harvard, Yale, Columbia, the University of Chicago, the University of Pennsylvania, and the University of Wisconsin set up influential publicity offices to spread the institutions' fame and to attract students and donors.

Nowadays, responsibility for recruiting students resides in the admissions office and fund raising with the development office, and a public relations officer or office may consult with them as well as handle other public relations tasks. The public relations office may monitor the institution's public image and advise administrators on areas of image strength and weakness. It may work with admissions and development officers to plan publications and manage their production. And the public relations office may prepare and distribute press releases about admissions and fund-raising activities as well as other campus stories.[5]

On some campuses, public relations and development/fund raising are all directed by a vice president for external relations. The person at this level sits in on all meetings involving public-sensitive information and actions and advises on policy and implementation. In other institutions, public relations means getting out publications and handling special events. In such cases, the public relations people are not involved in policy or strategy formulation, only tactics.

The institution can realize several advantages by formalizing its public relations operation: (1) better anticipation of potential issues; (2) better handling of these issues, (3) consistent public-oriented policies and strategies; and (4) more professional written and oral communications.

### The Public Relations Process

Public relations practitioners view themselves as the caretakers and enhancers of the institution's image. At various times, they are assigned the task of forming, maintaining, or changing attitudes. In this connection, they carry out the five-step process shown in Figure 14-2. We will examine each step in the following paragraphs.

**Identifying the Institution's Relevant Publics.** An institution would like to have the goodwill of every public that it affects or is affected by. But given limited public relations resources, it has to concentrate its attention on certain publics.

An educational institution's primary publics are those that it relates to on an active and continuous basis—its students, donors, faculty and staff, trustees, and the community. If the goodwill of any of these groups disappears—students stop coming, donors stop giving, faculty and staff start quitting, trustees lose their interest, or the community becomes hostile—the institution is in deep trouble.

The publics are related not only to the institution but also to each other in many important ways. A particular public may strongly influence the attitudes and behavior of other publics toward the institution. Consider a school whose students are highly satisfied. Their enthusiasm will be transmitted to their parents and to friends who might be potential students. Their enthusiasm will reinforce the faculty's attention to teaching. As alumni, they will be more generous donors and supporters of the school. Thus, students influence the attitudes and behavior of other school publics.

FIGURE 14-2　The public relations process

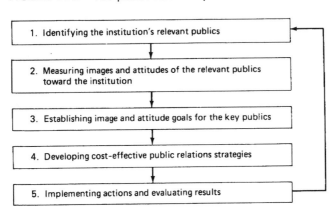

**Measuring Images and Attitudes of the Relevant Publics.** After identifying its various publics, the institution needs to assess how each public thinks and feels about it. Some idea of each public's attitude can be obtained simply through regular contacts with members of that public. But impressions based on casual contact cannot necessarily be trusted.

A college wanted to rent its stadium facilities to a professional football team for five Sundays as a way to acquire more revenue. The college's administrators thought that most local residents and city council members would be agreeable. However, when the plan became public, local citizens organized themselves and attacked the college, calling it insensitive and arrogant. They complained that the football crowd would use up parking space, leave litter, walk on lawns, and be rowdy. Many citizens, including city council members, revealed negative attitudes toward the college. The college's administration dismissed the community spokesperson as unrepresentative of community opinion, and were shocked when the vote went against the college.

Formal marketing research is essential to effective public relations. A focus group discussion with six to ten members of a key public can reveal their knowledge and feelings about the institution. Although the resulting observations may not be fully representative, they normally contribute valuable perspectives and raise questions that the institution will want to explore more systematically. Eventually, the institution may find it worthwhile to conduct formal field research on its image and issues of concern in the form of a public opinion survey. The public opinion survey measures such variables as awareness, knowledge, interest, and attitude toward the institution.

**Establishing Image and Attitude Goals for the Key Publics.** Through periodically researching its key publics, the institution will have some hard data on how these publics view it. The findings can be assembled in the form of a scorecard, such as the one illustrated for a college in Table 14-1. The scorecard becomes the basis for developing a public relations plan for the coming period. The college's scorecard shows that high school counselors have a medium amount of knowledge about the college and a negative attitude. Since high school counselors have a role in the college-choice decision, the institution needs to develop a communications program that will improve high school counselors' knowledge and attitudes toward the college. The objective should be made even more specific and measurable, such as "80 percent of the high school counselors should know at least four key things about the college, and at least 60 percent should report having a positive opinion about the college, within two years." Making the objectives concrete helps determine the necessary activities and budget and provides a basis for evaluating the success of the plan.

The next item on the scorecard indicates that communication also has

TABLE 14-1    Scorecard on a college's publics

| PUBLIC | KNOWLEDGE | ATTITUDE | PUBLIC'S IMPORTANCE |
|---|---|---|---|
| High school counselors | Medium | Negative | High |
| High school juniors and seniors | Low | Neutral | High |
| Alumni | High | Positive | High |
| General public | Low | Neutral | Low |

to be directed at high school juniors and seniors to increase their knowledge and improve their attitudes toward the college. As for alumni, their knowledge and attitude are ideal, and the college's job is simply to maintain their enthusiasm. As for the general public, the college may decide to do nothing. In this case, the general public's knowledge and attitude are not that important in attracting students, and the cost of improving the situation would be too high in relation to the value.

**Developing Cost-Effective Public Relations Strategies.** An institution usually has many options in trying to improve the attitudes of a particular public. Its first task is to understand why the attitudes have come about, so that the causal factors can be addressed by an appropriate strategy.

Let us return to the college that found it had weak community support when it wanted to rent its stadium to a professional football team. In digging deeper into the negative citizen attitudes, administrators discovered that many local citizens harbored resentments against the college, including complaints that (1) the college never consulted citizens or citizen groups before taking actions, (2) the college discriminated against local high school students, preferring to draw students from other parts of the country, (3) the college did not actively inform the local community about campus events and programs, and (4) the college owned extensive local property that was not on the tax rolls and thus raised the taxes of the citizens. Essentially, the community felt neglected and exploited by the college.

The diagnosis suggests that the college needs to change its ways and establish stronger contacts with the community. It needs to develop a *community relations program*. Here are some of the steps it might take:

1. Identify the local opinion leaders—prominent businesspeople, news editors, city council members, heads of civic organizations, school officials—and build better relationships through inviting them to campus events, consulting with them on college-community issues, and sponsoring luncheons and dinners.
2. Encourage the college's faculty and staff to join local organizations and participate more actively in community campaigns such as the United Way and the American Red Cross Blood Bank program.

3. Develop a speaker's bureau to speak to local groups such as Kiwanis, Rotary, and so on.
4. Make the college's facilities and programs more available to the community.
5. Arrange open houses and tours of the campus for the local community.
6. Participate in community special events such as parades, holiday observances, and so on.
7. Establish a community advisory board of community leaders to act as a sounding board for issues facing the college.

Each of these actions involves money and time. The institution will need to estimate the amount of expected attitude improvement with each project in order to arrive at the best mix of cost-effective actions.

**Implementing Actions and Evaluating Results.** The actions must be assigned to responsible people, along with concrete objectives, time frames, and budgets. The public relations office should oversee the effort and monitor the results. Evaluating the results of public relations activities, however, is not easy, since it is hard to separate them from the effects of other marketing activities.

Consider the problem of measuring the value of the institution's publicity efforts. Publicity is designed with certain audience-response objectives in mind, and these objectives determine what is measured. The major response measures are exposures, awareness/comprehension/attitude change, and changes in behavior.

The easiest and most common measure of publicity effectiveness is the number of *exposures* created in the media. Most publicists supply the client with a "clippings book" showing all the media that carried news about the institution. This exposure measure is not very satisfying. There is no indication of how many people actually read, saw, or heard the message, and what they thought afterward. Furthermore, there is no information on the net audience reached, since publications have overlapping readership.

A better measure calls for finding out what change in public *awareness/comprehension/attitude* occurred as a result of the publicity campaign (after allowing for the effect of other promotional tools). This requires the use of survey methodology to measure the before-after levels of these variables. The best measure is the effect of the campaign on people's actions—donating to the college, applying, and so forth.

Certain public relations activities will be found to be too costly in relation to their results and might be dropped. Or the public relations objectives might be recognized as too ambitious and require modification. Furthermore, new issues will arise with certain publics and require redirection of the public relations resources. As the public relations office implements these actions and measures the results, it can return to the earlier steps, reassess where the institution stands in the minds of specific publics, and determine what improvements to pursue. Thus, the public relations process is continually recycling, as the arrow in Figure 14-2 indicates.

## Public Relations Tools

Here we want to examine the major public relations media and tools in more detail. They are (1) written material, (2) audiovisual material and software, (3) institutional-identity media, (4) news, (5) events, (6) speeches, (7) telephone information services, and (8) personal contact.

**Written Material.** Institutions rely extensively on written material to communicate with their target publics. Colleges use annual reports, catalogs, employee newsletters, alumni magazines, posters, flyers, and so on.

In preparing each publication, the public relations office must consider *function, aesthetics*, and *cost*. For example, the function of an annual report is to inform interested publics about the institution's accomplishments during the year, with the ultimate purpose of generating confidence in the institution and its leaders. It should also further the institution's chosen strategy, including its positioning.

The annual report should be readable, interesting, and professional. A mimeographed annual report suggests a poor and amateurish organization. On the other hand, if the annual report is too slick, readers may question why the institution is spending so much on printing instead of on other things. Cost acts as a constraint in that the institution will allocate a limited amount of money to each publication. The public relations department has to reconcile considerations of function, aesthetics, and cost in developing each publication.

**Audiovisual Material and Software.** In the old days, college recruiters would make a presentation, answer questions, and pass out brochures to the high school seniors gathered to hear about the college. Today's recruiters, in contrast, come prepared to deliver an effective audiovisual presentation. Emerging technologies have created cost-effective ways to produce and distribute videotapes, videodisks, and informational software, virtually eliminating films, slides, and audio cassettes. Videocassettes are inexpensive enough to mail directly to prospects, while the more expensive videodisks of campus tours are more often available at college-guidance centers.

**Institutional-Identity Media.** In many schools there is little or no effort to achieve institutional consistency. Each of the institution's separate items takes on its own look, a situation that not only creates confusion but also neglects an opportunity to create and reinforce an *institutional identity*. In an overcommunicated society, educational institutions have to compete for attention. They should at least try to create a visual identity that the public immediately recognizes. The visual identity is carried through the institution's permanent media, such as logos, stationary, catalogs, brochures, signs, business forms, business cards, buildings, and—as appropriate—into fund-raising appeals and admissions literature.

The institutional-identity media become a marketing tool when they are attractive, memorable, and distinctive. The task of creating a coordinated visual identity is not easy. The institution should select a good graphic design consultant. A good consultant will try to get the institution's key decision makers to identify the essence of the institution, and then will try to turn it into a big idea backed by strong symbols. The symbols are adapted to the various media so that they create immediate institutional recognition in the minds of various publics.

**News.** The public relations office should also find or create favorable news about the institution and make that news interesting and available to the appropriate media. The appeal of publicity is that it is "free advertising." As someone said, "Publicity is sent to a medium and prayed for, while advertising is sent to a medium and paid for." However, publicity is far from free, because special skills are required to write good publicity and to "reach" the press. Good publicists cost money.

Publicity has three qualities that make it a worthwhile investment. First, it may have *higher veracity* than advertising, because it appears as normal news and not sponsored information. Second, it tends to catch people *off guard* who might otherwise actively avoid sponsored messages. Third, it has high potential for *dramatization* because news of a noteworthy event arouses attention.

Consider a college suffering from low visibility that adopts the objective of achieving more public recognition through news management. The public relations director will review the college's various components to see whether any natural stories exist. Do any faculty members have unusual backgrounds, or are any working on unusual projects? Are any new and unusual courses being taught? Are any exceptional students with unusual backgrounds enrolled? Are any interesting events taking place on campus? Is there a story about the architecture, history, or aspirations of the college? Usually a search along these lines will uncover hundreds of stories that can be fed to the media with the effect of creating much more public recognition of the college. Ideally, the stories the institution selects to publicize will symbolize the college's mission and goals, thus furthering achievement of the institution's strategy and supporting its desired market position.

A good public relations director understands that the media seek interesting and timely stories, and that educational institutions must compete for attention with all the other events of the day. The director will make a point of knowing as many news editors and reporters as possible and providing them with press releases.

In addition to press releases, the public relations office should also respond to media requests to interview faculty and other campus figures. When a news story breaks, various media seek out academic experts for comment. The public relations director should be knowledgeable about faculty areas of expertise and be able to recommend appropriate interviewees. Some campus public relations directors help faculty prepare for such interviews.

**Events.** An institution can increase its newsworthiness by creating events that attract favorable attention from target markets. Thus, a college seeking more public attention can host academic conferences, present well-known speakers and public figures, mark important occasions in the life of the college, and provide press releases on notable people and events at the college. Each well-run event impresses the immediate participants and provides the basis for several stories directed to relevant media vehicles and audiences.

**Speeches.** The public relations director will look for effective spokespersons for the institution and will try to arrange speaking engagements. If a college's president is articulate and attractive, the public relations director will try to line up appearances on national and local television and radio talk shows and at major conventions. The director can also set up a speakers' bureau for delivering appropriate talks to community organizations.

**Telephone Information Services.** Many institutions have dedicated telephone information lines, some offering 800 service (with no charge to the caller). Triton Community College, for example, set up a telephone number that gives recorded information about the college, registration times, and costs. Some school districts have set up "homework hotlines" where the teachers are available in the evenings to help students—and their parents—with homework problems. These telephone services are ways for the institution to show that it cares about the public and is ready to serve it.

**Personal Contact.** We have already referred to the importance of top administrators as spokespersons for the institution. Others associated with the school also have a public relations role: admissions officers, development officers, volunteer fund raisers, faculty, staff, current students, and alumni, among others. The impressions they make can have a significant impact on how the institution is perceived.

## MARKETING PUBLICATIONS

Every educational institution has marketing publications, whether it realizes it or not. Whether the school sends out photocopied fact sheets or elaborate four-color viewbooks, these materials communicate about the institution to those who see them. Schools and colleges prepare materials to support public relations, admissions, and development objectives. For example, posters can be very effective in attracting and informing certain prospect groups, when the recipient is well chosen and will display the poster. In this section we will review the range of materials, their unique roles, and guidelines for their preparation and use.

Direct mail is the major medium for reaching potential students and donors. In direct mail, the institution makes an offer to the recipient and seeks to obtain a direct response. The format of a direct mailing ranges from a self-mailer brochure to a package that includes a letter, four-color viewbook, application, and response card. Direct-mail experts strongly recommend including a letter in most cases: "Let a brochure do the telling, but a letter do the selling." Mailings that include a letter usually get a much better response rate than identical mailings without a letter.

Institutions that use direct mail skillfully are enthusiastic about its performance. Here are some guidelines for enhancing the effectiveness of direct mail:

**1.** *Target your most promising audiences.* The institution should take pains to purchase lists that carefully match the target-market segments. To purchase lists that are not well matched can be extremely costly in wasted time, materials, and postage, which could be better used on more appropriate audiences. Prospective-student lists that generate the highest response rate usually correspond closely to the institution's current student profile.

**2.** *Frame the right message for the right audience.* The materials must reflect an understanding of the recipients and of how your program or institution can meet their needs. The average person will spend only a few seconds glancing at a piece of third-class mail. The message must pique the reader's interest or it will be discarded.

High school students interviewed about college mailings said they liked letters personalized with their names; concise fact sheets that helped them sort out the colleges that would interest them; and prepaid return postcards to ask for information or to indicate they were not interested in the college. They did not like first-contact letters that "came on too strong," in some cases virtually guaranteeing admission; initial packets that contained too much material, including application forms and catalogs; and manila envelopes.

**3.** *State the benefits to the reader of making a positive response.* People usually respond best to a clearly stated personal benefit of taking the requested action. Direct-mail pieces often reflect some confusion between features and benefits. Features are attributes of the program or institution: "The college is located in downtown Manhattan" is a feature; but "At XY College you can see the best of America's performing arts in your own backyard" is a benefit. The benefits may be stated as testimonials from satisfied students or donors.

To clarify which benefits to offer, the staff preparing the mailing pieces should answer such questions as these: What benefits will people receive from attending this program, making a donation, or enrolling in this institution? Why should people come and/or donate? What will they get out of it?

**4.** *Send the message at an appropriate time.* The best-prepared message will be ignored if it comes at the wrong time, whether too early or too late. Since high school students start actively thinking about colleges in their junior—or even sophomore—year, direct mail from colleges that comes during junior year tends to get more attention. Continuing education programs usually send out announcements about eight weeks before a scheduled program: Earlier, the mailing may be put away and forgotten; later, the recipient may have already made conflicting commitments. Fund raisers select times that are likely to be attractive to prospective donors, such as end-of-the-year appeals to those who are considering the tax advantages of contributing.

**5.** *Tell the reader what response you want.* Some fund raisers and admissions staff feel shy about coming out and asking the reader to take some action, and thereby fail to get any response at all. They hope that the reader will draw the desired conclusion from the materials without being told. The letter and brochure should state the desired response—to send for further information, to write for an application, to send a check—and the response card should be easy to complete and be postage-paid. Gone are the days when educational institutions could fall back on the excuse that if people really cared, they would respond anyway.

**6.** *Plan follow-up mailings or other contact.* Don't assume that once is enough. A college admissions office may plan a succession of materials to send to those who ask for more information—a brochure on the student's area of interest, financial aid information, a campus viewbook, application materials, an invitation to the campus, perhaps phone calls from admissions staff. Those who do not respond may receive one or two additional mailings inviting an expression of interest before the school concludes the recipient is no longer a prospect.

**7.** *Measure your results.* Only by keeping track of response rates can the institution determine which lists and which materials are most effective. Those using direct mail should code each response card to indicate from which list the name came. By selecting the best segments to target and using the most effective approaches, the costs of direct mail can be greatly reduced over time.

## Direct Mail for Student Admissions

The admissions-office operation must have extraordinary procedures for sending out, receiving, responding to, and processing vast quantities of information, most of it on paper. Direct mail has become such a crucial tool for admissions that any admissions office without solid direct-mail expertise or access to outside expertise is at a distinct disadvantage.

Direct mail for admissions must meet several tests: It must reflect the school's mission and strategy, it must appeal enough to recipients that they are willing to read it, and it must communicate well enough to achieve its intended objectives. While these tests seem obvious, they are even more challenging in admissions because the primary audience for most of this direct mail is under age 18, has many interests besides college, and is probably being deluged with mail from dozens of other schools.

One father tracked and categorized every piece of direct mail his daughter received over one 50-day period in the spring of her junior year. He claimed that if all the materials were reformatted into a paperback book, the book would be 2,865 pages long! Not only was there "too much of it," much of it was "all the same," posed and lacking the glimmer of reality that a reader could identify with. Three-quarters of it was "off the mark," not relevant to the recipient and therefore a waste of the money spent to print and mail it to her.[6]

**Direct-Mail Materials.** The admissions office will typically make use of the following direct-mail pieces:

**1.** *The search piece.* The search piece is typically the very first introduction many students will have to the institution, since the college sends it out to selected students from lists purchased from American College Testing and/or the College Board in their "search" for prospects. The search piece should create awareness and arouse interest.

**2.** *The response vehicle.* The search piece—and every other mailing—must contain a response piece, typically a postcard, that makes it easy for the student to ask for more information.

**3.** *The "flagship piece"—either a viewbook or a prospectus.* A viewbook is like a conversation with the prospect, and usually includes many photographs and other visual elements. The prospectus contains more actual data about the institution, which is especially appropriate for sophisticated prospects who are likely to make thoughtful comparisons and want the data to do so.

**4.** *Department/program/major brochures.* Many prospects want and ask for details about specific programs in their areas of interest. Many such brochures are poorly done, either because they are boringly formal or because they don't give the information students really want. It is better to provide a good laser-printed fact sheet than a bad brochure. A useful brochure includes faculty biographies, lists of courses with distinctive courses highlighted, special department capabilities, and information on outcomes—what graduates do.

**5.** *Application form.* The application form is rarely viewed as a "marketing piece," yet good ones can make a difference in who decides to fill them out and whether they are filled out at all. The prenarrative on the application form can position the institution for the prospect, and the type of questions posed can either invite or repel student response. For example, Excellent School of Engineering introduces an application-essay question as follows: "At Excellent we prize students who show originality and inventiveness in addition to traditional measures of academic ability. Can you cite an example where you solved a challenging problem in a unique way?"

**6.** *Catalog.* The catalog is too expensive to serve only as a reference tool—it should also be a marketing tool. It should include necessary information about courses, regulations, and so forth, since the catalog constitutes a legal contract between the institution and the student, but it should also provide an historical sense of the college and its future, reflecting the institution's core values.

**7.** *Parents' piece.* For young students—most undergraduates—parents are major participants in the decision process. The admissions office should send a mailing with key information to the parents of strong prospects and admitted students.

**8.** *Financing piece.* Every student and family wants information on costs and on options for paying college costs.

**9.** *Campus visit piece.* Many prospects and their families will visit schools in the choice set. If they are coming from a distance and are unfamiliar with the school, they will probably be dealing with rental cars, motels, and highway maps, and will appreciate all the help the college's publications can provide. The visit piece should include a map of the area, a campus map with parking, a walking tour, and the admissions office clearly marked.

**10.** *A conversion piece.* The aim of this mailing is to motivate strong applicants and admitted students to apply and to send in their deposits. This mailing should revisit the core values of the institution presented in earlier communications, and confirm and reconfirm the match between the applicant and the institution.

**11.** *A candidate's reply kit.* Once a student has applied and been accepted to the typical college, the next flood of mail arrives—separate information sheets, forms to complete, checks to mail—from seemingly every office on campus. In the enrollment-management tradition of being thoughtful and responsive, some schools now combine all necessary information forms, print them in a unified set, and mail out this package complete with step-by-step directions and a return envelope.

## ADVERTISING

The idea of advertising strikes some educators as new, yet educators were using advertising as long as 2,000 years ago. The Greek sophists, like doctors and other wandering professionals of their day, publicly "made high display of their acquirements, and gave exhibitions of eloquence and of argument to show the value of their wares."[7] In more recent times—1869—an ad for Harvard College appeared on the outside cover of Harper's Magazine, and created an uproar. According to one commentator, "Such a thing had never been heard of before. It was as if Noah had put up posters on the cliffs of Armenia to announce that the ark was to open on such a day."[8]

Because of—or despite—these early practitioners, some educators resist the idea of paid advertising, feeling that it demeans educational programs and should be unnecessary. On the other hand, some educators may expect too much from advertising or try to accomplish large objectives with inadequate skills and resources, and thus be disappointed. In fact, advertising can play a role in an institution's communications program and can enhance rather than demean the institution that uses it appropriately.

Advertising consists of nonpersonal forms of communication conducted through paid media under clear sponsorship. Advertising can involve such varied media as magazines and newspapers, radio and television, outdoor displays (such as posters, signs, billboards, sky-writing), direct mail, novelties (blotters, calendars, pens, pencils), cards (bus, subway), catalogs, directories, and circulars. Advertising can serve to build the long-term image and reputation of the institution (institutional advertising) or of a particular division or program, to provide information about a specific program or event, and for other purposes.

To develop an effective advertising program, the institution must make five major decisions. It must:

1. Set advertising objectives.
2. Determine the advertising budget.
3. Decide on the message.
4. Select media.
5. Evaluate advertising effectiveness.

These decisions are diagrammed in Figure 14-3 and are discussed in the following sections.

### Set Advertising Objectives

An effective communications program must start with clear communications objectives. These objectives must flow from prior decisions on the institution's strategy—the target market, market positioning, and marketing mix. Some of the objectives will be addressed with public relations and other

FIGURE 14-3    Major decisions in advertising management

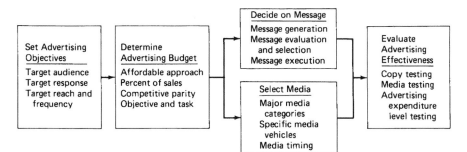

communications approaches, and others can best be addressed by advertising. The overall marketing strategy defines the role advertising will play in the total marketing mix.

Developing advertising objectives calls for defining the target audience, target response, and target reach and frequency.

**Identifying the Target Audience.** A marketing communicator must start with a clear target audience in mind. (*Target audience* is analogous to *target market* and refers to the audience we particularly want to reach with our communications.) The audience may be potential users of the institution's services, current users, deciders, or influencers. It may consist of individuals, groups, particular publics, or the general public. The target audience will critically influence the communicator's decisions on what is to be said, how it is to be said, where it is to be said, and who is to say it.

Consider the case of a small private college called Pottsville. In addition to its daytime courses, Pottsville offers evening courses for adult learners. It wants to reach adults living within 30 miles of the campus who might be interested in participating in these evening courses. It may want to appeal to several audiences—working adults and senior citizens who want something interesting to do with their leisure time. Each target audience might warrant a different communications campaign, of which advertising might be a part.

**Defining the Target Response and Audience Readiness.** Once the target audience is identified, the marketing communicator must define the target response that is sought. The ultimate response is usually some action, but action is the end result of what may be a long process of consumer decision making. The marketing communicator needs to know in which stage the target audience stands at present and to which stage it should be moved.

Any member of the target audience may be in one of the six action-readiness states with respect to the institution or its offerings. These states— *awareness, knowledge, liking, preference, conviction,* and *action*—are described next.[9]

**1.** *Awareness.* The first step is to determine the target audience's awareness of the institution. The audience may be completely unaware of the school, know only its name, or know one or two things about it. If most of the target audience is unaware, the communicator's task is to build awareness, perhaps even just name recognition. This calls for simple messages repeating the name. Even then, building awareness takes time. Pottsville College may have little or no name recognition among adults living 20 miles away. The college might set the objective of making 70 percent of these adults aware of Pottsville's name within one year.

**2.** *Knowledge.* The target audience may be aware of the college but not know much about it. Therefore, the communicator's objective will be to transmit some key information. Thus, Pottsville College may want its target audience to know that it is a private four-year college with distinguished programs in ornithology and thanatology, and that its evening programs for adult learners offer opportunities for in-depth study of these fields with outstanding experts. After the communications campaign, it can sample the target-audience members to measure whether they have little, some, or much knowledge of Pottsville College, and the content of their knowledge. The particular set of beliefs that the audience has of an institution is called its *image*. Institutions must periodically assess the images held by their publics as a basis for developing communications objectives.

**3.** *Liking.* If the target-audience members know the institution, the next question is, How do they feel about it? If the audience holds an unfavorable view of Pottsville College, the communicator has to find out why and then develop a communications program to build up favorable feeling. If the unfavorable view is rooted in real inadequacies of the college, then a communications campaign would not do the job. The task would require first improving the college and then communicating its quality.

**4.** *Preference.* The target audience may like the institution but may not prefer it over others. In this case, the communicator's job is to build the audience's preference. The communicator needs to present information on the institution's quality, value, performance, and other attributes. The communicator can gauge the success of the campaign by surveying members of the audience to see if their preference for the college is stronger after the campaign.

**5.** *Conviction.* Members of the target audience may have some level of interest in the courses offered but they may not have come to a firm decision to attend Pottsville. The communicator's job is to build conviction that attending is the right thing to do. Building conviction that one should select a particular institution is a challenging communications task.

**6.** *Action.* A member of the target audience may be convinced but may not quite get around to taking action. He or she may be waiting for additional information, may plan to act later, and so on. A communicator in this situation must encourage the consumer to take the final step.

The six states simplify to three stages known as the *cognitive* (awareness, knowledge), *affective* (liking, preference, conviction), and *behavioral* (action). The communicator normally assumes that consumers pass through these stages in succession. The communicator must then identify the stage that characterizes most of the target audience and develop a communications message or campaign that will move them to the next stage. Rarely can one message move the audience through all three stages. Most communicators try to find a cost-effective communications approach to moving the target audience one stage at a time.

Some marketing scholars have challenged the idea that a consumer passes from knowing to liking to taking action, in that order. Michael Ray has suggested that some consumers instead pass from knowing to taking action to liking.[10] An example would be a student who has heard of Pottsville, enrolls there without much feeling, and afterward develops a strong liking (or disliking) for the place. Ray has also suggested that sometimes consumers pass from taking action to liking to knowing. Thus, a student may sign up for a course that he or she knows nothing about except that it fits nicely in his or her class schedule, then enjoy the professor's teaching style and the content, and finally begin to understand the subject. Each version of the sequences has different implications for the role and influence of communications on behavior.

**Determining Target Reach and Frequency.** The third decision is the determination of the optimal target reach and frequency of the advertising. Since funds for advertising are usually limited, not everyone in the target audience can be reached with sufficient frequency. Therefore, the communicator must decide what percentage of the audience to reach with what exposure frequency per period.

Pottsville College might use radio advertising to publicize a special course for adult learners. Since the college may be unable to afford the cost of reaching everyone, the communicator must decide what percentage of the audience to reach with what exposure frequency. For example, the college could buy radio time during a particular program with an audience of about 25,000 listeners. Since an estimated 40 percent of the audience is adults over age 25, the reach would be 15,000 people. But one exposure to the radio spot, while enough to create awareness, may not be enough to inform listeners and convince them to sign up. The college will want to have the radio spot repeated enough times—enough frequency—that the audience will have time to reflect on what the college has to offer.

## Determine Advertising Budget

Setting the adverting budget will depend on the advertising objectives and the advertising program to carry them out. Some media will be far more expensive than others, and the communications planner must develop an affordable budget to carry out the identified tasks.

Pottsville College could approach the area radio stations, obtain information about audience size, demographic characteristics, and listening habits, then select the times and days for the spot to be aired.

In addition to setting the total size of the advertising budget, marketers must plan how to allocate the budget over different market segments, geographical areas, and time periods. In practice, advertising budgets are allocated to different segments depending on some indicator of market potential.

For example, Pottsville might spend twice as much on advertising in the city where the college is located, and less on advertising in small towns at a greater distance, on the premise that distant adults are less likely to enroll. Thus, the budget would be allocated to different segments according to their expected marginal response to advertising. A budget is well allocated when it is not possible to increase total market response by shifting dollars from one segment to another.

Some educational institutions receive donated or reduced-cost advertising. A notable example is the United Negro College Fund campaign. The copy is produced by a volunteering advertising agency, which provides this service as a member of the Advertising Council of America, and the media donate broadcast time and media space as a public service. The colleges that benefit from this advertising have no control over the place or timing of its appearance, but they have many of the advantages of a professional advertising program.

Perhaps the local radio station would give Pottsville some "free air time" for its spots. The one drawback of "free time" is that the college's spot might air at times when most working adults and senior citizens are unlikely to be listening.

### Decide on the Message

Given the advertising objectives and budget, the next step is to develop a creative message. Advertisers and their agencies go through three steps: message generation, message evaluation and selection, and message execution.

**Message Generation.** Message generation involves developing several alternative messages (appeals, themes, motifs, ideas) that are planned to elicit the desired response in the target market.

Messages can be generated in several ways. As we have already emphasized, every element of the school's communication mix should further the school's strategy and position while meeting one or more specific marketing objectives. Message generation must build on very careful attention to the target audience and the communications objectives.

Ideas for messages often emerge from the intensive groundwork that underlies the entire communications program—reviewing the institution's history, mission, goals, and achievement; talking with members of the school community and with members of the target market, individually or in focus groups; and gathering other information about the target audience and the subject of the communication to suggest ways to express the idea in the most compelling way. Trying to save time and money by reliance on clever "plays on words" and other products of casual brainstorming is usually ineffective, wasteful, or even disastrous.

The planners may use some formal deductive framework for coming up with advertising messages. One framework calls for generating three types of messages: rational, emotional, and moral.

1. *Rational messages* aim at passing on information and/or serving the audience's self-interest. They attempt to show that the institution or program will yield the expected functional benefits. Examples would be messages discussing a program's quality, economy, value, or performance.

2. *Emotional messages* are designed to stir up some negative or positive emotion that will motivate action. Communicators have worked with fear, guilt, and shame appeals, especially in connection with getting people to start doing things they should (brushing their teeth, practicing breast self-examination) or stop doing things they shouldn't do (smoking, overimbibing, overeating). Advertisers have found that fear appeals work up to a point, but if too much fear is aroused, the audience will block out the message. Communicators have also used such positive emotional appeals as love, humor, pride, and joy.

3. *Moral messages* are directed at the audience's sense of what is right and proper. They are often used in messages exhorting people to support such social causes as a cleaner environment, equal rights for women, and support for higher education. An example is the United Negro College Fund's appeal: "A mind is a terrible thing to waste."

Figure 14-4 shows a United Negro College Fund ad that combines both moral and rational appeals. The "waste not, want not" proverb sets the tone of the ad, which points out to businesspeople that a donation to the United Negro College Fund helps ensure that they will be able to hire well-qualified college graduates as employees in the future.

John Maloney proposed another deductive framework.[11] He suggested that buyers may be expecting any of four types of reward from a product: rational, sensory, social, or ego satisfaction; and that they may visualize these rewards from results-of-use experience, product-in-use experience, or incidental-to-use experience. Crossing the four types of rewards with the three types of experience generates 12 types of advertising messages, illustrated in Table 14-2.

Another approach examines the product's actual and desired positions and looks for the themes that would shift the market's view of the product in the desired direction. The advertisement may try to change the belief about the product's level on some attribute or the perceived relative importance of different attributes, or to introduce new attributes not generally considered

FIGURE 14-4   United Negro College Fund ad

When you need to fill a position.
you'll have a qualified graduate
that you helped educate.

**GIVE TO THE
UNITED NEGRO COLLEGE FUND.
A MIND IS A TERRIBLE THING
TO WASTE.**

Photographer: Dwight Carter
A Public Service of This Magazine &
The Advertising Council
© 1981 United Negro College Fund, Inc.

TABLE 14-2  Examples of 12 types of appeals

| TYPES OF POTENTIALLY REWARDING EXPERIENCE WITH A PRODUCT | POTENTIAL TYPE OF REWARD | | | |
| --- | --- | --- | --- | --- |
| | RATIONAL | SENSORY | SOCIAL | EGO SATISFACTION |
| Results-of-use experience | 1. Get the training to get ahead | 2. Yoga classes to relax body and mind | 3. Join a selct group—our alumni | 4. For women who are going places |
| Product-in-use experience | 5. The program based on your schedule | 6. Excitement in learning | 7. The friendly college | 8. Add some class to your life |
| Incidental-to-use experience | 9. Free child care while you attend class | 10. The thrill of the Homecoming game—autumn at the U. | 11. Make the friends you'll keep all your life | 12. The school for the discriminating student |

Source: Framework from John C. Maloney, "Marketing Decision and Attitude Research," in *Effective Marketing Coordination*, George L. Baker, Jr., ed. (Chicago: American Marketing Association, 1961).

by the market. For example, Drake University wanted to attract more students from the Chicago area by emphasizing that Drake was "away from home" but near enough to Chicago to get home quickly. Billboards were used near O'Hare Airport and a Loop-bound expressway announcing, "Drake University: Only 65 minutes from O'Hare to Des Moines."

**Message Evaluation and Selection.** The task of selecting the best message out of a large number of possibilities calls for evaluation criteria. Dick Warren Twedt has suggested that contending messages be rated on three scales: *desirability, exclusiveness,* and *believability.*[12] He believes that the communications potency of a message is the product of the three factors because if any of the three has a low rating, the message's communications potency will be greatly reduced.

The message must first say something desirable or interesting about the program or institution. This is not enough, however, since others may be making the same or very similar claims. Therefore, the message must also say something exclusive or distinctive. Finally, the message must be believable or provable. If consumers are asked to rate different messages on desirability, exclusiveness, and believability, these messages can be evaluated for their communications potency.

Messages can be tested through focus groups (including electronic focus groups described in Chapter 3) and other methods described later under ad pretesting.

**Message Execution.** The *words* must be memorable and attention-getting, especially in the headlines and slogans that lead the reader into the ad. There are six basic types of headlines: news ("New Music Program for Senior Citizens"); question ("Having Trouble Helping Johnny Do Homework?"); narrative ("I'll Be Marching Down the Aisle with My Son in June"); command ("Put Some Class in Your Life"); 1-2-3 ways ("6 Ways to Get Ahead at Work"); and how-what-why ("What You Should Know About College").

Any message can be put across in different execution styles. Suppose a multicampus community college district wants to encourage enrollment in evening programs for career training and job upgrading. The budget will stretch to allow locally broadcast 30-second television spots to motivate people to sign up for this program. Here are some major advertising execution styles that can be considered:

**1.** *Slice-of-life.* An interviewer regretfully tells a woman in her mid-thirties that she just doesn't have the educational requirements for the job she wants. The same woman, in a number of quick shots, is similarly turned down by other interviewers. She thinks to herself, "I'm going to take advantage of Western Community College's new programs." In the next scene, an interviewer (perhaps the original one!) stands up, shakes her hand, and congratulates her on earning the qualifications and getting the new job.

**2.** *Lifestyle.* A small group of men and women on a coffee break wearily share their ideas on what they have planned for that evening. When the round robin of mundane, boring suggestions finally comes around to Jane, she says brightly, "I'm starting my new class at Western Community College. It sounds really interesting, and I can upgrade my skills to get that promotion in the data-processing department." Everyone congratulates her and then sinks back—thinking of his or her own dull evenings ahead.

**3.** *Fantasy.* Jane steps forward to get a transfer from the bus driver. She imagines him as the college president in a cap and gown, proudly handing her a diploma. The bus full of weary commuters becomes a smiling crowd of well-wishers as she joyfully realizes her dream of finishing college.

**4.** *Mood.* The camera catches campus scenes of students laughing and joking, helping each other with homework, asking questions in lectures, and cheering a school team. The entire mood is upbeat, aware, alert, fast paced, and convivial.

**5.** *Musical.* The strains of "Pomp and Circumstance" are interspersed with collegiate songs and currently popular music while the film shows appropriate scenes from college life matching the music.

**6.** *Personality symbol.* "Western Woody," the college's cartoon mascot, gives a Western College cheer and urges listeners to come to the Open House.

**7.** *Technical expertise.* A number of job-placement counselors and employment recruiters introduce themselves and talk briefly of the success they've had in placing graduates of Western Community College's evening programs.

**8.** *Scientific evidence.* An economist presents the evidence of increased earnings potentials for graduates of programs similar to those of Western Community College, and the results of studies on the increased job satisfaction for the graduates.

**9.** *Testimonial evidence.* The ad shows a number of recent program graduates saying such things as, "This is my new office!" and "This is my new paycheck!"

The communicator must also choose the *tone* for the ad. The ad could be serious, chatty, humorous, and so on. The tone must be appropriate to the target audience and target response desired.

*Format* elements such as ad size, color, and illustration will make a difference in an ad's impact as well as its cost. A rearrangement of elements within the ad may also improve its attention-getting power. For example, large ads and four-color ads gain more attention, but these advantages must be weighed against the additional cost.

The importance of specific formal elements varies from one medium to another. If the message is to be carried in a print ad, the communicator has to develop the elements of headline, copy, illustration, and color. If the message is to be carried over the radio, the communicator has to carefully choose words and voice qualities (speech rate, rhythm, pitch, articulation). The "sound" of an announcer promoting an educational program has to be different from that of one promoting a used-car dealer. If the message is to be carried on television or given in person, then all of these elements plus body language (nonverbal cues) have to be planned. Presenters have to pay attention to their facial expressions, gestures, dress, posture, and hair style.

A study of television and print advertising found that the ads that scored above average in recall and recognition had the following characteristics: innovation (new product or new uses), "story appeal" (as an attention-getting device), before-and-after illustration, demonstrations, problem solution, and the inclusion of relevant characters that become emblematic of the brand (cartoon figures or actual people, who are not necessarily celebrities).[13]

### Select Media

Media selection is another major step in advertising planning. Some media thinking should take place before the message-development stage and even before the advertising-budget stage to determine which media are used by the target audience and which are most efficient costwise in reaching it. This information affects the size of the advertising budget and even the type of appeal to use.

There are three basic steps in the media selection process: choosing among major media categories, selection of specific media vehicles, and timing.

**Choosing Among Major Media Categories.**  The first step is to determine how the advertising budget will be allocated to the major media categories. The media planner has to examine the major media categories for their capacity to deliver reach, frequency, and results. Table 14-3 presents the major advertising media in order of their advertising volume: newspapers, television, direct mail, radio, magazines, and outdoor. Each major media category has its own advantages and limitations, listed after each media category in the table. Media planners make their choice among these major media types by considering target-audience media habits, what is being offered (can it be demonstrated?), the message, and cost. On the basis of these characteristics, the media planner has to decide on how to allocate the given budget to the major media categories.

**Selecting Specific Media Vehicles.**  The next step is to choose the specific media vehicles within each media type that would produce the desired response in the most cost-effective way.

Consider a business school that wants to advertise executive education programs in the San Francisco area. Possible vehicles include *The Wall Street*

TABLE 14-3   Profiles of major media categories

| MEDIUM | ADVANTAGES | LIMITATIONS |
|---|---|---|
| **Newspapers** | Flexibility; timeliness; good local market coverage; broad acceptance; high believability | Short life, poor reproduction quality; small "pass-along" audience |
| **Television** | Combines sight, sound, and motion; appealing to the senses; high attention; high reach | High absolute cost; high clutter; fleeting exposure; less audience selectivity |
| **Direct mail** | Audience selectivity; flexibility; no ad competition within the same medium; personalization | Relatively high cost; "junk-mail" image |
| **Radio** | Mass use; high geographical and demographic selectivity; low cost | Audio presentation only; lower attention than television; nonstandardized rate structures; fleeting exposure |
| **Magazines** | High geographical and demographic selectivity; credibility and prestige; high-quality reproduction; long life; good pass-along readership | Long ad purchase lead time; some waste circulation; no guarantee of position |
| **Outdoor** | Flexibility; high repeat exposure low cost; low competition | No audience selectivity; creative limitations |

*Journal, Time,* and *Business Week* (each in specially targeted local editions), the *San Francisco Chronicle,* the *San Jose Mercury-News,* and so on. The media planner contacts each vehicle or turns to several volumes put out by Standard Rate and Data that provide circulation and cost data for different ad sizes, color options, ad positions, and numbers of insertions.

Beyond this, the media planner evaluates the different publications on qualitative characteristics such as credibility, prestige, geographical editioning, occupational editioning, reproduction quality, editorial climate, lead time, and psychological impact. The planner makes a final judgment as to which specific vehicles will deliver the best reach, frequency, and results for the money. Professional media planners and buyers are knowledgeable about all these factors and their efforts often make the difference between a well-targeted, high-credibility campaign within budget and a lackluster effort.

Media planners normally calculate the *cost per thousand* persons reached by a particular vehicle. The cost-per-thousand criterion provides a crude initial measure of a media vehicle's exposure value. Several adjustments need to be applied to this initial measure. First, the measure should be adjusted for audience quality. For an executive-program advertisement, a newspaper read by 1 million executives will have an exposure value of 1 million, but, if read by 1 million retirees, would have close to a zero exposure value. In this instance, the media planner will want to weigh the preponderance of top business executives who read *The Wall Street Journal* against the fact that a smaller percentage of *San Jose Mercury-News* and *San Francisco Chronicle* readers happen to be executives. In fact, each publication supplies potential advertisers with detailed readership profiles, so they can evaluate the appropriateness of the publication. Also, many publications now have multiple editions—for example, in a city the size of Chicago a major newspaper would probably have a dozen or more customized editions. The advertiser could have a specific ad placed only in those editions with a heavy representation of business executives.

Second, exposure value should be adjusted for the audience attention probability. Readers of the San Jose and San Francisco papers may pay more attention to ads than do the readers of *The Wall Street Journal*. Third, the exposure value should be adjusted for the editorial quality (prestige and believability) that one vehicle might have over another. Business executives may be more attracted to a program that is advertised in *The Wall Street Journal*.

The business school would also use direct mail to reach executives in area firms. Assuming that appropriate mailing lists are available, direct mail is the most carefully targeted and usually most cost-effective medium. For this reason, colleges purchase mailing lists from American College Testing or use the College Board's Student Search Service, while the executive program would seek out and rent lists of business executives.

**Deciding on Media Timing.** The third step in media selection is timing. One aspect is that of seasonal timing. For most institutions and programs, there is a natural variation in the intensity of interest at different times of the year. Interest in school issues wanes during the summer; high school students may be apathetic about considering colleges until their junior or even senior year. Most marketers prefer to spend the bulk of the advertising budget just as natural interest is beginning to ripen and during the height of interest.

The other aspect is the *short-run timing* of advertising. How should advertising be spaced during a short period—say, a week? Consider these possible patterns: The first is called *burst advertising* and consists of concentrating all the exposures in a very short space of time—say, all in one day. Presumably, this will attract maximum attention and interest, and if recall is good, the effect will last for a while. The second pattern is *continuous advertising*, in which the exposures appear evenly throughout the period. This may be most effective when the audience needs to be continuously reminded. The third pattern is *intermittent advertising*, in which intermittent small bursts of advertising appear in succession, with periods of no advertising in between. This pattern is presumably able to create a little more attention than continuous advertising and yet has some of the reminder advantages of continuous advertising.

## Evaluate Advertising

The final step in the effective use of advertising is that of *advertising evaluation*. The most important components are copy testing, media testing, and expenditure-level testing.

*Copy testing* can occur both before an ad is put into actual media (copy pretesting) and after it has been printed or broadcast (copy posttesting). The purpose of *ad pretesting* is to make improvements in the advertising copy to the fullest extent prior to its release. There are two major methods of ad pretesting:

**1.** *Direct ratings.* Here a panel of target consumers or of advertising experts examines alternative ads and fills out rating questionnaires. Sometimes a single question is raised, such as, "Which of these ads do you think would influence you most to enroll at Pottsville?" Or a more elaborate form consisting of several rating scales may be used, such as the one shown in Figure 14-5. Here the person evaluates the ad's attention strength, read-through strength, cognitive strength, affective strength, and behavioral strength, assigning a number of points (up to a maximum) in each case. The underlying theory is that an effective ad must score high on all these properties if it is ultimately to stimulate taking action. Too often, ads are evaluated only on their attention- or comprehension-creating abilities. At the same time, it must be appreciated that direct-rating methods are judgmental and less reliable than harder evidence of an ad's actual effect on a target consumer. Direct-rating scales help to screen out poor ads rather than to identify great ads.

**2.** *Portfolio tests.* Here respondents are given a dummy portfolio of print ads and asked to take as much time as they want to read them. After putting them down, the respondents are asked to recall the ads they saw—unaided or aided by the interviewers—and to "play back" as much as they can

FIGURE 14-5    Rating sheet for ads

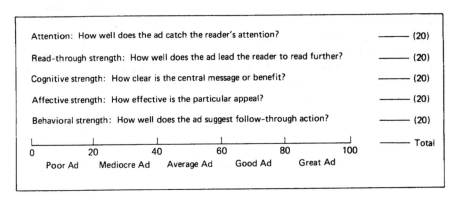

about each ad. The results are taken to indicate an ad's capacity to stand out and to be understood.

There are two popular *ad posttesting* methods, the purpose of which is to assess whether the desired effect is being achieved:

**1.** *Recall tests.* These involve finding people who are regular users of the media vehicle and asking them to recall advertisers and products contained in the issue under study. They are asked to describe everything they can remember. The administrator may or may not aid them in their recall. Recall scores are prepared on the basis of their responses and are used to indicate the power of the ad to be noticed and retained.

**2.** *Recognition tests.* Recognition tests call for sampling the readers of a given issue of the vehicle—say, a magazine—asking them to point out what they recognize as having seen and/or read.

It must be stressed that all these efforts rate the communications effectiveness of the ad and not necessarily its effects on attitudes or behavior, which are much harder to measure. Most advertisers are satisfied to know their ads have been seen and comprehended and are unwilling to spend additional funds to determine the ads' effectiveness.

Another advertising element that is normally tested is media. *Media testing* seeks to determine whether a given media vehicle is cost-effective in reaching and influencing the target audience. A common way to test a media vehicle is to place a coupon ad and see how many coupons are returned. Similarly, an institution can keep track of media vehicles used, their cost, and the number of inquiries generated by each. Another media-testing device is to compare the ad readership scores in different media vehicles as a sign of media effectiveness.

Finally, the advertising-expenditure level itself can be tested. *Expenditure-level testing* involves arranging experiments in which advertising-expenditure levels are varied over similar markets to see the variation in response. A "high-spending" test would consist of spending twice as much money in a territory similar to another to see how much more response (inquiries, applications, and so on) this produces. If the response is only slightly greater in the high-spending territory, it may be concluded, other things being equal, that the lower budget is adequate.

When testing expenditure level it is very important to assign *all* the relevant costs to each project. For example, the media cost for coverage of a campus event may be zero, but the college's public relations office spent parts of many days working with the event's organizers to plan and carry out the event, writing press releases about it, and talking with media representatives to encourage them to cover the story. The staff time alone may be in the thousands of dollars.

## THE EFFECTIVE COMMUNICATIONS PROGRAM

An educational institution's communications program involves public relations, marketing publications, and advertising. A typical school or college issues many communications and wants to get the most benefit from the time and money spent on them.

An effective marketing communications program has several hallmarks. First, effective marketing communications are *coordinated*. Rather than issuing a jumble of bulletins, brochures, and press releases, the institution analyzes its various markets and publics to determine each group's communications needs. It considers what response it wants from each group—for example, donations from alumni and applications from well-prepared high school seniors—and develops a communications program for each. Rather than depending on one communications form or medium, the institution will want to use a carefully planned combination of direct mail, advertising, publicity, and special events to achieve its communications objectives.

The institution will want to use a *single logo* and theme on publications and other communications to increase institutional recognition as well as identification of each communication with the institution. The quality of content and style will be consistent, and layout and production qualities will be appropriate to the communications objective. (For example, a brochure for potential large donors will be more lavish than a listing of the coming semester's course schedule.) To achieve quality and consistency, the institution will need one or more highly skilled professionals who review all official publications and, at the very least, have an opportunity to recommend improvements before publication and dissemination. This function may be headed by a director of communications.

Where possible, the institution will want to *personalize* its communications. With word processing and computerized address lists, the admissions office can send personalized communications even in very large mailings. Other communications to current students, parents, and donors can likewise include a personal salutation. Despite broad awareness that many letters are "computer generated," such touches still reflect well on the institution that uses them. Beware of defeating their effect by "signing" such personalized communications with a rubber stamp!

Effective marketing communications are *authentic*. There is no place for deception or puffery. Those who visit the college or decide to enroll will soon find the gaps and be resentful. Furthermore, an educational institution cannot and should not present inconsistent pictures of itself and its offerings to different groups. For example, admissions brochures and other recruiting communications should meet a "reality-test" review by currently enrolled students and others who are knowledgeable about the institution. And of course the institution should not tell falsehoods in the name of making the institution "look good." Exhibit 14-2 presents the credo of Bob Beyers, formerly Director of the News Service at Stanford.

Finally, educational institutions must remember that an effective marketing communications program, although important, is but one element in the institution's marketing effort. The institution must ensure its performance and viability through sound program, pricing, and distribution decisions as well.

## SUMMARY

Every educational institution constantly communicates about itself through its programs, students, alumni, campus, and formal communications program. Communications form one of the key elements of the marketing mix. The main types of marketing communications are public relations, marketing publications, and advertising.

Planning an effective communication involves (1) identifying the target audience, (2) clarifying the response sought, (3) developing a message, (4) choosing the medium or media, (5) selecting source attributes, and (6) collecting feedback.

The task of public relations is to form, maintain, or change public attitudes toward the institution. The process of public relations consists of five steps: (1) identifying the institution's relevant publics, (2) measuring the images and attitudes held by these publics, (3) establishing image and attitude goals for the key publics, (4) developing cost-effective public relations strategies, and (5) implementing actions and evaluating results.

Public relations practitioners must be skilled communicators, adept at developing written material, institutional-identity media, news releases,

EXHIBIT 14-2    Telling the truth

Few if any educational institutions set out to mislead their publics, but some, driven by the desire to "put their best foot forward," may issue communications that present a sanitized version of reality, which may ultimately hurt the institution.

In contrast, Bob Beyers, the long-time director of Stanford University's News Service (now retired), always started from the position that "in times of crisis, candor pays:" "If the institution makes no effort to tell both sides of a controversy, it relinquishes that function to the media . . . and/or its critics." He added a remark sometimes attributed to Henry Ford II: "The facts about this place can never be as bad as the fiction."

What makes Bob Beyers's approach remarkable is that it stands in stark contrast to what is routinely considered good college public relations. On most campuses, the emphasis is still on telling only what's good about the college, while doggedly trying to prevent bad news from getting out. Beyers held that such an approach was ineffective: "Any institution that tries to hide its warts will lose its esteem first with its own constituents, later with the general public."

Over the years, Beyers had a good deal of experience with skeptical colleagues at other colleges who are convinced—probably with good reason—that similar devotion to candor would threaten their job security. He had an object lesson for them: "Bad news may have good results. Once, quite a few Stanford faculty members were upset when one of their colleagues was quoted in *Time* magazine as saying that the library was the worst he'd ever seen at a major university. Yet that frankness helped the campus attract an outstanding librarian—and he, in turn, promptly enlisted the critic's support in building a better collection."

Source: Based on Fred M. Hechinger, "To Tell the Truth," *Change* (April 1978), pp. 56–57. Reprinted with permission of The Helen Dwight Reid Educational Foundation. Published by Heldref Publications, 1319 18th Street N.W., Washington, DC 20036.

events, speeches, and telephone information services, and at facilitating favorable personal contact by administrators and others associated with the institution.

Marketing publications include direct-mail pieces including viewbooks, prospectuses, catalogs, brochures, fact sheets, and many other publications addressing specific marketing needs. Virtually every institutional publication is a marketing publication, and the most obvious use of marketing publications is in admissions, development/fund raising, and public relations.

Advertising consists of nonpersonal forms of communication conducted through paid media under clear sponsorship. While some educators resist the idea of paid advertising, every institution that produces catalogs, bulletins, and direct mail is already engaged in advertising. With careful planning, the institution can make its advertising more effective.

An advertising program calls for five major decisions: (1) setting the advertising objectives, (2) determining the advertising budget, (3) deciding on the message, (4) selecting media, and (5) evaluating advertising effectiveness. The institution should identify the target audience, describe the desired response, and determine the target reach and frequency. The advertising budget can be set based on what is affordable and what is required to accomplish the institution's advertising objectives.

The message decision calls for generating messages, evaluating and selecting among them, and executing them effectively. The media decision calls for choosing among major media categories, selecting specific media vehicles, and deciding on media timing. Finally, evaluating advertising results helps to determine the cost-effectiveness of the advertising and to suggest changes in future advertising.

An effective communications program requires strong professional skills and cannot be left to chance. The institution's publications should be reviewed for quality and consistency of content and style. Wherever possible, communications should be personalized. The institution should ensure that communications are accurate and do not use puffery.

## Notes

1. See Thomas S. Robertson, *Innovative Behavior and Communications* (New York: Holt, Rinehart & Winston, 1971), Chap. 9.

2. Herbert C. Kelman and Carl I. Hovland, "'Reinstatement' of the Communicator in Delayed Measurement of Opinion Change," *Journal of Abnormal and Social Psychology*, 48 (1953), pp. 327–335.

3. Ken Arnold, "Principal: The First Two Letters are P.R.," *Thrust* (October 1977), p. 28.

4. Gerald S. Nagel, "How Can I Improve the Image of the College?" *Community College Review* (Summer 1981), pp. 24–27.

5. Thomas Huddleston, Jr., "Getting It Together," *Techniques* (American College Public Relations Association), April 1974, pp. 7–8.

6. Richard M. Canterbury, "Fifty Days of Unsolicited Mail from Colleges," *The Journal of College Admissions*, no. 125 (Fall 1989), pp. 11–14.

7. See Arthur H. Glogau, "Advertising Higher Education," *College and University Journal* (Spring 1964), pp. 34–39, for examples of higher education advertising through the centuries.

8. Edward Everett Hale, *Harvard*, Outlook, February 27, 1909, p. 457.

9. There are several models of buyer-readiness states. For a discussion of these models and their implications for advertising, see Richard Vaughn, "The Consumer Mind: How to Tailor Ad Strategies," *Advertising Age*, June 9, 1980, pp. 45–46.

10. Michael L. Ray, *Marketing Communication and the Hierarchy of Effects* (Cambridge, MA: Marketing Science Institute, November 1973).

11. See John C. Maloney, "Marketing Decisions and Attitude Research," in George L. Baker, Jr., ed., *Effective Marketing Coordination* (Chicago: American Marketing Association, 1961).

12. Dick Warren Twedt, "How to Plan New Products, Improve Old Ones, and Create Better Advertising," *Journal of Marketing* (January 1969), pp. 53–57.

13. David Ogilvy and Joel Raphaelson, "Research on Advertising Techniques That Work—and Don't Work," *Harvard Business Review* (July-August 1982), pp. 14–18.

# V

# Applying Marketing

# 15

# Attracting and Retaining Students

*Hood College, in western Maryland, blossomed in the 1970s. Enrollments tripled, annual giving shot up more than sevenfold, budgets roller coasted from surplus to deficit to surplus again, and a graduate school came into being—all signs of vitality that seers would hardly have predicted for a small-town liberal arts college for women, particularly in early 1973.*

*In that year, Hood's admissions picture was bleak. In seven of the eight preceding years, the number of students enrolled declined. The outlook for the fall term of 1973 was grim, for even the most optimistic estimates indicated that fewer than 160 students would matriculate. Hood's situation was not unique: Many women's colleges were experiencing application declines, and in response, many went coed; but Hood decided to remain a women's college. The key question for Hood was how to stop and reverse the enrollment decline.*

*Fortunately, in 1973 Hood College enjoyed a reputation as a sound, well-managed institution, providing a quality liberal arts education for young women, and was highly regarded in the region—the Middle Atlantic states and southern New England. Furthermore, Hood revitalized its academic program, incorporating practica, internships, and volunteer work in career-relevant areas. These strengths did not prevent Hood from facing an enrollment decline but did make it better prepared to take action to reverse it.*

*The new president brought two consultants to campus in April 1973. Their first task was to institute measures to attract every possible prospect for that fall. One stopgap measure involved the design, production, and distribution of a poster-folder, which was sent to selected high schools for posting as well as to every high school student whose name was still on Hood's prospect list. The poster-folder was sent to alumnae to give them an understanding of the college at that time, as well as to urge them to refer the names of prospective students. Under the direction of the consultants, the admissions staff phoned every admitted student who had not yet made a commitment to attend Hood. When the college opened in the fall, 170 of the 176 new students who had made deposits matriculated.*

*But these were only temporary measures. The real job lay in creating and implementing a program to attract many more students for the next year. The president's goal was to enroll 250 new freshmen in September 1974, an increase of almost 50 percent over 1973, and then to further strengthen the college to increase its attractiveness to students.*

*In the 1980s the college undertook an extensive planning process. Every department proposal must correspond to specific all-campus goals and objectives. In 1982 President Martha Church said, "We really do know what we want to do over the next several years. We want to be recognized at the national level as being an outstanding women's college that responds to the educational concerns of women at any age. We're not there now, but that's a goal."*

*Hood College has achieved many of its forward-looking goals, and as of 1993 the college had been highly ranked for academic excellence numerous times in published rankings of college quality. The college promotes the fact that*

- *its location "combines small city convenience and metropolitan resources"*
- *its programs and services are designed specifically for the students it serves*
- *its emphasis is on teaching*
- *it prepares students for the future*
- *and that it offers outstanding academic and physical resources.*

*The college's mission is the touchstone for its actions. The first paragraph of its mission statement, adopted by the Board of Trustees in 1990, states:*

> *Hood College is a contemporary, private institution of higher learning whose mission is twofold: to educate*

*women from throughout the nation and abroad and to pro-
vide professional preparation of women and men from the
region. Drawing on a deep and longstanding commitment
to the principles of a liberal arts education, Hood offers a
comprehensive curriculum of academic programs. Distinctive of a Hood education are the blending of the liberal arts
with preparation for professions and the balance between
general and specialized learning that serves as the best
foundation for life.*

**Sources:** Based on Donna Shoemaker, "Institutional Strategies: Hood College," *Educational Record* (Winter 1982), pp.
53–57; "A Case History of How a College Increased Its Freshman Enrollment 100% in One Year," *Insights* (June–July 1974),
pp. 1-14; George Keller, *Academic Strategy* (Baltimore, MD:
The Johns Hopkins University Press, 1983), pp. 77–80; and the
*Hood College Catalog 1993–94.*

Students provide most educational institutions with their reason for being.
Without students, schools would close their doors, not just because tuition
revenues would drop but because the schools would no longer have clients to receive the classes, counseling, and other services that the institutions were established to provide. And they would stop graduating new
alumni who in future would provide financial support and recognition for
the institution.

Recruiting students has been going on for millennia. Itinerant teachers
in ancient Greece relied on tuition from their student followers. In the nine-
teenth century, new American land-grant colleges frequently had to promote
the advantages of college study among a primarily rural population, using brochures and scholarship offers to attract first-time college-goers.

The rapid post-World War II expansion of public colleges, universities,
and community colleges, together with increased financial aid and government loan programs, encouraged many more high school graduates to consider higher education. During this era of expansion, many institutions were
flooded with applicants. At many private colleges the admissions director's
task was to select the best applicants for admission and send rejection letters
to the rest.

Times changed. The complacency that characterized many college admissions officers in the late 1970s evaporated during the 1980s and the competition to attract the most desirable students has intensified in the 1990s.
Many educational institutions are preparing new promotional literature, in-

creasing recruiting budgets, increasing travel, and spending more time and money on marketing research studies and direct mail.

As competition increases, colleges usually adopt one of three responses. Some proceed to do more of what they have been doing in the past: The admission director hires more admissions counselors to make more high school visits; the brochures are printed in four colors with new photographs, and more are mailed. This approach may temporarily attract more interest but is doomed to failure from the start. This we would term a *selling* approach, focusing on ways to "sell" the college and its programs.

A second group of schools takes the selling approach a step further, turning to the *hard sell*, believing that since heavy media advertising seems to sell beer and toothpaste, it will have a tremendous effect on applications and enrollment. The school may even come up with gimmicks and "deals" to attract more of the available students to attend. As part of the hard sell approach, admissions counselors are urged to try to convince each prospect that the school can deliver exactly what he or she wants. In desperation, some schools turn to recruiting wealthy if not always academically able students, and/or hire aggressive recruiters who receive commissions for each student who enrolls.

The result of a hard-sell approach is often an advertising glut, potential applicants turned off on the school, and disappointed enrollees who will soon drop out and discourage their friends from applying. Moreover, the admissions director will be looking for new admissions staff, since the professional admissions counselors will balk at misrepresenting what the school has to offer. In fact, if the school has so little to offer prospective students, the trustees and top administration should take a searching look at the school's mission and programs and consider if it should redirect its efforts or even close down.

A third group of schools turns to a marketing approach. They conduct marketing research to understand students' wants and needs. They provide programs and services that match the institution's mission and resources as well as students' needs. They schedule and locate, price, and promote offerings to attract and serve students' needs. These institutions reflect a commitment to educate and to serve.

The preceding chapters have presented the marketing approach. In this chapter, we consider the steps in applying marketing to student recruitment, from identifying problems through designing programs for student retention. We will use Hood College's experience and that of other institutions to illustrate the process. Although most of the examples are drawn from colleges and universities, the underlying issues and the critical tasks are quite similar for private elementary and secondary institutions.

This chapter presents the steps in the student-recruitment process and then discusses ways to measure and increase student satisfaction to improve retention.

## THE STUDENT-RECRUITMENT PROCESS

The student-recruitment process consists of the following steps:

1. Identify enrollment problems and needs in relation to resources and mission.
2. Define enrollment goals and objectives in line with institutional strategy.
3. Conduct research to segment the potential student market, to identify target markets, to understand the student decision process, and to determine market size and potential.
4. Determine the marketing strategy for recruitment, including the target market(s), marketing mix, and marketing expenditure level.
5. Plan and implement action programs.
6. Evaluate results and procedures, including cost-effectiveness of recruitment efforts and satisfaction of enrolled students.

We will consider each step in turn.

### Identify Problems

The first step is to identify the institution's problems as they may affect the institution's ability to attract and retain students. Declining enrollment is rarely the only problem an educational institution faces, but other problems are often overlooked until significant difficulties in enrolling new students galvanize the administration into full consciousness of the institution's plight. The curriculum may be outdated, or nearby institutions may have built up higher-quality, competitive programs, but these may not be perceived as serious threats until they take their toll on enrollment.

To get a picture of the institution's application and enrollment situation, the trends should be graphed. Figure 15-1 shows Hood College's total applicants, total acceptances, and total new students enrolled for 15 years. The highest number of applications and acceptances came in 1965, after which the number of applications began to decline sharply at Hood and most other women's colleges. The graph shows that as applications declined, a higher percentage were admitted. The admissions staff worked doubly hard to keep in contact with those admitted to encourage them to enroll.

What can the college expect if no corrective action is taken? The college should make enrollment estimates based on the most objective data available, perhaps indicating two or three alternative scenarios. Figure 15-2 projects what would happen to Hood's enrollment if the trends of the previous five years were to continue. The modest increases in new transfer students could not compensate for continued declines in new freshmen. Corrective action was necessary if Hood was to regain the enrollment levels of the past.

Graphing application and enrollment trends and projections can help document the extent of the enrollment problem, but alone they shed little light on the factors contributing to the decline. In Chapter 6, we presented approaches to assessing the institutions' strengths, weaknesses, threats, and op-

FIGURE 15-1 Applicants, acceptances, and matriculants at Hood College, 1960–1974

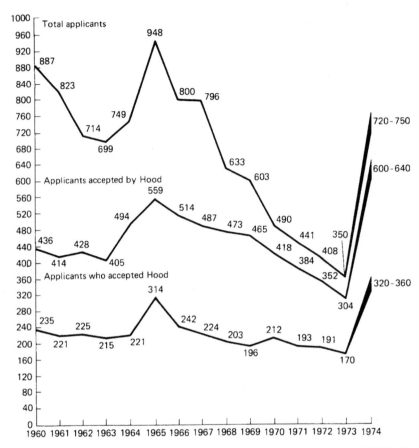

Source: "A Case History of How a College Increased Its Freshmen Enrollment 100% in One Year," *Insights*, June–July 1974, p. 2.

portunities. At the end of this chapter, we present guidelines for enrollment management. In Chapter 17, we present a checklist for auditing the institution's marketing effectiveness. The institution's leaders must thoroughly review the findings of these analyses to guide necessary changes in curriculum, services, teaching quality, and other aspects in addition to admissions.

## Define Goals and Objectives

The school's administration must decide on appropriate recruitment and admissions goals and objectives in line with its overall institutional strategy. For

FIGURE 15-2    Projections of enrollment trends

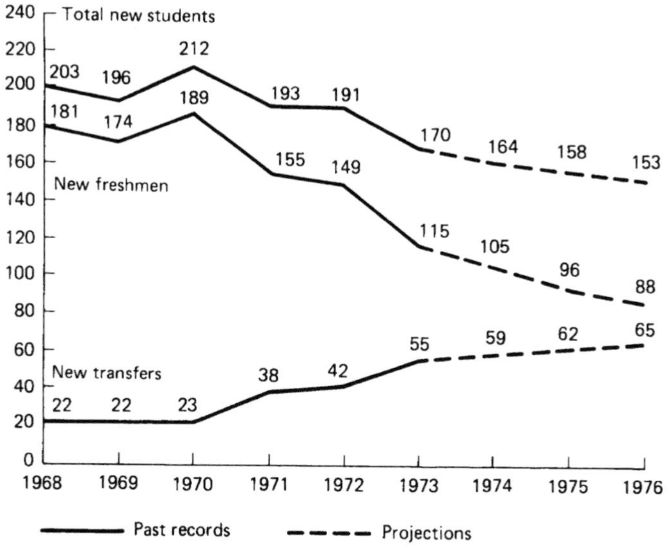

Source: "A Case History of How a College Increased Its Freshmen Enrollment 100% in One Year," *Insights*, June–July 1974, p. 3.

example, a college's goal may be to maintain the number and quality of students enrolled; to increase overall enrollment; to improve the quality of admitted students; to attract a certain number of students to a new program; or
some other goal. A school's specific situation and goals will shape its admissions objectives and specific actions to achieve them.

In Hood's case, admissions had become increasingly less selective over
the years preceding 1973. The president's stated objective was to enroll 250 new
freshmen in September 1974. The longer-term objective was to increase the
total number of new students (freshman, transfer, and continuing education) to
350, the capacity of the existing physical facilities. Then, by increasing the number of applicants, the college hoped to become progressively more selective.

Setting enrollment objectives raises three questions. First, what is the
institution's optimal level of student enrollment? This number is often based
on historical experience or on the highest number of students ever enrolled.
As long as residence-hall space and other housing do not impose constraints
on size, tuition-dependent schools often yearn to accommodate as many tuition-paying students as possible by increasing class size. Calculating optimum
class size is difficult. There is no formula for answering the question, Will the
freshman writing courses be more effective if each section is capped at 20 students rather than at 22 students?

The second question is, What level of enrollment can the institution realistically expect to draw? Setting realistic enrollment objectives requires good data and careful analysis. The initial enrollment objective may be based on strong optimism, but the operational enrollment objective—for determining budgets and staffing—must be based on strong data. Chapter 8 on forecasting market size provides useful approaches.

Third, what level of student quality does the school want to serve? Most schools want to attract academically talented students, but many do not have the faculty, curricula, and other attributes that permit them to compete with academically elite institutions for these students. Nonelite colleges need to be realistic about whom they can serve well, keeping in mind that an effective college academic program can make a tremendous contribution—"added value"—to students who may enter with weak academic backgrounds and skills. For example, Erskine College, a Presbyterian college in South Carolina, enrolls students with average SAT scores in the mid-to-high 400s. It graduates three-fourths of its entering freshmen, 32 percent of whom continue to graduate and professional schools.[1]

When application rates are softening may be a constructive time to consider these questions. Top administration and the admissions office should review the institution's resource commitments (people and buildings), along with financial, demographic, and other marketing-relevant data that bear on these decisions. The result should be a realistic target enrollment and quality level to guide planning for housing, student services, faculty hiring, and course planning and scheduling, as well as admissions.

In addition to setting goals for the number and quality of entering students, the admissions director should consider other recruiting and admissions goals and objectives. Hood's admissions office established five promotion goals:

1. To change the image of the college from a good traditional girls' school to an exciting, high-quality college for women, which emphasizes the new women's concerns and careers in a personable atmosphere.
2. To more effectively communicate the "new" image of the college to a target audience in particular market segments.
3. To improve the publications program—better appeals and more information, expanded use of printed materials.
4. To expand the inquiry base through increased mailings, posters, advertising, special events, career workshops, counselor luncheons, and alumnae.
5. To better promote financial aid, early acceptance, transfer programs, and career-oriented curricula.[2]

To carry out these goals the admissions office established specific objectives—school visits, campus events, interviews, and professional training, among others. This listing of goals and objectives, combined with marketing research, provides the basis for setting marketing strategy.

## Conduct Marketing Research

Marketing research can help the institution answer such questions as these:

- What have been our rates of applications, acceptances, and enrollments over the past several years?
- What are the market size and potential?
- Who are our primary and secondary markets?
- What are the characteristics of our current students?
- What are the characteristics of applicants who are accepted and do not enroll?
- What sources of information do they use in the college-decision process?
- Who are the college's competitors?

Many admissions offices already have vast amounts of data on inquiries, school visits made, number of interviews, applications, and so forth. These data are often ignored when times are good; and when demand shifts, the admissions staff is often so pressured to "do something" that the data continue to gather dust while the staff intensifies its activities. Yet these data are important indicators of what the institution has done with what effect, and they must receive close scrutiny. Hood's admissions-office staff pulled together records on the number of inquiries, applications, deposits, rejections, acceptances, matriculants, high school and junior college visits, campus interviews, annual reports, monthly breakdowns, and any other data relevant to the admissions picture. Where unavailable, the data were reconstructed as closely as possible. Past admissions efforts were reviewed.[3]

The data must be compiled and presented in a format that can be used in decision making. This usually means graphing it to show trends over the past five to ten years. The school will want to graph (as with Figure 15-1 on Hood College) the number of applicants, acceptances, and matriculants. In addition, the admissions staff can easily calculate the various *yield ratios* and graph those—number of acceptances divided by number of applications, number of acceptances divided by number of applications, number of matriculants divided by number of acceptances, and number of matriculants divided by number of applications. With a spreadsheet and graphics software, these data can be recorded and displayed quickly.

Where tuition revenues are based on number of courses taken rather than number of students enrolled, the admissions staff should also review trends in the total number of credit hours taken each term over the past several years. For example, the part-time M.B.A. program in a university school of business found enrollment numbers down, but the total number of credit hours was equal to that of the previous year—indicating that there were fewer students, but they were taking more units. Schools with significant part-time enrollments should graph the average number of units per student over a period of several years to determine trends in course loads. If a school wants to maintain a certain level of tuition revenue and the average number of units per student is dropping, the school must either encourage students to take more courses or recruit additional students to close the tuition-revenue gap.

Analyzing the characteristics of current students helps to identify where the college should recruit and what types of students it is likely to attract. As a rule, an educational institution will have an easier time attracting students like its current students than attracting prospects who are significantly different. From student records, the institution can create a profile of current students by age, sex, place of residence, type of prior school attended, academic background, test scores, and academic performance at the current institution. A residential college can usually identify its primary and secondary markets by noting the locations and characteristics of the high schools from which applicants come. Much of these data can come from the College Board and can be combined to show differences in yield over several years.

An institution's *primary market* is one from which it receives a large number of applications over time and from which a high percentage of accepted students typically decide to enroll. The primary market may be defined in terms of individual secondary schools, a number of secondary schools, or a given geographical area. Typically, a high percentage of primary-market candidates who submit applications are accepted and elect to attend the institution. Often an institution will find that its primary market is located within a 300- or even 100-mile radius of the institution, although this is not always the case. One small Kansas college has a primary market in Pennsylvania, where many members of the college's sponsoring church make their homes.

A *secondary market* is one from which the school has received a steady flow of applications over a period of three to five years but from which few of the admitted students have enrolled. The secondary market is substantially larger in area and number of potential applicants than the primary market, but the institution's yield rate is lower.[4]

Colleges that use the Scholastic Aptitude Test of the College Entrance Examination Board can obtain detailed analysis of applicant and enrollment data. The College Board can provide participating schools with the school's yield ratios with respect to characteristics of the school's applicants, accepted students, and enrollees and those of college-bound high school seniors in the region and nation, as well as the school's success in relation to its major competitors. With this information, the school can examine its success in attracting students.

Colleges receiving at least 100 SAT score reports automatically receive a listing of the top high schools from which applicants come. More detailed information can be obtained, including breakdowns for each high school by sex, SAT mean score, high school percentile rank, estimated parental contribution, and chosen area of study. This report helps identify the high schools that should receive admissions-office attention. A comparison with past years would reveal changes in the importance of specific feeder high schools. Another report helps define the college's competition by ranking the colleges most frequently applied to by applicants to the college. The American College Testing Program provides similar reports for colleges that use its score results.

In summary, the most important information for recruiting and admissions purposes may already exist in some form. The task is to locate it, organize it, express it in usable form (often graphically), and then draw conclusions from the data that can guide the choice of actions. The most crucial step is to implement the plan that grows out of the data. Too often, the available data are ignored, and planning is based on hunches rather than on available information.

Although existing data can answer many questions, institutional research is usually needed to answer questions that will affect recruiting strategy. The institution will want to know what attracted some students to apply and enroll, whereas others chose to attend another school. Many institutions survey admitted students and those who inquired, whether or not they followed through with an application. Typical surveys ask for respondents' personal and academic characteristics; their evaluation of the school in comparison with specific other colleges to which they applied; their evaluation of various contacts with the school and other sources of information; and a comparison of financial aid offers. The process of conducting a "matriculant/nonmatriculant survey" has been greatly simplified by the service offered by the College Board, which provides standard "admitted student questionnaires," with one version tailored (and color-coded) to go to admitted students who plan to enroll and another form to go to admitted students who have decided to attend elsewhere. Extensive analyses, including detailed comparisons with competing institutions, are provided.

Hood College conducted a survey as part of its admissions research program. A key part of the market research was an opinion-and-attitudes questionnaire that produced an 87% return from 1,000 students and young women who had inquired about Hood in 1972-73. The questions were framed by professionals so the answers would best reveal the respondent's evaluation of the weaknesses and strengths of the college as well as the factors that played a part in the candidate's decision—whether that decision was for or against the college.

This questionnaire was administered, in written form, to freshmen and upperclassmen at Hood, keeping the responses of these two groups separate for analysis. The same questionnaire was administered by phone to a list of "lost acceptances" and "lost inquiries" to see what motivated these women to turn down Hood for another college.[5]

With the results of such surveys, the school can prepare a profile description of the students who choose to attend and those who go elsewhere.

This *student profile* summarizes the student characteristics that will influence the recruiting and admissions process. If the college is satisfied with students who fit the current profile, the admission staff may decide to continue recruiting in the same or similar high schools. The college may believe it can take steps to attract and serve those who now attend other colleges; or it may conclude that those students would be dissatisfied and/or would not be good prospects for the college.

If it finds it is losing good prospects, the college will want to determine what changes in recruiting, financial aid, academic programs, or other areas would be required to successfully attract them, and then institute changes where appropriate. To attract students who are significantly different from the current profile, the college will need to segment and select target markets, then develop an attractive marketing mix to reach and serve each target market.

The institution will also want to carry out studies of the factors that weigh most heavily in students' application and enrollment decisions, of who has an influence on such decisions, of rates of retention and of transfer to other institutions, of the relative attractiveness of competing institutions, and of other factors that bear on student attraction and retention. To attract participants to short courses and special events, the institution should ask current participants what media they use in order to identify places to promote future programs.

The college will also want to know the size of its potential student market by various categories, discussed in Chapter 8. The potential market for any one institution will be shaped by numerous institutional characteristics and by demographic realities.

### Determine Marketing Strategy

Marketing strategy includes selecting the most promising target markets; setting the various components of the marketing mix; and setting the marketing expenditure level. Once the strategy is determined, the school can plan for implementation.

**Selecting Target Markets.** If recruiting resources were unlimited, every institution could attempt to appeal to each potential student. In practice, such a strategy is unworkable and wasteful, since recruiting is expensive and each institution can serve only a small percentage of the total available market. Instead, each institution focuses its attention on selected target-market segments.

At the undergraduate level, state universities focus their recruiting on graduates of high schools in their states. At the graduate level, specific departments may target the best graduating seniors in those disciplines from colleges in the region or the entire nation. Church-sponsored institutions usually target church members, although some are broadening their appeals. For example, North Park College in Chicago is the only college in the United States under the auspices of the Evangelical Covenant Church and recruits church members nationwide. But as church members are no longer as concentrated in the Chicago area and increasingly attend other colleges, North Park College has begun serving neighborhood teenagers whose Korean-immigrant families want them to attend a conservative, safe college nearby.

Target-market selection requires a thorough understanding of the topics presented in earlier chapters, including determining the characteristics of current students, consumer decision-making processes, key demographic and other macroenvironmental trends, and the institution's mission, resources, and goals. The institution must then segment its current and potential markets and determine where it can best meet the needs of potential students. Existing data, together with additional marketing research, can reveal the most important student characteristics and the sources of information upon which students base their decisions to apply and enroll. This understanding is essential for planning a sound recruitment program.

Hood College's decision to remain a women's college guided its choice of three target markets. First, the college continued to seek recent high school graduates who would be attracted to a women's college for "the modern woman." Second, the college set up a continuing education program to attract older women students. Third, it began an intensive program for Hispanic women, often underrepresented in higher education. In addition, the college now enrolls some local men as commuter students, but this is not a target market for Hood.

**Setting the Marketing Mix.** Previous chapters have discussed the seven elements of the marketing mix for services: people and processes, programs and packaging, price, place—location and delivery systems—and promotion. Each selected target market may require a different marketing mix, or at least some modification of the basic marketing mix. For example, when Hood decided to serve Hispanic women, it built on a strong Spanish department and a three-year grant from the Fund for Improvement of Post-Secondary Education to develop a bilingual, bicultural curriculum and to sensitize the campus to the special needs of these women.

Developing the appropriate marketing mix calls on aspects of the entire institution. To be attractive to prospects, an educational institution must provide a sound and appropriate educational program, at a price students and their families are willing and able to pay (with assistance as necessary), in a reasonably attractive place. All these features need to be communicated to prospective students in a timely, interesting, and accurate manner.

Often this communications task is deemed the only responsibility of the admissions office. In fact, the chief enrollment/admissions officer should be involved in all institutional planning that affects programs and services for students (including residence life), tuition and financial-aid planning, and other key decisions that will influence the institution's attractiveness to current and prospective students. The admissions officer knows the school's enrollment history and trends and has information directly from students about their desires and impressions.

Where joint planning is ignored or when key decisions are not communicated to the admissions director, unanticipated problems can arise:

A university seeking to increase occupancy rates in the residence halls decided to upgrade all the rooms by installing cable-TV and computer connections to the university computer network. This was a very attractive combination for enrolled students considering moving off-campus, and was also featured in a colorful brochure on housing options that was mailed to all admitted freshmen students.

Only then was it learned that the cost of upgrading the electrical wiring to support TVs and computers was greater than budgeted, and that the project would have to be delayed, perhaps for a year. The admissions director faced the prospect of disappointed students when they discovered the university had not delivered on its promise.

The chief admissions officer should also have a sound grasp of societal trends that may affect enrollment, and opportunities to share those insights. Ignoring these insights in the planning process leads to situations like this one:

When the first information-science major in the country was developed at a private college some time ago, the enthusiastic chairman of the department anticipated that several hundred freshmen would be attracted to it the first year. The admissions director suggested that 25 would be more realistic; and the matriculated statistic in September proved to be 23.

While the chairman knew that information science was a good program for eventual employment, he did not realize that high school counselors were not yet briefed that this major dealt with computers; parents were not prepared to pay for a course of study they did not understand; and, for the most part, high school seniors had already made other career college choices by the time the college's new program was announced.[6]

Had the admissions director been closely involved in planning, he could have pointed out the need to train admissions staff and high school counselors on information science and could have curbed the enthusiasm of the department chairperson.

The admissions office typically controls the communications function as it relates to recruiting students. The admissions staff will prepare (or direct the preparation of) brochures, letters, and other mailings to prospects and applicants; attend college fairs and college nights; arrange campus visits and make visits to high schools; and maintain contact with high school and community college personnel who may advise or refer students. (Private pre-collegiate institutions will use variations of these activities.)

The admissions office must plan an appropriate, cost-effective communication program for each target market. Figure 15-3 shows the questions the planners should consider in preparing the recruitment strategy. A community college mandated to serve the entire community will probably send periodic mailings to all area households in addition to holding information sessions for high school seniors, reentry students, and other defined groups. A school launching a new program needs to identify the best prospects and determine the best ways to reach them. Some schools enjoy such high demand that they do no advertising or direct mail to prospects and do not attend college fairs; instead, they will emphasize alumni and admissions office contacts with the best applicants.

FIGURE 15-3  Elements of core strategy

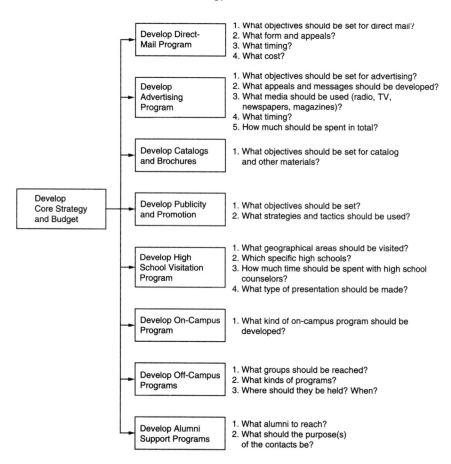

**Setting the Marketing Expenditure Level.** The admissions-office budget should be set to cover the necessary marketing tasks to accomplish the institution's admissions goals. A 1983 national survey found that the average cost of recruiting and admitting one college student in 1981–82 was $151. Selective liberal arts colleges spent the most, an average of $709; private colleges averaged $455, and public colleges spent $64.[7] These costs included salaries of admissions directors, counselors, and other staff; and travel, telephone, printing, supplies, postage, and other items. Comparable averages in the early 1990s were approximately $1,500 to $1,900 per enrolled student at private colleges, and about $540 at public institutions.

Most educational institutions find they must work harder and "smarter" to attract students. The growing importance of direct mail and increasing costs of printing and postage are factors increasing recruiting costs. The admissions director and staff must determine which recruiting activities are most important and allocate funds accordingly. By the same token, an institution can rarely afford to "squeeze" the admissions-office budget without serious risks to enrollment numbers and/or quality. It is, however, quite possible that the admissions office could be more effective by *reallocating* funds from one admissions-related activity to another.

## Plan and Implement Action Programs

The admissions office needs to translate its strategy into action programs, including what will be done, who will do it, and when. The action plan answers each of the questions shown in Figure 15-3 in detail, as well as any other specific institutional concerns. The action plan should provide for periodic reviews of how well the plan is succeeding, so changes can be made where indicated.

Planning should lead to improved performance. To be useful, the plan must be carried out in a smooth, professional, and timely manner. The plan should be appropriate for the institution and for the target markets it is designed to attract and serve.

**Handling Inquiries.** The admissions office will need smooth procedures for responding to inquiries. The simple mailing of a catalog and an application form has been largely superseded by direct-mail pieces, phone conversations, campus visits, and personal contacts. Admissions-office staff must be prepared to respond promptly and thoughtfully to requests for information.

Office procedures should be periodically reviewed to make sure they are working as intended. One simple but underutilized review technique is to "follow the inquiry"—that is, walk through the entire process that occurs from receipt of an inquiry letter or call to the mailing of a suitable reply to gauge whether the process is efficient and well suited to the needs and expectations of the school's prospects.

The following story documents what can happen when processes are inadequate or not well communicated to staff who must carry them out:

One college sent inquiries to the campus computer center, where the data-entry operator was to code and enter records on inquiries, then mail out application packets. However, the operator was not briefed on the need to send packets out on a daily basis, and by November she was six weeks late in mailing out 1,600 applications.

Needless to say, the admissions office took back the task of mailing applications.[8]

**The Admissions Decision Process.** The timetable for admissions decisions varies by type of institution. Many selective colleges and universities have established fairly uniform admissions-decision dates in early April, so that prospects can receive and evaluate all college notifications before making enrollment deposits in early May.

Some institutions have implemented "immediate-decision" programs to speed the review and notification process and thereby encourage qualified applicants to enroll. The School of the Art Institute of Chicago offers prospective students the opportunity to visit the school for a full day, to tour the school and the museum, and to get information about student services and financial aid. On the same day the prospect has an interview with an admissions counselor, who reviews the applicant's portfolio of artistic work and his or her academic qualifications (submitted two weeks in advance). At the end of the day the applicant is notified of the school's decision.

**Coordination with Financial Aid.** The effective cost (tuition minus financial aid) is a major factor in prospects' college-decision process. The admissions staff must work closely with the campus financial aid office to ensure that prospects receive and complete aid forms and that each eligible student is offered an equitable and attractive aid package. Where a comprehensive enrollment management approach has been implemented, admissions, financial aid, and student-records experts are already integrated to coordinate all aspects of the process as a team. This group (or the separate functions in concert) must determine how to allocate aid between continuing students and new students and how to implement programs of strategic financial aid packaging to affect yields.

**Notification of Applicants and Yield Management.** Applicants should be notified of acceptance or rejection as promptly as possible in accordance with announced procedures. Some schools use a "rolling admissions" process, making and sending notification of admissions decisions throughout the year; others have one or more notification dates.

The admissions process does not conclude when notifications have been sent. The school needs to encourage accepted applicants to enroll through *yield-management* events such as parties, special on-campus events for the top prospects, and calls from faculty and current students.

By maintaining close, positive contact with newly admitted students throughout the period between acceptance and registration, the school can start to bond the admitted student to the institution. Not only does this continuing contact build student morale, but at the same time it helps to reduce "summer melt-down"—admitted students' decisions not to enroll at the school where they sent a deposit. At fairly strong institutions this summer melt-down can be 10 percent of admitted freshmen; clearly less selective institutions are more likely to experience an even larger loss. The importance of yield management is obvious in such circumstances.

The school also needs to provide information about housing, orientation schedules, advising, and registration. Additional timely information about the institution and its programs may help students confirm their decision to enroll. Rollins College in Florida helps freshmen preregister by telephone in early June with a faculty advisor. At the same time, students can get answers to other questions about the college. These and other follow-up efforts can encourage the transition from admitted student to enrolled and committed student.

What of the applicants the school does not accept? By applying, applicants are expressing a serious interest in the school. How rejected applicants are treated shapes their future image of the school and what they say to others about it. Admissions officers often make special efforts to handle notification of rejection as sensitively as possible, recognizing the time, effort, and dreams that each application represents.[9] A responsive, marketing-oriented school notifies rejected applicants as promptly as possible so that they can make other plans.

## Evaluate Results and Procedures

Five types of evaluation should be routinely carried out. First, the admissions office will want to review the *total number and quality of applications* received and the institution's success in meeting its enrollment number and quality objectives. Close examination of yields at each stage of the recruitment funnel—and of the same numbers for microfunnels for particular segments—will reveal a great deal about the admissions office's effectiveness.

Second, the admissions office should *survey admitted students* who enroll and those who do not enroll to find out how they differ in demographic characteristics, interests, abilities, and perceptions of the institution, as discussed earlier.

Third, the *cost-effectiveness* of advertising, school visits, and other recruitment efforts should be evaluated. An evaluation of advertising effectiveness is shown in the preceding chapter. In a similar manner, the school can evaluate travel expenditures by how many contacts were made, how many applied and enrolled, and the salary and travel costs involved. Table 15-1 shows an example of such an evaluation for Cornell College, which combines yield information at each stage in the admissions "funnel"—from inquiry to enrollment—with the admissions-office and other activities that initiated the student-college contact.

Of course, recruitment efforts are likely to have a wider effect than such evaluations can reveal. For instance, visits to high schools may increase the visibility of the college with younger students and with guidance counselors, and the results may not be measurable for several years. The school will still reap benefits by striving to measure the impact of current efforts and by testing proposals for new activities.

Bradley University surveyed matriculants and nonmatriculants about the importance of various recruiting activities and used these ratings to evaluate the cost-effectiveness of each technique. Bradley considered two recruiting programs that would each cost about $5,000 a year: purchasing a toll-free telephone line, and flying high school counselors to the campus. The survey results showed that 69 percent of students think that college response to their questions is important, whereas only 38 percent believe that the high school counselor's advice is important. On this basis, the admissions office decided to install a toll-free line.[10]

Fourth, the admissions director and staff should review their *recruiting procedures* qualitatively. Improved procedures might reduce paperwork and delays for applicants, identify new information needs or formats, provide an enhanced image for the institution, and/or increase staff time for other tasks. The review may also suggest places where additional training would enhance staff confidence and performance.

Fifth, the admissions office should later review data on students' satisfaction, academic performance, and retention to assess how well the students they admit match what the institution offers. Satisfaction and retention are considered in the following section.

## IMPROVING RETENTION

Retaining matriculated students is just as important as attracting and enrolling them. Students are not a captive audience—each matriculated student renews his or her enrollment decision every term. The busy or dissatisfied student may cut back on the number of courses or drop out completely. Nondegree "leisure" students may decide to take courses at a different institution each term or to take none at all.

Attrition rates vary greatly by type of institution:

- In four-year institutions, roughly half the students who enter never graduate from the same institution. Among the half who leave the institution, however,

TABLE 15-1   1991–92 applications and enrolled students, by source of first contact

| SOURCE CATEGORY | INQUIRIES | PERCENT OF INQUIRIES | APPLICANTS | CONVERSION RATE APP/INQ | PERCENT OF ALL APPLICATIONS | ADMITS | CONVERSION RATE ADM/APPS | PERCENT OF ALL ADMITS | ENROLLED STUDENTS | YIELD RATE ENROLLED/ INQ | PERCENT OF ALL ENROLLED STUDENTS |
|---|---|---|---|---|---|---|---|---|---|---|---|
| Travel Initiated | 2,797 | 11.1 | 142 | 5.1 | 9.2 | 129 | 90.9 | 9.7 | 37 | 1.3 | 8.9 |
| Student Initiated | 3,083 | 12.3 | 627 | 20.3 | 40.7 | 479 | 76.4 | 36.1 | 150 | 4.8 | 36.0 |
| Referral Initiated | 1,028 | 4.1 | 94 | 9.1 | 6.1 | 83 | 88.3 | 6.3 | 20 | 2.0 | 4.8 |
| Direct Mail/ Solicited | 18,217 | 72.5 | 677 | 9.1 | 44.0 | 637 | 94.1 | 48.0 | 210 | 1.2 | 50.3 |
| TOTAL | 25,125 | 100.0 | 1,540 | 6.1 | 100.0 | 1,328 | 86.2 | 100.0 | 417 | 1.7 | 100.0 |

Source: Peter Bryant and Kevin Crocket, "The Admissions Office Goes Scientific," *Planning for Higher Education*, 22 (Fall 1993), 3.

a substantial number transfer to other colleges and eventually finish. Still, roughly 30 percent of the freshmen entering four-year colleges never finish a bachelor's degree.

- Community colleges have a much higher dropout rate than four-year institutions have. Approximately 60 percent of the entering freshmen in community colleges never complete an associate degree, and over 80 percent never complete a bachelor's degree.
- Private four-year institutions have slightly higher graduation rates for students five years after admission than do public four-year institutions (roughly 53 percent).
- The more prestigious and selective the institution, the lower its attrition rate. Very selective institutions have low dropout rates; at the other end, "open-admission," unselective community colleges have extremely high dropout rates.
- Institutions that are heavily populated by commuter students have higher dropout rates, and institutions with strong residential dormitory programs have lower dropout rates.[11]

The retention issue is important for several reasons. A responsive institution wants to create as much satisfaction as it reasonably can. Pragmatically, satisfied students are less likely to drop out. Considering the effort and other costs of recruitment, the school should make a concerted effort to retain students who, with some help, could succeed at the institution.

The institutional costs of attrition are substantial. The institution loses the tuition revenue and enrollment-dependent public subsidies. A dropout may mean an unused residence-hall space and loss of a year's room and board fees. Serious dissatisfaction leads not only to a high dropout rate but also to a weakened institutional image among prospective candidates, making recruitment even more difficult.

The admissions staff must seek out and enroll more students to replace those who drop out, often accepting weaker candidates to meet enrollment quotas. Four-year public institutions (depending on type) must enroll from 160 to 311 freshman in order to graduate 100 seniors. The range among four-year colleges is 120 to 192.[12]

The importance of creating more satisfaction and improving retention cannot be overemphasized. In Chapter 2 we introduced the concept of satisfaction and discussed its relationship to the goals of the institution. In the following section, we present specific ways to assess student satisfaction. Then we discuss the steps in a successful retention program.

## Assessing Student Satisfaction

In spite of its central importance, student satisfaction can be difficult to measure. Students will differ in what characteristics of the school are related to their satisfaction and how much of each characteristic they feel is essential. Some students may be disappointed because the foreign language department is weak; others will be oblivious to the foreign language department but be tremendously disappointed if the school's football team is on probation and can't play in bowl games.

To overcome the difficulty of measuring satisfaction directly, some institutions look primarily at objective measures related to enrollment. They reason that if a student enrolls and stays, the student is probably satisfied. Such schools will look at the following measures:

- Rates of increase in number of applications and in percentages of those admitted who matriculate.
- The school's share of the relevant target market. For example, of all National Merit Scholars living west of the Rockies, what percent chose this school? (Or, for a parochial school, of all the school-age children of families belonging to this parish, what percentage are sending their children to the parish school?)
- The number of well-qualified children of alumni who enroll and the number of families in which two or more children choose to attend the school. These measures may indicate high satisfaction.
- The school's retention rate. Of those students who matriculate, what percentage stay through graduation?

These indirect, objective measures are important, but by themselves they are insufficient to assess satisfaction. When a school has no competitors or when there are more applicants than it can serve, these measures may be high and yet not reflect actual satisfaction. Even when a school does not have a monopoly, applications and enrollments may remain strong for a while even after satisfaction has started to decline because enrolled students are close to graduating or because transferring would be difficult or costly.

The school needs to supplement these indirect measures of satisfaction with other information obtained from students themselves. We will turn to these *direct measures* of satisfaction next.

**Student Panels.**  Students may be selected to make up a *panel* that will be sampled from time to time about their feelings toward the school or any of its services. In marketing research a panel is a set of respondents from whom information and opinions are solicited on more than one occasion, but they will not necessarily ever meet as a group. The panel members may be asked to respond to mail or telephone surveys and/or be invited to participate in focus groups.

Panel members may volunteer, be named by the student government as liaisons to the administration, or be selected at random and invited to participate. Some provision is usually made to rotate membership on the panel to get fresh views from new people. Such panels often provide valuable information. At the same time, the panel may represent only the views of those who are involved enough to be willing to serve on a panel. It is even possible that those who will serve are more loyal to the school and thus less likely to see its faults.

**Exit Interviews.** Some institutions interview—or try to interview—each student who decides to withdraw. The interview may be carried out by a member of the dean of students' staff, and may be rather general or may follow a carefully designed list of questions. The exit interview can be a source of problem identification, and—occasionally—an opportunity to address students' personal situations and make it possible for them to choose to stay.

The University of Rochester focuses not solely on withdrawing students, but also on graduating seniors. Graduating seniors are asked to complete an extensive questionnaire about many aspects of their college experience. For those students who prefer to respond to the survey questionnaire in the context of a personal interview, a large number of university staff are trained to conduct these one-on-one interviews and to record responses.

**Student Satisfaction Surveys.** Some schools conduct periodic surveys of student satisfaction. They send questionnaires or telephone a random sample of students to determine what they like and dislike about the school. Three types of questions for measuring student satisfaction will be described here.

*Directly reported satisfaction.* A school can distribute a questionnaire to a representative sample of students, asking them to state their felt satisfaction with the school as a whole and with specific components. Students can be interviewed in person, on the telephone, or through a mail questionnaire.

To measure felt satisfaction, the questionnaire would contain questions of the following form:

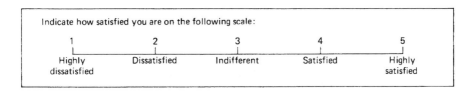

The student responds by circling the number on the scale from 1 to 5 that describes his or her level of satisfaction. Although five intervals are used in this example, some scales use as few as three intervals, others as many as eleven. The numbers assigned to the intervals are arbitrary, except that each succeeding number is higher than the preceding one. There is no implication that these are unit distances—that the respondent who marks 5, "highly satisfied," is twice as satisfied as the student who marks 3, "indifferent."

When the results are in, a histogram can be prepared showing the percentage of students who fall into each group for each questionnaire item. Of course, students within any group such as the "highly dissatisfied" group, may have very different intensities of dissatisfaction, ranging from feelings of mild disappointment with the school to intense anger.

If the histogram is highly skewed to the left, with the preponderance of students dissatisfied, the school is likely to be in deep trouble. If the histogram is bell-shaped, the school has some satisfied and some dissatisfied students, and a large group that is more or less neutral. If the histogram is highly skewed to the right, the school can be assured that it is delivering satisfaction to most students. Repeating this survey at regular intervals points up any significant changes in the distribution. Furthermore, the respondents should be asked to respond to similar scales for the various components of the school, such as its academic program, extracurricular program, housing, and the like. With this information, the institution could investigate the contribution of satisfaction with various components to overall satisfaction with the school.

The data may also be presented as shown in Figure 15-4, which reports percentages of college sophomores and seniors who said they were generally pleased with each area surveyed. The survey found that the vast majority of

FIGURE 15-4    Student satisfaction with college

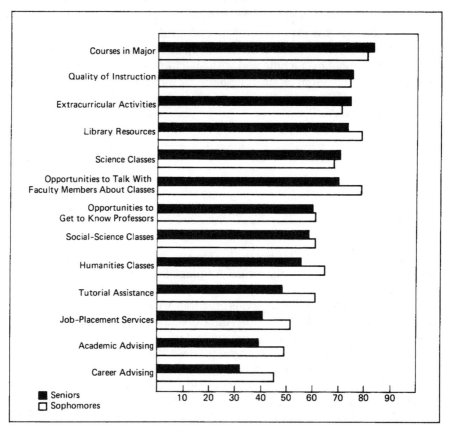

Source: Higher Education Research Institute, University of California, Los Angeles. Chart by Tyler Young appeared in *The Chronicle of Higher Education*, July 27, 1983, p. 2. Copyright by *The Chronicle of Higher Education*. Reprinted with permission.

college students are satisfied with their academic programs and professors, but many complain that support services—such as academic advising, career counseling, and job placement—are inadequate. Seniors tend to be more dissatisfied with the services than sophomores are.

*Derived dissatisfaction.* The second approach measures derived dissatisfaction on the premise that a person's satisfaction is influenced by his or her expectations as well as the perceived experience. Two excellent ways to measure dissatisfaction are described in Chapter 2: importance-performance analysis and the SERVQUAL questionnaire.

## Key Steps in a Retention Program

An institution interested in increasing retention will enjoy more success if two conditions are met. First, there must be visible institutionwide commitment to student retention, reflected in formal and informal reward systems. Second, all units of the school that come in contact with students must be part of the solution, not admissions or advising alone.[13]

**Set Up a Retention Steering Committee.** A retention program needs designers and champions. The committed institution should establish a retention steering committee to fill these roles. Each department and other functional area of the school should set up its own retention committee to develop plans for its own area. Each area committee should send one member to serve on the university committee to ensure representation. Steering committee members should be committed to the shared goal of improving programs and services for students.

**Assess the Retention Situation.** Most schools have highly accurate counts of applications received, applications accepted, students enrolled in a given term, and the degrees granted, yet they may be unaware of their retention rate. To understand the institution's retention situation, the steering committee needs to (1) determine the institution's past record on retention, and (2) determine factors related to attrition. These steps help determine in what ways the institution is successful and what aspects need to be changed to enhance retention.

Retention can be assessed by individual student and/or by cohort. *Individual retention* means that the school can trace the enrollment history of each student, and then keep track of how many students reach various milestones, such as completing the freshman, sophomore, junior year of study, and graduating within four years or within five or six years. The retention rate is the percentage of those entering who graduate within a certain period, typically four or five years for a four-year program.

*Cohort retention* involves tracking the number of students moving from one milestone to the next, for example, freshmen who enroll for the sophomore year, sophomores enrolling for junior year, juniors enrolling for senior year, and seniors graduating. The precise composition of each year's "classes" will shift as some entering students drop out and transfer students replace them.

While cohort retention data are harder to interpret, they can at the very least lead to some institutional introspection. Figure 15-5 illustrates the retention problem of one part-time graduate-degree program that takes an average of three years to complete. Simply comparing the number of new students enrolled and the number of degrees granted each year shows that about one-third of matriculating students do not complete the program. To improve the diagram's accuracy, it is more comparable to match the number of matriculants in a given year with the number of graduates three years later. Such an analysis reveals that approximately 40 percent do not complete the program.

This noncompletion statistic of 40 percent should raise questions about student selection and satisfaction, and about curriculum and teaching quality. The high attrition rate might reflect conditions outside the school's—and the students'—control, such as job transfers out of the area, increased work responsibilities that prevent part-time study, or transfer to a full-time program. Still, the graduate program should try to determine various reasons for leaving and their frequency.

The school could carry out a longitudinal study assessing each student's enrollment status at several intervals. The most comprehensive type of longitudinal study examines the complete enrollment histories of all students in an entering class over a period of several years on a term-by-term basis. Once longitudinal data files are compiled, researchers can (1) identify the cumulative percentage of an entering class in each of several retention and attrition categories at several points over a period of time; and (2) place each student into the appropriate retention or attrition category at the end of the set longitudinal period.

FIGURE 15-5    The attrition gap for a part-time graduate program

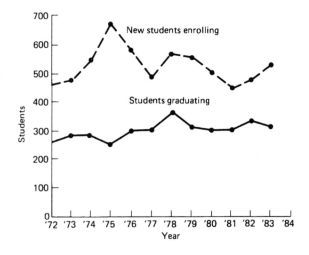

Where complete individual enrollment histories are conveniently available, students who entered several years before can be studied.[14] The steering committee may also launch a retention study of the current entering class, with the results used to track the effectiveness of retention efforts in future years. In either event, each student's enrollment status is noted each term—enrolled, voluntarily withdrawn while in good standing (including reason, if known), disciplinary dismissal, academic dismissal, graduated, and so forth. Some students labeled "dropouts" may be "stopouts" who will return within a year or two, or "attainers" who have achieved their personal goals (such as to prepare to transfer or for a job) and then leave without graduating.[15] A longitudinal approach can best differentiate between attrition categories.

**Determine Why Students Leave.** Getting at the "real" reasons why students leave can be very difficult. In some cases, the reasons for withdrawal appear obvious—academic or disciplinary dismissal, for example. But the concerned institution seeks to identify the controllable factors that lead to such events. For example, in the case of academic dismissal, should the student have been admitted? Was the student inadequately prepared for the academic demands of the institution? Could these deficiencies be identified in the applicant file? Did the student get inadequate guidance in identifying areas needing improvement? Did the student have personal problems that could have been alleviated by appropriate counseling, financial assistance, or other help?

Students who leave voluntarily should be interviewed or surveyed to determine their reasons for leaving and their future plans. They may drop out because of family obligations, illness, financial problems, lack of academic skills or motivation, desire to work or travel, or dissatisfaction with the school. They may drop out for a time and then return, or they may transfer to schools that are closer, or less expensive, or that in other ways better meet their needs. Many "dropouts" eventually complete degree requirements at the same or other institutions. By understanding the reasons for transferring or dropping out, the institution can determine how to improve its programs and other factors that affect retention.

At some institutions the quality of student life and instruction may be so poor that the institution should be asking not why students *leave*, but why students *stay*. Emergency attention to "plugging a leaky bucket" should not come at the expense of institutional efforts to improve overall quality and satisfaction.

**Encourage an Attitude of Service to Students.** Enhancing retention may call for substantial changes in programs, facilities, support services, and other areas. But often the first and most important step is to foster a campuswide attitude of serving students. The official tone of the campus is set by faculty, administrators, secretaries, and other staff. Important steps include making current personnel aware of their importance, providing training, and hiring with students in mind. Exhibit 15-1 illustrates the importance of serving students.

EXHIBIT 15-1    Influences on student retention

During her senior year in high school, Jane wrote to Eucalyptus University as part of the routine of applying to colleges. After two weeks, she received a mimeographed letter outlining the personal nature of a Eucalyptus U. education. The accompanying application forms were more complex than an income tax form and, of course, asked for $20.

Several days later, Jane telephoned Eucalyptus U. After 17 rings, an operator answered and placed her on "hold" for four minutes. When the operator returned to the phone, she asked, "Are you through?" And when Jane finally reached the admissions office, a secretary told her, "The director is not taking any calls, and the rest of the staff is out. Could you call back tomorrow?"

Jane was persistent and scheduled a visit to Eucalyptus. There were no directional signs when she drove onto the campus, so she found a parking space near what looked like an administration building. It wasn't. She met two professors and a student—and none of them knew where the admissions office was.

Twenty minutes later, success. The admissions office was busy and loud, but finally a receptionist confronted Jane: "Do you have an appointment?" Jane said she did, but the receptionist informed her that the director was not available and that she would have to see a student assistant (who turned out to be transferring from Eucalyptus and was less than enthusiastic about the university).

In spite of her experience, Jane enrolled that fall. Registration was like a lottery; she was enrolled in two classes, via computer, that were completely out of her field. She was interested in pre-law, and her assigned counselor was from the chemistry department. There was a major error in her tuition bill. Her dorm room had not been cleaned, and her roommate was taking drugs. It took two weeks to get her room changed, and she fell behind on her homework.

One of Jane's professors made her buy two textbooks—both of which he had written. Another was late every day and missed several classes altogether. Another just read his notes—and didn't even do that very well.

But one professor cared, counseled, and gave Jane the attention that made the difference. Jane is still attending Eucalyptus U. because one person understood that colleges exist to serve their students.

Young, sensitive minds need support, not confrontation—and this does not apply only to the classroom. Telephone operators, secretaries, groundskeepers, business-office personnel, and other staff members are part of the lifeblood of a college. They often lack degrees and professional training, but their roles are important. They greet students, bill them, comfort them, delay them, frustrate them, inform them.

Administrative personnel in student-affairs offices have a special function. They provide the "home-away-from-home" counsel that makes a student comfortable. Theirs should not be a job but a labor of love. They ought to ask themselves questions of this sort:

EXHIBIT 15-1    (continued)

- Are the forms, guidelines, rules, and regulations necessary? Or are they part of a system that just evolved?

- Can students understand the regulations that *are* important? Or are they written in "educationese"?

- Within reason, is the office door open, or just slightly ajar?

- Are students involved in the planning and implementation of policies that affect them?

The role of the faculty member is even more basic: to be the teacher he or she always wanted to be. A caring professor sees a student as both a consumer and a product. While the student is learning and paying a price in time and money, a product is developing. The result can be positive or negative, and those who influence the result have a grave responsibility. The most positive words a college can hear about itself are, "The professors really care." If faculty members approach each class, each term, each year with enthusiasm, the college is alive and well.

Source: Dennis L. Johnson, "One Professor Cared," *The Chronicle of Higher Education*, April 19, 1976. Copyright 1975 by Editorial Projects in Education. Reprinted with permission of *The Chronicle of Higher Education.*

**Establish a Good Student-Institution Match in Recruiting and Admissions.** Programs to enhance retention begin when the admissions office plans its recruiting strategy. The college should recruit and admit students who are qualified to benefit from its programs and who "match" the current student body in interests and ability. If the college decides to attract a new market—for example, older commuting students—it should consider in advance the necessary staff, support services, and facilities to succeed with this new group.

The institution must provide complete, accurate, and timely information to help students make the enrollment decision. A student who makes a poor choice of institution or program of study will probably have low morale, perform poorly, and drop out.

**Facilitate the Student's Transition into the Institution.** Once the new student is admitted, the college needs to help the student get started "right" through appropriate placement in courses, orientation to procedures and support services, and activities that create a sense of identification and belonging. Table 15-2 lists the most frequently used retention activities, and orientation tops the list.

**Provide Counseling and Advising.** Counseling and advising should be available from the very beginning. On a residential campus, many students are living away from home for the first time and are dealing with complex per-

TABLE 15-2    Frequently used retention activities

| | |
|---|---|
| Improve delivery of freshman intake services (orientation) | 93% |
| Improve academic support services | 86% |
| Improve effectiveness of academic advising program | 86% |
| Improve classroom instruction | 85% |
| Integration of individuals into the educational and social life of the institution | 82% |
| Respond more systematically to the needs of "at risk" students | 81% |
| Conduct retention/attrition research | 80% |
| Address major areas of student concern | 80% |
| Make improvements in physical plant | 80% |
| Encourage wider participation in extracurricular activities | 79% |
| Provide faculty/staff development programs | 78% |
| Revise admissions material and procedures to improve student/institutional fit | 78% |
| Provide programs/services for special student groups | 77% |
| Mandated assessment and course placement | 75% |
| Offer special workshops for students | 73% |
| Increase frequency and out-of-class contact between faculty, staff, and students | 70% |
| Enhance the quality of residential life | 69% |
| Implement an "early alert" system | 66% |
| Make modifications in financial aid program | 62% |
| Provide enriched or accelerated academic experiences | 58% |
| Implement an extended orientation program | 53% |
| Provide special services for adult learners | 53% |
| Develop a comprehensive approach to undecided/exploratory students | 37% |
| Implement an institutionwide service management strategy | 36% |
| Offer a preadmission bridge program | 30% |

Source: *Williams-Crockett 1992 National Enrollment Management Survey* (Littleton, CO: Williams-Crockett, 1992).

sonal issues of identity, competence, and choice. They also face family illness, death, and other human crises and may well need personal counseling at these times. If such circumstances lead them to drop out, they will be more likely to return if they have received such help.

Academic advising is often mentioned as important to retention. Students who are performing well academically and who have a sense of purpose (such as a career direction) are less likely to drop out. To some extent, academic advising can be effective in helping students identify strengths and weaknesses, improve study skills, and determine academic and career interests. But to be effective, such advising must be of high quality, and students must make use of it. A survey of deans found that although 95 percent of undergraduate students consider dropping out at some time, only a third seek advice from professors.[16] Often students withdraw without any interaction with college faculty, administrators, or staff. The institution that waits for students to come for help will probably have little or no influence on their decisions to withdraw.

Providing high-quality advising requires committed, competent advisors. If professors are unprepared, uninterested, or unavailable—or are perceived as such—students will not go to them for advice. Good academic advising cannot be mandated. At some institutions, faculty advisors are selected and receive additional training and released time, while other institutions have professional academic advisors.

Most institutions would like to concentrate their retention efforts on the most dropout-prone students. Unfortunately, prediction is difficult. The only reliable predictor is college grades, but that predicts only academic dropouts. Counseling and advising programs to reduce attrition need to be directed toward all students and need to begin as soon as students arrive on campus.

**Create a Caring, Responsive Environment.** The purpose of these efforts is to create the academic and social conditions that foster personal growth, academic success, and a sense of belonging. The institution committed to retaining students needs to examine its efforts and take steps to create the kind of atmosphere that encourages students to stay.

## ENROLLMENT MANAGEMENT

As the concern for student enrollment has increased, institutional leaders have come to realize that retaining matriculants is just as important as attracting them. The need to manage college enrollments from the point of initial student contact to the point of graduation has become increasingly apparent. As a result, the concept of enrollment management is quickly replacing the admissions model that focuses only on attracting and admitting qualified students. Enrollment management has generated a great deal of interest, yet it remains a new concept and one that is ill-defined.[17]

These words, written by Don Hossler in his landmark book *Enrollment Management* in 1984, are just as true over a decade later. The concept of enrollment management was not new in 1984. In 1974 John Maguire and Frank Campanella integrated Boston College's enrollment-related activities. Maguire became the first dean of enrollment management and wrote the first article on the topic (p. 327, note 2). The mystery is that over two decades have passed and few educational institutions have yet adopted even the fundamental principles of enrollment management.

The slow diffusion of enrollment management cannot be explained by lack of need: More schools and colleges than ever are "running to catch up" with changing demographics, shifting student preferences, and other factors which call for even greater attention to recruiting and retention. Programs of merit and other forms of no-need financial aid have intensified competition for strong students. Never before has there been such an obvious need for coordination between all the areas that affect enrollments. Figure 15-6 illustrates the interconnections between enrollments and many different areas of the institution.

Yet the traditional pattern of separate functional areas remains. A 1992 national survey of 599 colleges found that "the concept of an integrated enrollment management unit in higher education is more theory than practice."[18] Of the chief enrollment officers responding, most had direct administrative responsibility for only two of a number of functional areas associated with enrollment management (Table 15-3).

In many institutions, the division of responsibility is such that key enrollment-related areas may report to distinct vice presidents: admissions, advising, curriculum, and student records to the academic vice president; financial aid and student financial services to the vice president for business and finance; residence halls, career planning and placement, and student activities to the vice president for student services; and alumni, development, and university communications and publications to the vice president for institutional relations.

FIGURE 15-6    Institutional participation in enrollment management

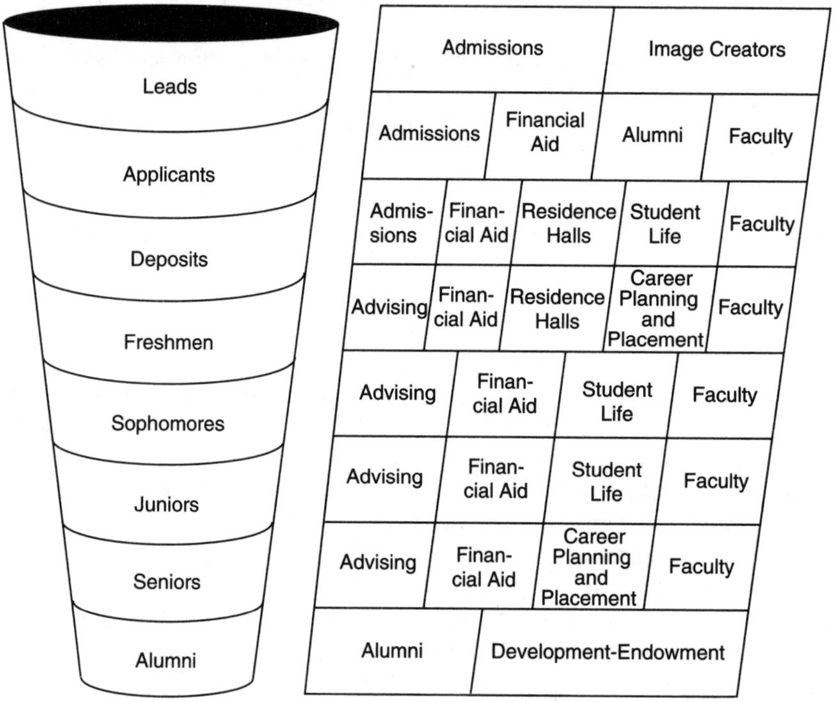

Source: Jan Janzen, "Enrollment Management: The Model, the Manager, and the Message," Proceedings of the 1989 Symposium for the Marketing of Higher Education (Chicago, IL: American Marketing Association, 1989), P. 383.

TABLE 15-3   Areas of responsibility
of chief enrollment
officers

| | |
|---|---|
| Recruitment | 89% |
| Admissions | 94 |
| Orientation | 33 |
| Financial aid | 47 |
| Institutional research | 21 |
| Student retention | 35 |
| Registration | 43 |
| Academic advising | 22 |
| Learning assistance | 13 |
| Career planning and placement | 24 |
| Residential life | 13 |
| Institutional strategic planning | 26 |
| Graduation | 29 |

Source: Data from *Fall 1992 National Enroll-ment Management Survey Report* (Littleton, CO: Williams-Crockett, The Noel-Levitz Center for Enrollment Management, 1992), p. 10.

This dispersion of lines of responsibility leaves the coordination task to the institution's president or council of vice presidents, rather than integrating the functions closer to the point of decision making and action. The functional divisions traditional to academic institutions have probably been the highest barrier to implementation of enrollment management.

In contrast, Figure 15-7 shows an organizational chart for an institution with an enrollment-management organization. The vice president of enrollment management provides the integration of functions. According to Robert Sevier,

> The most compelling reasons for adopting an enrollment management approach to student recruiting is to have a single, knowledgeable authority oversee as many internal/institutional variables that affect recruiting [and retention] as possible.

> Over the years I have seen many institutions waste enormous amounts of time, money, and prestige because they did not have a single source of authority and accountability. They had conflicting recruiting and marketing goals, vague and overlapping areas of responsibility, and contested budgets. An enrollment management approach solves these problems.[19]

For institutions interested in the components and key tasks of an enrollment-management program, Exhibit 15-2 presents a useful list of six goals and a checklist of questions prepared by John Maguire.

FIGURE 15-7   Organizational chart for an enrollment-management model

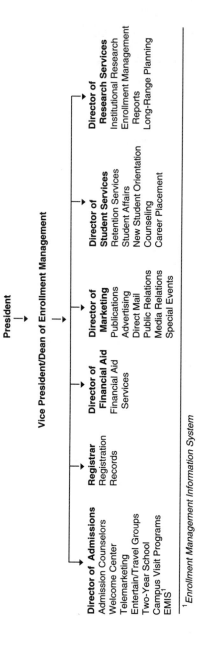

**President**

**Vice President/Dean of Enrollment Management**

**Director of Admissions**
Admission Counselors
Welcome Center
Telemarketing
Entertain/Travel Groups
Two-Year School
Campus Visit Programs
EMIS[1]

**Registrar**
Registration
Records

**Director of Financial Aid**
Financial Aid
Services

**Director of Marketing**
Publications
Advertising
Direct Mail
Public Relations
Media Relations
Special Events

**Director of Student Services**
Retention Services
Student Affairs
New Student Orientation
Counseling
Career Placement

**Director of Research Services**
Institutional Research
Enrollment Management
Reports
Long-Range Planning

[1]*Enrollment Management Information System*

Source: Robert A. Sevier, "Is Demography Destiny?," *The Journal of College Admissions*, no. 135 (Spring 1992), p. 21.

EXHIBIT 15-2  Enrollment management checklist

---

*Goal #1: Organization for Enrollment Management*

*To organize appropriate departments in a way that facilitates the coordination of staff, the flow of information, and the integration of enrollment-management decisions.*

( )  Are you generally satisfied with the coordination among marketing, recruiting, pricing/financial aid, and retention functions at your institution? Who is responsible for bringing new students to your institution? Who has responsibility for maintaining overall enrollments?

( )  Is a designated official at your institution responsible for relating academic planning to long- and short-range student demand?

( )  Which departments within your institution are involved in both admissions and retention?

( )  Does your admissions office have immediate access to decision makers at your institution—by reporting either directly to the president or to someone else who can make important decisions quickly? Where are the financial aid and the registrar's offices placed in your table of organization? What about the office of institutional research? Who is responsible for enrollment-management research?

*Goal #2: Student Information Systems and Research*

*To create an integrated student database and a capacity to use student information systems for coordinated research and planning.*

( )  Do you undertake more than straightforward demographic analysis of your applicant pool? Do you understand you own strengths and weaknesses as perceived by the accepted applicant pool?

( )  Do you investigate your competition to understand (a) why students make choices, (b) which institutions are perceived as most similar to yours in image, and (c) where there is the greatest application overlap?

( )  Do you know how your institution rates among its competition on factors that influence students' decisions? On what factors you most want to rank favorably? Where are the "image/reality" gaps in perceptions?

( )  How do you attempt to position yourself advantageously within the student marketplace as well as among your competitors? What kind of student would be the best match with your institution? How do you define student quality as it relates to a realistic positioning strategy?

( )  Do you periodically seek the opinion of your own students and alumni in order to determine, among other things, how fully their original expectations have been met, how valuable their overall educations have proved to be, and how well specific programs have served them?

EXHIBIT 15-2    (continued)

( )    Are your student information systems integrated, reports prepared and research generated in the area of enrollment in such a way as to easily cut across the boundaries of departments and functions?

( )    Do you use College Board Validity Studies in an effort to understand which predictors best correlate with your most important criterion variables? Do you have a layperson's appreciation for research terminology such as correlation and multiple regression analysis?

( )    Do you display the number of applications, acceptances, deposits in tabular and graphical form on a daily, weekly, monthly, and yearly basis? Do you know precisely how many applications you are up against compared to the previous year? Can you use the computer to combine present and past data to extrapolate trends?

( )    Does your admissions system include a careful tracking of inquiries and their yield in applications? Do you know, through research, why inquiries do or do not apply to your institution? Are you able to determine the perceptions of your institution among students who do not go beyond the inquiry or applicant stage, but who have characteristics compatible with the students you seek?

( )    Do you encourage graduate students (and in some cases undergraduate honors students) as well as faculty members in such departments as sociology, economics, and marketing to do research relating to enrollments? Do you have staff members, who can write or supervise doctoral theses, working on research papers that will improve the management of enrollments.

### Goal #3: Admissions Marketing

***To develop admissions and marketing programs in order to attract qualified students in sufficient numbers during periods of possible enrollment declines.***

( )    Is your institution preparing a contingency plan for possible enrollment declines? What is the likelihood that your institution will experience a significant decline?

( )    How do you involve faculty, alumni and students in admissions? How many are active from each group? Do you have an adequate budget, staff, and orientation program to ensure success?

( )    How many high schools does your admissions staff visit in a given year? How many major feeder secondary schools provide you with 50 percent of your applications? Is this figure closer to 30 percent or 10 percent of the total number of schools sending at least one application? Could you be using staff travel time more productively?

( )    What percent of your applicants actually visit your campus? Is their overall impression favorable? Do you allocate adequate resources for pro-

EXHIBIT 15-2    (continued)

grams that will attract students and their parents to your campus? Can they attend classes and/or stay overnight?

( )    To what extent are parents important in the overall decision-making process? What special programs have been devised to give parents the opportunity to assist their sons and daughters in considering your institution?

( )    Who prepares your marketing literature? Are the opinions of student consumers sought? Do you have confidence in the impact your publications have on prospective families' opinions of your institution? What tests do you apply to determine how they are being received?

( )    Do you periodically employ experimental marketing ideas that can then be analyzed for cost and benefit? Taking everything into consideration (time, costs, results, etc.), are you able to assess which approaches to the market work best and under which circumstances?

( )    Do you use your admissions application and the process itself as positive marketing tools? Do you require applicants to respond to offers of admission, housing, and financial aid before they have had the opportunity to weigh offers from all institutions to which they apply?

( )    How well do students from your most important feeder schools perform at your institution? Do you compare levels of achievement at various schools with their performance at your institution?

( )    Do you use the Student Search Service of the College Board or other direct-mail strategies to stimulate new interest in your institution? How do you target mailings to achieve the best results? Do you know the yield for inquirers within specific market segments?

( )    If you have any graduate programs, does your institution apply enrollment-management techniques to recruitment, retention, and funding of graduate students?

### Goal #4 Pricing and Financial Aid Strategies

*To implement pricing and financial aid strategies that will optimize the institution's ability to attract and retain the desired academic and socioeconomic mix of students.*

( )    Do you have a comprehensive financial aid policy at your institution? Are your goals consistent with the College Scholarship Service's "Principles of Student Financial Aid Administration"? Can you operationally define *equality of educational opportunity*?

( )    In addition to supporting national goals with your policy, do you pursue well-defined institutional goals? Do you offer no-need scholarships? Athletic scholarships? Minority scholarships?

EXHIBIT 15-2 (continued)

( ) Are you able to meet the full financial need of every accepted financial aid applicant? If not, how do you establish priorities for deciding who is eligible for your limited funds? By meeting equal percentages of need or underfunding by a fixed dollar amount? By fully funding the neediest first and denying aid to others? Or by fully funding the best first and denying aid to others?

( ) How do students manage to stay at your institution if they arrive with less money than they need? Do they know what their alternative sources of funds are (if any)? Do you set aside a pool of money for students who have distinguished themselves academically or who have taken on excessive self-help burdens through loans and employment?

( ) Do you know how much financial aid is forfeited by students who withdraw from your institution? How do you redistribute this money among freshmen, transfers, and returning students?

( ) How are institutional and government funds apportioned among divisions and classes at your institution? Do you have special budgets for part-time work and loans for new students?

( ) Do you continually analyze financial aid yield data in an effort to optimize certain quantifiable goals such as overall enrollment, minority representation, academic quality, net tuition, and yield?

( ) Do you have a centralized office of student employment to assist all students in identifying sources of income for potential use in defraying educational expenses? Do you attempt to link students to jobs by areas of interest and location? Are alumni integrated into the job locator network?

( ) Are you satisfied that you are positoned properly in the marketplace with respect to pricing? Do you consider financial aid budgets as you contemplate the best institutional pricing strategy?

( ) Do you offer all students and their families, even those not eligible for financial aid, financial counseling?

### Goal #5: Demand Analysis and Institutional Response

*To develop a capability to anticipate immediate and long-term student interest and methods for improving the institution's ability to provide for these interests.*

( ) Has your institution prepared long-range (five- to ten-year) academic and fiscal plans that identify institutional goals and that include enrollment objectives? Do you have a long-range enrollment plan?

( ) Can you obtain an accurate "snapshot" of student enrollments at all levels at all times of the year? Is student flow at your insitution such that you should think in terms of semesters rather than academic years?

EXHIBIT 15-2 (continued)

( ) To what extent are persons responsible for enrollments involved in re-source allocation decisions at your institution? Can you project student demand by studying applications for admission, internal transfers, and the job market? Have you prepared an institutional study on this subject re-cently for distribution to the academic and administrative communities?

( ) Does your institution use the formal registration process as a means to assess student demand with respect to optimal course selection and dis-tribution (time and place)?

### Goal #6 *Retention and Transfer Students*

*To formalize an institutional retention program in order to determine reasons for attrition, to minimize it to whatever extent desirable, and to enroll qualified transfer students as replacements.*

( ) Do you know exactly how many students leave your institution in a given year, semester, month, week, or day? What percent of all students in a typical class graduate in eight to ten semesters?

( ) Do you have a centralized, adequately staffed transfer admissions pro-gram to expand your applicant pool and to maintain enrollment stabil-ity in all, and especially upper-level, classes? Once transfer students have been admitted to your institution, do they have the same opportu-nities for financial aid, housing, and course selection as their peers who started as freshmen?

( ) If you have been able to assess why students come to your institution, do you understand why they leave and where they go? Do their reasons vary from year to year? Do transfers enter your institution making the same erroneous assumptions that prompted your dropouts to leave in the first place (the "revolving door" syndrome)?

( ) Do all departments within your institution feel responsible for helping to maintain retention?

( ) Do you have an advisement program (faculty, staff, peers, graduate stu-dents) that attempts to relate curriculum and student life to overall per-sonal and career goals?

( ) Do you have a mechanism for helping students leave your institution in cases where they would obviously be better served elsewhere (new career objectives, need to "find themselves," an interest in an academic area not offered by your institution)? Do you have an "exit interview" process?

Source: Updated by John Maguire from a list that appeared in his article "Enrollment Management Checklist," *Handbook of Institutional Advancement*, A. Westley Rowland, ed. (San Francisco, CA: Jossey-Bass, 1986), pp. 643–673

## SUMMARY

Attracting students is often an educational institution's key marketing task. Schools and colleges seek to enroll students who will benefit from what the institution has to offer. Although publicly supported colleges accept students who meet specific criteria, selective public and private institutions want to attract many applicants so that they may admit the very best. Once the institution has enrolled qualified students, the next task is to ensure that each student's reasonable expectations are met so that the student will complete the program and become a satisfied graduate.

The student-recruitment process consists of six steps: identifying enrollment problems, defining enrollment goals and objectives, researching the potential student market, setting marketing strategy, planning and implementing action programs, and evaluating results and procedures.

Retaining students is just as important as attracting and enrolling them, since students are not a captive audience. The institution will want to create a high level of satisfaction. Responsive educational institutions will measure satisfaction and make changes and improvements to increase satisfaction.

An effective retention program must include all points of contact between the student and the institution. The retention process should include eight steps: set up a retention steering committee, assess the retention situation, determine why students leave, encourage an attitude of service to students, establish a good student-institution match in recruiting and admissions, facilitate the student's transition into the institution, provide counseling and advising, and create a caring, responsive environment.

Enrollment management coordinates all the functions that directly affect the attraction, admission, financing, and retention of the students the school most wants to serve. Despite its many advantages in coordination and effectiveness, the enrollment-management model has been slow to be adopted.

### Notes

1. David Riesman, "The Evangelical Colleges: Untouched by the Academic Revolution," *Change* (January/February 1981), pp. 13–20.

2. *Master Plan 1973-1984*, Hood College Admissions Office.

3. "A Case History of How a College Increased Its Freshman Enrollment 100% in One Year," *Insights* (June-July 1974), pp. 1–14.

4. William Ihlanfeldt, *Achieving Optimal Enrollments and Tuition Revenues* (San Francisco: Jossey-Bass, 1980), pp. 77–81.

5. "A Case History," p. 5.

6. Clifford C. Campbell, "The Administration of Admissions," in *Marketing Higher Education: New Directions for Higher Education* (San Francisco: Jossey-Bass, 1978), pp. 52–53.

7. Beverly T. Watkins, "The Cost of Recruiting a Student Is on the Rise," *The Chronicle of Higher Education*, May 4, 1983, p. 7.

8. Campbell, "The Administration of Admissions," p. 62.

9. Herbert L. David, Jr. reports his survey results in "Strategies and Philosophies Used by Colleges and Universities to Minimize the Trauma of Non-Acceptance (Rejection) Letters," *The Journal of College Admissions*, no. 139 (Spring 1993), pp. 14–20.

10. Thomas Huddleston and Frank A. Wiebe, "Understanding the Nature of the Student Market for a Private University," *Journal of College Student Personnel* (November 1978), p. 522.

11. J. Victor Baldridge, Frank R. Kemerer, and Kenneth C. Green, *The Enrollment Crisis: Factors, Actors, and Impacts*, AAHE-ERIC/Higher Education Research Report No. 3 (Washington, DC: American Association for Higher Education, 1982), p. 37.

12. C. Henderson and J. C. Plummer, *Adapting to Changes in the Characteristics of College-Age Youth*, Policy Analysis Service Reports, 4, no. 2 (Washington DC: American Council on Education, 1978), p. 31.

13. Lee Noel, "First Steps in Starting a Campus Retention Program," in Lee Noel, ed., *Reducing the Dropout Rate* (San Francisco: Jossey-Bass, 1978), pp. 87–88.

14. The College Board nows offers a service that, using college-supplied data, analyzes "student persistence" from the inquiry stage through graduation from the institution.

15. Edwin A. Rugg, "Design and Analysis Considerations for Longitudinal Retention and Attrition Studies," *College and University* (Winter 1983), pp. 119–134.

16. Judi R. Kesselman, "The Care and Feeding of Stop-outs," *Change* (May 1976), pp. 13-15.

17. Don Hossler, *Enrollment Management: An Integrated Approach* (New York: College Entrance Examination Board, 1984), p. 5.

18. *Fall 1992 National Enrollment Management Survey Report* (Littleton, CO: Williams-Crockett, The Noel-Levitz Center for Enrollment Management, 1992), p. 10.

19. Robert A. Sevier, "Is Demography Destiny?" *The Journal of College Admissions*, no. 135 (Spring 1992), p. 21.

# 16

# Attracting Financial Resources

*The Charles E. Merrill Trust contributed $114 million to charity over its 23-year existence, which ended in 1983.*

*Merrill, the founder of the brokerage firm Merrill Lynch, grew up poor in a small town in Florida. When he was a boy his four-year-old sister Mary fell sick and died. Their father, although a practicing small-town doctor, did not have money for the medicines, or the equipment and skill that might have saved her.*

*Merrill went north to Amherst College in 1904 with little money. Money for his college expenses came from his mother's income from running two rooming houses, and Merrill was the business manager. He never forgot the humiliation of being poor at Amherst. Dropping out of Amherst after two years, he attended and dropped out of law school at the University of Michigan, and went to Wall Street. He made a million dollars, lost it in the crash, and came back to make it again.*

*His love of Amherst came only after he left it. He attended every reunion, not just those of his class of 1908. He admired the leadership in finance and law that Amherst produced, the ambitious young men it attracted. He was quick to help those who lacked money for their education. Amherst gave Charles Merrill his life-long belief in the value of education, and his loyalty to the college had an almost religious fervor to it.*

*The foundation he created under the Merrill Trust gave the majority of its grants to educational institutions. Merrill specified that 40 percent of the trust's income had to go to eight named beneficiaries. Half of that 40 percent went to Amherst, and one-*

432

*quarter to Deerfield Academy, with smaller fractions going to Stetson University in Florida (whose preparatory school Mr. Merrill had attended), Kenyon College in Ohio (because he respected its president), and four hospitals. The remaining 60 percent was divided into thirds: one for education, one for religion (10 percent Protestant, 5 percent apiece Catholic and Jewish), and one for established charitable, scientific, or religious institutions. The first measurement of any appeal was whether it helped people to help themselves.*

*Many of the schools receiving grants were elite private institutions, but the number also included public and private institutions of wide variety.*

*In his book* The Checkbook, *Merrill's first-born son and namesake Charles Merrill provides an insider's view of setting priorities and policies. He details the motives and purposes for making grants to specific institutions and causes, as illustrated in the following examples:*

United Negro College Fund, New York City, 1963, 1978—$175,000. *Started in 1944 to coordinate and monitor the appeals by separate colleges, the UNCF is the most important funding source for black institutions. It has always had strong corporate backing. Bob Magowan [a trustee and son-in-law of the trust's founder, and president of Safeway Stores] helped raise $600,000 for it one year in San Francisco, and he presented the appeal to us its first time. The weaker colleges would never have survived without these annual gifts. "A mind is a terrible thing to waste" is their current slogan, an argument worth respect.*

Navajo Community College, Chinle, Arizona, April–June, 1971, 1972—$55,000. *Chinle opened in 1969, the first college located on an Indian reservation and the first controlled by an Indian board of regents. Two-thirds of its curriculum was devoted to vocational-technical subjects like agriculture and forestry, auto repairs and operation of heavy equipment, nursing, and office training; and one-third was devoted to liberal arts courses that would enable a student to transfer to a four-year college.*

Berea College, Berea, Kentucky, 1960–1981—$135,000. *Berea is the archetypal Appalachian college and it was one of my father's favorite charities. Berea had been founded in 1855 to supply educational opportunities for Southern mountain people and, protected by its isolation, accepted women and blacks at that early date.*

*Our grants went for salaries, construction, and curriculum re-organization that demanded retraining of faculty to be able to handle the new interdisciplinary courses, and strengthening of the Afro-American Studies Program.*

**Source:** Adapted from Charles Merrill, *The Checkbook: The Politics and Ethics of Foundation Philanthropy* (Boston, MA: Oelgeschlager, Gunn & Hain, 1986).

In addition to attracting students, educational institutions must attract financial support to carry on their activities. Most private educational institutions are not-for-profit organizations and rely on tuition from students, on income from endowment funds, and on donations and grants. Public elementary and secondary schools are tax supported, but the funding formula has been undergoing changes in many states. The concept of foundations and fund raising for public elementary and high schools no longer raises eyebrows, as many groups apply professional fund-raising approaches to provide funding for arts, music, and other programs cut from public school budgets.

State colleges and universities, as we noted in Chapter 1, often are better described as state assisted than state supported. After decades of primary reliance on allocations from the public treasury, many public colleges and universities are raising tuition levels (and facing student protests), while also increasing the size of their fund-raising staffs to actively solicit alumni donations, and foundation and corporate grants. Public institutions are also launching ambitious capital campaigns.

Fund raising has evolved through various stages. Its earliest stage was begging, with needy people and groups importuning more fortunate people for money and goods. Some schools and colleges still believe that the more needy they present themselves to be, the more willing people will be to give money.

The next stage of fund raising relied on the premise that people would be more willing to give if they got something tangible in return. Of course, to make a surplus, the fund-raising institution had to rely on volunteers to make cakes for bake sales or on donated goods for auctions, and so forth. The success of such fund-raising activities often depended more on people's interest in the products for sale than on their interest in supporting the institution.

The modern view of fund raising is *development,* whereby educational institutions build up different classes of loyal donors who give consistently and receive benefits in the process of giving. A development perspective starts from the position that the school or college is worthy of support and that prospective donors who value what it has to offer will contribute if an opportunity is presented. Exhibit 16-1 contrasts the development orientation with the former (and narrower) fund-raising orientation. We do use the term

EXHIBIT 16-1   The contrast between a development orientation and a fund-raising orientation

| DEVELOPMENT | FUND RAISING |
|---|---|
| **BASIC APPROACH/CONCEPTS** | **BASIC APPROACH/CONCEPTS** |
| • Commitment of chief administrator and board to the development program | • Panic reactions to negative deficits start process of fund raising |
| • Complete integrity | • Crisis orientation |
| • Principal concern is top-quality education | • Project-oriented; year-to-year |
| • Good business management procedures are absolute necessity | • Temporary solutions |
| • Long-range planning | • Limited objectives—short range |
| • Public relations as prerequisite | • Shaky, unreliable, insecure |
| • Invite substantial investments | • Immediate solution demanded |
| • Goals and objectives clearly written | • Amateur approach; stopgap measures |
| • Negotiate from position of strength | • No planned continuing efforts: hit and miss; no long-range plan Band-Aid approach |
| • A positive attitude is paramount and permanent | • Negotiate from position of weakness—"help," "need," "poor," "assist" |
| • Publics must be involved with the institution on a continuing basis | • Rely on gimmicks and events |
| *PROGRAMS AND PROJECTS* *(activities)* | *PROGRAMS AND PROJECTS* *(activities)* |
| • Establish endowment fund | • Bingo (a major form of financial support) |
| • Estate—planning programs | • Car wash |
| • Annuity programs | • Annual bazaar |
| • Marketing research program—needs people | • Thanksgiving raffle |
| • Life insurance benefits solicited | • $10-a-plate dinner |
| • Business and industry grants | • Cadillac ball |
| • Research major prospects | • Sales program and advertising |
| • Involve influential, affluent people | • Magazine sales |
| • Encourage bequests | • Candy drives |
| • Scholarship programs | • Festivals |
| • Proposals to foundations | • Annual book fair |
| • Long-range planning | • Las Vegas Night |
| • Written, distinctive philosophy | • Mardi Gras |
| • Policy, practice, and procedure manuals | |
| • Stewardship programs to encourage repeat donations | |

EXHIBIT 3-2 (continued)

| DEVELOPMENT | FUND RAISING |
| --- | --- |
| *RESULTS (effects)* | *RESULTS (effects)* |
| • Large private donations received on a consistent annual basis | • Recurring financial crisis |
| • Money programmed for five to ten years down the road | • Confused job specs |
| | • Job descriptions out of date |
| • Working from clearly projected 5-year plan | • Working one year at a time |
| • Positive attitude developed | • Raising money on crisis orientation |
| • Problems are looked upon as challenges | • No clear-cut goals or objectives |
| | • High staff turnover |
| • Obstacles are seen as opportunities | • Vague financial reporting |
| • Annual reports of progress to all publics | • No records of past progress or reasons for change |
| • Supporters of program have strong interest in programs | • Changes made for the sake of change |
| • Function charts developed | • Unwritten assumptions |
| • Life insurance policies/dividends received | • Vague organization chart |
| | • Does nothing to educate public about values of education nor their role in supporting education |
| • Foundation grants | |
| • Private dollars generated | • Fails to get people involved in programs |
| • Insurance dollars attracted | |

Source: Adapted from Rev. John Flynn, cited in *Catholic School Management Letter* (24 Cornfield Lane, Madison, CT 06443 September 1980), p. 2.

*fund raising* in this chapter, but we use it to describe obtaining financial resources within a planned, organized, and well-implemented development program.

Virtually everything the institution does has an effect on its ability to attract and maintain the support and enthusiasm of its markets and publics—not only of donors, but also of students, faculty, staff, the community, and others. In this view, development is really a part of an overall institutional advancement program that includes public relations, communications, alumni programs, and anything else that generates satisfaction and potential support—including campus landscaping and the reputation of the school's athletic teams.

For example, in 1957 Stanford University received a letter in pencil on a scrap of paper:

> Gentlemen, My name is Max Herman Stein, born Nov. 12, 1883.
>
> I have an estate which I believe to be worth in excess of $200,000. This I intend to bequeath to Stanford.

Stein's only previous contact with the university came during a period of work as a gardener on a nearby estate. He chose Stanford partly because of its clean record in the Pacific Coast Conference football scandal of the time. A visit to the campus convinced him he had made the right choice. Since his death in 1958, the Max H. Stein Professorship in Physics has supported two Nobel laureates.[1]

Some institutions are short of both fund-raising expertise and money. Many rely on short-range fund-raising tactics when they should be working to establish their schools' credibility and worthiness so that people will want to support them. In Exhibit 16-1, the director of education for a Catholic archdiocese contrasts a long-term *development* approach and a short-term *fund-raising* approach.

We use *fund raising* in this chapter to refer to the institution's activities to obtain financial support. The development approach to fund raising reflects the marketing view that the institution must:

- Analyze its position in the marketplace.
- Concentrate on those donor sources who have resources and whose interests are well matched to the institution.
- Design solicitation programs to satisfy each donor group.

This approach involves carefully segmenting the donor markets; measuring the giving potential of each donor market; assigning executive responsibility for developing each market through research and communication approaches; and developing a plan and budget for each market based on its potential.

There is a dynamic new element in development—stewardship. Institutions receiving donations are taking steps to demonstrate to donors that their investments in the institution are being utilized and managed well.

This chapter will analyze fund raising from a marketing perspective, considering the following topics:

1. Laying the groundwork for fund raising.
2. Setting fund-raising goals.
3. Organizing for fund raising.
4. Researching and approaching donor markets, including individual givers, foundations, corporations, and government agencies.
5. Coordinating fund-raising activities.
6. Evaluating fund-raising effectiveness.

## LAYING THE GROUNDWORK FOR FUND RAISING

The contribution of institutional strategic planning is nowhere more apparent than in fund raising. The institution that has gone through the strategic planning process presented in this book has the following advantages:

- The institution is aware of the major threats and opportunities that the environment poses and has developed contingency plans for dealing with them.
- The institution has identified its key publics, has determined their images of

the institution, and has developed communications programs for them.
- It has a thorough understanding of its major markets—students, donors, and others—and their expectations of the institution.
- The institution has identified its competition and has determined how to position itself in ways that are valued by its markets and publics.
- The institution has analyzed its strengths and weaknesses as a basis for remedying weaknesses and communicating its strengths.
- It has clarified its mission and has identified the overall goals and objectives it will pursue.
- The institution has analyzed the programs and services it offers and has made decisions about which to drop, modify, build, add, and feature.
- It has reviewed its organizational design to provide the structure and organizational culture that support its other activities.
- The institution has effective systems for obtaining and disseminating important information to support research, planning, implementation, and control tasks.
- It has rank-ordered its goals and objectives and has determined the financial resources needed to attain them.
- The institution can answer the prospective donor who wants evidence that the institution knows where it is going and will spend donated money wisely to further significant goals.

With this preparation at the institutional level, the development staff can proceed to determine (through additional research, if necessary) the best features of the institution that would merit donor support; set fund-raising goals; research donor markets; and develop and implement fund-raising action plans.

## SETTING FUND-RAISING GOALS

Educational institutions typically set annual and long-range goals for fund raising. One university set the following goals for a five-year campaign to raise $50 million:

1. To provide the annual operating support needed for ongoing university programs and operations and to expand and strengthen annual giving programs.
2. To increase the university's endowment so that income from endowment investments will underwrite at least 10 percent of the educational and general expenses.
3. To provide the funds for the construction of two urgently needed facilities and the renovation of four existing structures.

In this case, the goals state the uses for the donated funds, rather than just the desired total amount. In the process of developing fund-raising goals, the school's leadership will consult with key people, including deans and department chairs, to determine their most pressing needs, as well as the projects they would undertake if additional resources were available. These needs and wishes should reflect strategic planning at the university as well as school and department level, and should be prioritized as a basis for determining the amount the institution would like to raise.

A frequently used, parallel first step is to conduct a *feasibility study*. The school, often in conjunction with fund-raising consultants, will want to determine if its goals and campaign target amount are sound. The feasibility study entails presidential visits with a great many alumni and other key individuals in the life of the school, seeking their opinions about the school's goals and aiming to engender enthusiasm—and eventually financial support—to carry them out.

The institution may set goals for particular donor groups. For example, one large university set the following goals for a class that was marking its twentieth-year reunion:

1. Participation by 75 percent of class members.
2. $500,000 overall class dollar goal, which, if reached, will earn an additional $100,000 in challenge grants from five classmates.
3. Establish a $100,000 class endowment fund composed of gifts that are over and above regular annual contributions.

For the class that was graduated only five years ago, the goals are much more modest: to increase class participation and to establish a $50,000 class endowment fund with gifts that are over and above annual contributions.

Most institutions set a total goal each year for contributions because this allows the institution to (1) establish a budget for fund-raising activities, (2) motivate the staff and volunteers to high exertion, (3) measure fund-raising effectiveness, and (4) help establish university budget planning goals.

Educational institutions arrive at their fund-raising goals in different ways, such as these:

1. *Incremental approach.* Here the institution takes last year's contribution total, increases it to cover inflation, and then modifies it up or down depending on the expected economic climate.
2. *Need approach.* Here the institution forecasts its financial needs and sets a goal based on them. Thus, a university's administration will estimate the future building needs and costs, faculty salaries, energy costs, and so on, and set the portion that has to be covered by fund raising as its target.
3. *Opportunity approach.* Here the institution makes an estimate of how much money it could raise from each donor group with different fund-raising approaches and expenditures, with the objective of maximizing the net surplus. This approach is often used before a major capital campaign; the development office conducts a feasibility study before announcing the campaign goal.

Educational institutions often use a combination of these three approaches. They look for growth from year to year, they keep in mind the continuing and special needs for which the institution needs money, and they consider the giving potential for each donor group.

After setting its fund-raising goal, the institution has to develop an overall fund-raising strategy, identifying the most promising donors and determining how to present its case to them. The institution needs to prepare a *case statement*, explaining the institution's worthiness, its needs, and reasons why support is justified. It may base its appeal on loyalty, on identification with earlier distinguished benefactors, or on some other major motive for giving, identified through prospect research and segmentation. The institution also must determine how to allocate scarce staff time to different donor groups and geographical areas.

The role of the vice president for development in influencing the institution's objectives and strategies varies greatly. Some institutions treat the development officer as a technician rather than a policymaker. The president and/or board decides how much money is needed, selects the broad fund-raising strategy, and then assigns its implementation to the development officer. This constrained role unfortunately robs the institution of a valuable contribution that the development officer can make.

Some institutions give more scope to the development officer, recognizing this person's expertise and central role in the institution's development efforts. He or she participates *with* the institution's top administrators and trustees in setting dollar goals and fund-raising strategy, and in developing the institutional positioning strategy. When the development task calls for the involvement of high-level administrators (for example, to ask a major donor prospect for a gift), the president or other key persons make this a top-priority responsibility.

The rewards of this level of involvement are substantial. The institution's positioning strategy is likely to be significantly strengthened by the development officer's insight, and the dollar goals and fund-raising strategy will be more realistic. Of equal importance, the necessary solid partnership between the chief development officer and the president (or other institutional head) will be strengthened by the shared responsibility for planning the direction of the campaign. Finally, the development officer will be able to raise money more effectively.

## ORGANIZING FOR FUND RAISING

Educational institutions must develop an organized approach to fund raising. Small schools—particularly private elementary and high schools—may have one person who is chiefly responsible for fund raising. This person may be the school's head or have the title of director of development. He or she will be responsible for identifying fund-raising opportunities and activating others—administrators, trustees, faculty, alumni, and other volunteers—to assist when needed.

Larger colleges and universities will have development offices with dozens or even hundreds (in the case of Ivy League schools) of full-time development staff, plus volunteers who may number into the hundreds. In these large institutions, development staff members take responsibility for either specific donor markets (segmented in various ways), services, marketing tools, or geographical areas. We shall illustrate this by showing how a large private university organizes its fund raising.

A model organization for university fund raising is shown in Figure 16-1. The board of trustees has the ultimate responsibility for overseeing the financial health of the university. They do this by making personal and company contributions, arranging donor contacts, and advising on development strategy, as well as by oversight of endowment and investment strategy. The college president is the chief fund raiser when it comes to meeting major prospects and asking for their support. The vice president for development is the chief planner of the fund-raising strategy for the institution and also personally asks for money from potential donors. Day-to-day administration is often handled by a director of development, to free the vice president for development for strategic planning and coordination of the functions that report to him or her, which may include public relations, publications, and alumni affairs.

The remaining development staff carries out specialized activities. Some of the staff are specialized to donor markets—thus, there are directors of an-

FIGURE 16-1   A large university fund-raising organization

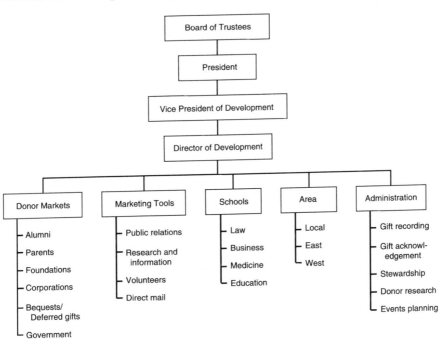

nual giving, planned giving (trusts and bequests), foundations, corporate giving, and so on. Other staff members manage marketing functions, such as donor relations, research, stewardship, and event planning. Still others handle various divisions within the university (i.e., medicine, business, and so on), where they get to know the faculty and fund-raising needs and opportunities. The development program also needs to have skilled staff and well-developed procedures for recording and acknowledging gifts, stewarding the gifts, researching donor prospects, and planning recognition and other events.

Reliance on volunteers is somewhat controversial among development professionals. The school's top administrators and development officer should consider to what degree, how intensively, in what capacities, and over what time period individual volunteers are willing and able to serve. In some instances the staff's effectiveness can be amplified by volunteers—such as alumni, friends of the institution, deans, faculty, students, and so on—who take on fund-raising responsibilities. But the use of volunteers isn't without drawbacks. In many situations the use of volunteers places heavy time demands on development staff and administrators who must recruit, train, motivate, and monitor volunteers. The institution needs to consider the necessary and most effective roles volunteers can play—for example, class representatives for annual giving—and arrange for most of the tasks to be carried out by paid staff.

The institution's effectiveness in fund raising is also affected by the quality of its information system. The development office needs to maintain up-to-date and easily accessible files on donors and prospects (individuals, foundations, corporations, donor contacts, and so on) so that past and/or potential giving can be identified and previous solicitations can be reviewed. The computerization of development files means that data can now be retrieved by the donor's affiliation, year of degree receipt, school, giving level, giving history, residence location, occupation, and other key variables. This database places the fund raiser in a much better position to allocate his or her time effectively to the most promising donors and prospects.

## RESEARCHING AND APPROACHING DONOR MARKETS

Educational institutions obtain their donated funds from four major donor markets: *individuals, foundations, corporations,* and *government.* In this section, we will examine the characteristics of each donor market and show how these shape fund-raising activities.

Effective fund raising relies heavily on marketing research. The development staff needs to understand thoroughly actual and potential donor groups and to determine ways to segment these groups further into more homogeneous groups that predict their ability and/or willingness to give. The staff members need to conduct *prospect research* to identify specific prospects for larger gifts, to develop a profile of their interests and affiliations, and to rate them on their giving potential and the strength of their motivation to give.

The development office needs to draw on results of prior or new image studies on how donor segments perceive the institution. To tailor the case for giving still further, the development staff needs to understand the donor decision process, including identifying the most salient motivations for giving, strengthening and creating ties with the institution, and encouraging a habit of giving. Accurate identification of donors, appropriate cultivation, and evidence of sound stewardship are at the heart of successful fund raising.

One of the most successful approaches is to present giving as an *investment* in some aspect of the institution that the donor cares about. For some individual donors, this will be the athletic program; for others, the business school, and for still others, scholarships for students. Corporations typically support projects that offer them some short- and/or long-term potential benefits, such as goodwill or better-trained employees. When the institution presents the prospective donor with an attractive investment opportunity, the possibility for a gift is greatly enhanced. We will have more to say about motives for giving as we take up each broad source of funds.


## Individual Donors

Individuals are the largest single source of donations to educational institutions, accounting for half of all voluntary support for higher education in 1991-92.[2] Of course, individual institutions vary greatly in the percentage of funding received from individuals.

In order to develop effective approaches, the development staff needs to segment this group in a meaningful way. Donor markets can be segmented on geographic, demographic, psychographic, and behavioristic variables (see Chapter 9). Segmentation can suggest the benefits which each group wants from giving. Of course, the development office should be careful to check its hunches about donor motivations by asking them what benefits are most important to them. Some people give, and *say* they expect nothing back. But actually they have expectations. They expect the institution to use the money efficiently; they expect the school to show gratitude; and they expect continuing contact from the institution to assure them that their contribution is valued. Even the anonymous giver, while wanting no acknowledgment, may privately enjoy the self-esteem of being "big enough" to give money without requiring recognition. One group of donors to a university might respond to pride, another to "let's catch up to the competition."

Another important basis for segmentation is the donor's giving potential. Fund raisers distinguish between small, medium, and large donors. Educational development officers typically find that about 90 percent or more of the money is donated by less than 10 percent of the donors. Thus, many fund raisers prefer to concentrate all or most of their staff's energy on large potential donors, feeling that attracting a few large gifts would produce more funds than attracting many small gifts. If a college development officer spends 30 hours with a wealthy alumnus who ends up giving $1 million, the fund raiser's productivity is much greater than spending weeks in a direct-mail or telemarketing campaign to raise $100 from each of 10,000 alumni. For this reason many development officers in the past neglected building up the number of alumni givers and concentrated instead on increasing the size of the average gift received. This point of view has changed, as more schools are seeking to involve all alumni in school support and giving, while maintaining efforts to attract large gifts. This effort is based on evidence that the small donor, over time, will become the medium or large donor if the donor is cultivated and "stewarded" through the years.

The usual approach for attracting large gifts is *personal solicitation,* either by someone in the development office, an administrator (the president, a dean, or a principal, for example), a trustee, or another highly credible spokesperson for the institution. If the spokesperson is a trustee or graduate, he or she should already be donating at the level expected from the prospect. For example, a trustee calling on a prospect for a $5,000 donation to a capital campaign should ideally have already given that amount or more, since the prospect should find the requester to be both credible and worthy of emulation.[3]

Personal solicitation consists of five steps: *identification, introduction, cultivation, solicitation,* and *stewardship.* The development office first identifies wealthy individuals who could conceivably have a strong interest in the institution.[4] The staff then identifies others who might supply information (about their inclinations toward the school, their current financial situation, and so on) and arranges an introduction. The development director, trustee, or other representative cultivates the person's interest without asking for any money. Asking too early may result in a refusal or in a smaller donation than is possible or desirable. Fund raisers will spend considerable time cultivating wealthy individuals. Eventually they do ask for money, having carefully considered what level of donation and purpose to propose to each specific donor. Upon receiving a donation, the development office staff and the appropriate school administrator make a point of expressing their appreciation and providing appropriate recognition to the donor.

Some schools are skillful in hosting events for wealthy prospects to attract their financial support. One well-known (formerly all-male) private university invited 50 of its wealthiest alumni to an all-expense-paid weekend on the campus, flying them in on private planes from their homes in various parts of the country. These alumni were put up in the best hotel, treated to some fine lectures, led in a religious service by the university president, and treated to a football game won brilliantly by the school's team. The spirits were so high that the average alumnus attending that weekend gave a check to the university for over $100,000.

If the institution has qualified volunteers (often alumni), this same approach can be very successful in soliciting smaller donations. But for gifts below a certain amount, the development office will probably choose to use other approaches (described later) which are more cost-effective and time-effective.

Major-gift fund raising is often most effective when the institution has developed a "wish list" of exciting projects and endowment opportunities and lets the prospective donor see the list. Large institutions classify their wished-for capital gifts in several financial sizes, ranging from the purchase of library books and periodicals for under $10,000 to the construction of an entire building for over $20 million. One of the most powerful appeals is an offer to have donors' names (or the names of loved ones) attached to campus buildings, distinguished chairs, and the like. In addition, fund raisers can offer these donors several ways to make their gifts, including direct cash payment, gifts of stock and other property, deferred gifts such as trusts and annuities, and bequests whereby donors assign part or all of their estates to the institution upon their death. Schools and colleges have developed a variety of gift plans that can be tailored to the needs of individual donors.

The majority of donors will not be especially wealthy, but their support is critical for three reasons. First, from a fund-raising perspective, their donations contribute to achieving the institution's financial objectives. Second, today's modest donors may become generous as their financial wherewithal and interest in the institution grow. Third, educational institutions do not live by money alone. By the act of contributing money, donors are acknowledging and reinforcing their ties to the institution. Donors at any level will typically feel more interest in the institution and its success. They are in a position to speak well of the school and to encourage others to attend, to donate, or to support the school in other ways.

The use of direct mail, phonathons, and telemarketing has made it possible for educational institutions to reach and stay in contact with small donors.

**Direct Mail.** Direct mail is the least expensive way to communicate with individual donor prospects. A further advantage of sending mail solicitations is that mailing lists can be updated by requesting an address correction from the U.S. Postal Service.

A typical direct-mail communication may include three items:

- A letter from a member of the donor's graduating class (if an alumnus), from the president or principal, or from some other person who is likely to be known and respected by the recipient, asking the recipient to contribute.
- A brochure that presents the case for supporting the institution.
- A reply card and envelope or other response piece for the recipient to send in a contribution.

A brochure without a letter is rarely as effective as a combination of the two. A truism of fund raising is that people give to people; a brochure alone does not establish the personal connection that prompts people to give. The letter establishes a personal link between the requester and the prospect.

The skilled development officer recognizes the importance of making it easy for the prospect to give. Without a reply card, the prospect may never get around to writing to the development office; without a postage-paid envelope, the prospect may never get around to finding a stamp and putting the contribution in the mail.

Designing and producing effective solicitation letters, brochures, and response pieces is ideally carried out by people with skill and experience in preparing direct mail. Fund-raising professionals recognize the importance of communications that appropriately reflect the institution's character and quality.

**Phonathons and Telemarketing.** *Phonathons* have become an important fund-raising tool because they are more personal and thus more effective than direct mail. In addition, phonathons are less time-consuming and less costly than face-to-face contact.

A phonathon consists of a group of volunteer callers who meet in a room specially equipped with a telephone for each person, for the purpose of calling donor prospects and asking for contributions. Since most phonathons are scheduled in the evening hours when volunteers and prospects are not at work, the facilities may be a large office donated by a company for the evening. Volunteers usually have something in common with the people they will be calling. For example, they may have graduated the same year or majored in the same field. Parent volunteers will call other parents. Each volunteer caller receives printed information explaining the aim of that evening's phonathon and answering such essential questions as, "Why are alumni gifts important?" "Who are our prospects?" and "How much should I ask for?" The instructions usually include a sample conversation "script" as a guide.

After completing a successful call, the volunteer writes a short thank-you note to accompany the card for the donor to return with the contribution. For example, for a donor who says yes and names an amount, the note might read, "Dear Paul, Your thoughtful gift of $100 means a lot to the university. Sure hope you can make it to the campus for the reunion." For someone who says "maybe": "Dear Sue, Thanks for considering a gift to the university. Your $25 can make a difference when you add it to other gifts made by our classmates. I hope you'll participate. Regards." Such personal notes cement the person-to-person contact made over the telephone.

The development office needs to remember that volunteers are donors too. The office might provide sandwiches and a pep talk before beginning in on the evening's calls, with coffee and snacks during the evening. The organizers should, of course, warmly thank the volunteers for their contributions of time, effort, and loyalty in helping the institution. Some development offices strive toward making the experience "fun" as well as gratifying, by giving each caller a bell to ring after each call yielding a pledge, and giving school souvenirs (for example, a school pin) to all the callers and perhaps a special token gift—such as a mug—to the person who happened to raise the most money during the calling period.

A more recent development is the use of commercial *telemarketing* carried out by paid employees—sometimes the school's students, sometimes professional telemarketers. Some people resent being asked for a donation by a paid caller and would prefer a call from a volunteer. Volunteer phonathons require a great deal of paid-staff time to organize (inviting and motivating enough volunteer callers), train, and supervise, and can only be done on an occasional basis.

Professional telemarketers are skilled, need far less supervision, and should be able to raise far more money than the cost of their salaries. In the best case the professional telemarketers will be the institution's students, since they can answer donors' questions as well as reflect their personal enthusiasm for the school and their appreciation for how donations improve the educational experience. Whether students or others, the telemarketers need excellent model scripts, training, and a regular source of advice when they have questions.

For those critics who feel the callers should always be volunteers, it is worth noting that the vice president for development and the development staff are all paid employees, and their participation in soliciting gifts is quite accepted by donors.

## Foundations

Colleges and universities are the primary beneficiaries of foundation grants, receiving 40 percent of all foundation-grant dollars awarded. These grants total about 20 percent of all gifts to higher education in the United States.

There are some 22,000 active grant-making foundations in the United States. There are four basic types:

**1.** *Family foundations* set up by wealthy individuals to support a limited number of activities of interest to the founders. Family foundations typically do not have permanent offices or full-time staff members. Decisions tend to be made by family members and/or counsel. Development offices often find that soliciting donations from a family foundation consists of soliciting the founders of the trust as they would other wealthy individual donors.

**2.** *General foundations* set up to support a wide range of activities and usually run by a professional staff. General foundations range from extremely large organizations—such as the Ford Foundation and the Rockefeller Foundation—that support a wide range of causes and give most of their money to large, well-established institutions, to more specialized general foundations that give money to a particular cause, such as education (Carnegie Foundation).

**3.** *Community trusts* set up in cities or regions and made up of smaller, personal foundations whose funds are pooled for greater effect.

**4.** *Corporate foundations* set up by corporations with funds coming from endowment or from current income. (Corporations may donate up to 5 percent of their adjusted gross income to charitable causes.)

We will first discuss issues relevant to all four types of foundations and then turn to corporate foundations for further attention.

**Researching Foundations.** With 22,000 foundations, the fund raiser needs to know how to locate the few that would be the most likely to support a given project or cause. Fortunately, there are many resources available for researching foundations.[5] The best single source is the Foundation Center, a nonprofit organization with reference collections in New York, Washington, Cleveland, and San Francisco and cooperating collections in every state. Many libraries around the country also carry valuable materials describing foundations. The most important materials include these:

**1.** *The Foundation Grants Index,* which lists the grants that have been given in the past year by foundation, subject, state, and other groupings. The fund raiser could, for example, look up medical education, find all the grants made to support medical education, and identify the most active foundations in this area of giving.

**2.** *The Foundation Directory,* which lists more than 3,100 foundations that either have assets of over $1 million or award more than $100,000 annually. The directory describes the general characteristics of each foundation, such as type of foundation, type of grants, annual giving level, officers and directors, location, particular fields of interest, contact person, and so on. The directory also contains an index of fields of interest, listing the foundations that have a stated interest in each field and whether or not they gave money to this field last year.

**3.** *The Taft Foundation Reporter,* which presents comprehensive profiles and analyses of private foundations, and the *Taft Corporate Directory,* which covers corporate foundations and corporate nonfinancial support, such as loaned executives and equipment donations. Entries contain extensive information on each foundation, including recent giving pattern by type of grant, areas of interest, and geographical emphasis, as well as the history of the donors and of the foundation, and application procedures.

**4.** *The National Data Book*, which includes all the currently active grant-making foundations in the United States. *The Data Book* lists foundations by state in descending order of their annual grant totals, and gives information on location, principal officer, market value of assets, grants paid, and gifts received. This book includes community foundations.

**5.** *The Foundation News*, which is published six times a year by the Council on Foundations and describes new foundations, new funding programs, and changes in existing foundations.

**6.** Annual reports from foundations that look promising. Such reports include the foundation's history, current assets, geographical limitations to its giving, the range of grants, the current focus of activity, and whom to contact. The annual report will also give specific guidelines for making an application to the foundation, including whether to submit a letter of inquiry or preliminary proposal, or to submit only completed proposals.

**7.** *COMSEARCH Printouts*, produced by the Foundation Center, which are computer-sorted listings of foundation grants in more than 60 major giving categories.

The key concept in identifying foundations is that of *matching*. The educational institution should search for foundations matched to its interests and scale of operation. Too often, a small college will send a proposal to the Ford Foundation because it would like to get this well-known foundation's support. But the Ford Foundation accepts only about one out of every 100 proposals and may be less disposed toward helping small colleges than more regional or specialized foundations would be.

**Preparing the Proposal.** After identifying several foundations that might have high interest in its project, the institution should try to determine their level of interest before investing a lot of time in proposal preparation. Most foundations are willing to respond to a letter of inquiry, phone call, or personal visit to determine how interested they are likely to be in the project. If the foundation officer is encouraging, the fund-seeking institution can then make the investment of preparing an elaborate proposal for this foundation.

Writing successful grant proposals is becoming a fine art, with many guides currently available to help the grant seeker.[6] Each proposal should contain at least the following elements:

1. A cover letter describing the history of the proposal, and who, if anyone, in the foundation has been contacted.
2. The proposal, describing the project, its uniqueness, and its importance.
3. The budget for the project.
4. The personnel working on the project, with their resumes.

The proposal itself should be compact, individualized, organized, and readable. In writing it, the institution should be guided by knowledge of the selection criteria that the particular foundation uses to choose among the many proposals it receives. Many foundations describe their criteria in their annual reports or other memos; or their criteria can be inferred from the characteristics of the recent proposals they have supported, or by talking to knowledgeable people. Among the most common guiding criteria used by foundations are these:

1. The importance and quality of the project.
2. The neediness and worthiness of the institution.
3. The institution's ability to use the funds effectively and efficiently.
4. The importance of satisfying the people who are doing the proposing.
5. The degree of benefit that the foundation will derive in supporting the proposal.
6. The contribution this project might make if it serves as a model for other institutions.

If the proposing institution knows the relative importance of the respective criteria, it can do a better job of selecting the features of the proposal to emphasize. For example, if the particular foundation is influenced by the person or group who presents the proposal, the institution should sent its highest-ranking officials to the foundation. On the other hand, if the foundation attaches greatest importance to the quality of the written proposal, the institution should edit and present the proposal very carefully.

Educational institutions should not contact foundations only on the occasion of a specific proposal. Many colleges and universities cultivate a handful of appropriate foundations in advance of specific proposals to establish the shared interests of the institution and the foundation. One major university sees the Ford Foundation as a "key customer account." The development officer arranges for various people in the university to meet people at their corresponding level in the foundation. One or more members of the university's board call on corresponding board members of the foundation each year. The university president visits the foundation's president each year for a luncheon or dinner. Members of the university's development staff cultivate relations with foundation staff members at their level.

When the university has a proposal, it knows exactly who should present it to the foundation and whom to see there.[7] Furthermore, the foundation is more favorably disposed toward the university because of the long relationship and special understanding they enjoy. Finally, the university is able to do a better job of tracking the proposal as it is being reviewed by the foundation because of the multilevel relationships between the institutions.

### Corporations

Corporations represent another distinct source of funds. In 1991–92, American business contributed $2.26 billion of the $10.7 billion that was given to higher education.[8] Corporate giving differs from foundation giving in three important ways. First, corporations regard gift giving as a minor activity, whereas for foundations it is the major activity. Corporations may vary their giving with their levels of current and expected income. They have to be sensitive to the feelings of their stockholders, to whom they have a primary obligation, in terms of both how much to give to charity and what charities and causes to support. Corporations are more likely to avoid supporting controversial causes than are foundations.

Some large corporations handle the many requests for support they receive by establishing a foundation so that corporate officers are not personally drawn into gift decision making. Alternatively, some companies target some or all of their corporate charitable contributions to causes supported by their employees. They do this by matching each employee's contribution to a particular cause according to some formula, for example, dollar for dollar.

Second, corporations pay more attention than foundations do to the direct and indirect benefit that any grant might return to them. If they can show that a particular grant will increase community goodwill, train students in specialties the company may need, expand potential sales of the company's products in the future, or otherwise benefit the company, this grant will be more acceptable to the board of directors and stockholders. Some companies achieve all three ends. For example, Apple has donated its computers to grade schools, high schools, and colleges to increase students' computer skills. The donations enhance the company's reputation as a good citizen, involved in education. Apple also knows that people tend to buy what they are already familiar with, and that the students and their families will be more likely to purchase the same brand of computer they learned on.

Third, corporations can make more types of gifts than foundations can. An educational institution can approach a business firm for money, goods, and/or services. Effective corporate fund raising requires the institution's development office to know how to identify good corporate prospects. Of the thousands of business enterprises that might be approached, relatively few are appropriate to any specific institution. Furthermore, educational institutions may have the staff and other resources to cultivate only a few corporate givers. The best prospects for corporate fund raising have the following characteristics:

1. *Local corporations.* Corporations located in the same area as the school or college are excellent prospects. A university, for example, can base its appeal on the continuing education and other benefits to the corporation's employees, and a business school can point to well-prepared graduates employed by the corporation. Corporations find it hard to refuse support to worthwhile institutions in their area.
2. *Kindred activities.* Corporations located in a kindred field to the institution's are excellent prospects. The leading automobile manufacturers are inter-

ested in supporting mechanical engineering programs, and accounting firms support accounting education and related programs.

3. *Declared areas of support.* An institution should target corporations that have a declared interest in supporting its type of institution. Some corporations channel all or most of their contributions to education, with some favoring grants to small institutions, others to faculty research, and so on.

4. *Large givers.* Large corporations and those with generous giving levels are good prospects. Yet fund raisers must realize that these companies receive numerous requests and may favor those educational institutions in the local area or a kindred field. A recent survey of corporate giving found that corporations tend to keep giving to the same institutions, so those currently receiving aid may find it easier in the future than those who are not currently recipients. Regional offices of major corporations are often not in a position to make a donation without the approval of the home office.

5. *Personal relationships or contacts.* Educational institutions should review their personal contacts as a clue to corporations that they might solicit. A university's board of trustees often consists of influential people, including CEOs or retired executives, who can open many doors for corporate solicitations. Corporations tend to respond to peer influence in their giving.

6. *Specific capability.* The fund raiser may identify a corporation as a prospect because it has a unique resource needed by the institution. Thus, a school might solicit an instrument company for a donation of science laboratory equipment.

The preceding criteria will help the institution identify a number of corporations that are worth approaching for contributions. Corporations in the institution's geographical area or field are worth cultivating on a continuous basis aside from specific grant requests, increasingly through "affiliates" programs. However, when the institution is seeking to fund a specific project, it needs to identify the best prospects and develop a marketing plan from scratch.

We will illustrate the planning procedure in connection with the following example:

A well-known private university's outmoded biology classrooms and laboratories were located in a solid and historic 40-year-old building. The interior facilities were wholly inadequate for research and instructional purposes, while a modernization would keep the biology programs in the forefront and attract the best faculty and students.

The university was seeking to raise $5 million for a substantial renovation and modernization of the building's interior. The university was willing to name the remodeled building after a major corporate donor that would supply at least 60 percent ($3 million) of the money being sought. This donor would be the "bell cow" that would attract additional corporate donors to supply the rest of the funds.

The university would need to begin by developing a description of the proposed improvements, an estimate of construction and equipment costs (factoring in inflation), and an explanation of how these improvements would have a positive impact on the university's educational programs, student and faculty recruitment, the quality of the school's graduates and research, and the benefits to biological science and industry.

The next step calls for the university to identify one or more major corporations to approach. The fund raisers recognized that major prospects would have two characteristics: They would be established corporations, and they would have a history of recruiting biology graduates of the university. The fund raisers developed the matrix shown in Figure 16-2 and proceeded to classify corporations by their giving potential and their interest potential. In classifying corporations, they realized that pharmaceutical and biotechnology companies fell in the top left cell. Some of these companies have strong profits (giving potential) and a high interest in biological science programs (interest potential). They also want to give money to good causes to win public goodwill. The university decided that approaching a pharmaceutical company would make good sense.

Which pharmaceutical company? Here the university applied additional criteria. A pharmaceutical company located in the same geographical area had already given a major donation to this university for another project; it was ruled out. The university considered whether it had any good contacts with some of the other pharmaceutical companies. It identified one corporation in the East in which several of the university's graduates held important management positions. In addition, a member of the university's board of trustees—a major-bank president—knew the chairperson of the company. It was decided on the basis of this and other factors to approach this pharmaceutical company for support.

The next step called for preparing a *prospect solicitation plan.* As a start, the university fund raisers researched the company's revenues, profits, major officers, recent giving record, and other characteristics. The information was useful in deciding whom to approach at the corporation, how much to ask for, what benefits to offer, and so on. A decision was made to approach the corporation's chairperson, ask for $3 million for the modernization project, and offer to name the building after the corporation or after someone the corporation championed.

FIGURE 16-2 Classifying prospective corporate donors by level of interest and giving potential

| | | Giving Potential: High | Medium | Low |
|---|---|---|---|---|
| Interest Potential | High | | | |
| | Medium | | | |
| | Low | | | |

The final step called for *plan implementation.* The university trustee arranged an appointment to visit the corporation's chairperson, an old friend. He was accompanied by the university's president and also the vice president for development. When they arrived, they met with the chairperson and the company's foundation director. They made their presentation, and the chairperson said the proposal would be given careful consideration. A subsequent meeting was held on the university's campus to demonstrate to the company how its gift would be used and to introduce the faculty and students who would benefit from the company's commitment. The pharmaceutical company ultimately donated the money to the university.

The company responded positively to this solicitation because the proposal met its four major criteria:

1. The proposal had to be worthwhile from a societal point of view. In this case, an enhanced biology building would contribute toward better-trained biological scientists in the United States.
2. The corporation had to feel that the soliciting institution was worthwhile and would handle the grant well. Here the company had full confidence in the university and its faculty.
3. The proposal should create some direct benefit, if possible, for the pharmaceutical company. In this case, the company recognized a number of benefits: It would have a recruiting advantage; it would memorialize its name on the campus; and it would get good publicity for supporting this private university.
4. The company foundation placed value on the personal relationships involved. The fact that an important bank president and university trustee had taken the time to present the proposal personally to the company chairperson was an important factor in the careful consideration of the proposal.

In general, corporations pay attention to these criteria in considering whether to fund a particular proposal; therefore, the institution should weave them into its planning and proposal presentation.

### Government

Another major source of funds is government agencies—typically federal or state—that support various types of research, equipment, training, and scholarship/fellowship support. For example, the National Endowment for the Humanities and the Fulbright Commission both make grants to faculty and other scholars to carry out special projects or overseas teaching assignments, and the National Science Foundation may support particular areas of scientific inquiry.

Many colleges and universities appoint a director of contracts and grants or "sponsored projects"—which include both contracts and grants from corporations and other nongovernmental sources as well as government grants.[9] The director of sponsored projects strives to cultivate opportunities to obtain government funding. Large universities will have a sponsored projects office with a director and staff. The sponsored projects office staff will monitor announcements of government (and other) funding opportunities that might have potential for the institution, and will track areas of particular interest to identified faculty and other researchers. The director of sponsored projects may also spend time in Washington, DC and elsewhere getting to know key program officers at relevant agencies, although more frequently this contact needs to take place directly between faculty researchers and the relevant government agencies.

Government agencies normally require the most detailed paperwork in preparing proposals. On the other hand, the agencies are very willing to review proposals, placing the main weight on the proposal's probable contribution to the public interest. Certain topics become hot, and the granting agencies look for the best proposals they can find on these topics. They pay less attention to agency benefit or to personal relations with the requesting institutions. Furthermore, some government agencies are mandated to ensure wide geographical dispersion of grants, which offers advantages to otherwise isolated institutions.

## COORDINATING FUND-RAISING ACTIVITIES

We have described the most frequently used approaches for each major donor market. The development office must decide which donor segments should receive the most attention and then design a plan for each segment. The totality of fund-raising activities must be carefully scheduled and coordinated to ensure that they will reinforce each other and yield the desired results.

For most educational institutions, the fund-raising focus is on donations for current needs (operating expenses) and for endowment. From time to time, an institution will undertake a *capital campaign* to raise a very large amount for specific building projects and other capital needs. Whether this is an *annual-giving campaign* or a capital campaign, the principle is the same:

> A *campaign* is an organized and time-sequenced set of activities and events for raising a given sum of money within a particular time period.

Capital campaigns require the most careful planning. Here are some major considerations.

1. An educational institution should not run a capital campaign too often. After one university ended its five-year capital campaign, it would not launch another one for at least three to five years. This spacing is necessary if the capital campaigns are to retain their integrity in the minds of donors.
2. The institution has to make decisions on the capital campaign's goal and duration. The goal should be achievable, for there is nothing more embarrass-

ing than failing to reach the goal. And the campaign should not last too long because it will eventually lose its momentum.

3. The institution should try to add a matching-gift feature to the campaign, whereby some wealthy donors or foundations promise to match—say, dollar for dollar—the money raised. Early in the planning, the institution has to find and cultivate challenge grants. Even later, when the campaign may begin to slow down, challenge grants can help to increase enthusiasm and momentum toward reaching the campaign goal by the designated time.

4. The institution should prepare an attractive booklet showing the main priorities of the campaign and how donors' gifts will be applied.

5. The campaign strategy calls for approaching various potential donor groups in a planned sequence. First, board members should be asked for large gifts to be in hand even before the campaign begins. Next, potential large donors should be approached. These steps will reinforce the message that the campaign is generating much support and enthusiasm, and others will want to get on the bandwagon.

Despite careful planning, prospecting, and other activities, some contributions come as a complete surprise. An example is Max Herman Stein's donation to Stanford, cited earlier. Many experienced fund raisers know of large donations from people who happened to visit the campus or see a press release about the school and who developed an interest in supporting the institution; and also of seemingly rather small donations that increased tremendously in value, such as that described in Exhibit 16-2. Such surprises add to the excitement of fund raising and remind fund raisers that each donor is important and that each impression the institution makes may have long-term consequences.

EXHIBIT 16-2    A gift that grew

In 1976 a graduate of Santa Clara University's master of business administration program, grateful for the program's role in his career success, dropped by the school and gave an unrestricted gift of 2,500 shares of a company he had started three years before. Glenn Klimek's Dysan Corporation was privately owned and the stock had no established market value.

Santa Clara's controller's office had the stock appraised, and placed a value of $12,000 on the gift.

By the time it was sold in the mid-1980s the stock had a value of about $700,000. With the money the university established an endowed chair in Klimek's name in its school of business. First to hold the chair was Dr. Albert V. Bruno, a professor of marketing under whom Klimek studied.

Source: Based on Donald K. White, "Santa Clara U. Struck It Rich," *The San Francisco Chronicle*, June 30, 1981.

## EVALUATING FUND-RAISING EFFECTIVENESS

Each institution must make a continuous effort to improve its fund-raising effectiveness through evaluating its recent results, especially in the face of increasingly sophisticated competition and scarce funds. Fund-raising effectiveness must be evaluated by results, not merely by effort, as in Figure 16-3.

The institution can evaluate its fund-raising results on a macro and a micro level. We will consider each in turn.

FIGURE 16-3

Source: Cathy Carlson, *The Chronicle of Higher Education*, September 21, 1983, p. 33. Copyright © 1983 by *The Chronicle of Higher Education*. Reprinted with permission.

## Macroevaluation

We have consistently emphasized the importance of measuring the results of marketing activities, and fund-raising activities are no exception. Even small schools can and should analyze the results of their fund-raising efforts. Figure 16-4 shows a straightforward matrix to summarize the results of a longer analysis of fund-raising effectiveness for a private elementary or high school.[10]

Educational institutions use several methods to evaluate their overall fund-raising effectiveness.

**Percentage of Goal Reached.** Institutions that set an annual goal start by reviewing how close they came to achieving the goal. Every institution wants to achieve or exceed its goal. This creates a temptation to set the goal low enough to ensure success. The development director may favor a low goal so that he or she will look good. The institution's president, however, may

FIGURE 16-4   An annual-fund evaluation matrix

| Constituent | Goal | Actual (Pledge/Cash) | Non-monetary Benefits | Strengths | Weaknesses | Potential Leadership |
|---|---|---|---|---|---|---|
| Major Gifts | | | | | | |
| Board | | | | | | |
| Parents | | | | | | |
| Alumni | | | | | | |
| Alumni Parents | | | | | | |
| Grand-parents | | | | | | |
| Businesses | | | | | | |
| Faculty/ Staff | | | | | | |
| Other | | | | | | |

Source: "Evaluating the Annual Fund," *Catholic School Management Letter*, vol. XIV, no. 6 (May 1993), p. 4. A publication of Catholic School Management, Inc., 24 Cornfield Lane, Madison, CT 06443.

be tempted to push for a high goal to induce the development office to work harder to improve the university's economic security.

**Composition of Gifts.** The institution should examine the composition of the money raised, looking at trends in the two major components:

Gifts = Number of donors × Average gift size

*Number of Donors.* Each institution hopes to increase the number of donors each year. The institution should pay attention to the number of donors in relation to the potential number of donors. For example, suppose that about 20 percent of Northwestern's alumni contribute each year. The development office should ask not only why 20 percent give, but also why 80 percent do not give. The development officer should interview a sample of alumni nongivers and identify the importance of such reasons, for example, did not enjoy Northwestern as a student, do not like the way Northwestern is evolving, disagree with policies of the school in which I graduated, couldn't care less, was never asked, and so on. Every refusal suggests a possible plan of action.

*Average Gift Size.* A major objective of the fund-raising institution is to increase the size of the average gift. The development office should review the size distribution of gifts. Table 16-1 shows the size distribution of gifts to a major university. This table shows the importance of the major gift: The top nine donors contributed more dollars than are found in any other gift-size class. The table also shows that the gift-size class of $10,000 to $25,000 does not have as many members as it should have. The development office should estimate the potential number of additional gifts that might be obtained in each size class against the current number to determine the size classes of gifts that deserve targeted effort in the next period.

**Composition of the Donor Base.** The institution will want to examine the number and size of gifts and the number of donors by categories or segments of the donor group. For example, it will want to track the percentage of donors and donations coming from alumni, and from other donor groups such as parents, faculty, and trustees. Trends up or down may be sig-

TABLE 16-1   Size distribution of gifts to a university

| SIZE OF GIFT | DONORS | AMOUNT |
|---|---|---|
| $5,000,000 and above | 9 | $ 59,000,000 |
| $1,000,000–$5,000,000 | 28 | 44,000,000 |
| $500,000–$1,000,000 | 34 | 23,000,000 |
| $100,000–$500,000 | 210 | 43,000,000 |
| $25,000–$100,000 | 350 | 16,000,000 |
| $10,000–$25,000 | 400 | 6,000,000 |
| Less than $10,000 | | 14,000,000 |
| All bequests | | 20,000,000 |
| Total | | $225,000,000 |

nals that the institution is doing a better or worse job of appealing to specific groups and that adjustments should be made. The institution will also track funds from foundations and corporations in the same way.

**Market Share.** For some institutions, their share or rank in fund raising among comparable institutions can indicate whether they are doing a competent job. For example, a private midwestern university compared its results to the results of five comparable universities and found it was trailing in the number of alumni givers and in the amount raised through government grants. The university took steps to give more attention to these two areas.

**Expense/Contribution Ratio.** The fund-raising institution is ultimately interested in its net revenue, not gross revenue. Donors want their contributions to be used for significant purposes and are more reluctant to give if they feel that an excessive share of contributed dollars goes for fundraising expenses. An average-size college or university will spend about 10 percent of the amount raised on direct fund-raising expenses. There are some economies of scale in fund raising, so that a large institution may spend as little as 5 percent, whereas a small school may spend 15 percent or more.[11]

### Microevaluation

The institution should also rate individual development-staff members on their fund-raising effectiveness. This is not always done. One university vice president for development said he had a general idea of the funds brought in by each staff member, but not specific numbers. Many gifts were the result of several staff people working together—one identifying the prospect, others cultivating the prospect, and still another getting the donation. Still, it would be worthwhile to evaluate each individual's performance as a basis for praise, additional training and supervision, or dismissal. As an example, one university rates staff members who work with foundations by using the indicators in Table 16-2. In the case of a one-person or very small development office— as in a small private school, or when a new staff person is hired to handle a particular area—it is exceedingly important to measure individual fund-raising productivity. The person's efforts must bring in enough to cover—and considerably exceed—the person's salary and other institutional costs.

This sort of productivity assessment is difficult in the first year or so when the development office is new, since it takes time to put a development plan into action and start seeing results. If the development officer's productivity is ultimately low or even just adequate to cover salary and overhead, the institution's top administration should question whether the institution could be getting better results from a different development officer.

Finally, volunteers—including faculty, students, and others—who participate in fund raising should also be kept informed of the results of their ef-

TABLE 16-2  Evaluation of the productivity
of a hypothetical development
officer

| | |
|---|---|
| Number of leads developed | 30 |
| Number of proposals written | 20 |
| Average value of proposal | $40,000 |
| Number of proposals closed | 10 |
| Percentage of proposals closed | 50% |
| Average value closed | $39,000 |
| Average cost per proposal closed | $6,000 |
| Cost per dollar raised | $0.20 |

forts, insofar as it is feasible and appropriate. For example, if a faculty member accompanies a development officer to visit a potential donor, the faculty member should be informed if the prospect eventually decides to donate. This record keeping and coordination can take time, but the reward is that faculty and other volunteers will be even more energized to participate in future efforts. To the extent that volunteers come from within the institution, they should receive not only praise but also acknowledgment during salary and performance reviews, as well as special events and thank-yous from the development office.

## SUMMARY

Fund raising is a major task for most educational institutions. Fund raising has evolved through several stages, from begging to an emphasis on short-term activities to, most recently, fund raising as development and part of institutional advancement efforts. Marketers assume that the act of giving is really an exchange process in which the donor invests in the institution in return for some largely intangible benefit.

Applying marketing to fund raising calls for laying the groundwork by developing a thorough strategic plan for the institution. Fund raising then becomes the means for attracting the financial resources to carry out the elements of the strategic plan. Once the overall institutional strategy is established, the institution needs to establish its fund-raising goals to guide the fund-raising effort. Goals are set on either an incremental basis, need basis, or some combination of these.

The development office has to be organized to conduct the necessary marketing research and other tasks required to plan and implement fund-raising activities. Each major donor market should be segmented according to interest in the institution, ability to donate, and other relevant segmentation variables. The development staff should select the most promising donor segments and prepare plans for contacting and appealing to each. These activities need to be sequenced and coordinated for maximum results.

Finally, the development office needs to conduct regular evaluations of fund-raising results. Macroevaluation consists of analyzing the percentage of the goal reached, the composition of the gifts, the average gift size, the composition of the donor base, the market share, and the expense/contribution ratio. Microevaluation consists of evaluating the performance of each individual fund raiser, to determine whether the person's efforts are yielding a positive return to the institution.

## Notes

1. "Bequests Come In All Forms and Sizes—But Each Is Vital," *The Stanford Observer* (April 1981), p. 9.

2. *The Chronicle of Higher Education Almanac*, August 25, 1993, p. 39.

3. As pointed out in Chapter 14, a credible communicator is attractive, expert in the topic, and likable.

4. A guide to prospect research is Helen Bergan, *Where the Money Is: A Fund Raiser's Guide to the Rich* (Alexandria, VA: BioGuide Press, 1985).

5. Two useful articles on researching foundations are F. Roger Thaler, "What You Need to Know in Researching Foundations," in J. David Ross, ed., *Understanding and Increasing Foundation Support* (New Directions for Institutional Advancement No. 11, 1981), pp. 19-24; and Carol M. Kurzig, *The Foundation Center and Its Role in Research*, in the same publication, pp. 25–40.

6. Here are some useful sources of advice on writing grant proposals: Lois DeBakey and Selma DeBakey, "The Art of Persuasion: Logic and Language in Proposal Writing," *Grants Magazine*, 1, no. 1 (March 1978), 43–60; F. Lee Jacquette and Barbara J. Jacquette, *What Makes a Good Proposal* (New York: The Foundation Center, 1973); Robert A. Mayer, *What Will a Foundation Look for When You Submit a Grant Proposal?* (New York: The Foundation Center, 1972); and Suzanne Perry, "Getting a Foundation Grant Takes More Than a Good Idea, Program Officers Say," *The Chronicle of Higher Education*, October 20, 1982, p. 25.

7. See W. Noel Johnson, "Using Total Institutional Resources in Foundation Solicitation," in Ross, *Understanding and Increasing Foundation Support*, pp. 59–67. Johnson explains how various groups beyond the administration and the development office can help in this process.

8. *The Chronicle of Higher Education Almanac*, August 25, 1993, p. 39.

9. Two useful guides are Kenneth L. Beasley, Michael R. Dirgerson, Oliver D. Hensley, Larry G. Hess, and John A. Rodman, *The Administration of Sponsored Programs* (San Francisco, CA: Jossey-Bass, 1982); and Philip Des Marais, *How to Get Government Grants* (New York: Public Service Materials Center, 1980).

10. The discussion questions on which the matrix is based appear in "Evaluating the Annual Fund," *Catholic School Management Letter*, XIV, no. 6 (May 1993), 1–3.

11. This is the subject of an issue of New Directions in Institutional Advancement entitled *Analyzing the Cost Effectiveness of Fund Raising*, Warren Heeman, ed., no. 3, 1979.

# VI

# Evaluating Marketing Activities

# 17

# Evaluating Marketing Performance

Even schools that are currently successful in carrying out their missions will need to respond to inevitable changes. And even though adapted to meeting many present needs, the school may be overlooking some important programs and services that would strengthen the institution and enhance its contribution to the community.

How does an educational institution determine how well it is performing? Most educational institutions focus attention on student numbers and on budgets, but many rarely take a long look at their accomplishments and problems. They wait for major problems to overtake them before considering how to alter their course. Other educational institutions want to take steps to improve their performance, but the administration and faculty may be unsure how to proceed. The institution that seeks to be excellent, to be distinctive, and to provide a high level of satisfaction usually develops a strategy in line with its mission, resources, and potential. It must plan how best to match the resources it has to offer with the needs and wants of defined groups of potential students, donors, and others.

Evaluating marketing performance can take place at several levels in the institution. The type of evaluation will depend on the institution's commitment to marketing and on its stage in the implementation process. For example, in earlier chapters, we described methods for identifying marketing problems, and for analyzing marketing performance, including market-share analysis, analysis of competition, enrollment and fund-raising yields, performance-to-expense ratios, image analysis, attitude tracking, student-satisfaction measures, retention/attrition measurement, and other indicators of effectiveness. Each one of these measures can and should become part of the institution's monitoring system.

From time to time, educational institutions should undertake a critical review of their overall marketing effectiveness. Each school and college should periodically reassess its performance in serving its desired markets. Two such assessment tools are presented in this chapter: a marketing-effectiveness rating review and a marketing audit.


## MARKETING-EFFECTIVENESS RATING REVIEW

Suppose a college president wants to know how well the institution is performing. He or she could review application and enrollment trends, fundraising records, faculty teaching performance ratings, levels of grants and funded research, and other objective measures of performance. The president might assume that reasonably consistent performance in each area would indicate that the institution was on course, and that any declines signaled a problem.

In fact, institutional marketing effectiveness is not necessarily revealed by current performance. The college's good results may be due to luck in having the right programs at the right time, rather than having a strategic plan for continuing to offer appropriate programs. Additional improvements in program offerings might attract better students and increase the effectiveness of the institution beyond current expectations. Another component of the institution may be encountering difficulties in spite of excellent marketing planning. It would be premature to change direction too soon.

The marketing effectiveness of an institution or school or department is reflected in the degree to which it exhibits five major attributes of a marketing orientation: *a consumer-oriented philosophy, an integrated marketing commitment, adequate marketing information, a strategic orientation,* and *effective implementation.* Each attribute can be measured. Table 17-1 presents a marketing-effectiveness rating instrument based on these five attributes. This form is tailored for the admissions office but can be adapted for use by the development office or by other functional areas of the institution. The instrument in Table 17-1 would be filled out by key people involved in enrollment management and admissions, as well as others in the admissions office. The scores would then be summarized and the results examined and discussed.

Few educational institutions achieve scores within the superior range of 26 to 30 points in each of the five areas. Most receive scores in the fair range, indicating that people in the institution see room for marketing improvement. The scores on each attribute indicate which elements of effective marketing action need the most attention. The responsible area of the school can then establish a plan for correcting its major marketing weaknesses.

The marketing-effectiveness rating review process does not address the

TABLE 17-1   Marketing-effectiveness rating instrument for admissions (*Check one answer for each question*)

### CONSUMER-ORIENTED PHILOSOPHY

SCORE

A.  Does the admissions officer participate in the overall college planning process?
0   ☐ The admissions officer does not participate in college planning. The officer is simply given recruitment goals set by the central administration.
1   ☐ The admissions officer is asked for certain data and suggestions relative to college needs but does not participate in the formal college planning process.
2   ☐ The admissions officer is a participant in the annual and long-range planning of the college's future.

B.  What is the dominant philosophy of the admissions office?
0   ☐ Wait and see how many applications come in and go out and beat the pavement to fill the sales gap.
1   ☐ Reach out everywhere and anywhere students can be found.
2   ☐ Identify major college sources, rate them on their potential student yield, and allocate time and choose strategies accordingly.

C.  How aware and responsive is the admissions office to major environmental trends and developments?
0   ☐ The admissions office pays little attention to the changing environment.
1   ☐ The admissions office keeps informed but is slow to respond to new opportunities.
2   ☐ The admissions office is on top of changing trends and opportunities and is quick to respond.

### INTEGRATED MARKETING COMMITMENT

SCORE

D.  Does the admissions officer have sufficient influence or control over the resources that matter to effective recruitment?
0   ☐ No.
1   ☐ Somewhat.
2   ☐ Yes.

E.  Is the admissions officer in close touch with the faculty and deans?
0   ☐ The admissions officer rarely meets faculty members to learn what they are doing.
1   ☐ The admissions officer occasionally attends faculty functions to sense possible opportunities for admission strategy.
2   ☐ The admissions officer cultivates close relations with the faculty or specific faculty members to sense possible admissions opportunities.

F.  Does the admissions office make good use of volunteers?
0   ☐ Volunteers are expected to work hard for the college, and little motivation is provided.
1   ☐ Volunteers are thanked in the course of their work.
2   ☐ Volunteers are treated to special benefits and acknowledgment and helped to feel like a major force in the total effort.

TABLE 17-1 (continued)

---

### ADEQUATE MARKETING INFORMATION

SCORE

---

G. Is the information system adequate and easy to use?
0 ☐ The information system is missing some important data and is not conveniently organized.
1 ☐ The information system contains most of the needed data and is conveniently organized.
2 ☐ The information system contains all of the needed data and is conveniently organized.

H. When were the latest studies conducted of the perceptions and attitudes of key college sources toward the institution?
0 ☐ Several years ago.
1 ☐ A few years ago.
2 ☐ Recently.

I. What effort is expended to measure and improve the cost-effectiveness of different recruitment approaches?
0 ☐ Little or no effort.
1 ☐ Some effort.
2 ☐ Substantial effort.

---

### STRATEGIC ORIENTATION

SCORE

---

J. What is the extent of formal recruitment planning?
0 ☐ The admissions office does little or no formal recruitment planning.
1 ☐ The admissions office develops an annual recruitment plan.
2 ☐ The admissions office develops a detailed annual recruitment plan and a careful long-range plan that is updated annually.

K. What is the quality of the current recruitment strategy?
0 ☐ The current strategy is not clear.
1 ☐ The current strategy is clear and represents a continuation of traditional strategy.
2 ☐ The current strategy is clear, innovative, data-based, and well reasoned.

L. What is the extent of contingency thinking and planning?
0 ☐ The admissions officer does little or no contingency thinking.
1 ☐ The admissions officer does some contingency thinking but little formal contingency planning.
2 ☐ The admissions officer formally identifies the most important contingencies and develops contingency plans.

---

### EFFECTIVE IMPLEMENTATION

SCORE

---

M. How well are the recruitment strategies, policies, and techniques communicated and implemented up and down the line?
0 ☐ Poorly.
1 ☐ Fairly.
2 ☐ Successfully.

N. Does the admissions office have adequate resources, and does it use them effectively?
0 ☐ The resources are inadequate for the job to be done.
1 ☐ The resources are adequate but they are not employed optimally.
2 ☐ The resources are adequate and are employed efficiently.

TABLE 17-1    (continued)

| EFFECTIVE IMPLEMENTATION |
|---|

SCORE

O.  What are the quality and adequacy of written communications going to the market?
0    ☐  The written communications are inadequate and poor in execution.
1    ☐  The written communications are adequate but uneven in execution.
2    ☐  The written communications are adequate and high in quality.

| TOTAL SCORE |
|---|
| The instrument is used in the following way. The appropriate answer is checked for each question. The scores are added—the total will be between 0 and 30. <br>   The following scale shows the level of marketing effectiveness: <br>        0–5 = None     16–20 = Good <br>        6–10 = Poor     21–25 = Very good <br>       11–15 = Fair    26–30 = Superior |

institution's quality, which is ultimately of great importance to any educational institution. The rating process reveals areas in which the institution can improve its marketing efforts, but the institution must undertake other analyses to assess the actual and potential quality of its faculty, students, and academic programs. Monitoring an institution's overall quality is more straightforward when colleges define their educational services in performance terms, including academic programs, cost, time, access, and program completion. The institution may use reputational ratings of academic institutions and departments, site reviews (as by accreditation teams or experts brought in as consultant/reviewers), faculty publications and research grants received, teaching evaluations, graduate school acceptances and honors received by graduates, and other measures of quality.

Table 17-2 presents Linda Delene's list of institutional performance factors, which can be further customized to specific institutions. Note that no one of these factors explains the institution's quality or performance, but each is an *indicator* of quality. Most institutions could gather the *range* of information she recommends, but very few currently do so, and fewer still are in a position to use these indicators to track improvements over time. Yet attention to changes in these indicators can give an "early-warning system" for detecting changes in the institution's performance.

TABLE 17-2    Institutional performance measures

1. Attrition or retention rates by class of student customers.
2. Completion or graduation rates by program and class level.
3. On and off-campus work placements during matriculation.
4. Availability of internships, volunteer, and/or cooperative work-study programs in designated fields of study.
5. Library study space, computer terminal access, and electronic network systems and availability.
6. Enrollment access to first and second choice of classes.
7. Proportion of voluntary and involuntary change of majors by class levels.
8. Staffing credentials and levels of personnel in advising, career exploration and placement, and health/counseling services.
9. Average financial aid packages (all sources) by income ranges.
10. Student ratings of instruction by major fields and college.
11. Job or graduate school placement rates in majors or desired field of study.
12. Employer and graduate school satisfaction ratings with graduates' knowledge, skills, and abilities.
13. Pass/fail rates for graduates in licensure/certificate programs upon course completion.
14. Campus housing, health, fitness, and other extramural facilities.

Source: Linda M. Delene, "Market Driven Promotion: An Ethical Dilemma," in *Proceedings of the 1993 Symposium for the Marketing of Higher Education* (Chicago: American Marketing Association, 1993), p. 247.

## THE MARKETING AUDIT

At some point, the college's president and trustees may conclude that developing an integrated institutional marketing strategy requires a more thorough approach. The recommended approach for assessing overall marketing effectiveness is a *marketing audit*.[1]

A marketing audit is a comprehensive, systematic, independent, and periodic examination of an institution's marketing environment, objectives, strategies, and activities with a view to determining problem areas and opportunities and recommending a plan of action to improve the institution's marketing performance.

A complete marketing audit exhibits four characteristics:

**1.** *Comprehensive.* The marketing audit covers all the major marketing-related issues facing the institution, not just a few trouble spots. It would be called a functional audit if it covered only the admissions office, or student services, or some other component of the institution's contact with markets. Although functional audits are useful, they are sometimes misleading in locating the real source of the problem. For example, a decline in enrollment may be a symptom not of an inadequate admissions office, but of a weak curriculum or changing demographics. A comprehensive marketing audit is usually more effective in locating the real source(s) of an institution's marketing-related problems.

**2.** *Systematic.* The marketing audit involves an orderly sequence of diagnostic steps covering the institution's marketing environment, internal marketing organization, programs and services, and specific marketing activities. The diagnosis is followed by a corrective-action plan involving both short-term and long-term actions to improve the institution's effectiveness.

**3.** *Independent.* The marketing audit is normally conducted by an outside consultant—or by someone inside the institution who has sufficient independence to obtain the confidence of the top administration and to exercise the needed objectivity.

**4.** *Periodic.* The marketing audit should be carried out periodically instead of only when there is a crisis. The results of an audit should be useful for an institution that is seemingly successful, as well as for one in deep trouble.

Some educators resist the term *audit* because it connotes an after-the-fact analysis of quantifiable data in a formalistic manner. Leslie Goldgehn, the leader in adapting the marketing-audit process to higher education, reports that the term *marketing audit* has aroused feelings of hostility and apprehension from administrators and faculty who "feared the marketing consultant would come to campus armed with a flashy Madison Avenue advertising campaign and all the charm of an IRS auditor."[2] So she retitled her marketing-audit instrument a *marketing opportunity analysis.* Regardless of the term used, the marketing audit includes the same issues and tools.

A marketing audit is typically carried out by an outside evaluator, a consultant with expertise in marketing and marketing research who is knowledgeable about educational institutions and their environments. Such a consultant typically brings experience from working with a number of institutions and can work with the contracting institution's administration, faculty, and staff in laying out a marketing plan and guiding them in its implementation. The consultant becomes a trainer and guide. The institution should be prepared to listen to bad news as well as good from the consultant, and administrators and others should not try to keep the consultant away from sensitive areas.[3]

### The Components of a Marketing Audit

A marketing audit consists of examining the major components of the institution's marketing situation. Our list of components is drawn from the marketing audit developed by Goldgehn.[4]

- *Historical and cultural analysis* includes current information, history of the institution, history of programs and services, the events leading to the initiation of the study, and the current institutional climate. This part of the audit places the current institutional environment in historical perspective.

- *Marketing environment analysis* is an assessment of the internal and external trends and significant groups that affect the institution. The following aspects of the institution's environment are analyzed: curricular programs, student services, publics, markets, students, distribution, competition, demographic trends, economic and political factors, social and cultural factors, and technology.

- *Marketing planning analysis* assesses how the institution's mission has been translated into planning, including a marketing plan. This phase includes an evaluation of the planning function and planning mechanisms of the institution.

- *Marketing strategy analysis* reviews the institution's strategies relating to program selection, positioning, market segmentation, and competition, and the extent to which the current strategy is appropriate in the light of the existing and anticipated environment and opportunities.

- *Marketing organization analysis* is an evaluation of the formal marketing structure of the institution, or, when no formal marketing structure exists, of the various functions that support marketing.

- *Marketing information analysis* evaluates the information and research capabilities and needs of the institution.

- *Pricing analysis* evaluates the monetary and budgetary needs of the institution, including an analysis of tuition, costs, fund-raising effectiveness, and the market response to tuition.

- *Administrative-department analysis* reviews the administrative departments that support the marketing effort of the institution, typically including admissions, financial aid, development, and institutional relations.

- *Curricular-program analysis* considers the institution's programs, degrees, majors, and courses in relation to student markets, publics, and societal trends. This analysis has implications for recruitment programs in the various program areas. Supporting resources, including the library and student services programs, can be reviewed in this phase.

The complexity of the marketing audit will vary with the size and complexity of the institution and its current situation. Many institutions conduct an audit for the first time when there are major problems or opportunities, and top administrators and trustees face crucial decisions. The relative emphasis given to each audit component may vary depending on the institution's circumstances.

## Steps in the Audit Process

Carrying out a marketing audit involves several tasks that may be spread out over several weeks or months. The following five steps are typical of most marketing audits.

**Preparation for the Audit.** The marketing audit begins with a meeting between the auditor and the institution's president (and other top administrators, as determined by the president) to work out an agreement on the objectives, coverage, depth, data sources, and timing of the audit. A major objective of this meeting is to establish shared expectations about what the audit should accomplish, and to ensure that the audit is being conducted with the full support and involvement of the institution's top administration. Following the meeting, the auditor should provide a detailed plan covering who is to be interviewed, the themes to be covered, and other issues that will affect the scheduling and cost of the audit. Once the proposed plan and terms are accepted, the auditor can proceed to gather information.

**Information Gathering.** The most time-consuming step in the auditing process is the gathering of information. The cardinal rule in marketing auditing is: Don't rely solely on the institution's administrators for information and opinions. The auditor will interview faculty, staff, students, alumni, community members, and other people and groups who are knowledgeable about the institution and/or whose opinions about it can have an effect. The auditor constantly keeps in mind the aims of the audit, so that each interview or other data-collection step contributes information relevant to the analysis.

**Analysis of Information.** The auditor next faces the task of identifying themes in the information and making evaluative judgments about the institution's current status and potential. It is at the analysis step that the auditor's experience, independence, and objectivity are most essential. In the process of analyzing the available information, the auditor may decide to conduct additional interviews or seek out other information to fill in gaps.

**Preparation of Findings and Recommendations.** The auditor then prepares a written report presenting the major findings and recommendations of the audit.

**Presentation of Findings and Recommendations.** In addition to delivering the written report, the auditor may also be asked to present the audit findings and recommendations to the institution's president, other administrators, and the board of trustees. Such sessions give the participants an opportunity to clarify their understanding of the report and initiate the process of developing or revising the institution's marketing plans.

## From Audit to Marketing Plan

The purpose of a marketing audit is to improve the institution's marketing effectiveness. The audit may reveal that some aspects of the institution's functioning could be improved. It may disclose a growing divergence between the institution's present activities and current or emerging trends. To realize the full benefits of a marketing audit, the institution's leaders must be willing to listen to bad news as well as good, and they must be willing and able to make recommended changes in the institution's functioning.

The recommendations of a marketing audit should direct the institution's subsequent marketing planning. The auditor often consults in the planning process, working with administrators, faculty, and staff who actually develop the marketing plan and carry it out.

At this point, we have returned to the theme with which we began—the importance of sound strategic planning. This book has described the steps in the strategic planning process and how strategic planning is reflected in marketing activities. The marketing-audit process is a checkpoint in the continuing cycle of planning and implementation that leads to improved institutional effectiveness.

### SUMMARY

Enhanced strategic marketing planning and implementation depend upon periodic assessment of marketing performance, in addition to ongoing programs to assess institutional performance in the quality of its offerings and outcomes.

Two assessment tools can be used to monitor marketing effectiveness. The marketing-effectiveness rating instrument profiles the institution's marketing effectiveness in terms of consumer-oriented philosophy, integrated marketing commitment, adequate marketing information, strategic orientation, and effective implementation. The marketing audit is a comprehensive, systematic, independent, and periodic examination of the institution's marketing environment, objectives, strategies, and activities. The purpose of a marketing audit is to determine marketing problem areas and to suggest corrective short-term and long-term action plans to improve the institution's overall marketing effectiveness.

### Notes

1. Although marketing audits have been conducted in the for-profit sector for over 40 years, their use by educational institutions is relatively recent. For background on marketing audits, see Philip Kotler, William Gregor, and William Rodgers, "The Marketing Audit Comes of Age," *Sloan Management Review* (Winter 1977), pp. 25–43. The framework for a marketing audit for higher education and an example of a marketing audit for small, less-selective liberal arts colleges is provided in Leslie A. Goldgehn's *A Marketing Opportunity Analysis: Application of a Strategic Marketing Audit to Higher Education,* unpublished doctoral dissertation, Northwestern University, 1982.

2. Goldgehn, *A Marketing Opportunity Analysis,* p. 140.

3. Ibid., pp. 35–36.

4. These components are based on Goldgehn, *A Marketing Opportunity Analysis,* pp. 128–143. Specific audit questions for eight of the nine components appear on pp. 235–269.

# Index of Subjects

# Index of Names

# Index of Organizations